SOCIETY OF BIBLICAL LITERATURE

I0356406

DISSERTATION SERIES

Number 173

EGYPTIAN PROPER NAMES AND LOANWORDS IN NORTH-WEST SEMITIC

by
Yoshiyuki Muchiki

Egyptian Proper Names and Loanwords in North-West Semitic

Yoshiyuki Muchiki

Egyptian Proper Names and Loanwords in North-West Semitic

Society of Biblical Literature
Atlanta, Georgia

Egyptian Proper Names and Loanwords in North-West Semitic

by
Yoshiyuki Muchiki

Library of Congress Cataloging-in-Publication Data
Muchiki, Yoshiyuki
Egyptian proper names and loan words in North-West Semitic/ Yoshiyuki Muchiki.
p. cm. — (Dissertation series; no. 173)
Includes bibliographical references and index.
ISBN 0-88414-004-0 (cloth : alk. paper) — ISBN 1-58983-133-0 (paper : alk. paper)
1. Semitic languages, Northwest—Phonology, Comparative—Egyptian. 2. Egyptian language—Phonology, Comparative—Semitic languages, Northwest. 3. Semitic languages, Northwest—Foreign words and phrases—Egyptian. 4. Names, Egyptian. I. Title. II. Series: Dissertation series (Society of Biblical Literature) ; no. 173.
PJ4127.M83 1999
492—dc21 99-40507
CIP

08 07 06 05 04 6 5 4 3 2

Printed in the United States of America
on acid-free paper

To my Mother,
Tamae Muchiki

Contents

PREFACE xiii

ABBREVIATIONS xv

SYMBOLS xxv

INTRODUCTION 1

CHAPTER I
EGYPTIAN PROPER NAMES AND LOANWORDS
IN PHOENICIAN AND PUNIC 9

A. Phoenician and Punic Documents: Dates and Provenances 10
B. Inventory of Egyptian Names and Loanwords 14
[1] Personal Names 14
[2] Divine Names 14
[3] Geographical Names 45
[4] Loanwords 45
C. Analysis of Phonological Correspondences 46
[1] Ph : Eg Phonetic Correspondences 46
[2] Eg : Ph Phonetic Correspondences 48
[3] Table of Correspondences 50
[4] Notes on the Correspondences 51
a) Glottal Stops 51
b) Labials 52
c) Sibilants 52

d) Laryngals and Pharyngals (Eg *hs*) 52
e) Alveolars 53
[5] The Possible *Matres Lectionis* in Ph and Pu 54

CHAPTER II
EGYPTIAN PROPER NAMES AND LOANWORDS IN ARAMAIC

IN ARAMAIC 55

A. Aramaic Documents: Dates and Provenances 56
B. Inventory of Egyptian Names and Loanwords 63
[1] Personal Names 63
[2] Divine Names 156
[3] Geographical Names 159
[4] Loanwords 165
[5] Month Names 176
C. Analysis of Phonological Correspondences 179
[1] Aram : Eg Phonetic Correspondences 179
[2] Eg : Aram Phonetic Correspondences 183
[3] Table of Correspondences 186
[4] Note on the Correspondences 187
a) Glottal Stops 187
b) Semi-Vowels 188
c) Pharyngals and Laryngals (Eg *hs*) 189
d) Velars 189
e) Alveolars 190
f) Labials 191
g) Nasals 191
h) Sibilants 192
[5] *Matres Lectionis* 192
a) *Yodh* 192
b) *Waw* 193
c) *He* 193
d) *Aleph* 193
e) Notes on the Use of *matres lectionis* 194
[6] Spirantization 196
a) Phoenician Evidence 196
b) Hebrew Evidence 198

c) Aramaic Evidence 199
d) New Evidence (through Egyptian) 200
[7] N-Assimilation 203

CHAPTER III
EGYPTIAN PROPER NAMES AND LOANWORDS IN HEBREW

EGYPTIAN PROPER NAMES AND LOANWORDS IN HEBREW 205

A. Hebrew Documents: Dates and Provenances 206
B. Inventory of Egyptian Names and Loanwords 207
[1] Personal Names 207
[2] Divine Names 229
[3] Geographical Names 229
[4] Loanwords 236
C. Analysis of Phonological Correspondences 259
[1] Heb : Eg Phonetic Correspondences 259
[2] Eg : Heb Phonetic Correspondences 262
[3] Table of Correspondences 264
[4] Notes on the Correspondences 265
a) Glottal Stops 265
b) Semi-Vowels 266
c) Labials 266
d) Nasals 266
e) Sibilants 266
f) Pharyngals and Laryngals (Eg *hs*) 267
g) Velars and Alveolars 267
[5] Notes on the Hebrew Vocalizations 268
a) Eg article *p3* 268
b) Eg feminine ending *t* : Heb ה 270
c) Other Vowel Changes 271

CHAPTER IV
EGYPTIAN PROPER NAMES AND LOANWORDS IN UGARITIC

[1] Personal Names 276
[2] Divine Names 280
[3] Loanwords 280
B. Analysis of Phonological Correspondences 284
[1] Ug : Eg Phonetic Correspondences 284
[2] Ug Akk : Eg Phonetic Correspondences 284
[3] Eg : Ug Phonetic Correspondences 284
[4] Eg : Ug Akk Phonetic Correspondences 285
[5] Table of Correspondences 286
[6] Notes on the Correspondences 287

CHAPTER V
EGYPTIAN PROPER NAMES AND LOANWORDS IN THE EL-AMARNA TABLETS 289

A. Inventory of Egyptian Proper Names and Words 290
[1] Personal Names 290
[2] Divine Names 297
[3] Geographical Names 297
[4] Loanwords 298
B. Analysis of Phonological Correspondences 304
[1] Akk : Eg Phonetic Correspondences 304
[2] Eg : Akk Phonetic Correspondences 304
[3] Table of Correspondences 308
[4] Notes on the Correspondences 309
a) Glottal Stops 309
b) Semi-Vowels 309
c) Labials and Nasals 309
d) Pharyngals and Laryngals (Eg *hs*) 310
e) Sibilants 310
f) Velars and Alveolars 310
[5] Phonetic Changes between EA and The Late Period 311
a) Consonants 311
b) Vowels 311

CHAPTER VI

CONCLUSIONS 313

[1] Consonantal Correspondences 313
[2] Notes on the Correspondences 314
a) Glottal Stops 314
b) Sibilants 315
c) Pharyngals and Laryngals 315
d) Alveolars 317
[3] Phonetic Changes 318
a) Changes of Consonants 319
b) Dropping of Consonants 320
c) N-assimilation 320
d) Prosthetic *Aleph* 321
[4] *Matres Lectionis* 321
[5] Quantitative Analysis of the Eg Loanwords 322
[6] Light on the Age and Character of Eg Termst in the Old Testament 324
[7] Hybrid Names (Eg religious Influences) 325

BIBLIOGRAPHY 327

INDEXES 347
A. Eg Personal Names 347
B. Hybrids Personal Names. 353
[1] with Eg gods 353
[2] with Semitic gods. 354
C. Eg Divine Names 354
D. Eg Place Names 355
E. Eg Loan Words 355

Preface

This is the revised edition of my PhD dissertation submitted to the University of Liverpool in 1990. Thanks are due to my two supervisors, Profs. K. A. Kitchen and A. R. Millard, with whom I discussed identifications and phonological problems every week. Their suggestions and solutions which were incorporated in my discussions are numerous. If I had not been able to work so closely with them, I would never have accomplished this work. I would like to extend my sincere thanks to Prof. A. F. Shore (Liverpool) for his helpful advice on Demotic; and to my two external examiners, Drs. D. J. Ray (Cambridge) and J. F. Healey (Manchester) for their helpful comments. I considered their comments made in the oral examination when I revised it for publication. Fortunately, just before the end of this revision, Prof. B. Porten (Jerusalem), who had read through my thesis, kindly sent me a long list concerning the readings of Aramaic texts, in which he dealt with more than 85 Aramaic names and words. The certainty of the reading was greatly enhanced by his professional skill in dealing with original texts.

The research been supported by generous grants from Tyndale House, Cambridge, and the First Congregational Church in Revere (USA), and my many friends in Japan. I am also thankful to Mrs Susan Tsumura who read through the whole manuscript carefully and corrected my English.

My sincere thanks go to my wife Sachiko and our two sons, Tomoya and Masaya, who so long shared the burden and assisted me.

Yoshiyuki Muchiki

Kawasaki, Ikuta, JAPAN
March, 1999

Abbreviations

a	Achmimic
AAG	R. Degen, *Altaramäische Grammatik*
Abel	F. M. Abel, *Géographie de la Palestine*
AD	G. R. Driver, *Aramaic Documents of the Fifth Century B.C.*
AE	*Ancient Egypt*
AEO	A. H. Gardiner, *Ancient Egyptian Onomastica*
AfO	*Archiv für Orientforschung*
AHw	W. von Soden, *Akkadisches Handwörterbuch*
AION	*Annali dell' Istituto Orientale di Napoli*
Aist	J. Aistleitner, *Wörterbuch der Ugaritischen Sprache*
AJSL	*American Journal of Semitic Languages and Literatures*
Akk	Akkadian
Albright	"Cuneiform Material for Egyptian Prosopography 1500–1200 BC" *JNES* 5 (1946) pp. 7–25
ANG	J. J. Stamm, *Akkadische Namengebung*
AO	*Acta Orientalia*
AÖAW	*Anzeiger der phil.-hist. Klasse der Österreichischen Akademie der Wissenschaften*
AP	A. Cowley, *Aramaic Papyri of the Fifth Century B.C.*
APN	K. L. Tallqvist, *Assyrian Personal Names*
APNMT	H. B. Huffmon, *Amorite Personal Names in the Mari Texts*
APO	E. Sachau, *Aramäische Papyrus und Ostraka aus einer jüdischen Militär-Kolonie zu Elephantine*
Aram	Aramaic
Aram Texts	B. Porten, *Jews of Elephantine and Arameans of Syene (Fifth century B.C.E.): Fifty Aramaic Texts with*

	Hebrew and English Translations
ÄRAT	W. Spiegelberg, *Aegyptologische Randgloßen zum Alten Testament*
ARES	*Archivi Reali di Ebla Studi*
ASAE	*Annales du Service des Antiquités de l'Égypte*
Assy	Assyrian
Assurb	Assurbanipal
b	Bohairic
BA	Biblical Aramaic
BA	*Biblical Archaeology*
Baby	Babylonian
BASOR	*Bulletin of the American Schools of Oriental Research*
BCH	*Bulletin de Correspondance Hellénique*
BDB	F. Brown-S. R. Driver-C. A. Briggs, *Hebrew and English Lexicon of the Old Testament*
BE	*The Babylonian Expedition of the University of Pennsylvania*
Beeston	A. F. L. Beeston-M. A. Ghul-W. W. Müller-J. Ryckmans, *Dictionaire Sabéen*
Benz	F. Benz, *Personal Names in the Phoenician and Punic Inscriptions*
Bergsträßer, *Introduction*	G.Bergsträßer, *Introduction to the Semitic Languages*
BHS	*Biblia Hebraica Stuttgartensia*
Bibl. Or	*Bibliotheca Orientalis*
Biella	J. C. Biella, *Dictionary of Old South Arabic: Sabaean Dialect*
BIFAO	*Bulletin de l'Instiut français d'Archéologie Orientale*
BMB	*Bulletin du Musée de Beyrouth*
BMQ	*British Museum Quarterly*
BP	E. G. Kraeling, *The Brooklyn Museum Aramaic Papyri. New Documents of the Fifth Century B. C. from the Jewish Colony at Elephantine*
Brugsch, *Wb*	H. Brugsch, *Hieroglyphisch-Demotisches Wörterbuch*
"Brief"	E. Edel, "Der Brief des ägyptischen Wesirs Pasijara an den Hethiterkänig Hattusili und verwandte Keilschriftbriefe"
*Beziehungen*2	W. Helch, *Die Beziehungen Ägyptens zu Vorderasien*

	im 3. und 2. Jt. v. Chr
Bulletin	J. Teixidor, *Bulletin d'Epigraphie Semitique*
Burchardt	M. Burchardt, *Die Altkanaanäischen Fremdworte und Eigennamen im Ägyptischen*
c / cent	century
CAD	*The Assyrian Dictionary of the Oriental Institute of the University of Chicago*
Calice	F. Calice, *Grundlagen der Ägyptisch-Semitischen Wortvergleichung*
Caminos	R. Caminos, *Late-Egyptian Miscellanies*
Cd'E	*Chronique d'Égypte*
CDME	R. O. Faulkner, *A Concise Dictionary of Middle Egyptian*
Černý	J. Černý, *Coptic Etymological Dictionary*
CIS	*Corpus Inscriptionum Semiticarum*
Clay	A. T. Clay, *Business Documents of Murashû son of Nippur*
Copt	Coptic
Crum	W. E. Crum, *A Coptic Dictionary*
Demot	Demotic
DemNB	E. Lüddeckens, *Demotisches Namenbuch*
DG	H. Gauthier, *Dictionnaire des Noms Géographiques*
"Difficult Words"	G. R. Driver, "Difficult Words in the Hebrew Prophets," in *Studies in Old Testament Prophecy* ed. by H. H. Rowley
DISO	Ch. F. Jean-J. Hoftijzer, *Dictionnaire des Inscriptions Sémitiques de l'Ouest*
DN	Divine Name(s)
Dyn	Dynasty
EA	El-Amarna tablets
Eg	Egypt(ian)
EG[3]	A. Gardiner, *Egyptian Grammar*[3]
El-Hoffra	A. Berthier-R. Charlier, *Le sanctuaire punique d'El-Hofra à Constantine*
Eleph	Elephantine
Ellenbogen	M. Ellenbogen, *Foreign Words in the Old Testament*
Eph	M. Lidzbarski, *Ephemeris für semitische Epigraphik*
Erichsen	W. Erichsen, *Demotisches Glossar*

f	female
f	Fayyumic
fem	feminine
frag	fragment
G	P. Grelot, *Documents araméens d'Égypte*
GAG	W. von Soden, *Grundriß der akkadischen Grammatik*
Géographie	P. Montet, *Géographie de l'Égypte Ancienne*
Gesenius	*Gesenius' Hebrew Grammar*
Gk	Greek / the Greek Period
GM	*Göttinger Miszellen*
GN	Geographical Name(s)
GNNLB	R. Zadok, *Geographical Names according to New- and Late-Babylonian Texts*
Grammaire	A. de Buck, *Grammaire Élémentaire du Moyen Égyptien*
Gröndahl	F. Gröndahl, *Die Personennamen der Texte aus Ugarit*
GVG	C. Brockelman, *Grundriss der vergleichenden Grammatik der Semitischen Sprachen*
Handbuch	M. Lidzbarski, *Handbuch der nordsemitischen Epigraphik*
Harding	G. L. Harding, *An Index and Concordance of Pre-Islamic Arabian Names and Inscriptions*
Harris, *Grammar*	Z. S. Harris, *A Grammar of the Phoenician Language*
Harris, *Development*	Z. S. Harris, D*evelopment of the Canaanite Dialects*
Harris, *Lex.Stud.*	J. R. Harris, *Lexicographical Studies in Ancient Egyptian Minerals*
Heb	Hebrew
Herr, *Seals*	L. G. Herr, *The Scripts of Ancient Northwest Semitic Seals*
Heuser	G. Heuser, *Die Personennamen der Kopten*
HG	Bergsträsser, *Hebräische Grammatik*
*HG*2	G. Beer-R. Meyer, *Hebräische Grammatik*
Hist. Gram	H. Bauer-P. Leander, *Historische Grammatik der Hebräischen Sprache des Alten Testamentes*
Hoch	J. E. Hoch, *Semitic Words in Egyptian Texts of the New Kingdom and Third Intermediate Period.*

HTR	*Harvard Theological Review*
IAM	*Inscriptions Antiques du Maroc*
IDB	*The Interpreter's Dictionary of the Bible*
IEJ	*Israel Exploration Journal*
IFP	M. G. Amadasi, *Le Iscrizioni Fenicie e Puniche delle Colonie in Occidente*
IFO	P. Magnanini, *Le Iscrizioni Fenicie dell'Oriente*
IPN	M. Noth, *Die israelitischen Personennamen im Rahmen der gemeinsemitischen Namengebung*
JA	*Journal Asiatique*
Jackson, "Ammonite PNs"	K. P. Jackson, "Ammonite Personal Names in the Context of the West Semitic Onomasticon"
Jackson, *Ammonite Lang.*	K. P. Jackson, *Ammonite Language of the iron Age*
JAOS	*Journal of the American Oriental Society*
JARCE	*Journal of American Research Center in Egypt*
JB	*Jerusalem Bible*
JCS	*Journal of Cuneiform Studies*
JEA	*Journal of Egyptian Archaeology*
JEOL	*Jaarbericht Ex Oriente Lux*
JKF	*Jahrbuch für Kleinasiatische Forschung*
JNES	*Journal of Near Eastern Studies*
Johns	C. H. W. Johns, *Assyrian Deeds and Documents*
Jones, *Glossary*	D. Jones, *A Glossary of Ancient Egyptian Nautical Titles and Terms*
JPOS	*Journal of the Palestine Oriental Society*
JQR	*Jewish Quarterly Review*
JRAS	*Journal of the Royal Asiatic Society of Great Britain and Ireland*
JSS	*Journal of Semitic Studies*
JTS	*Journal of Theological Studies*
K	W. Kornfeld, *Onomastica Aramaica aus Ägypten*
KAI	H. Donner-W. Röllig, *Kanaanäische und aramäische Inschriften*
KAT^3	H. Zimmern, *Die Keilinschriften und das Alte Testament*^{3}
KB^3	L. Köhler-W. Baumgartner, *Hebräisches und aramäisches Lexikon zum Alten Testament*
KHw	W. Spiegelberg, *Koptisches Handwörterbuch*

KM	H. Ranke, *Keilschriftliches Material zur Altägyptischen Vocalisation*
Knudtzon	J. A. Knudtzon, *Die El-Amarna-Tafeln*
KRI	K. A. Kitchen, *Ramesside Inscriptions*
Krug	M. Lidzbarski, *Phönizische und aramaische Krugaufschriften aus Elephantine*
KTU	M. Dietrich-O. Loretz-J. Sanmartin, *Die Keilalphabetischen Texte aus Ugarit*
L	T. O. Lambdin, *Egyptian Loanwords and Transcriptions in the Ancient Semitic Languages*
LÄ	*Lexikon der Ägyptologie*
Lambdin	T. O. Lambdin, "Egyptian Loanwords in the Old Testament," *JAOS* 73 (1952) pp.145–155
Laroche	E. Laroche, *Les Nomes des Hittites*
Late	the Late Period
Leander	P. Leander, *Laut- und Formenlehre des Ägyptisch-aramäischen*
LEG	J. Černý, *A Late Egyptian Grammar*
LH	E. Bresciani-M. Kamil, *Le lettere aramaiche di Hermopoli*
Liddell & Scott	H. G. Liddell-R. Scott, *Greek-English Lexicon*
LR	M. H. Gauthier, *Livre des Rois d'Egype*
Lw	Loanword(s)
LXX	Septuagint
m	male
masc	masculine
MB	Middle Babylonian
MDIK	*Mitteilungen des Deutschen Archäologischen Instituts, Ableitung Kairo*
MDOG	*Mitteilungen der Deutschen Orientgesellschaft*
Moran	W. L. Moran, *Les Lettres d'El-Amarna*
MK	Middle Kingdom
Moscati	S. Moscati, *An Introduction to the Comparative Grammar of the Semitic Languages*
N(aveh)	J. Naveh, *The Development of the Aramaic Scripts*
NA	Neo-Assyrian
NAT	Parpola, *Neo-Assyrian Toponyms*
NB	Neo-Babylonian

NB	F. Preisigke, *Namenbuch*
NBD	J. D. Douglas (ed), *The New Bible Dictionary*
n.d.	no date
NEB	*New English Bible*
NEph	R. Degen-W. W. Müller-W. Röllig, *Neue Ephemeris für semitische Epigraphik*
"Neue Deutungen"	E. Edel, "Neue Deutungen Keilschriftlischer Umschreibungen Ägyptischer Wörter und Personennamen"
NK	New Kingdom
n.p.	no provenence
NPN	I. J. Gelb-P. M. Purves-A. A. Mcrae, *Nuzi Personal Names*
NSI	G. A. Cooke, *A Text-Book of North-Semitic Inscriptions*
NW	North-West
OA	Old Aramaic
OAP	D. Foraboschi, *Onomasticum Alterum Papyrologicum*
OB	Old Babylonian
OK	Old Kingdom
OLZ	*Orientalistische Literaturzeitung*
OPP	M. Mayrhofer, *Onomastica Persepolitana. Das altiranische Namengut der Persepolis Täfelchen*
Or An	*Oriens Antiquus*
Or NS	*Orientalia* Nova Series
Peckham	B. Peckham, *The Development of the Late Phoenician Scripts*
Ph	Phoenician
Phonétique	J. Vergote, *Phonétique Historique de 'Egyptien*
PN	Personal Name(s)
PNCP / (Clay)	A. T. Clay, *Personal Names from Cuneiform Inscriptions of the Cassite Period*
Porten A	B. Porten, *Textbook of Aramaic Documents from Ancient Egypt,* Vol 1
Porten B	B. Porten, *Textbook of Aramaic Documents from Ancient Egypt*, Vol 2
Porten C	B. Porten, *Textbook of Aramaic Documents from Ancient Egypt*, Vol 3
PPG	Friedrich-Röllig, *Phönizisch-Punische Grammatik*
PRU	C. Virolleaud, *Le Palais royal d'Ugarit*

PSBA	*Proceedings of the Society of Biblical Archaeology*
Pu	Punic
Pyr	Pyramid (Period)
Ranke	H. Ranke, *Die ägyptischen Personennamen*
RB	*Revue Biblique*
RdE	*Revue d'Égyptologie*
Rec. de Trav.	*Recueil de Travaux Rélatifs à la Philologie et à l'Archéologie Égyptiennes et Assyriennes*
Reisner, *HES*	G. A. Reisner-F. C. Stanely-L. D. Gordon, *Harvard Excavation at Samaria*
REJ	*Revue des Études Juives*
RES	*Repertoire d'Épigraphie Sémitique*
RESem	*Revue des etudes Semitiques*
Revue d'Assy	*Revue d'Assyriologie et d'Archéologie Orientale*
rev	reverse
RS	Ras Shamra
RSO	*Rivista degli Studi Orientali*
RSV	*The Revised Standard Version*
s	Sahidic
S I	W. Spiegelberg, *Ägyptisches Sprachgut in den aus Ägypten stammenden aramäischen Urkunden der Perserzeit*
S II	W. Spiegelberg, "Die ägyptischen Personennamen in den kürzlich veröffentlichten Urkunden von Elephantine," *OLZ* 15 (1912) pp. 1–10
S III	W. Spiegelberg, "Zu den ägyptischen Personennamen der Urkunden von Elephantine," *OLZ* 16 (1913) pp. 346–347
SAK	*Studien zur Altägyptischen Kultur*
Saqq(ara)	J. Segal, *The Aramaic Texts from Norht Saqqara*
SB	Standard Babylonian
SBPA	*Sitzungsberichte der Preußischen Akademie der Wissenschaften*
SE I	F. Vattioni,"I Sigilli ebraici," *Biblica* 50 (1969) pp. 357–388
SE II	F. Vattioni, "I Sigilli ebraici II," *Augustinianum* 11 (1911) pp. 447–454
SE III	F. Vattioni, "I Sigilli ebraici III," *AION* 38(1978) pp.

	227–253
Sem	Semitic
SF	F. Vattioni, "I Sigilli fenici" *AION* 41 (1981) pp. 177–193
SG	M. A. Levy, *Siegel und Gemmen*
SSEA	*Society for the Study of Egyptian Antiquities*, Toronto
Stark	J. K. Stark, *Personal Names in Palmyrene Inscriptions*
TAÉ	N. Aimé-Giron, *Textes araméens d'Égypte*
*TIP*2	K. A. Kitchen, *The Third Intermediate Period in Egypt*
Tomback	R. S. Tomback, *A Comparative Semitic Lexicon of the Ph & Pu Languages*
Ug	Ugaritic
UF	*Ugarit-Forschungen*
UHP	M. Dahood, *Ugaritic-Hebrew Philology*
UMBS	*The University Museum, Publication of the Babylonian Section*
Urk	*Urkunden des Ägyptischen Altertums*
UT	C. H. Gordon, *Ugaritic Textbook*
VESO	W. F. Albright, *The Vocalization of the Egyptian Syllabic Orthography*
V I	G. Vittmann, "Zu den in den phönikischen Inschriften enthaltenen ägyptischen Personennamen" *GM* 113 (1989) pp. 91–96
V II	G. Vittmann, "Zu den ägyptischen Entsprechung aramäisch überlieferter Personennamen" *Or* NS 58 (1989) pp. 213–229
VA	*Varia Aegyptiaca*
Verbum	K. Sethe, *Das Ägyptische Verbum im Altägyptischen, Neuägyptischen und Koptischen*
VT	*Vetus Testamentum*
VTS	*Supplement to Vetus Testamentum*
Vycichl	W. Vycichl, *Dictionnaire étymologique de la langue Copte*
Wb	A. Erman-H. Grapow, *Wörterbuch der ägyptischen Sprache*
"Weitere Beiträge"	E. Edel, "Weitere Beiträge aus der Heiratskorrespondenz Ramses' II: KUB III 37 + KB I 17 und KUB 57"
Welt Or	*Die Welt des Orients*

Worrell	W. H. Worrell, *Coptic Sounds*
WZKM	*Wiener Zeitschrift für die Kunde des Morgenlandes*
Yahuda, *Language*	A. S. Yahuda, *The Language of the Pentateuch in its Relation to Egyptian.*
ZAH	*Zeitschrift für Althebräistik*
ZÄS	*Zeitschrift für Ägyptische Sprache und Altertumskunde*
ZAW	*Zeitschrift für die Alttestamentliche Wissenschaft*
ZDMG	*Zeitschrift der Deutschen Morgenländischen Gesellschaft*
ZVS	*Zeitschrift für vergleichende Sprachforschung auf dem Gebiet der indogermamischen Sprachen.*

Symbols

[ ]	restored letter(s)
]	end missing
[	beginning missing
-	unidentifiable letter
ב֯	major damage
בׄ	minor damage
**	certainly Egyptian
*	probably Egyptian

INTRODUCTION

Purpose

The purpose of this study is to establish, from the North-West Semitic side, the phonetic correspondences between North-West Semitic (Phoenician, Aramaic, Hebrew and Ugaritic) and ancient Egyptian chronologically. In other words, the present study deals with how North-West Semitic scribes wrote Egyptian in their Semitic writing systems, with concentration on consonantal correspondences.

Between Semitic and Egyptian there are three directions in relationship: (1) cognates[1], (2) Semitic loanwords in Egyptian[2], and (3) Egyptian loanwords in Semitic. However there has been considerable confusion over phonetic correspondences between the two languages, because most scholars were unaware of or ignored the fact that Semitic

[1] The studies on Semito-Hamitic cognates are A. Erman, "Das Verhältniss des Ägyptischen zu den semitischen Sprachen" *ZDMG* 46 (1892) pp.93–129. Ember, "Kindred Semito-Egyptian Words" *ZÄS* 51 (1912) pp.110–121; *ZÄS* 53 (1917) pp.83–90; Egypto-Semitic-Studies (Leipzig, 1930). W. F. Albright, "Note on Egypto-Semitic Etymology I" *AJSL* 34 (1918) pp.81–98; "Notes on Egypto-Semitic Etymology II" *AJSL* 34 (1918) pp. 215–255; "Notes on Egypto-Semitic Etymology III" *JAOS* 47 (1927) pp.198–237; F. Calice, *Grundlagen der Ägyptisch- Semitische Wortvergleichung*, (Wien, 1936); M. Cohen, *Essai comparatif sur le vocabulalre et la phonétique du chamito-Semitique,* (Paris, 1947). For a bibliography since 1844, see A. Ember, *Egypto-Semitic-Studies*, pp. IX–XIV.

[2] The most notable older ones are M. Burchardt, *Die Altkanaanäischen Fremdworte und Eigennamen im Ägyptischen* (Leiptig, 1910); W. F. Albright, *The Vocalization of the Egyptian Syllabic Orthography* (NY, 1934). Recently James E. Hoch published *Semitic Words in Egyptian Texts of the New Kingdom and Third Intermediate Period* (Princeton, New Jersey, 1994); cf. Thomas Schneider, *Asiatische Personennamen in ägyptischen Quellen des Neuen Reiches* (Göttingen, 1992).

and Egyptian scribes transliterated each other's languages differently. An example is the correspondence between Eg *ṯ* and Sem ס. Egyptian scribes used *ṯ* for Semitic ס. Therefore it was naturally assumed that Semitic scribes also used Sem ס for Eg *ṯ*.[3] However the facts are quite contrary to this general assumption. Therefore there is need to establish the correspondences in terms of the Semitic side, and the present work is devoted to this.

This comparative study between Semitic and Egyptian should bring at least four more results of interest to the philologist. First of all, it should enable us to see the historical changes and real sound values of Egyptian consonants. It is well known that the Egyptians were extremely conservative in their writing system. Therefore it is very difficult to discuss their sound values on the basis of the hieroglyphs. However, when Semitic scribes wrote Egyptian they tried to transcribe it as they heard it. Therefore, their records reflect directly the real sound values of Egyptian.[4] Secondly, the study could also reveal some of the phonetic values of Semitic, because the number of consonants is different, *e.g.*, Egyptian has three strong *h*s (*ḥ*, *ḫ*, *ẖ*), while Ugarit has two and the rest of North-West Semitic have only one ח. When we observe how Semitic scribes deal with the three Egyptian *h*s, some differences in sound values of Semitic consonants may appear. At the same time, the study could show differences, if any, in sound values of consonants in North-West Semitic which have been regarded as virtually the same, when we look into the way the same Egyptian consonant was differently represented by four North-West Semitic languages. Thirdly, it could make it possible to bring out the meaning of the Semitic word distinctly, when an Egyptian etymology has been established, especially in cases of loanwords. Finally, Aramaic, Hebrew and Ugaritic might shed light on Egyptian vocalization, because Aramaic and Hebrew frequently used *matres lectionis* in order

3 The most notable case of this correspondence is Heb GN סכת which has been identified with Eg *ṯkw*. This is a Semitic place name transcribed into Egyptian, not vice versa. Another type of confusion should be noted here, the correspondence between Eg ʿ and Sem ח. Eg ʿ is represented by Akk *ḫ* because Akk does not have ʿ. Scholars mistakenly use the correspondence between Eg ʿ and North West Sem ח, which has ʿ, *e.g.*, Ph פער is identified with *p3-ḫr.y* "the Syrian" (Benz, *PN* p. 193).

4 With this idea A. Millard worked on Assyrian royal names in Semitic (Aramaic and Hebrew), "Assyrian Royal Names in Biblical Hebrew" *JSS* 21 (1976) pp. 1–14, which shows that the method is sound and the result can be fruitful.

to indicate pronunciation of foreign names and words, and Ugaritic has three *alephs*. We can also expect to see Egyptian vocalization more directly in the El-Amarna tablets.

Method

Appropriate materials for this purpose are (1) Egyptian Personal names, (2) Egyptian Divine names, (3) Egyptian Geographical names, and (4) Egyptian loanwords transcribed into Semitic. First, therefore, I collected these Egyptian elements from North-West Semitic documents and identified them. Then I analysed the consonantal correspondences by using identifications in the collected material which are sure. Because of the goal of the study, when we work on identification we should start with well established correspondences, and pursue the explanation within those correspondences as far as possible. We should accept another correspondence only when the evidence clearly requires it. For example, we start with the correspondence between Ph כ and Eg *k*. However, when a certainly Egyptian name *p3-di-ẖns.w* is found under פטכנס, we must accept the correspondence between Ph כ and Eg *ẖ*. On the other hand, we do not identify מחפרע with *w3ḥ-ib-rʿ* because the correspondence between Aram מ and Eg *w* is not certain, and the name could be explained as *mnẖ-ib-rʿ* or *mn-ẖpr-rʿ*. The acceptance of the representation of Eg *w* by Aram מ is rejected in this case. To accept a new correspondence, at least two certain examples are required unless the identification is perfectly clear, because scribal mistakes or dialectal variants are always possible.

Identification

It is obvious, therefore, that the identification plays a key role in the study. Just as the consonantal correspondences are made on a strict basis, the identification also should be investigated until beyond doubt. The following are our criteria for identification;

First of all, negatively, the name does not have any possible Semitic explanation. Not only is it not attested as a Semitic name, but also the name or its element is not attested as a Semitic root. If the identification is open to both Egyptian and Semitic possibilities, the name cannot be used for the analysis.

Positively, the name has a good Egyptian explanation; that is, (i) the name is attested as Egyptian with proper phonetic correspondences[5] in the appropriate period. (ii) the name has the same pattern as Egyptian names, *i.e.*, פט (*p3-di-*) + DN; אס (*ns-*) + DN etc. which are attested in the appropriate period. (iii) the name has a typical Egyptian name element, *e.g.*, ענח (*ʿnḫ* "life"), Egyptian divine name, *e.g.*, אס "Isis"; אסר "Osiris" etc. and (iv) the name itself, its element, and/or the name type is attested in the appropriate period; *e.g.*, all Ph and Aram names should be attested after the New Kingdom.

Additional pieces of information on each name or word are also helpful; (i) the context where the name or word occurs, the affiliation which the name bears, and the provenance where the documents containing Egyptian names and words were found, (ii) the frequency of attestation which offers an aid to determine the identification, *e.g.*, *amanmaššu* (Ug Akk) would seem to be identified with *imn-m-š*, because of the correspondence between *š* and *š*. However, *imn-ms* is so common in the New Kingdom period that we can safely choose *imn-ms* for its identification. (iii) For investigation of the later pronunciation of Eg words, Coptic should bring considerable information. Especially when we check the vocalization of Eg words, which is often apparent from the *matres lectionis* in Aram, since the Coptic forms reflect the later condition of Eg pronunciation, their information on vocal aspects is quite useful. (iv) Finally other forms of Egyptian names, such as Greek, Coptic, Akkadian, enable us to see the historical stages of Egyptian names and consonants, though each language has its own weakness in transcribing Egyptian, *e.g.*, the Greek forms cannot reflect *aleph*, *'ayn*, etc..

As for loanwords, further considerations seem to be required; (i) The word should show proper consonantal correspondences, (ii) It must also correspond well to Egyptian in meaning, and the meaning should fit the context of the Semitic text. (iii) The possibility of it being a

[5] The expression "proper correspondences" may invite an accusation of circularity of argument, because the purpose is to establish the proper correspondences. However, we must start somewhere. Therefore, as I mentioned previously, we start with widely accepted correspondences. The certainty of the correspondences can only be reached after the evidence for the correspondence is piled up and reexamined.

Hamito-Semitic cognate must be carefully examined, because the cognates have often undergone secondary changes, *e.g.*, Eg *ib* "heart"and Heb לֵב, Akk *libbu*. (iv) The Egyptian word should be attested at least since the Middle Kingdom. If the word is attested in Eg since the Old Kingdom, because of the great time span in which the word could be borrowed, it is more likely to be an Egyptian loan word. (v) If the word is commonly attested in Semitic documents, and has been given a Semitic form, it is more difficult to distinguish a loan word from a cognate. However, if the word occurs only in the context of Egyptian contact, the possibility of an Egyptian loan is high.

After all these examinations, these Eg names and words are classified in three categories;

1. Names or words which, though possibly Egyptian, cannot be identified with certainty (no mark).

2. Names or words which are probably Egyptian, but not confirmed (marked with *)

3. Names or words which are certainly Egyptian (marked with **)

Those which others have thought to be Egyptian but which are not, or are at best very doubtful, are marked with ?. Only those which have two asterisks will be used for the final analysis.

Problems

Because our goal is to establish phonetic correspondences on the basis of the correspondences of letters, the fundamental problem is, needless to say, the conservative Egyptian writing system itself, which hardly reflects the phonetic changes.[6] The reconstruction of the phonetic value of the Egyptian consonants in the case of the present study is made possible to some extent through the following:

1) The knowledge of the historical course of the changes of

---

[6] The reconstruction of Eg phonology can be made possible through (1) Coptic and transcription of Greek, Aramaic, Hebrew, Akkadian etc.; (2) foreign or loanwords in Egyptian; (3) sound-shift in Egyptian. Osing *LÄ* III p.944.

Egyptian consonants and morphemes[7]; *e.g.*, final *r* and fem. *t* dropped in Late Egyptian.

2) The check of progressive spellings; *e.g.*, *ḏb3.t* "box" has been also spelled as *tbi͗* (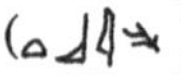), *tb.t* () in the Middle Kingdom; *db.t* (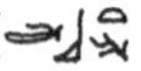) in the New Kingdom. The collected spellings seem to indicate that its pronunciation changed from something like *ḏb3.t* to *tb.t* / *tbi͗* to *db.t*. However the knowledge of the historical changes of Egyptian consonants tells that the course of change of the consonant *ḏ* is *ḏ* > *d* > *t*. Therefore, the real change is *ḏb3.t* > *db.t* > *tb.t* / *tbi͗*, through which we know that the New Kingdom spelling *db.t* is a historical spelling, the pronunciation had already become [tbi] in the Middle Kingdom.

3) Investigation of Coptic, *e.g.*, the Coptic form of *ḏb3.t* is ⲦⲎⲎⲂⲈ, ⲦⲀⲒⲂⲈ

4) Comparison with transcriptions into cuneiform.[8]

5) Greek can also provide us with the historical stages of Egyptian consonantal values.

6) Vowel shifts which took placed in Egyptian between Ramesses II and the Assyrian period are known to us;

/ŭ́/ > /ḗ/, /ŭ/ > /ĕ/, /ắ/ > /ṓ/ (after nasal > /ū́/)[9]

A second problem is dialectal differences in Egyptian, about which we know very little. All that we can do to resolve this problem is to look into the dialectal differences in Coptic forms.

The problems are not only on the side of Egyptian: the Semitic languages also could not escape phonetic changes in the course of the history. In this study we assume that Semitic phonemes did not change in sound values (*e.g.*, /d/ is always [d]). It is possible that Egyptian words and names underwent a secondary change or were Semiticized in pronunciation, after being transcribed into Semitic. It is also possible that the divine names and words which were borrowed and found a permanent place in Semitic remained as historical spellings even after

[7] Historical study of Egyptian consonants has been done by J. Vergote, *Phonétique Historique de l'Egyptien* (Louvain, 1945); *Grammaire Copte* (Louvan, 1973); W. Worrell, *Coptic Sounds* (Ann Arbon, 1934); J. Osing, "Lautsystem" *LÄ* III pp. 944–947.

[8] H. Ranke, *Keilschriftliches Material zur Altägyptischen Vokalisation* (Berlin, 1910).

[9] J. Osing, *LÄ* III, pp. 947–8; For other references, see Heb GN פתרוס.

the pronunciation changed in Egyptian.[10] In this case the first contact in which word or names are transcribed is the most important.

Previous Works

There are two previous studies devoted entirely or partially to Eg proper names and words in North-West Semitic languages. In 1906 W. Spiegelberg published "Ägyptisches Sprachgut in der aus Ägypten stammenden aramäischen Urkunden der Perserzeit" (in *Orientalisches Studien Theodore Noeldeke zum 70 Geburtstag*, pp. 1093–1115, Giessen), in which he collected 56 PNs, 30 DNs, 4 GNs, 5 month names, and 5 loanwords (total 99) from the Aramaic documents[11] and put forward the following correspondences between Aramaic and Egyptian consonants;

Aram	Eg	Aram	Eg
ʾ	*i҆*	*m*	*m*
	prosthetic *aleph*	*n*	*n*
b	*b m*	*s*	*s/ś*
g	*g* (?)	ʿ	ʿ
h	(vowel letter)	*p*	*p f*
w	*w* or (vowel letter [u/o])	*ṣ*	*ḏ* (Ѫ)
ḥ	*ḥ ḫ ẖ*	*q*	*g ḳ*
ṭ	*ḏ d ṯ*	*r*	*r*
y	*3* (Copt ו/Є in initial or final)	*š*	*š*
k	*k*	*?*	*ṯ*
l	*l*	*t*	*t* (< *t*, *ṯ*, *ḏ*, *d*)

Though many identifications and discussions in his study are still valuable, the phonetic correspondences are still incomplete and wrong correspondences crept into the table because the number of

10 For this case, see Ph אסר "Osiris."

11 Six years later, he again studied Egyptian personal names in Aram documents from Elephantine, and added 24 PNs in "Die ägyptische Personennamen in den Kürzlich veröffentlichten Urkunden von Elephantine" *OLZ* 15 (1912) pp. 1–10. In an additional work, "Zu den ägyptischen Personennamen der Urkunden von Elephantine" *OLZ* 16 (1913) pp. 346–347, he made two corrections. These works are not included in his analysis of the correspondences between Egyptian and Aramaic given below.

Egyptian elements is limited and misunderstandings are included. Furthermore, the correspondences are only between Egyptian and Aramaic, leaving other North-West Semitic languages untouched.

The second major attempt was made by T. O. Lambdin, *Egyptian Loanwords and Transcriptions in the Ancient Semitic Languages* (unpublished Ph. D dissertation submitted to the Johns Hopkins University, 1952). However, this work was a little unfortunate from the viewpoint of our goals, because of its uneven achievement. First of all, his main concern was, as the title suggests, with Egyptian loanwords in Old Testament and El-Amarna tablets.[12] As a result Egyptian proper names in the Old Testament and Egyptian in other North-West Semitic documents were largely neglected. There is little progress in his study concerning Egyptian in Aramaic and Phoenician. Furthermore his main interest was in identifications, not in the phonetic relationship between two languages.

Finally perhaps it is legitimate to mention in this section Kornfeld's *Onomastica Aramaica aus Ägypten*, pp. 77–97, because of the bulky collection of Egyptian PNs in Aramaic in which he studied 229 Egyptian PNs. However his work suffers from its failure to check the original publications and the Coptic forms, and from the acceptance of the wider correspondence between Egyptian and Aramaic. Recently G. Vittmann has remedied many of these weaknesses, "Zu den ägyptischen Entsprechung aramäisch überlieferter Personennamen" *Or.* NS 58 (1989) pp. 213–229.

The present study differs from those of Spiegelberg and Lambdin in bringing together all Egyptian elements in all North-West Semitic documents and analysing them historically and geographically with concentration on phonetic aspects. It affords a more consistent comparison between Egyptian and North-West Semitic, even some comparison among North-West Semitic languages. The continuing discoveries of ancient texts in Egypt and the Near East also enable the present work to take much more material into account than the earlier studies.

12 Parts were later published as independent articles; "Egyptian Loanwords in the Old Testament," *JAOS* 73 (1952) pp. 145–155; "Egyptian Words in Tell-El Amarna Letter No. 14" *Or.* NS 22 (1953) pp.362–369.

I

EGYPTIAN PROPER NAMES AND LOANWORDS IN PHOENICIAN AND PUNIC

The personal names in Phoenician and Punic documents have been collected and analysed by F. Benz, who published his dissertation *Personal Names in the Phoenician and Punic Inscriptions* in Rome in 1972. I am indebted to his work for my collection of Egyptian personal names and for checking the possibility of Semitic explanations of the names. For discoveries after 1970, which was when his work virtually ended, I used the Semitic proper names found every year in the index of "Bulletin d'Epigraphie Semitique" by J. Teixidor in *Syria* 44 (1967) –56 (1979).[1] These two works are the main sources of my collection of Egyptian names, though I have checked each publication of new Phoenician and Punic inscriptions wherever possible.

As for Egyptian names in Phoenician texts, T. Lambdin first collected 4 Egyptian DNs and 15 Egyptian PNs in his dissertation.[2] All these possibilities except one were followed by Benz (p. 192f) and he added six names, though most of his identifications are not certain.

1 This was republished as a single volume: Javier Teixidor, *Bulletin d'Epigraphie Sémitiqine* (1964–1980), (Paris: Librairie Orientaliste Paul Geuthner, 1986).

2 Thomas O. Lambdin, *Egyptian Loanwords and Transcriptions in the Ancient Semitic Languages* (unpublished Ph. D dissertation subimitted to the Johns Hopkins University) Baltimore 1952. For the previous studies of Egyptian names in Phoenician, see p. 116 and 131. Among them the most important is W. Spiegelberg, "Die Ägyptischen Personennamen in den kurzlich veröffentlichten Urkunden von Elephantine," *OLZ* 15 (1912) pp. 1–11.

Recently G. Vittmann reexamined these Egyptian names and added seven more Eg names.[3] In the present paper 53 personal names, 11 divine names, 3 geographical names, and 2 loanwords are collected. Only those which have two asterisks will be used for the final analysis.

A. PHOENICIAN AND PUNIC DOCUMENTS: DATES AND PROVENANCES

It is not only impossible but also unnecessary to enter into an exhaustive discussion on the dating of Phoenician inscriptions, because it is not our main purpose. It is important, however, to give a date for each document in which the Egyptian names occur for the purpose of the chronological correspondences of Egyptian and Phoenician forms. Therefore, in the following list I usually followed the widely accepted dates, while trying to accept recent discussions on the dates as much as possible.

The dates of the documents are determined by two different criteria: (1) Historical information mentioned in documents (*e.g.* Pumiyaton 362/1–312 BC; the Nubian campaign of Psammeticus II 593 BC[4]) and (2) paleography. Since dated inscriptions are quite limited, the majority of the inscriptions are dated on the basis of the paleography. The accuracy of the paleographical determination is enhanced to a considerable extent by B. Peckham, *The Development of the Late Phoenician Scripts*, 1968. When he discussed the dates of the documents, I have mostly followed him. The grounds of each date are found in footnotes. If there is no footnote the dates of the documents are those given by the scholars who published the document I quoted. The dates of a few documents in *CIS* are based upon Harris' *A Grammar of the Phoenician Language* p. 157. The dates are given only for the documents which have Egyptian names used for the later analysis.

---

[3] G. Vittmann, "Zu den in den phönikischen Inschriften enthaltenen ägyptischen Personennamen," *GM* 113 (1989) pp.91–96.

[4] K. A. Kitchen *TIP* § 368.

[1] ***CIS* I**

9	2nd cent. BC	Umm el-'Awamid
11 (*KAI* 33)	325 BC[5]	Cition
12	4th (–3th) cent. BC	Cition
13	*ca.*300 BC[6]	Cition
46 (*KAI* 35)	end of 4th cent. BC	Cition
53	early 3rd cent. BC[7]	Cition
58	4th–3rd cent. BC	Cition
86 (*KAI* 35)	450–400 BC[8]	Cition
88	386 BC[9]	Idalion
93 (*KAI* 40)	255/4 BC[10]	Idalion
102a (*KAI* 49.34)	5th–3rd cent. BC[11]	Abydos
102c (*KAI* 49.36)	5th–3rd cent. BC	Abydos
111	592 BC[12]	Abu Simbel
112	592 BC	Abu Simbel
118 (*KAI* 58)	3rd cent. BC[13]	Piräus (Greece)
122 (*KAI* 47)	2nd cent. BC[14]	Malta
144 (*KAI* 46)	mid 9th cent. BC[15]	Nora
154	5th–4th cent. BC[16]	Tharros
197–375	400–146 BC[17]	Carthage
617	3rd cent. BC[18]	Carthage
670–3557	400–146 BC	Carthage
3778 (*KAI* 78)	3rd cent. BC	Carthage
3919–5522	400–146 BC	Carthage
5523 (*KAI* 96)	2nd half of 3rd cent. BC	Carthage

---

5 Peckham, pp. 18, n. 27; 21. *KAI* 33.

6 *Ibid.*, p. 7 and 24.

7 *Ibid.*, p. 37

8 *Ibid.*, p. 7. Cf. J. P. Healey's date: *ca.* 550 BC in "The Kition Tariffs and the Phoenician Cursive Series,"*BASOR*, 216 (1974) pp. 53–60.

9 *Ibid.*, p. 9 and 24.

10 *Ibid.*, p. 23f.

11 *KAI* 49.

12 Peckham, p. 106 and 161.

13 *KAI* 58.

14 *Ibid.*, p. 69. F. Cross dated it late 2nd cent. BC (*IEJ*, 14, 1964, p. 186, n. 9).

15 W. Röllig, "Paläographische Beobachtungen zum ersten Auftreten der Phonizier in Sardinien" in *Antitiron Jürgen Thimme* p. 128.

16 G. Amadasi, *IFP*, p. 94.

17 Peckham, p. 195ff. Note the fall of Carthage in 146 BC.

18 *Ibid.*, p. 182.

5852–5991 (*KAI* 91)	400–146 BC	Carthage
[2] ***Krug***	mid 5th cent. BC	Elephantine
[3] ***RES***		
1 (*KAI* 48.2)	2nd–1st cent. BC[19]	Memphis
235 (*KAI* 48.3)	same as above	
297		
298	mid–5th cent. BC[20]	Sidon
307	2nd half of 2nd cent. BC[21]	Umm el-'Awamid
662 (*KAI* 118)	15–17 AD[22]	Ras el-Haddagia
800 (*KAI* 17)	2nd cent. BC[23]	Tyre
928	n.d.	n.p.
1216 (*KAI* 68)	3rd cent. BC[24]	Terranova-Pausania
1332 (*KAI* 49.37)	5th–3rd cent. BC[25]	Abydos
1340	5th–3rd cent. BC[26]	Abydos
1507 (*KAI* 52)	4th–2nd cent. BC[27]	unknown (Egypt)
[4] ***KAI***		
12	3rd–2nd cent. BC[28]	Byblos
29	mid–7th cent. BC[29]	Ur
50	6th cent. BC[30]	Saqqara
51	4th–3rd cent.BC	n.p.
100	n.d.	Dougga
124	53 AD	Leptis Magna

19 *KAI* 48.

20 A. Vonel, "Six Ostraca phéniciens trouvés au temple d'Echmoun près de Saïde," *BMB*, 20 (1965) pp. 45–95 esp. p. 58f.

21 M. G. Amadasi, *IFP*, p. 18

22 *KAI* 118.

23 Peckham, p. 77; also *KAI* 17.

24 *KAI* 68.

25 *KAI* 49; G. Amadasi, *IFP* p.66.

26 M. Lidzbarski, *Eph.* III, p.96.

27 Peckham, p. 128, n. 69.

28 *Ibid.*, p. 45 and 54; cf.*KAI* and Dussaud (*Syria*, 6 p. 269) dated it as 1st cent. AD.

29 *Ibid.*, p. 105 and 127.

30 *Ibid.*, p. 128 and *KAI*.

[5] *APO*

82 n.d.

[6] **Journals**

N. Aimé-Giron, *BIFAO*, 23 (1924) p. 3: end of 5th cent. BC, Egypt

M. Chéhab, *BMB*, 13 (1956) p. 43–52, No. 4.1, 2: end of 3rd– end of 2nd cent. B C, Umm el-'Awamid.

A. Dupont-Sommer, *JKF*, 1 (1950) p. 44.1: 9th– 8th cent. BC, Cilicia

M. Dunand, *BMB*, 18 (1965) p. 106: 2nd half of 5th cent. BC[31], Sidon.

R. Barnett, *BMQ*, 27 (1963– 1964) p. 85: 5th cent.BC[32] , Egypt.

A. Honeymann, *JRAS*, (1960) p.111.1: 327 BC[33] , Cyprus.

M. Lidzbarski, *OLZ*, 30 (1927) p. 458: n.d., Byblos

W. Kornfeld, *AÖAW*, 115 (1978) p. 203: Abydos.

F. Vattioni, *SF*, p.180, No.4 and 5: n.d., n.p.

[7] **Other Works**

M. Amadasi, *IFP*, p. 39: 5th– 4th cent. BC, Malta.

————. *IFP*, p. 93: 5th– beginning of 4th cent. BC[34] Tharros

E. Babelon, *Traité des monnaies*, p. 758f.: 361– 312 BC.

A. Berthier-R. Charlier, *El-Hofra*, p. 256.1

————. *El-Hofra*, p. 138.3

G. Cooke, *NSI*, 149, B6: 361– 312 BC, Cition

N. Dunand, *Fouilles de Byblos*, vol.1 no. 1111a, Byblos

G. Hill, *Catalogue of the Greek Coins of Cyprus*, p. 21– 22: 361– 312 BC, Cition

J. Fevrier, *IAM*, p. 116: 3rd cent. BC, Maroc

M. A. Levy, *SG*, p. 24: n.d./n.p.

————. *SG*, p. 25: n.d./n.p.

P. Magnanini, *IFO*, p. 63: n.d., Abu Simbel.
p. 122: 3rd cent. BC, Idalion.
p. 21: 2nd cent. BC, Umm el-'Awamid.
p. 77: 5th cent. BC, Elephantine.

J. Segal, *Saqqara* : 5th cent. BC, Saqqara.

---

31 Teixidor, *Bulletin*, p. 210.

32 *Ibid.*, p. 126 and 334; Röllig, *Welt Or.*, 5 (1968) p.118–120.

33 Peckham, p. 18, n. 27.

34 M. L. Uberti, "Scarabeo Punic del Museo Archeologico Nazionale de Cagliari,"*Atti del 1° Convegno Italiano Vicino Oriente Antico*, (1978) p. 160.

B. INVENTORY OF EGYPTIAN PROPER NAMES AND LOANWORDS

[1] Personal Names

אבאי

--- *ibi* 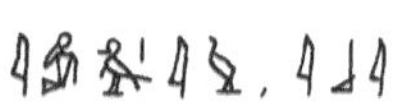

[Ph] papyrus: *KAI* 51.Rs.3 “son of פטבנטט”

[Eg] Ranke I.20.9 m. Late; I.20.10 m./f. OK– Dyn 26; *DemNB* I.61(*iby*); [Gk] cf. 'Ιβοϊς,'Ειβοϊς, 'Ιβῶϊς, 'Ιβόεις (*NB* p. 146)

Cf. Aram אבא

The reading אבאי is not sure. Yet the Egyptian origin of this name is also suggested by *KAI* (III, p. 69). Both affiliation and provenance support אבאי as an Egyptian. What is more, there seems to be no Semitic explanation. Eg common name *ibi* is the nearest equation, though it does not correspond exactly to אבאי.

אבראס (hybrid) **

--- אבר-*3s(.t)* “Isis is strong”

[Pu] Berthier-Chaarlier, *El-Hophra* p. 155 no. 256.1

[Eg] see DN אס.

אחמן (hybrid) **

--- אח-*mn(.w)* “Brother of Min”

V I p. 93

[Ph] *Krug* 150

[Eg] for *mn.w* see *Wb* II.72.11.

Vittmann explained it as a pure Eg name *i(ʿ)ḥ-mn* “moon-Min” (*DemNB* I.58), which is equally possible.

אחמס **

--- *i(ʿ)ḥ-ms* 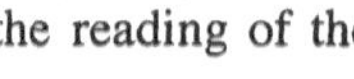 “The moon is born”

V I p.93

[Ph] *CIS* I.111.1

[Eg] Ranke I.12.19 m. Mk– Gk; *DemNB* I.58; [Aram] אחמס [Gk] 'Αχμασις, 'Αμασις, 'Αμοσις, 'Αμωσις (*NB* p. 69, 22, 27, 29)

As for the reading of the final letter ([-]אחמ), see Peckham, p.

106, no. 7, and p. 161. See also his discussion about the date of this inscription p. 127f. The loss of Eg *'ayn* appears from NK *i(ʿ)ḥ* (*Wb* I.42) and Copt. ᵇⲓⲟϩ , ˢⲟⲟϩ, ᶠⲁⲁϩ. cf. Heb ירח, Akk *warḫu*; they perhaps share a common ancestor (Spiegelberg, II. p. 8).

אלאמן (hybrid) **

--- אל- *imn* "Amon is god"

[Ph/Pu] seal: Levy, *SG* p. 24 no. 5; *CIS* I.1331.3/4]אמן

[Eg] see Heb DN אמון.

אמחפי *

--- **im(y.t)-ḥpy*

[Ph] ostracon: Saqqara, IV (corrected to אמחפי by J. Naveh, *IEJ* 35 p. 211)

[Eg] cf. *im.y-ptḥ* (Ranke I.25.24 f. NK); *im.y-p.t* (Ranke I.25.23)

Likewise possible is a hybrid name אמ-*ḥpy* "Mother of Apis."

אמננך **

--- *imn-nḫ(w)* "Amun is a protector"

[Ph] seal: Vattioni, *SF* no. 5 לפתח בן אמננך

[Eg] Ranke I.29.20 m. NK.

The reading of is not *nḫ* (Ranke I.29, n. 2), but *nḫw* "protector" (*Wb* II.304.14f).

אמתאסר (hybrid) **

--- אמת-*3s-ir* "Servant of Osiris"

[Ph] *CIS* I.93.2

[Eg] see DN אסר.

אסברך (hybrid) **

--- *3s(.t)*-ברכ "Isis has blessed"

[Ph] Magnanini, *IFO* p. 21, no. 12.2

[Eg] see DN אס.

אסעא **

--- **3s(.t)-ʿ3(.t)* "Isis is great"

[Ph] *KAI* 12.3
[Eg] cf. *imn-ʿ3* (Ranke I.26.26), *ptḥ-ʿ3* (I.138.18), *ḥr-ʿ3* (I.246.9), *mw.t-ʿ3* (I.147.12)
Cf. Aram אסיתעא (*3s.t-t3-ʿ3* "Isis the great"); Ph עחר (*ʿ3-ḥr* "Horus is great").

Donner-Röllig (*KAI* 12) considered that אסעא is a hypocoristicon of *אסעמם, which does not exist. The *aleph* of *ʿ3.t* was possibly preserved by the feminine ending *-t*.

[א]סראדר (hybrid)
--- *3s-(i)r-*אדר "Osiris is mighty"
[Ph] Magnanini, *IFO* p. 122, no. 12.1
[Eg] see DN אסר.

אסרגן (hybrid) **
--- *3s-(i)r-*גן "Osiris is a protector"
[Pu] *CIS* I.821.4
[Eg] see DN אסר.

אסרשמר (hybrid) **
--- *3s-(i)r-*שמר "Osiris is a keeper"
[Ph] *CIS* I.122.2, 3
[Eg] see DN אסר.

אסרתני (hybrid) **
--- *3s-(i)r-*תני "Osiris, give him"
[Ph] *Krug* 1
[Eg] see DN אסר

For the interpretation of this name, see Benz p. 217.

אסתכ̊י̊נ̊ (hybrid)
--- *3s(.t)-*תכני "Isis establishes" (Benz p. 209)
[Pu] *CIS* I.1159.2
[Eg] see DN אס.

אפן
--- *ipn* 𓇋𓊪𓈖 (meaning unknown)
[Pu] J.-B. Chabot "Punica" *JA*, Series II. vol 10 (1917) pp. 53–71.

[Eg] Ranke I.24.10 m.Late/f.MK.

Benz did not explain the name, yet he suggested a possible connection with the Ug name *apn* (*UT* 19.307).

אשפמד

--- *(n)s-p(3)-md(w)* 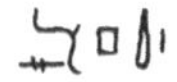 "He belong to the (sacred) staff" (?)

[Ph] *APO* 69.11

[Eg] see Aram אספמת

B. Porten pointed out that the name is Phoenician. The correspondence between Ph ד and Eg *d* could be justified by Aram אבוט/אבוד *(3bḏw)* "Elephantine." However the second letter ש, corresponding to Eg *s* is troublesome.

Cf. Aram אספמת.

את **

--- *it(f)*  "Father"

[Ph] *CIS* I.6059; seal: Vattioni, *SF* no. 44.

[Eg] Ranke I.50.13 m. Dyn 6–Late/f. MK.

אתם *

--- **itm* "Atum"

[Pu] *CIS* I.5548

[Eg] cf. *Wb* I.144.5.

The Eg god Atum is not attested as a PN. Nevertheless, it is quite possible that Atum was used as a PN, because many other DNs, such as *ḥr, ptḥ, imn* etc., were frequently used alone as PNs.

בבא

--- *bb.i, bb.i(w), b(3)b3* 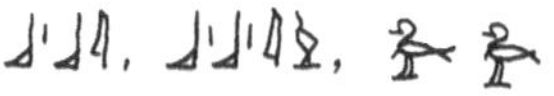

[Pu] *CIS* I.3025.2 בבא

[Eg] Ranke I.95.16, 19; 96.3–9 m./f. OK–Late; [Aram] בבא

Semitic possibilities are Akk *babu* (*APN* p. 49); Ug *bn bb*(*UT*. 19.440); Heb בֵּבָי (Neh 10:16, Ezr 2:11); Talmudic *bābāʾ*, *bēbay* (see Benz p. 282), though the Egyptian name is equally possible.

בבי

--- Var. of בבא

[Pu] *CIS* I.3108.3; *KAI* 100.7 בבי

[Eg] see אבב.

בדסי (hybrid) *

--- בד-*3s(.t)* "By the hand of Isis"

[Pu] *CIS* I.5684.2

[Eg] see DN אס

It is most likely that סי is a deity (Benz p. 364). That סי is *3s.t* is perhaps supported to some extent by the Aramaic form נפסי (*nfr-3s.t*), פטסי (*p3-di-3s.t*). Yet this is the sole case where Isis occurs as סי in Pu texts.

בכא **

--- *b(3)k.i*

[Ph] seal: Levy, *SG* p. 25 (no. 6)

[Eg] Ranke I.90.13; cf. Ranke I.93.19 and 20; 98.25 and 26 m. MK– Late/f. NK. The entry of Ranke I.90.13 should be divided into *b3k* and *b3ki*; [Gk] [B?]ακκις, Βαχη, Βαχιος, Βηκις, Βοκως, Βυκης (*NB* p. 70ff); [NA] *bak-ki-e* (Postgate, *Fifty NA Legal Docum.*, no. 18.36; see Zadok, *GM* 26 p. 64).

בלא *

--- *br* 

[Pu] *CIS* I.132.7

[Eg] see Aram בלא.

בנאס (hybrid) **

--- בנ-*3s(.t)* "Son of Isis"

[Ph] Magnanini, *IFO* p. 77, no. 39

[Eg] see DN אס.

בנחף (hybrid) **

--- בנ-*ḥp* "Son of Apis"

[Ph] *Krug* 34b

[Eg] for *ḥp* see *Wb* III.70.

Cf. Gk Απις; Copt ^{S}ϩⲁⲡⲉ, ^{B}ϩⲁⲡⲓ ; Aram חפי.

בעלחנת (hybrid) **

--- בעל-*ẖnt(y)* "(a crocodile god) *ẖnty* is lord"

[Ph] *CIS* I.52.2

[Eg] For *ḫnty* see *Wb* III.308.6f.

בשא

--- *bš3(w)*

[Ph] *KAI* 50.2

[Eg] Ranke I.98.22 m. NK(?); [Aram] cf. בשאה; [Akk] cf. *Ba-sa-a* (*APN* p. 53a)

Eg *bš3w* corresponds to בשא. Though בשא is feminine in the Ph text while Eg *bš3w* is masculine, it is to be remembered that many Eg names are used without distinction of sex.

הר *

--- *hr(.t)* "Contentment, Joy"

[Pu] *CIS* I.2511.5

[Eg] Ranke I.230.21 f. Late

There is a Semitic root *hr* "mountain," which once occurs in הרבעל. Yet there seems to be no example of Semitic הר alone as PN.

הרב

--- *hr-(i)b* "The contented"

[Pu] *CIS* I.375.5; 1386.2

[Eg] Ranke I.230.5–7 m. OK–Gk/f. Late–Gk; [Aram] הריו;

[Gk] cf 'Εριεῦς (*NB*.p. 103).

Only if the *ib* () of *hr-ib* is not a determinative, is the identification possible (see the discussion in Aram הריוטא). Another possibility is **hrw-ip.t* "the day of festival of the 12th month" (cf. *hrw-nfr* "happy day" Ranke I.231.4 m. OK–NK; For *ip.t* see *Wb* I.68.11).

הרבעל (hybrid) **

--- *hr-*בעל "Ba'al is contented"

[Ph] Dunand, *Fouilles de Byblos*, no. 1111a

[Eg] cf. *hr* + DN type names, such as *hr-b3st.t* (Ranke I.230.20f Late).

Cf. הרב, הר.

וא

--- *wỉ(3)*  "Boat"
Benz p. 192; K p. 121; V I p. 91
[Ph] *Krug* 11b לוא בר צחפמו
[Eg] Ranke I.75.24 m./f. MK–NK; [Gk] cf. Οὔϊος (*NB* p. 248)

Benz considered the name to be Eg *w3r* (Ranke I.72.14), which is attested once in the Late period. Since Eg final *r* dropped in NK, it is possible, yet we have to admit that the final א would function as a vowel letter indicating [i], which is unlikely. In terms of its affiliation, an Eg name is preferable, though it does not offer a strong support. If this is an Eg name *wỉ(3)* is more likely. The preservation of Eg *ỉ* of *wỉ3* at the end is demonstrated in such names in Aram as פתחמוא (*ptḥ-m-wỉ3*), פנוא (*p3-n-wỉ3*). Lidzbarski suggested that the name is a short form of a Semitic name such as אבא (so attested in Talmud; *Krug* p. 7). Yet as Vittmann pointed out, it is more likely that the name is a לוא (ל is not a preposition). For this name attested in Ph, see Teixidor *Bulletin*, p. 489.

וחפרע **

--- *w(3)ḥ-(ỉ)b-rʿ*  "Reʿ is kindly"
Benz p. 192
[Ph] Nöel Aimé-Giron, *BIFAO* 23 p. 5.
[Eg] Ranke I.72.28 m. Late–Gk; II p. 348; *DemNB* I.113; [Gk] Ουαφρῆ (LXX), Οὔαφρις (Manetho), 'Απρίης (Herodotus and Diodorus), 'Οαφρῆς, Ουαφρης (*NB* p. 239, 246), 'Απριας (Ctesias, Athenaeum 13); [Heb] חפרע (Eg king Dyn 26, Jer 44:30); [Akk] cf. *uḫ-pa-ra-sa-a, u-uḫ-pa-ra-sa-a* (E. Weidner, in *Mélanges Syriens offerts à R. Dussaud*, II, pp. 931f; for Eg *w3ḥ-ib-rʿ-s* Ranke II.348); [Aram] וחפרע; [Copt] cf. ΟΥΒΦΡΗ (*w3ḥ-ib-p3-rʿ DemNB* I.132).

It is noteworthy that Heb חפרע does not have an initial weak consonant *w*. The loss of the initial *w* is probably connected with the general feature that in Hebrew the *waw* can hardly come at the initial position in words. For example, at the beginning of a word, when the *waw* is not supported by a full vowel, it drops (cf. דַע for וְדַע, see Gesenius, §19h). Perhaps the change is *w(3)ḥ-(ỉ)b-rʿ* *[wăḥparaʻ] > *[uḥparaʻ] (cf. Akk. *Uḫ-pa-ra*) > *[ḥoparaʻ] (Anaptyxis) > [ḥopraʻ] (vowel syncope).

It is certainly interesting that Eg *b* corresponds to פ in Ph, Heb,

Aram, and even Akk probably because it is placed before [r]. Notice that Akk forms *uḫ-*, *ʾu-uḫ* do not indicate an initial consonant; if there were an initial consonant, it should have been written as *mu-uḫ*.

חאר

--- *ḥr*  "Horus" (?)
Teixidor, *Bulletin* p. 129 (no. 72)
[Ph] Masson, *BCH* 93 pp.694–700
[Eg] see חר

Teixidor considered the name to be Horus. Yet the identification is open to question, because of the middle *aleph*.

חב **

--- *ḥb(.y)*  "He of festival"(?)
[Ph] seal: Vattioni, *SF* no. 8
[Eg] Ranke I.236.15 m. NK

This root is not attested in Ph and Pu. Harris suggested it is an abbreviation of a name (Harris, *Grammar*, p. 99). There is a Heb PN חֹבָב (Num 10:29) which is not quite comparable, because of the gemination of ב, though BDB suggests a possible connection. An Eg name, therefore, is most likely because *ḥb* is common as a word (*Wb* III.57.5) and a PN since OK.

In terms of name-giving, Eg PN *ḥb.y* perphaps shows the same practice as Heb חגיה "feast of Yah" and Ebla *du-bu-hi*-DN, *Ard-nubatti, Ardrssesu* indicate. They were most likely born on a day of festival (A. Millard, *ARES*, I, p. 164).

חלבס[35]

--- *ḥrbs* "The face of Bes"

[Ph] *Krug* 10.2 חלפס (Reading quite uncertain. The following discussions are based on the assumption that the reading חלבס is correct).

[Eg] Ranke I.253.27 m. Late; *DemNB* I.205 (*p3-ḥr-bs*/*ḥrbs*); [Gk] χάλβης, 'Αλαβῆσις (*NB* p. 17. see also A. Leahy, *Cd'E* 55 p. 57–58; Fraser, *JEA* 40 p. 135); [NA/NB] *ḫa-la-bé-e-su* (Niseman, *Iraq*, 28 p. 156); *ḫal-la-bi-še, ḫa-la-bi-e-si, ḫa-la-bi-e-še*. See also R. Zadok, *GM* 64 p. 73 for these cuneiform correspondences.

J. D. Ray suggested that חלבס is perhaps *Ḥalebēs (**ḥr.ỉ-bs*) "Bes has flown" (note that *ḥr.ỉ* is ϩⲱⲗ in Copt). This solution is phonetically better, though *ḥr.ỉ* "to fly" seems not to be used in PNs.

חמבעל (hybrid) **

--- *ḥm*-בעל "The servant of Ba'al"

[Ph] *CIS* I.4734.3

[Eg] cf. *ḥm* + DN type name, Ranke I.239.17ff. *ḥm-ptḥ* "the servant of Ptah" (m. Late), *ḥm-mn.w* "the servant of Min" (m. OK), *ḥm-ḥtḥr* (m. OK).

חמי *

--- *ḥm(.t)* "Maidservant"

---

35 Since Ranke cited this name wrongly (Ranke I.253.27), it has been spelled חלבס, rather than חלפס (Lidzbarski) by most scholars (J. Griffith, D. Wiseman, A. Leahy, R. Zadok). Although Lidzbarski stated that the reading of this name is certain (*Krug*. p. 6), we can be sure from the photograph of only two letters; namely, the first letter ח and the last letter ס. The second letter, which most scholars have considered ל, is not likely to be ל, in comparison with another ל which occurs in the previous line in עבדבעל. It could be the trace of an erased letter. The third letter can not be ב, because we have in this inscription three othe בs which show a consistent form of ב. The ב of חלבס does not look like the other three בs. פ is more likely, as Lidzbarski read it.

For the discussions of this name, see J. Gwyn Griffiths "Is Cholbe a Greek name?" *ASAE* 51 (1951) pp. 219f., and A. Leahy, "«ḤARWA» and «ḤARBES»" *Cd'E* 55 (1980) pp. 43–63, esp. 56–62. He observed that Eg. *ḥr* "Horus" is always written as חר in Semitic, while the other *ḥr* (, ,) could be rendered by חל in Semitic (The phonetic change of Eg. *r* to Semitic ל was discussed by W. A. Ward (*Or* NS 32, p. 419 n. 1). Benz (p. 109 and 311) identified a Semitic root חלף "to change", "to substitute" in חלבס, which he explained as חלפ(א)ס. Yet we should remember that חלף is not found in Ph but in Aram, Heb, and Arab (Lidzbarski, *Krug*. p. 6).

[Ph] *CIS* I.3179.5; 3709.5; 4924.4/5; 5730.3; 5951.2;
[Eg] Ranke I.240.3 f. NK–Dyn 22

Equally possible is *ḫm.i* , (Ranke I.269.14 m/f. MK); *ḫm.y* (Ranke I.259.15 f. NK).

חמנכת **

--- **ḥm-nḫt* "Servant of (god) the Mighty"
[Pu] *CIS* I.336.3
[Eg] For *ḥm* as a PN element, see Ranke I.239.16, also *ḥm* + DN type names: *ḥm-ptḥ, ḥm-mn.w, ḥm-rʿ* etc. For *nḫt* as an epithet for a deity, see *p3-n-nḫt* "He who belongs to the Mighty" (Ranke I.109.6 and 7 m. Dyn 20–Gk).

חנתס

--- *ḥnt(3)s(w)* "Lizard"
Benz p. 192; V I p. 91
[Ph] statue: *RES* 1507.2 (*KAI* 52)
[Eg] *Wb* III.122; [Demot] *ḥnts* (Erichsen p. 315); [Copt] ⲁⲛⲑⲟⲩⲥ as a PN ϩⲁⲛⲧⲟⲩⲥ (Crum p. 11b)

Benz suggested the Eg origin of this name and identified it with *ḥnw.t-š3* (Ranke I.244.4). However Eg *š* usually does not correspond to Ph ס. While *ḥnw.t.s* (quoted by *KAI* 52) is attested only in OK, *ḥnts.w* (Ranke I.245.13) is attested in MK. Vittmann compared it with Demot *ḥnts* "Lizard." If the name is Eg, Vittmann's solution is most likely.

חף **

--- *ḥp*
[Ph] ostracon: Saqqara, XX
[Eg] Ranke I.237.1 m. MK–NK / f. OK–MK.
Cf. Aram DN חף.

חפיו **

--- *ḥp-iw* , "the Apis has come"
L p. 131; Benz p. 192
[Ph] *krug* 47.2, 54.1.
[Eg] Ranke I.237.5 m. NK(?)–Late; [Gk] 'Απιεῦς, 'Επεῦς (*NB* p. 39, 100) "Απιος, "Αππιος, 'Απιοῦς, 'Απεων, 'Απιων; [Aram]

חפיאו, חפיו

Phonetic correspondence is a little difficult. The following other forms give us some clues for the phonetic reconstruction; Aramaic form fully written חפיאו (cf. חפיו); [Copt] ^{s}ϩⲁⲡⲉ, ^{b}ϩⲁⲡⲓ (Apis); Copt ⲉⲓ[ⲓ] "to come"; Akk ^{m}*Na-aḫ-tu-ḫa-ap-pi-i* (Ranke *KM*, p. 39), ^{m}*Uk-ḫa-ap-pi-i* (*Ibid.*, p. 41); [Gk] 'Απιευς; therefore, [*Ḥapi'i/ew] < [*Ḥapi-i(a).w(u)], then intervocalic *aleph* droped or merged [Ḥapīw] > Ph חפיו, Aram חפיו, Gk 'Επευς, ῎Απιος, 'Απιοῦς. The final ו is an element of *sḏm.w* form (old perfective).

חפת

--- *ḥpt* "Embrace"

[Ph] seal: Clermont-Ganneau, *JA* Series 8 vol.1

[Eg] Ranke I.239.1 m/f. MK–Late.

חר **

--- *ḥr* "Horus"

V I p. 93

[Ph] *CIS* I.46.1; *RES* 1340; [Ph] 4319.5, 4945.3/4

[Eg] Ranke I.245.18 m. OK–Gk /f. MK–NK; [Gk] ʽΩρος, ῞Ωρ, ῞Ωρο, ῞Ωρρος, ῞Ωρως, ῞Ορος, ῞Ορ, ʽΑρους (*NB* p. 52, 242f, 497); [Copt] ϩⲱⲣ, ϩⲁⲣ-; [Aram] חר, חור; [Heb] חור; [Ug] *ḥr* (Gröndahl, p. 136); [NA] ^{m}*Ḫu-u-ru* (*APN* p. 90a; Ranke, *KM* 29; Zadok, *GM* 26, p. 64; cf. *CAD* H p. 256 *ḫuru* "son").

חרוץ **

--- *ḥr-wḏ(3)* , "Horus is prosperous"

L p. 131f; Benz p. 192

[Ph] *Krug* 40

[Eg] Ranke I.246.23; p. 378; 251.24 m. Late–Gk; [Gk] ʽΑρουωθις, ʽΑρουώθης, ʽΑρυώτης (*NB* p. 52, 57); [Aram] חרוט, חרוץ; [Copt] ϩⲉⲣⲟⲩⲟϫ; [NB] *Ḫar-ma-ṣu, Ḫa-ar-ma-ṣu* (Wiseman, *Iraq* 28 p. 155).

חרכף *

--- **ḥr-k(3)p* "Horus is Bird catcher"

[Ph] *Krug* 54.2.

[Eg] cf. *p3-k3p.w* "The bird catcher" (Ranke I.120.5 m. Late–Gk).

cf. *p3-ir-k3p* (Ranke I.101.15 m. Late).

Another possibility is **ḥr-kf3* "Horus is trust-worthy" (cf. *kf3* "the Trustworthy" Ranke I.334.15).

חרמס **

--- *ḥr-ms(.w)*  "Horus is born"

[Ph] Berthier-Charlier, *El -Hofra* 138.3

[Eg] Ranke I.249.1 m. MK–Gk / f. MK–NK; [Gk] Ἑρμᾶς (*NB* p. 104).

ימחת **

--- *i(i)-m-ḥt(p)* 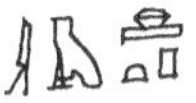 "Coming in peace"

V I p. 93

[Ph] *Krug* 14a.

[Eg] Ranke I.9.2 m. OK–Gk; *DemNB* I.55; [Gk] Ἰμούθης, Εἰμούθης, Ἰμουτ, Ἰμουτης, Ἰεμουθης (*NB* p. 149); [Aram] אמחות, ימחות

With respect to the dropping of the final *p* of *ḥtp*, we could compare it with its late form  (*Wb* III.188). Gk forms also support that the final *p* dropped. Yet it should be remembered that Coptic still preserves the final *p* as ϩⲱⲧⲡ, ϩⲱⲡⲧ̄. The root מחת is not attested in Semitic, so the interpretation as an imperfect form, which Benz offered, is impossible.

יפתא

--- *ipt.y*

[Pu] Berthier-Charlier, *El-Hofra* 161.2, 3.

[Eg] Ranke I.24.19 m. NK–Late

Considering that laryngals and pharyngals were merged in the Late Punic, a Semitic explanation; יפתח > יפתא is not impossible. However, the א for ח seems to be restricted in the initial position (Benz p. 204; cf. Friedrich-Röllig, *PPG*2 p. 14f.).

יתנחף (hybrid) **

--- יתן-*ḥpy* "Apis has given"

[Ph] *Krug* 2, 5, 16

[Eg] see *Wb* III.70.1ff.

כנמי

--- **k̟n-m(3) ỉ* "The lion is strong"
[Pu] *CIS* I.3785.3
[Eg] cf. *k̟n* + DN type names (Ranke I.334.18ff): *k̟n-mn* (m. NK–Dyn 21). For מי (*m3ỉ*), see Ph. פמי.
The equation of Ph כ for Eg *k̟* is a little questionable.

כנפון

--- **k(3.ỉ)-nf(r)-wp* "My beautiful ka exists"
[Pu] *CIS* I.4531.4/5.
[Eg] cf. *k3(ỉ)-nfr*  (Ranke I.340.10 m. OK–Late) and *nfr.w-wn* (Ranke I.203.23).

כנפי **

--- **k(3.ỉ)-nf(r)*  "(My) ka is good" or "(My) beautiful ka"
L p. 132; Benz p. 192.
[Ph] *Krug* 24
[Eg] Ranke I.340.10 m. OK–Late; [Gk] Κνοῦφις, Χνοῦφις (*NB* p. 181, 478); [Aram] כנופי
Loss of the final *r* of Eg *nfr* is common enough (מנף = *mn-nfr*, Copt. ˢⲚⲞⲨϤⲈ, ᵇⲚⲞⲨϤⲒ, Černý, *LEG* § 1.9). Yet the plural form or old perfective form *nfr.w* preserved the *r* with the protection of the final *-w* (cf. Copt ⲚⲞⲨϤⲢ). Hence the Eg Crrespondenc of כנפי is not *k3-nfr.w* as Benz suggested (Ranke I.338.6, 340.10). The final י is most likely to be a vowel letter (see the later discussion: [5] The Possible *matres ledtionis* in Ph).

כשי **

--- *(ỉ)kš*  + gentilic י "The Nubian"
L p. 132; Benz p.192; V I p.92
[Ph] graffito: *CIS* I.112 c. 1 [י]כש, c. 2 כשי; graftito: Magnanini, *IFO* p. 63.4; Lidzbarski, 30 p. 458[36]
[Eg] Ranke I.48.23; *DemNB* I.80; cf. Ranke I.102.4 m. Dyn 22; [Copt] ⲉϭⲱϣ, ⲉⲑⲱϣ "Nubian"; [Gk] 'Εκυσις, 'Εκουσιος, Κοῦσις, Χούσης (*NB* pp. 97, 185, 478) cf. πεκυσις, πεχυσιος, πεχῦσις (*NB* p. 259); [Heb] כוש, כושי; [Aram] כשי; [NA] *ku-ú/u-si* (Assurb. I.53, 78 as GN), cf. *ku-sa-a-a*, *ku-sa-ia-a* (*APN* p.

36 Dussud's reading בנפנמי (*Syria*, 6, 1925, p.270f.) was corrected by Lidzbarski. For the text from Abu Simbel, see also J Friedrich, *ZDMG* 114, 1964,

119a); [MB] *kōši* ; [NB] *kūšu*.

(*i*) of *iks* is a prothetic *aleph* which is not reflected in Ph. texts. The loss of the *aleph* could be explained: (1) the prothetic *aleph* simply dropped; (2) Eg word for "the Nubian" has two forms, namely, *ikš* and *kšy* (see Ranke I.348.26 *ksw*), which is supported by the Gk forms 'Εκυσις and κοῦσις. The final י of כשי is probably a gentilic. Lipinski pointed out the possibility that כשי is a Semitic name[37] attested in the cuneiform texts (*APN* p. 119a). Yet there is no difficulty in thinking that the same Eg name occurs also in the cuneiform texts.

מי **

--- *m(3)i* "Lion"

[Ph] *CIS* I.5852.1

[Eg] Ranke I.144.1 m. OK–NK

Cf. Ph פמי.

מנתחר

--- **mnṯ(.w)–ḥr* "Montu-Horus"

[Ph] seal: Bordreuil, *Catalogue des sceaux*. p. 26 (no. 12)

[Eg] cf. *mnṯ.w* + DN type: *mnṯ.w-imn* "Montu-Amun" (Ranke I.153.25 m. Dyn. 20); *mnṯ.w-mn.w* "Montu-Min" (Ranke I.154.15. m. NK).

מריחי

--- **mr-iḥy* "Beloved of *Iḥy*, son of Hathor"

[Ph] *CIS* I.60.3; I.93.3, 4, 5

[Eg] cf. *mr* + DN type names (Ranke I.155. 15ff.): *mr-ip.t* (m. NK), *mr-imn*, *mr-b3st.t* etc.. Eg god *iḥ* (Copt. ˢᵇⲉϩⲉ, ᶠⲁϩⲏ) (*Wb* I.119.15f) who is attested in PNs well, such as *p3-iḥ*, *p3-iḥ.y*, *p3-n-iḥ.w* (Ranke I.101.24–26; 106.16). For the loss of the *r* of *mry*, see the discussions in the entries of Heb מיאמן and מראל.

נבסך *

--- **nb(.i)-s(b)k* "My lord is Sobek"

[Pu] *CIS* I.531.3

[Eg] cf. *nb.i* + DN type names: *nb.i-rᶜ* (Ranke I.186.1), *nb.i-imn*

37 Lipinski, review of *Personal Names in the Phoenioian and Punic Inscriptions*, by F. Benz, in *Bibl.Or* 32 (1975) p.79; cf. *IPN* p.232, no.803.

(Ranke I.183.10). For the dropping of *b*, see Aram פטסבך.

נפר

--- *nfr(.w)* "Beauty"
Teixidor, *Bulletin*, p. 126; Aimé-Giron, *JA*, 17 p. 57f; V I p. 93
[Ph] *Krug* 50; Kornfeld, *AÖAW* 115 p. 203 (no. 20).
[Eg] Ranke I.203.16–18 m/f. Ok–NK; [Gk] Νεφερως, Νεφερ, Νεφερᾶς, Νεφεραῦς, Νεφερος (*NB* p. 230); [Aram] נפר

This name is not listed in Benz, although it occurs in Lidzbarski *Krug* no. 50 (p. 17), where he suggests the possibility of an Eg name. The name is not *nfr* (Ranke I.194.1), because of the preservation of *r* of *nfr* (Gk νουφις; see the discussion in כנפי). For the possibility of the name as Eg loan in Canaanite, see Ug *nfr* (*UT* 1680).

סכר *

--- *skr* "Sokar"
[Pu] *CIS* I.3751.4
[Eg] Ranke I.298.8 m./f. MK (Notice that *skr* is used as a theophoric element until the late Period (e.g. Ranke I.298.11; I.200.17; II p. 370).

There is a Ph root סכר "to remember" (זכר in Heb), which can be a PN, cf. זֶכֶר (1 Chr 8:31), זַכּוּר (Num 13:4), while Heb סכר "to shut" (not attested in Ph) is not used in PNs. As בעלסכר and סכרבעל are attested (*Eph* 395; *CIS* 1218, 1354), סכר could be a short form of a Ph name. The identification is open to choice.

סנר **

--- *s(3)-nr(.t)* "Son of Vulture goddess"
[Ph] *RES* 297.1
[Eg] Ranke II.312.13 m. Late

Notice that *snr* is attested as a GN, and PN (*UT* 19.1776). Yet a Semitic etymology is uncertain; so an Eg solution is probable.

ססר **

--- *s(3)-sr* "Son of the ram"
[Pu] *CIS* I.2882.3; 3351.7/8
[Eg] Ranke I.284.10 m. Gk.

ספתח **

--- *s(3)-ptḥ*  "Son of Ptah"

--- *s(3.t)-ptḥ*  "Daughter of Ptah"

L. p. 132; Benz p. 192; V I p. 92

[Ph] *Krug* 9.1

[Eg] Ranke I.282.1 m. NK–Late; Ranke I.288.22 f. MK; [NB] *ʾsi-ip-ta-ḫu* (Vittmann, *GM* 70 p. 65).

סראסר **

--- **sr-3s-ir* "Osiris is noble"

[Ph] seal: Vattioni, *SF* no. 4

[Eg] cf. the *sr* + DN type names (Ranke I.316.26-317.3 m. NK–Late): *sr(?)-imn*, *sr(?)-ptḥ*, *sr(?)-mnṯ.w*, *sr-ḏḥwty*.

עבדאבסת (hybrid) **

--- עבד-*b(3)s.t(.t)* "Servant of Bast"

[Ph] *CIS* I.86b.6; *Krug* 12, 15b.2, 39, 46 [א]בדאבסת; *RES* 800.2. 1332; [Pu] *CIS* I.3267.5 [עבד]אבסת.

[Eg] see DN אבסת; [Gk] ᾿Αβδουβαστίος.

עבדאמן (hybrid) **

--- עבד-*imn* "Servant of Amun"

[Ph] *Krug* 8.1; M. Dunand; *BMB*, 18 (1965) p. 106; *APO* 82.8 (according to Porten in his letter)

[Eg] see DN אמן; [Gk] ᾿Αβημονος (Josephus), ᾿Αβδμων (Diodorus of Sicile), ᾿Αβυμων (F. Jacoby)

F. Cross and P.McCarter compared the name with Ug *guru ʾammana*, Hittite *KUR Am-ma-na*, a mountain in Syria, perhaps the Anti-Cassios (*Rivista di Studi Fenici* 1 p. 4 n. 7), because the עבדאמן occurs as the name of a king of Sidon. However, it is conceivable that the name of a Phoenician king features an Eg deity (cf. פמי) and it is usual for עבד to be used with a divine name. In any case though there is no difficulty in thinking that the name on a jar from Elephantine contains an Eg deity (*Krug* 8.1).

עבדאס (hybrid) **

--- עבד-*3s(.t)* "Servant of Isis"

[Ph/Pu] *CIS* I.3523.2 עֹבְדֹאֹס; *RES* 298.1

[Eg] see DN אס.

עבדאסר (hybrid) **

--- עבד-*3s-ir* "Servant of Osiris"

[Ph/Pu] *CIS* I.9.1, 13.2, 46.1, 58.2/3, 122.2, 3, 2098.4, 2156.4, 2739.4, 4336.6/7 עבדא[ס]ר, 4551.4/5, 5182.2, 5991.2; *RES* 1.3, 235 עבדאסר; *Krug* 1, 34b; Chehab, *BMB* 13 no. 4.1, 2

[Eg] see DN אסר.

עבדבסת (hybrid) **

--- Var. of עבדאבסת

[Pu] *CIS* I.2082.4

[Eg] see DN אבסת.

עבדחר (hybrid) **

--- עבד-*ḥr* "Servant of Horus"

[Ph] *RES* 307.1/2; *CIS* I.53

[Eg] see PN חר.

עבדכרר (hybrid) *

--- עבד-*ḳrr* "Servant of the Frog"

[Pu] *CIS* I.2630.3

[Eg] for *ḳrr* see *Wb* V.61.5f. Copt [s]ⲔⲢⲞⲨⲢ,[b]ⲬⲢⲞⲨⲢ "the frog"; cf. NA *pa-aḳ-ru-ru* for Eg *p3-ḳrr* (Ranke, *KM* p. 31).

The correspondence between Ph כ and Eg *ḳ* is not certain. Notice that Eg *ḳ*, is represented by NA *ḳ*.

עבדמת̊ (hybrid)

--- עבד-*mw(.t)* "The servant of Mut"

[Pu] *CIS* I.2098.3

[Eg] cf. Ranke I.90.18f. *b3k-mw.t*  "the servant of the Mut"

Mut (*mw.t*) is one of the most common theophoric elements in Eg PNs.

עבדם (hybrid)

--- Var. of עבדאם (?)

[Pu] *CIS* I.308.4

[Eg] see Ph עבדאס.

עֺבֻדעֺס (hybrid)

--- Var. of עבדאס

[Pu] *CIS* I.4948.3

[Eg] see DN אס

Notice the confusion of א and ע in Punic. Cf. עבדס.

עבדפֺּמי (hybrid)

--- עבד-*p(3)-m(3)i* "The servant of פמי"

[Ph] *CIS* I.88.6

[Eg] see PN פמי.

עבדפתח (hybrid) **

--- עבד-*ptḥ* "The servant of Ptah"

[Ph] *CIS* I.111.1; *Krug* 27, 30 עֻבֻּדפתח

[Eg] for *ptḥ*, see *Wb* I.565; Copt ^{s}ⲡⲧⲁϩ; Gk Φθα.

עבדרע (hybrid) **

--- עבד-*rʿ* "The Servant of Reʿ"

[Pu] *CIS* I.3778.10

[Eg] for *rʿ* see *Wb* II.401; Baby. *rīʾa*; Heb רע; Gk -ρι; Copt ^{s,b}ⲣⲏ, ^{a}ⲣⲓ.

עחר **

--- *ʿ(3)-ḥr* "Horus is great"

Teixidor, *Bulletin*, p. 431; G p. 465; K p. 85; V I p. 93

[Pu] seal: Amadasi, *IFP* p. 93 No.10[38].

[Eg] cf. *ḥr-ʿ3*  "Horus is great" (Ranke I.246.9; II.377)

Notice an honorific transposition of *ḥr*. See also the composition of *ʿ3* + DN: *ʿ3-ptḥ* (Ranke I.57.17), *ʿ3-3ẖ.ty* (Ranke I.57.5), *ʿ3-ỉmn* (Ranke I.57.7). Cf. *ỉmn-ʿ3* (Ranke I.26.26), *ptḥ-ʿ3* (Ranke I.138.18). m. MK–NK (PN with *ḥr* is common enough throughout the history of Egypt, *e.g.* Ranke I.245.18ff. It seems there is no necessity to limit the composition *ʿ3* + DN to MK only; against Lambdin,

38 For the photo, see M. L. Uberti, "Scarabéo punic del Museo Archeologic Nazionale di Cagliari," *Atti del I° Convegno Italiano sul Vicino Oriente Antico*: Orientis Antiqvi Collectio XIII (Rome, 1978) pp. 157–162, pl. XIII.

Kornfelt p. 85, see Grelot p. 465). Vittmann explained it as *ʿnḫ-ḥr*, citing Aram עחרנפי. However, the merging of two different, strong Eg *h*s is unconceivable, and עחרנפי does not exist (see Aram עחמנפי).

עמסכר (hybrid) *

--- עמ-*skr* "(My) kinsman is Sokar"

[Pu] *CIS* I.3303.4

[Eg] for *skr* see *Wb* III.487.13. In PNs see Ranke I.200.17, II.370 *nfr-k3-skr* "fine is the ka of the god Sokar" (m. Late); Ranke I.298.8–11.

Two explanations proposed by Benz are (1) abbreviation for עבד + DN; (2) עמס "to carry" + DN. Yet he did not identify the deity (cf. עמסמלך, בעלעמס, מלקתעמס Benz p. 379). When we compare it with Heb names עמיאל "My kinsman is god", עמינדב "My kinsman is noble", עמישדי "My kinsman is Shaddai", although there is a Ph word סכר (Heb זכר) "to remember", it is most likely that סכר is a theophoric element.

ענבעל (hybrid)

--- *ʿn*-בעל "Fine is Baʿal"

[Pu] *CIS* I.5844.4

[Eg] see *ʿn* + DN type names: *ʿn-b3s.t.t* "Fine is Bastet (Ranke I.61.11 f. Late); *ʿn-mw.t* "Fine is Mut" (Ranke I.61.18)

Note the Ph roots ען I "to see", II "spring", III "sight", IV "now" (Tomback p. 251–2), which seem not to be used in PN (Benz p. 38f.), while *ʿn* + DN is a common Eg feminine name in the late Period. Considering that ענבעל is a feminine name, the Eg possibility is likely (see the discussion of Heb PN עניהו).

ענבתבעל (hybrid)

--- *ʿn*-בתבעל "The daughter of Baʿal is beautiful"

[Pu] *CIS* I.5893.4

[Eg] see ענבעל.

ענחפמס **

--- **ʿnḫ-p(3)-ms* "The child lives"

L p. 132; Benz p. 192; V I p. 92

[Ph] *Krug* 14b

[Eg] cf. *ʿnḫ-p3-ḫrd* "The son lives" (Ranke I.63.17 m. Late–Gk; *DemNB* I.99; *p3-ms* "The child" (Ranke I.105.11 m. NK)

The Eg form **ʿnḫ-p3-ms* does not occur in Eg documents. Yet both elements *ʿnḫ* and *p3-ms* are well attested in Eg PN. There is no difficulty in concluding that the Ph may have preserved a good Eg PN. Another possibility is **ʿnḫ-p3-ms(s)* where *ms(s)* is the Libyan word for "chief". This word entered Egyptian in Dyn 22/23.

עפתֿח **

--- *ʿ(3)-ptḥ* 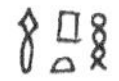 "Ptah is great"

[Ph] *Krug* 42 and 59

[Eg] Ranke I.57.17; 138,18; *DemNB* I.95. m. MK-Late

See עחר for the discussion of this type of name. פתח as a theophoric element is very common throughout Egypt.

פדס (hybrid)

--- פד-*(3)s(.t)* "Isis has ransomed"

[Pu] *CIS* I.3896.2; 3916.7

[Eg] see DN אס

Halff (*Karthage* 12 p. 139) suggested that פדס is פדאס (*p3-dỉ-3s.t*), However Eg *d* is exclusively equated with Ph and Pu ט. If we accept the elision of the *aleph* of *3s.t* (אס > ס), as suggested in ברסי, Aram נפסי etc., a hybrid name פד-*3s.t* is most likely, cf. פדיה "יה has ransomed" (Benz p. 389).

פֿוֹמי *

--- **p(3y).w-m(3)ỉ* "Their lion"

[Ph] *APO* 85.4 (pl. 72) (according to B. Porten this is Ph)

[Eg] cf. פמי

If פו stands for Eg article *p3* (see Aram פומון), *p3-m3i* "the lion" (Ranke I.105.5 m.Late) is possible.

פֹּוסך *

--- **p(3)-(n-)wsḫ(.t)* "He who belongs to a wide hall"

[NPu] seal: Vattioni, *SF* no. 46

[Eg] cf.*p3-n-t3-wsḫ.t* "He who belongs to the wide hall" (Ranke II.28.13).

J. D. Ray commented that in general *p3-n-* is followed by a definite noun, as shown in *p3-n-t3-wsḫ.t*. Yet the possibility of its being an Eg name cannot be excluded, because, negatively, no other explanation can be provided; positively, there are some Eg names which have *p3-n-* followed by an indefinite noun, such as *p3-n-ḥ(w).t, p3-n-ḥb, p3-n-ḥr, p3-n-ḫtyw, p3-n-ṯb, p3-n-ḏ3ḏ3* (Ranke I.110.3, 4, 6, 15, 112.7, 12) etc.

פטאס **

--- *p(3)-d(ỉ)-3s(.t)* 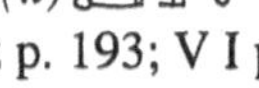 "He whom Isis has given"

L p. 132; Benz p. 193; V I p. 92

[Ph] *Krug* 39 בנאס (corrected to פטאס by Vittmann; yet the ט is uncertain), 48; a little box: *KAI* 29.1

[Eg] Ranke I.121.18 m. Dyn 22ff.–Gk; II p. 355; *DemNB* I.290 (*p3-ti-is.t*); [Copt] ⲡⲁⲇⲏⲥⲉ, ⲡⲁⲧⲉⲥⲉ, ⲡⲁⲧⲏⲥⲉ (*DemNB* I.290); [Gk] πατεῆσις, (πατῆσις), πετεῆσις, (πετῆσις), (πατισις), πετεησε, πετεησης, πετεισις, (πετησιος) (*NB* pp. 286f, 312, 318); [Aram] פטסי, פטאסי; [NB] *pa-ṭi-e-su* (Zadok, *GM* 26 p. 65); [Persia] *pa-ṭa-e- si-i'* (Ranke, *KM* p. 40).

פטאסי **

--- *p(3)-d(ỉ)-3s(.t)*

L p. 132; Benz p. 193; V I p. 92

[Ph] *Krug* 57

[Eg] see פטאס

Cf. Aram פטאסי

Possible explanations of the final י are (1) a *mater lectionis* (see "The possible *Mater Lectionis*" p. 74). (2) a caritative ending or feminine ending ַי; cf. שָׂרַי (Gen 11:30), נָעֳמִי (Ruth 1:2). F. Gröndahl observed a caritative ending *-y* [-iya] in Ug PN: *il(i)piya, kalbeya, gbᶜly, krny* etc. (Gröndahl p. 25), and Akk caritative endings are also *-(i)ya* and *-(y)atum*. Yet this element seems non-existent in the Ph names (Benz p. 242). (3) Eg bi-form of this name. First this possibility of a bi-form is suggested by Eg documents: (i) *p3-di-3s.t* and (ii) *p3-di-3s.t.ỉ* (Ranke I.121.18 and 19). Yet the final *ỉ* (𓇋) could be a male determinative (𓀀). Secondary cuneiform writings show this possibility: R. Zadok (*GM* 64,1983, p. 74) points out that the theophoric element Isis is spelled in two ways, *i.e.*, (1) [(d)]*e-si-ʾ* ([I]*A/Am-mat-*[de]*-si-ʾ* 423/2 BC; *Ab-di-*[de]*-si-ʾ* 217/6 BC) and (2) *e-su* (*Ra-ḫi-(i-)me/mé-(e)-su* 2nd cent. BC). Yet the Ph variations פטאס and פטאסי occur at the same time and place, so I am inclined to consider it as *mater lectionis*.

פטבנטט **

--- **p(3)-d(i)-b(3)-n(b)-ḏd(w.t)* "He whom the ram, the lord of Mendes, has given"
L p. 131f; Benz p. 192f; V I p. 91
[Ph] statue: *RES* 1507
[Eg] Ranke II.284.20; see Aimé-Giron, *BIFAO* 38, p. 29; [Gk] πετεμενδης (*NB* p. 313).

Harris (*Grammar* p. 137), followed by Lambdin, Benz, and *KAI*, divided this name into two names; "פט son of טט." However, *KAI* also quotes Aimé-Giron (*BIFAO* 38 p. 29) who first proposed the Eg equation of פטבנטט. A single name is more likely because we have Gk correspondence Πετεμενδης. The lack of *b* can be justified by *(n)s-b3-n(b)-ḏd(.t)* = Σμενδης (Ranke I.174.17). Cuneiform material ^{uru}*Bi-in-di-di (b3-nb-ḏd)* (Assurb. I 99) also proves that the *b* of *nb* has been lost.

Eg. *ḏd.w* ("Mendes") and *ḏd* ("to say") underwent different phonetic changes. The *ḏd* () became *ḏ* (probably *ḏd* > *ḏt* > *ḏ*) from MK (*Wb* V.618), and took no further change until Copt ϫ. cf. צחא (*ḏd-ḥr*). Contrarily the *ḏd.w* ( ) in question changed into *dd* (probably *ḏd.w* > *dd.w* > *dd*) from MK (*Wb* V.630). This was rendered as טט in Ph (cf. Ranke *KM* p. 93 *ṭeṭi* = *ḏd(.t)*. What is more, Eg *dd* (Ph טט) is not attested as a single name after Dyn 18 (Ranke I.401.3, 4, 7: notice I.401.5 has a foreign sign), though פט (*p3-di*) is attested well until Gk period. Therefore פטבנטט is most likely to be one name.

פטכנס̇] **

--- *p(3)-d(i)-ḫns(.w)* "He whom Khons has given"
L p. 132; Benz p. 193
[Ph] *Krug* 49.1
[Eg] Ranke I.125.21 m. NK-Gk; *DemNB* 1.336 (*p3-ti-ḫnsw*) ; [Gk] Πετεχωνσις, Πατεχων, Πετασονς, Πετεσων, Πετεχων(ς) (*NB* p. 318); [Aram] פטחנס; [NB] *pa-aṭ-ḫa-an-si* (Zadok, *GM* 64 p. 73); [Copt] cf. ^{s}ⲡⲁ-ϣⲟⲛ̄ⲥ, ^{b}ⲡⲁ-ⲭⲱⲛ.

פלסחר (hybrid) **

--- פלס-*ḥr* "Horus has watched"
[Pu] *CIS* I.4853.4
[Eg] see PN חר.

פמי **

--- *p(3)-m(3)i*  "The lion"
[Ph] *CIS* I.144.8 (Nora inscription), *CIS* I.4777.6
[Eg] Ranke I.105.5; *DemNB* I.186 m. Late; [Gk] Πμοις, Φυοις;
[Copt] ⲡⲁⲙⲱⲉⲓ (Heuser p. 23)
Cf. Aram פשנפמוי

פמי has been known as an unidentified god in Ph texts. Yet this deity is to be identified with the Eg lion god *p3-m3i*. For a full discussion on this identification, see Y. Muchiki, "The unidentified god *PMY* in Phoenician texts" *JSS* 36 (1991) pp. 7–10.

פמיחויא (hybrid)

--- *p(3)-m(3)i*-חויא "פמי has preserved him"
[Pu] *CIS* I.5981.1
[Eg] see PN פמי.

פמייתן (hybrid) **

--- *p(3)-m(3)i*-יתן "פמי has given"
[Ph] *CIS* I.11; *CIS* I.12; Honeyman, *JRAS* 1960 p. 111.1
[Eg] see PN פמי.

פמיסרכא (hybrid)

--- *p(3)-m(3)i*-סרכא "פמי is the Lord"
[Pu] *CIS* I.5981.1
[Eg] see PN פמי

For the interpretation see Benz p. 403 (סרכא = אדנא).

פמישמ[ע] (hybrid) **

--- *p(3)-m(3)i*-שמע "פמי has heard"
[Ph] *CIS* I.197.3
[Eg] see פמי.

פמישמר (hybrid)

--- *p(3)-m(3)i*-שמר "פמי has kept"

[Pu] *CIS* I.2379.6

[Eg] see PN פמי.

פמיתן (hybrid) **

--- *p(3)-m(3)i*-(י)תן "פמי has given"

[Ph/Pu] *CIS* I.617.4, 5; 670.2/3 פמיתן; 2106.3 פמ̊י̊תן; 5690.4/5; Babelon, *Traité des monnaies*, pp. 758–59 no. 709–724; Cooke *NSI*, 149.b.6 (coin) [פמי]תן; Hill, *Catalogue of the Greek Coins of Cyprus*, p. 21–22

[Eg] see PN פמי.

פמת **

---**p(3)-(n-)m(w).t* "He who belongs to Mut"

L p. 132

[Ph] *Krug* 56

[Eg] Ranke II.280.13 (cf. S I p. 1105 No. 40); [Gk] Παμουθις, Παμοῦτις (*NB* p. 263f.); [Aram] פמת.

פנפא *

--- *p(3)-(n-i)np(w)* "He who belongs to Anubis"

[Pu] *CIS* I.908.4; 2035.4/5; 2487.4; 3557.4; 3919.4: 5963.2 [פ]נפא; *CIS* I.3778.8; *CIS* I.3919.4; *CIS* I.5523.4.

[Eg] Anubis is a common element of Eg PNs, see Ranke I.115.5, 118.9, 122.11 etc.; [Gk] Πανουφις, Παανοῦφις, Πανούφιος, Πανουφ, Πεανοῦφις, Πανουπις, Πεουπις, Φανουφις, Πανουπ (*NB* p. 270f.); [Aram] פנפה.

Another possibilities are (1) *p3-nfr* "The beautiful one" (Ranke I.113.1 m. NK–Dyn 26; *DemNB* I.3 and 192). If this identification is correct, the final *aleph* is *mater lectionis* for [i]. Notice that the normal realization of Eg *nfr* is נף in Ph and נפי in Aram; (2) *p3-nfr-ii* "The beautiful one came" (Ranke I.113.2 m.Late), which explains the final א as Eg *i*. In terms of the Gk forms which are aboundantly attested, *p3-n-inpw* seems to be the more probable.

פסמסנית

--- *psm(ṯk)-s(3-)ny.t* 

S II p.9
[Ph] *Krug* 8.2
[Eg] see Aram פסמסנית.

פסר *

--- *p(3)-(n-)3s-(i)r* "He who belongs to Osiris"
L p. 132; Benz p. 193; V I p. 92
[Ph] graffito: *RES* 1322
[Eg] Ranke I.107.5 m. Dyn 21–Gk; *DemNB* I.360; [Gk] Πεσόρις, Πεσουρις, Πεσυρις, Παυσιρις, Παυσειρις, Παυσιρεις (*NB* p. 308); [Aram] פסרי

Benz (p. 193) suggests two possibilities for Eg names: *p3-sr* and *p3-šri*. *P3-šri* is well attested from Dyn 19 to Gk, yet the correspondence between Eg *š* and Ph ס is hardly justified. *P3-šri* should be compared with Ph פשר. *P3-sr* is more likely to be equated with פסר. The second possibility is *p3-n-3s-ir*, if we admit that *aleph* of אסר (*3s-ir*) has been lost as in Aram -סרי (תחסרי, פסרי).

פעלאבסת (hybrid) **

--- פעל-*b(3)s.t(.t)* "Bast has made"
[Ph] *CIS* I.102a; *Krug* 11a
[Eg] see אבסת.

פער

--- *p(3)-ʿr* "He who ascends"
Benz p. 193; V p. 92 (with negation)
[Ph] scarab: *RES* 903 (now lost). P. Bordreuil, *Catalogue des Sceaux*, p. 21 no. 4 פערחמן
[Eg] Ranke I.103.8 m. Late.

Benz compared it with *p3-ḫr.y* "The Syrian" (Ranke I.116.17). However, the correspondence between Eg *ḫ* and Ph ע is hardly acceptable. E. Ledrain suggested the mountain Pe'or in Moab as the origin of this name (*Revue d'Assy.*, 2, p. 93). Cf. Pu פער "marbles?" (*DISO* p. 233), Heb פערי (2 Sam. 23:35), Ug PN *pʿr* (*UT* 2078). Therefore an Eg origin is questionable.

פפי **

--- *ppy*

[Pu] *KAI* 100.7
[Eg] Ranke I.131.18 (perhaps 130.3, 5, 6; 131.12) m./f. MK-NK;
[Gk] Παπος, Παππος, Παποῦς, Πεποῦς, Πιποῦς, Πεπῆς, πιπης (*NB*p. 277 and 305)

There is no root פפי, no explanation from the Semitic side. Though *ppy* is a famous Eg name in Dyn 6, Ranke I.131.18 gives evidence that this name was still common in NK and used even in the Late period as a component of names (Ranke I.132.4). Gk forms show it was common at that time.

פפן **

--- *p(3)-(n-)pn(w)*  "He who belongs to the Mouse"
[Ph] *CIS* I.1435.4; 2946.4 [פפ[ן; 3140.3 [פפן]
[Eg] Ranke I.108.1 m. Dyn 26; [Gk] cf. Παπνου (*NB* p. 276)

There is no satisfactory Semitic explanation of this name. Ug *ppn* (*UT* 2084 *bn ppn*; *UT* 85.6 ᵐ*pa-pa-na*), which is probably from Eg (see Ug *ppn*).

פשמחי **

--- *p(3)-š(ri)-(n-)mḥy(.t)* 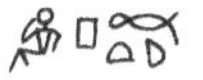 "The son of Meḥet"
V I p. 93
[Ph] statue: *RES* 1507.2
[Eg] Ranke I.118.24 m. Gk; II p. 355; *DemNB* I.250 (see Ranke I.118.7–119.11 for *p3-šri-n*-type names which are very common during the late and Gk. period); [Gk] Cf. Ψενε(μ)μοῦς, Ψενεμχοις (*NB* p. 485).

KAI presents a broken name פשמ[-]י[39]. Teixidor, however, reads it פשמחי with the comment that this reading is certain (*Bulletin*, p. 213, No. 124). With respect to the final י in Ph, it should be remembered that the goddess Meḥet is written as  *mḥy.t* (*Wb* II.127). It indicates that the final *y* was still pronounced in Eg in a final syllable, where final *-t* had been lost (Copt ⲙϩⲏ). For other cases in which the final *y* is recorded in the Late and Gk period, see Ranke I.108.15, 325.24, 387.21, 394.1, 411.5.

39 See also Lidzbarski, *Handbuch*, Vol., II. Plate X. 5; for the photo J. Ferron "La inscripcion cartaginesa en el Arpocrates madrileño," *Trabajos de Prehistoria*, N.S. 28 (1971) plates I–IV.

פשר *

--- *p(3)-šr(i)* "The lad"

[Pu] *CIS* I.5724.4

[Eg] Ranke I.118.5 m. Dyn 19–Gk; [Gk] Πασιρις, Πεσιρις, Πεσεῖρις, Πασῖρε, Πισῖρις (*NB* p. 282)

There is a Semitic root פשר in Akk. *pašāru* "loose, untie" in PN *pá-še-er; pa/išīru* "secret" in PN *Itti-GN-pa-šir/ši-ru/ri; pāširu(m)* in PN *lupa-ši-ri*, GN *pa-šer/še-er* (*AHw* II.844–845). Yet the meaning of the North West Semitic root פשר is obscure (*DISO* p. 238, see *AP* p. 168). Benz suggests a possible connection of פשר with the NPu name יפשר (Benz p. 396). Yet note the feminine form תשרי (*t3-šri.t*) in Aram. (*Saqqara* 95a.1).

פתא *

--- *p(3)-(n-)t(3)* "He who belongs to the land"

[Pu] *RES* 1216.4

[Eg] Ranke I.112.3 m. NK–Late; 120.17; *DemNB* I.6.420; [Gk] Πάτος (*NB* p. 289 and 292); [Aram] פתא

Copt forms of *t3* "land" are ˢⲦⲞ, ᵇⲐⲞ, which are reflected in Gk forms. Note other possible explanations; (1) Donner-Röllig's suggestion (*KAI* 68): פתחא > פתא; see also *DISO* p. 232. (2) Iranian name element *pata* "protect", *pati-* "lord" (Mayrhofer, *OPP* pp. 134, 350).

פתח **

--- *ptḥ* "Ptah"

[Ph] seal: Vattioni, *SF* no.5.

[Eg] Ranke I.138,9 m. MK–Late; [Gk] Πταΰας, Πτάϊς (*NB* p. 348).

פתחא **

--- *ptḥ* "Ptah"

[Pu] *CIS* I.154.2

[Eg] see above; [Copt] cf.ⲫⲐⲀⲘⲞⲚⲦ (Heuser p. 61).

The final *aleph* of פתחא is a feature of Punic PN, such as כנש / כנשא, יער / יערא, ארש / ארשא etc. as a hypocoristic (Benz p. 233).

פתחי **

--- *ptḥ.y* "He of Ptah"(?)

[Ph] graffito: *CIS* I.111
[Eg] Ranke I.142.4 m. Late.

פֿתׅיחו

--- **p(3)-(n-)t(3)-(n.t-)iḥw(.t)* "He who belongs to the Cow"
[Ph] *CIS* I.112a
[Eg] For this type of PN see *p3-šri-n-t3-iḥ.t* (Gk Ψενταης *NB* p. 489, Ranke I.119.9 and 10)

תיחו is comparable with *t3-iḥw.t* (Ranke II.278.8) and *p3-iḥw.t* (Ranke I.106.16). The singular article *t3 / p3* with a plural form must indicate *t3-n.t-iḥw.t* or *p3-n-iḥw*. The final ו is a reflection of the plural ending; cf. *p3-iḥ* (Ranke I.101.24); [Gk] Cf. Πετεεῦς (*NB* p. 310).
Cf. Copt. s,bⲉϩⲉ, fⲁϩⲏ for *iḥ.t*.

צחא **

--- *ḏ(d)-ḥ(r)*  ,  "The face speaks"
L p. 132; Benz p. 193
[Ph] *Krug* 34c; Fevrier, *IAM* p. 116 no. 75
[Eg] Ranke I.411.12 m. Late–Gk / f. Gk; [Gk] Ταχῶς, Τεῶς (*NB* p. 424 and 433); [Aram] צחא; [NA] *Ṣi-ḫa-a, Ṣi-ḫu-u* (*APN* p. 205b; Ranke, *KM* p. 34, 38); Cf. Copt ϫⲱ, ϫⲉ´ (construct Crum 754a); [Heb] cf. צִיחָא (Neh 11:21, Ezr 2:43, Neh 7:46)

Ph צחא (Benz p. 193, Estañol, *Vocabulario Fenicio*, p. 216) does not exist (print mistake?). *IAM* p. 116 no. 75 is not צחא but צחא. See plate VII. Since MK (*ca.*1800 BC) Eg *ḏd* became *ḏ* (see פטבנטט; *Wb* V.618).

צחפמו **

--- *ṯ(3y)-ḥp-(i)m.w*  "Apis can seize them"
L p. 132; Benz p. 193
[Ph] *krug* 11b; 21.1, 26, 34c
[Eg] Ranke I.388.2 m. Late–Gk/f. Late; [Aram] שחפמו, שחפימו; [Akk] *Saḫ-pi-ma-a-ú* (*APN* p. 190a)

The final consonant ו is a suffix pronoun (3.m.pl).

צכנסמו **

--- *ṯ(3y)-ḫns(.w)-(i)m.w* "Khons can seize them"

L p. 132; Benz p. 193
[Ph] *Krug* 48
[Eg] Ranke I.388.6 m. Late.

שמו *

--- *ṯ(3y)-(i)m.w*  "(DN) can seize them"
[Pu] *CIS* I.2760.3 שׁמו, 5255.1
[Eg] Ranke I.387.13; II.399 m. Late (a short form of *ṯ3i* + DN + *im.w*); [Gk] Σαμωους (bilingual), Σαμαυς, Θαμωυς, Θαμως; [Aram] שמו; [Akk] *šá-mu-ú* (Zadok, *The Jews in Baby.*, p. 33).

Benz left it unexplained. The possibility of the equation of Ph ש with Eg *ṯ* is suggested by the dialectical varieties in Copt ^{s}ϫⲓ, ^{b}ϭⲓ. Since Aram שמו is attested, Ph שמו = *ṯ3i-im.w* is possible. Yet this is the only case of the representation of Eg *ṯ* by Ph ש. (see [4] Notes on the Correspondences, c) Sibilants). Cf. also Aram פסמשך. As for the name, Harris suggested that it is an error (Harris p. 151). Therefore, the identification remains uncertain.

תחוא *

--- *t(3)-ḫ(3)w(.t)* "The altar"
[Pu] *CIS* I.320.3
[Eg] *ḫ3w.t* is a kind of altar used in PNs. *e.g.*, *ʿn-nfr-ḫ3w.t* (Rank I.61.23 f. NK), *nfr-ḫ3w.t* (Ranke I.199.1 m. Dyn 18), *ḥnw.t-ḫ3wt* (Ranke I.243.28 f. NK); [Aram] cf. תחוא

A feminine name beginning with ת indicates the possibility of an Eg name. If the identification is correct, the final *aleph* is to be considered as a *mater lectionis*. Another solution is *(p)tḥ-(m-)wi(3)* "Ptah is in the bark" (Ranke I.139.18 m. MK, with note that the preposition *m* can be elided). The dropping of the *p* of *ptḥ* is suggested by Akk *Taḫmaya, Ataḫmaya, Taḫmaš(š)i* (see Akk PNs in Chapter V).

תפט *

--- **t(3)-(n.t-)p(3)-d(i)* "Daughter of *p3-di*"
[Pu] *CIS* I.2683.3
[Eg] cf. *t3-n.t-p3-di-sbk* (Ranke I.360.2 m. Gk); *p3-di* (Ranke I.121.17 m. Dyn 22–Gk)

Benz, following *CIS*, considered תפט to be a misspelling of שפט (Benz p. 186). Yet פט (*p3-di*) is a common Eg name in the

Late period, which is attested in Aramaic as פטי. Therefore "Daugher of *p3-dì*" is likewise possible.

[2] Divine Names

אבסת **

--- *b(3)s.t(.t)* "Bast" (a goddess of Bubastis)

[Pu] Amadasi *IFP* p. 39, 31.2

[Eg] *Wb* I.423; [Aram] אבסת; [Akk] *ubešti* cf. *pa-aṭ-u-as-tú, pu-ṭu-biš-ti* (Assurb I.96)

Ph initial *aleph* is a prothetic *aleph* (Cooke *NSI* p. 69). Akk forms indicate that Eg *b3st* starts with /u/, Ph initial *aleph* is used to protect the initial vowel.

אמן **

--- *ìmn* "Amon" (a god of Thebes)

[Pu] *RES* 662.1

[Eg] *Wb* I.84.16f.; [Gk] 'Αμουν; [Copt] ^{k}ⲁⲙⲟⲩⲛ; [Baby] *amâna, amûnu*; [Heb] אמון; [Ug] *amn*

Estañol (*Vocabulario fenicio* p. 68) suggests that אמן is an error for חמן, because of the development Pu ח > א (Friedrich-Röllig *PPG* § 35; see a discussion of *KAI* III p. 123). Therefore the combination Baal-Ammon is reasonably deleted from this catalogue.

אס **

--- *3s(.t)* "Isis" (wife of Osiris)

[Ph] *RES* 1.2

[Eg] *Wb* IV.8; [Gk] 'Ισις, (Πετε)ησις; [Copt] ^{s}ⲏⲥⲉ, ^{b}ⲏⲥⲓ;

[Aram] אסי; [NA] *-èšu/-eš-* ; [NB] *-ēsi*ʾ (Ranke, *KM* p. 43).

אסר **

--- *3s-ìr* "Osiris" (god of the netherworld)

[Ph] *RES* 504.B.1 אס[ר]

[Eg] *Wb* I.359; [Aram] אוסר, אסר; [Copt] ⲟⲩⲥⲓⲣⲓ, ⲟⲩⲥⲓⲣⲉ, ⲟⲩⲥⲉⲣ

[Gk] 'Οσιρις; [NA] cf. PN *pu-ṭi-še-ri* (Zadok, *GM* 26 p. 65); GN *pu-ši-ru* (*pr-ws-ìr* "Busiris" Assurb. I.100)

It is to be noted that the correspondence between Ph א and Eg *w* occurs only in the case of **ws-ir* "Osiris." We have certain inscriptional indications that Osiris was written as*ws(i)r* in the Gk period 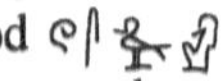 , 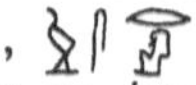 ,  (*Wb* I.359). Before that period, however, there is no inscriptional evidence with respect to the reading of Osiris. It was Erman who first advocated the reading of Osiris as *ws-ir* (*ZÄS* 46, pp. 92-95). It was unfortunate that his wrong treatment of the Aramaic equation אוסר / אסר led him to the wrong conclusion. There seems to be no difficulty acknowledging that the initial *aleph* retains its consonantal value, and the following *waw* is a *mater lectionis* /u/. This fact is confirmed by our Ph equation אסר (5th–1st cent. BC, 28 times), because of its rigorous consonantal system. Therefore, we can safely conclude that Eg reading of Osiris before the Gk period is not *ws-ir*, but *3s-ir*. After that period Ph א is preserved as a historical writing (for the full discussion, see Y. Muchiki, "On the transliteraton of Osiris," *JEA* 76 (1990) pp. 191–194 and 77 (1991) p. 197.

** חרפכרט

--- *ḥr-p(3)-ẖrd*  "Harpokrates (Horus the child)"
[Ph] statue: *RES* 1507; Barnett, *BMQ* 27 p. 85.
[Eg] *Wb* III.123.6; [Gk] 'Αρποκράτης, 'Αρποχράτης, 'Αρποκρατίων,'Αρποχρατιων (*NB* p. 53f)
Cf. Aram פטחרפחרט (For some differences between the Ph and Aram transcriptions, see Degen, "Der Name Harpokrates in Phönizischer und arämaischer Umschreibung" *Welt Or.* 5 pp. 218–221).

The following DNs are attested as theophoric elements in hybrid names: חף (*ḥp* "Apis"), חר (*ḥr* "Horus"), מן (*mn.w* "Min"), פמי (*p3-m3i* "the lion"), סכר (*skr* "Sokar"), רע (*r*ᶜ "Re").

[3] Geographical Names

אן **

--- *i(w)n(w)* "Heliopolis"

[Ph] *CIS* I.102a

[Eg] see Heb אן.

מנף **

--- *m(n)-nf(r)* "Memphis"

[Ph] *CIS* I.102a

[Eg] see Heb נף and מף

From the context it is likewise possible that מנף is מ[נ]נף "from Memphis." Yet notice the Aramaic form מנף.

תחפנחס **

--- **t(3)-ḥ(.t)-p(3)-nḥs(y)* "The mansion of the Nubian"

[Ph] *KAI* 50.3

[Eg] see Heb תחפנחס.

[4] Loan Words

אי "coastal land"

--- *iw* "island"

[Ph/Pu] *CIS* I.139 אינסמ; *KAI* 99.5; *CIS* I.266.3/4; *CIS* I.268.3/4; Cooke 56.4

[Eg] see Heb Lw אי.

חתם "seal" **

--- *ḫtm* "seal"

[Ph] *CIS* I.5522.5; *KAI* 51.Vs.9 ח[ת]מ; 51.Vs.9/10; *KAI* 124.4; Dupont-Sommer, *JFK* 1 p. 44.1; *CIS* I.118; scarab: *RES* 928.

[Eg] see Heb Lw חתמ.

C. ANALYSIS OF PHONOLOGICAI CORRESPONDENCES

[1] Ph : Eg Phonetic Correspondences

Ph א : Eg *3* (mid. 7th – 1st cent. BC)
PN = אמתאסר, אסעא, אסרגן, אסרסמר, אסרתני, סראסר, עדאסר, פטאס, פטאסי; DN = אס

Ph א : Eg *ỉ* (595 BC – 15/17 AD)
PN = אחמס, אמננך, את, בכא; DN = אמן; GN = אן

Ph א : Eg final *r*[40] (5th – 3rd cent. BC)
PN = צחא[41]

Ph prosthetic א : Eg ø (5th – 2nd cent. BC)
PN = אבסת

Ph ב : Eg *b* (5th – 2nd cent. BC)
PN = בכא, הרב, פטבנטט; DN = אבסת

Ph ה : Eg *h* (4th cent. – 146 BC)
PN = הרב

Ph ו : Eg *w* (5th cent. – 146 BC)
PN = וחפרע, חפיו, חרוצ, צחפמו, צכנסו

Ph ח : Eg *ḥ* (6th – 2nd cent. BC)
PN = אחמס, וחפרע, חמנכת, חפיו, חר, חרוצ, חרמס, ימחת, צחא, צחפמו, עחר, עפתח, פשמחי, פתח, פתחא, פתחי; DN = חף, חר, חרפכרט, פתח; GN = תחפנחס

Ph ח : Eg *ẖ* (9/8th cent. BC – 53 AD)
PN = ענחפמס; Lw = חתמ

Ph ט : Eg *d* (7th – 2nd cent. BC)
PN = פטאס, פטאסי, פטבנטט, פטכנס; DN = חרפכרט

Ph ט : Eg *ḏ* > *d* (4th cent. – 146 BC)
PN = פטבנטט[42]

Ph י : Eg *y* (593 – 146 BC)
PN = מי, פשמחי, פפי, פתחי

---

40 For the final Eg. *r* > *ỉ*, see Černý, *LEG* § 1. 9.

41 In the final position, Eg *r* is represented by Ph א like English [fa:ðər] > [fa:ðə']: צחא. Since Eg *ḥr* ( ) had already changed into [ḥo] at the final position (cf. Copt ϩⲟ, yet ϩⲣⲁ̋), the final *aleph* seems to function as a vowel letter: *aleph* = /o/. The א of פנפא (*p3-nfr*) could be explained in the same way (*aleph* = /e/). However it might be a feature of Punic personal names, to which the final א is sometimes added, like פתחא (see the later discussion on *Matres Lectionis* p. 54).

42 For the phonetic change Eg *ḏd* > *dd* (טט), see the entry of פטבנטט.

Ph י : Eg *i* (mid. 9th – 2nd cent. BC)
PN = חפיו, ימחת, פמי; DN = פמי

Ph י : Eg ø (593 BC)
PN = כשי[43]

Ph י (*mater lectionis*): Eg ø (5th cent. BC)
PN = כנפי, פטאסי[44]

Ph כ : Eg *k* (593 – 5th cent. BC)
PN = כנפי, כשי

Ph כ : Eg *ḫ* (mid. 5th – 2th cent. BC)
PN = אמננך, חמנכת, צכנסמו, פטכנס

Ph כ : Eg *ẖ* (5th – 2nd cent. BC)
DN = חרפכרט (cf. Aram חרפחרט)

Ph מ : Eg *m* (mid. 9th cent. BC – 53 AD)
PN = אחמס, אמננך, חרמס, חמנכת, ימחת, מי, צחפמו, צכנסמו, ענחפמס, פמי, פמת, פשמחי; DN = אמן, מן, פמי; GN = מנף; Lw = חתמ

Ph ן : Eg *n* (6th cent. BC – 15/17 AD)
PN = אמננך, חמנכת, כנפי, נפר, סנר, ענחפמס, פפן, פטכנס, פטבנטט, צכנסמו;
DN = אמן; GN = אן, מנף, תחפנחס

Ph ס : Eg *s* (7th – lst cent. BC)
PN = אחמס, אסעא, חרמס, סנר, ססר, ספתח, סראסר, ענחפמס, פטאס, פטאסי, פטכנס, צכנסמו; DN = אבסת, אס; GN = תחפנחס

Ph ע : Eg *ʿ* (5th – 1st cent. BC)
PN = אסעא, וחפרע, עחר, ענחפמס, עפתח; DN = רע

Ph פ : Eg *p* (mid. 9th – 2nd cent. BC)
PN = חפיו, ספתח, ענחפמס, עפתח, פטאס, פטאסי, פטכנס, פטבנטט, פמי, פמת, פשמחי, פפי, פפן, פתא, פתה, פתחא, פתחי, צחפמו; DN = חף, חרפכרט, פתח, פמי; GN = תחפנחס

Ph פ : Eg *f* (5th cent. – 146 BC)
PN = כנפי, נפר; GN = מנף
Notice that this correspondence is restricted to Eg *nfr*.

Ph פ : Eg *b* (mid. 5th cent. BC)
PN = וחפרע (after laryngal /b/ > /p/)

Ph צ : Eg *ḏ* (mid. 5th cent. BC)
PN = חרוץ, צחא

---

[43] The final *yodh* could be resolved as a Ph gentilic.

[44] The final *yodh* seems to be a *mater lectionis*. See the later discussion on the possible *matres lectionis* p. 54.

Ph צ : Eg *ṯ* (mid. 5th – 3rd cent. BC)
PN = צחפמו, צכנסמו
Ph ר : Eg *r* (5th – 1st cent. BC)
PN = הרב, וחפרע, חר, חרוץ, חרמס, נפר, סנר, ססר, סראסר, עחר; DN = חר, חרפכרט, רע
Ph ש : Eg *š* (593 – 2nd cent. BC)
PN = כשי, פשמחי
Ph ת: Eg *t* (9/8th cent. BC – 53 AD)
PN = את, ימחת, חמנכת, ספתח, עפתח, פמת, פתא, פתח, פתחא, פתחי; DN = אבסת, פתח; GN = תחפנחס; Lw = חתמ

[2] Eg : Ph Phonetic Correspondences

Eg *3* : Ph ø (mid. 9th – 2nd cent. BC)
PN = בכא, וחפרע, חרוץ, כנפי, ספתח, עחר, עפתח, פמי, פטבנטט, צכנסמו;
DN = אבסת, פמי (articles *p3* and *t3* excluded).
Eg *3* : Ph א (7th – 1st cent. BC)
Eg *i* : Ph ø (7th – 1st cent. BC)
PN = הרב, וחפרע, כשי, סראסר, פטאס, פטאסי, פטבנטט, פטכנס, פשמחי, צחפמו, צכנסמו; GN = אן
Eg *i* : Ph א (593 – 3th cent. BC)
Eg *i* : Ph י (mid. 9th cent. – 146 BC)
Eg *y* : Ph ø (6th – 5th cent. BC)
PN = צכנסמו, צחפמו; GN = תחפנחס
The reasons for the lack of Ph equivalents are; (1) the reduction of *ṯ3y*. cf. Copt ^{s}ϫⲓ, ^{b}ϭⲓ (Ph צ); (2) the loss of the final *y*. cf. *nḥsy* 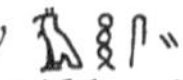 > *nḥs* Gk 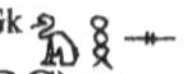 (*Wb* II.303)
Eg *y* : Ph י (6th – 3rd cent. BC)
Eg ᶜ : Ph ø (593 BC)
PN = אחמס (see the entry אחמס)
Eg ᶜ : Ph ע (5th – 3rd cent. BC)
PN = וחפרע, ענחפמס, עפתח, עחר, אסעא; DN = רע
Eg *w* : Ph ø (5th – 2nd cent. BC)
PN = פטכנס, פמת, צכנסמו; DN = מן; GN = אן
The lack of correspondence is due to loss in the Eg words, *e.g.*, *ḫns.w* > *ḫns*; Copt ⲡⲁ-ϣⲟⲛ̄ⲥ (Ph כנס)
Eg *w* : Ph ו (5th cent. – 146 BC)

Eg *b* : Ph ø (4th cent. – 146 BC)
PN = פטבנטט (bi-labial following *n* dropped)
Eg *b* : Ph ב (5th – 2nd cent. BC)
Eg *b* : Ph פ (end of 5th – end of 4th cent. BC)
Eg *p* : Ph ø (mid. of 5th cent. BC)
PN = ימחת (final Eg *p* dropped)
Eg *p* : Ph פ (mid. 9th cent. – 146 BC)
Eg *f* : Ph פ (5th cent. BC)
Eg *m* : Ph מ (mid. 9th cent.BC – 53 AD)
Eg *n* : Ph ø (4th – 2nd cent. BC)
PN = פתא, פשמחי, פפן
The losses of Eg *n* are due to assimilation.
Eg *n* : Ph נ (6th cent. – 2nd cent. BC)
Eg *r* : Ph ø (5th – 2nd cent. BC)
PN = פשמחי, כנפי; GN = מנף
Eg *r* : Ph א (5th cent. – 146 BC)
In the final position Eg *r* lost its consonantal value and functioned as a vowel letter (see each entry כנפי, צחא).
Eg *r* : Ph ר (6th cent. BC – 146 BC)
Eg *h* : Ph ה (4th cent. – 146 BC)
Eg *ḥ* : Ph ח (6th – 2nd cent. BC)
Eg *ḫ* : Ph ח (9/8th cent. BC – 53 AD)
: Ph כ (mid. 5th cent. – 146 BC)
Eg *ẖ* : Ph כ (5th – 2nd cent. BC)
Eg *s/ś* : Ph ס (7th – 2nd cent. BC)
Eg *š* : Ph ש (6th – 2nd cent. BC)
Eg *k* : Ph כ (6th – 2nd cent. BC)
Eg *k* : Ph כ (591 – mid. 5th cent. BC)
Eg *t* : Ph ø (7th – 2nd cent. BC)
PN, DN, GN = passim
Eg fem. ending *-t* lost its consonantal value since NK, except פמת (*p3-mw.t*).
Eg *t* : Ph ת (6th – 2nd cent. BC)
Eg *ṯ* : Ph צ (mid 5th cent. BC)
Eg *d* : Ph ט (7th – 2nd cent. BC)
Eg *ḏ* : Ph צ (mid. 5th – 3rd cent. BC)
Eg *ḏ* > /d/ : Ph ט (4th – 2nd cent. BC)

[3] Table of Correspondences

	Ph	primary	secondary	Eg	primary	secondary
glottal stops	א	*3 ỉ*	*r* ø	*3*	א	ø
				ỉ	א י	ø
	ע	ʿ		ʿ	ע	
semi vowels	י	*y ỉ*	ø	*y*	י	ø
	ו	*w*		*w*	ו	ø
labials	ב	*b*		*b*	ב	פ ø
	פ	*p f b*		*p*	פ	ø
				f	פ	ø
nasals	מ	*m*		*m*	מ	
	נ	*n*		*n*	נ	ø
latrals	ל	-				
trill	ר	*r*		*r*	ר	א ø
pharyngals & laryngals	ה	*h*		*h*	ה	
	ח	*ḥ ḫ*		*ḥ*	ח	
				ḫ	ח כ	
				ẖ	כ	
sibilants	ס	*s*		*s*	ס	
	ש	*š*		*š*	ש	
	צ	*ḏ ṯ*				
velars	ק	-		*ḳ*	-	
	כ	*k ḫ ẖ*		*k*	כ	
	ג	-		*g*	-	
alveolars	ת	*t*		*t*	ת	ø
	ד	-		*ṯ*	צ	
	ט	*d*	*ḏ*	*d*	ט	
	ז	-		*ḏ*	צ	ט

*The above arrangement is based on the Eg alphabetical order, not phonology.

[4] Notes on the Correspondences

a) Glottal Stops

It has been generally acknowledged that Eg *3* lost its consonantal value from NK on except for initial *3*.[45] This fact is observable among the Ph forms of Egyptian names. No Eg *alephs* are reflected in Ph forms, except in the initial position of אס (*3s.t*) and אסר (*3s-ir*) and possibly in the final position.

As אס and אסר are DNs (Isis and Osiris), it is possible to assume that the initial *aleph* remains as an historical spelling in Ph in the Late period. However, it is not necessary to think that Eg *3* does not correspond to Ph *aleph* at the initial position. We have inscriptional evidence that the *aleph* of *3s.t* was pronounced even in the late period; 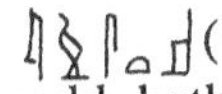 (*Wb* V. 8.11). Therefore, when *3s.t* and *3s-ir* entered the Ph world, both were rendered as אס and אסר, because of the existence of the Eg *aleph*. Some centuries later, Eg *aleph* was lost even in the initial position. Yet the *aleph* continued in Ph to protect the following vowels [e] and [o].

Probably אסעא (*3s.t-ʿ3.t*) is the best example to indicate the possibility that Ph א corresponds to Eg *3* in the final position. Eg *aleph* could be protected by the feminine ending. Another example in which Eg *3* seems to be described by Ph *aleph* is that of פתא (*p3-n-t3*). Yet the fact that Coptic rendering of Eg *t3* is ^{s}TO, ^{b}ΘO inclines us to consider it as a vowel letter. Yet Copt does not have an *aleph*-sign, so even if the final *aleph* was pronounced, they could not write it.

The assumption that Eg *ỉ* possesses two sound values in Egyptian[46] : (1) semi-vowel [i] and (2) *aleph* seems to be confirmed by Ph equations י and א. The correspondence of Eg *ỉ* to Ph א is clearly attested at the initial position (*e.g.* אחמס, אמן, אן) and at the final position (*e.g.* בכא; notice that the final *aleph* could be a vowel letter). Eg *ỉ* and Ph י correspond well. Yet חפיו (*ḥp-ỉw*) is not a case of the correspondence between Eg *ỉ* and Ph י, because here Eg *ỉ* was an *aleph* which was dropped in Ph by merging with preceding [i/y].

---

45 For examples, Osing, "Lautsystem," *LÄ*, III, p. 947; J. Vergote, *Phonétique*, p. 96; see the synoptic table after p. 122.

46 Gardiner, *EG*^{3}, § 20. cf. A. de Buck, *Grammaire*, § 13, he said the second value is any vowel with soft attack of progressive relaxation.

b) Labials

Due to the absence of a sign for the *f* consonant in Ph, Eg *f* is represented by Ph פ. It is natural that Eg voiceless *f* corresponds to Ph voiceless פ, rather than voiced ב. Eg *b* once corresponds to Ph פ (וחפרע: *w3ḥ-ib-r*ʿ). Since this Eg *b* is consistently represented by פ in all Semitic forms, it is probable that the internal change of sound value /b/ > /p/ took place in Eg, before this name was recorded by Semitic scribes. According to all Greek forms and the Hebrew forms, the *b* of *w3ḥ-ib-r*ʿ closes the syllable. Therefore it possible that this *b* became a voiceless aspirate which the scribes heard as פ (notice the Akk form *uḫ-pa-ra*).

c) Sibilants

The two sibilants ס and שׁ correspond well between Ph and Eg without confusion. There are two names, however, which slightly indicate that Eg *s* was recorded by Ph שׁ: אשרשלח (= אסרשלח? *CIS* I.65.1/2) and אבדשר (= אבדאסר? *CIS* I.4229.4)[47] . Though the Assyrian deity "Assur" is not a attested as a theophoric element in Ph and Pu inscriptions, אשר is more likely Assur in terms of phonology. If אשר is אסר (Osiris), then the following two explanations are possible; (1) Ph ס became שׁ under the influence of another שׁ of שלח. (2) Dialectic variation in Cyprus[48].

The correspondence between Ph שׁ and Eg *ṯ* is suggested only by Ph שמו (*ṯ3y-im.w*). Since שמו is unique this correspondence cannot be certain. Benz suggested that it is a misspelling of שמע (p. 420; cf. Harris, *Grammar*, p. 151).

d) Pharyngals and Larygals (Eg *hs*)

The different number of *h*-consonants in Eg (*h*, *ḥ*, *ḫ*, and *ẖ*) and Ph (ה and ח) compelled ancient scribes to conflate them. Yet the correspondences are very characteristic;

[47] Tsevat, *VT*, 4 (1954) p. 4, said "an example of a syncretism of Osiris and the Ph deity, Salah." Yet more likely to be שלח "to send."

[48] Friedrich and Röllig, *PPG*, § 47.

Eg *h* = Ph ה (1 x)
Eg *ḥ* = always Ph ח (42 x)
Eg *ḫ* = Ph ח (2 x); Ph כ (4 x)
Eg *ẖ* = Ph כ (2 x)

Notice that only Eg *ḫ* has more than one Ph equivalent, ח 2x and 4x. These data imply that spirantization (fricativization) of /k/ occured in Phoenician by the 5th century B.C.. As we shall see in the next chapter, there is no such evidence forthcoming from the Aramaic data. Accordingly, we conclude, contra the view of most scholars, that spirantization developed first in Phoenician and only later spread to Aramaic and other Northwest Semitic languages. A full discussion appears below in the next chapter, section [6] Spirantization.

e) Alveolar

Ph צ seems to represent two different Eg consonants; *ṯ* and *ḏ*:

צ	*ṯ*	Eg *ṯ3y*	2x	Elephantine
	ḏ	Eg *wḏ3, ḏd*	2x	Elephantine

It is generally assumed that Eg *ṯ* and *ḏ* have a parallel phonetic history. Yet kept their distinction even until Coptic as follows:

ṯ [tšh] / [tš] = Copt ϭ
ḏ [tš] / [dž] = Copt ϫ[49]

Yet as far as Eg *ṯ3y* is concerned, there are dialectical variations; ˢϫ and ᵇϭ. Since both names (צחפמו, צכנסמו) came from Elephantine the sound of Achminic is more likely, although the survival of *ṯ* and *ḏ* in the various Copt dialects is complex. We may perhaps safely conclude that Ph צ corresponds to Eg *ṯ*, when *ṯ* became /ḏ/ (Copt ϫ). Therefore, Ph צ basically corresponds to Eg *ḏ*[50] (cf. Aram and Heb ש corresponding to /ḏ/).

---

49 J.Vergote, *Phonétique*, p. 38ff; Osing, "Lautesystem," p. 947; de Buck, *Grammaire*, p. 26.

50 There is a unconfirmed PN שמו (*ṯ3y-im.w*), which seems to indicate correspondence between Ph ש and Eg *ṯ*. Considering that the provenance of שמו is Carthage, we also could assume that Eg *ṯ3y* was pronounced like Bohairic ϭι, not Sahidic ϫι, which is used in the Delta. The Greek form of this name, Σαμωους indicates that Eg *ṯ3y* was heard as a kind of sibilant. Cf. Aram representation of Eg *ṯ* is ש, not צ.

Finally it is noteworthy that Ph consonants ד and ז were never used to represent Eg consonants, though a full range of dentals (or alveolars) is attested in Eg.

[5] The Possible *Mater Lectionis* in Ph

It has been said that Ph writing was rigidly consonantal. Vowel letters are not used at all in Ph inscriptions, except for a very few foreign names found from Cyprus[51] . However, a few Eg names from Elephantine indicate the possibility of *matres lectionis*; צחא, כנפי, פטאסי.

(1) צחא (*ḏd-ḥr* *[ḏiḥo]): 5th– 3rd cent. BC

It is well known that the final *r* dropped in late Egyptian. Eg *ḥr* became ϩⲟ in Coptic. Therefore, the final *aleph* of צחא probably indicates an /o/ vowel.

(2) כנפי (*k3.i-nfr*): 5th cent. BC

Eg sg. *nfr*, after losing the final *r*, is represented by either נפ (מנף) or נפי. Even in Aram *nfr* is written without the final י (cf. נפסי = *nfr-3s.t*; ורסנף = *wrs-nfr* etc.). This strongly suggests י is a vowel letter. The Greek forms κονουφς, χονουφις, and Copt ⲚⲞⲨϤⲒ point to a /i/ or /e/ vowel in this final syllable like the Ph י.

(3) פטאסי (*p3-di-3s.t*): 5th cent. BC

The fact that the name is also realized as פטאס strongly supports that the final י is a *mater lectionis*. For details see the entry פטאס.

As far as the כנופי and פטאסי is concerned, there is no alternative explanation. The use of *aleph* and *yodh* in these names from the 5th century onwards indicates that the Phoenician scribes were aware of the function of the *matres lectionis* although they saw no need to use them in writing their own language.

[51] Z. Harris, p. 17f.

II

EGYPTIAN PROPER NAMES AND LOANWORDS IN ARAMAIC[1]

Egyptian proper names and loanwords in Aramaic documents were first collected to any extent by W. Spiegelberg in "Ägyptisches sprachgut in den aus Ägypten stammenden aramäischen Urkunden der Perserzeit." (C. Bezold, ed., *Orientalische Studien Th. Nöldeke zum 70. Geburtstag*, 1906, pp. 1093–1115; Abbr. S I). He also worked on Eg PN in the documents from Elephantine in "Die ägyptischen Personennamen in den kürzlich veröffentlichten Urkunden von Elephantine," (*OLZ* 15, 1912, pp. 1–10; Abbr. S II). Every later study on Eg names in Aram owes much to him.

When M. Noël Aimé-Giron published *Textes Araméens d'Egypte* in 1931, he added a number of identifications of Eg PNs. Then these three collections were combined by T. Lambdin in the third chapter of his unpublished Ph. D. thesis; *Egyptian Loanwords in the Ancient-Semitic Languages* (1952; Abbr. L). In 1970s two more important works with respect to foreign names in Aramaic texts were published ; (1) P. Grelot, *Documents Araméens d'Egypte* (1972; Abbr. G), in which, pp. 460–502, he identified and discussed a considerable number of Eg names, as well as others. (2) W. Kornfeld, *Onomastica Aramaica aus Ägypten.*(1978; Abbr. K) in which the number of Eg names reached 229. As I mentioned in the Preface, I owe many readings of Aram texts to Prof. Porten. His personal letter is quoted as

[1] What is meant by "Aramaic" here is mainly Imperial Aramaic. My collection of Eg names and words from Aram is mainly restricted to Imperial Aram documents, though sporadically collected from late Aram.

"his letter."

In the present work about 400 PNs, 9 DNs, 19 GNs and 51 Lws including 12 month names are discussed. Only those which have two asterisks will be used for the final analysis.

A. ARAMAIC DOCUMENTS: DATES AND PROVENANCES

The paleography and the dates of Aram documents were fully studied by J. Naveh, *The Development of the Aramaic Script* (1966). In the following list I have accepted his dates whenever he discussed the dates of the texts (Abbr. N). The grounds for each date are found in footnotes. If nothing is mentioned in footnotes the dates of the documents are those given in the publication quoted. The dates are given only for the documents which contain Egyptian names used for the final analysis.

[1] ***AP*** (Cowley): Papyrus, from Elephantine[2]

1	495
2	484
3	408
4	*ca.* 475[3]
5	471
6	465
7	late 5th cent. BC (461 or 401)[4]
8	460
9	460
10	456
11	2nd quarter of 5th cent. BC[5]
12	last quarter of 5th cent. BC[6]
13	447
15	441 or 435

[2] The following dates are mostly based on Naveh pp. 31–36, unless there is no indication.

[3] No. 4 is not a dated cocument. Cowley suggests the possible relation with No. 2 and 3.

[4] Cowley 461 BC (Artaxerxes I); Yaron 401 BC (Artaxerxes II), *JSS* 2 (1957) p. 34.

[5] Cowley's date *ca.* 455; Yaron's date *ca.* 479 (*JSS* 2, p. 42f.).

[6] Cf. Cowley's date: 450 – 440 BC.

16	2nd half of 5th cent. BC
17	428
18	434 – 420
20	420
21	419 (N. p. 33)
22	400 (N. p. 43)[7]
23	end of 5th cent. BC.
24	same as above
25	416
26	412
27	late 5th cent. BC
28	411
29	*ca.* 409
30	408
31	408
32	probably 408 or little later
33	*ca.* 408
34	last decade of 5th cent. BC
35	400
37	late 5th cent. BC
38	same as above
39	last quarter of 5th cent. BC
40	same as above
41	2nd half of 5th cent. BC
42	last quarter of 5th cent. BC
43	late 5th cent. BC
44	same as above
45	2nd half of 5th cent. BC
50	5th cent. BC[8]
51	end of 5th cent. BC
53	same as above
56	last decade of 5th cent. BC
63	5th cent. BC[9]
66 – 68	same as above[10]
69 (*CIS* II 149)	late 5th cent. BC

[7] Cf. Cowley 419 BC.
[8] "Year 13" is mentioned in line 3. Yet there is nothing to identify the date.
[9] "Year 13" and "year 6" are mentioned. Yet there is no clue for the date.
[10] No. 66 – 68: fragmentary inscriptions do not show any indication for dating.

70 (*CIS* II 144)	same as above
71 (*CIS* II 145)	3rd quarter of 5th cent. BC
72 (*CIS* II 146)	*ca.* 375 (N. p. 43f)
73 (*CIS* II 147)	late 5th cent. BC
74 (*CIS* II 148)	late 5th or early 4th cent. BC
75 (*CIS* II 150)	late 5th cent. BC
76 (*CIS* II 151)	late 5th cent. BC
81	beginning of 3rd cent. BC (N p. 43), Edfu
83 recto	before 400
83 verso	*ca.* 300
p. 317A	5th cent. BC, Saqqara

[2] ***APO*** (Sachau): ostraca

75.1	early 3rd cent. BC (N. p. 44)
75.2	end of 4th cent. BC (N. p. 37)
76.1–3, 5	*ca.* 475 BC (N. p. 44)
76.4	5th cent. BC (N. p. 39)
76.5	same as above
77.1–2	*ca.* 475 BC (N. p. 37)
77.3	4th cent. BC (N. p. 45)
78	*ca.* 475 (N. p. 37)
82	n.d.
83	n.d.
87	n.d.

[3] ***AD*** (Driver): 410 (N. fig. 6)[11], provenance unknown
1–13
Frag 1A, 1B, 3, 7, 10.

[4] ***BP*** (Kraeling)[12]: from Elephantine

1	451 BC (N. p. 36)
2	449 BC (N. fig. 5)
3	449 BC
4	434 BC
5	427 BC
6	420 BC (N. p. 36)

11 None of the letters are dated. Driver's dates 411/10 – 408 BC (cf. Naveh's fig. 6 for *AD* 3,4,5,7).

12 All documents are dated, except No. 16, which is a collection of fragments.

7	420 BC
8	416 BC (N. p. 36)
9	404 BC (N. fig. 5)
10	402 BC
11	402/1 BC (N. p. 36)
12	402/1 BC
13	399 BC (N. p. 36)
14	449 BC
16	

[5] ***CIS* II**

8	722–705 BC (N. p. 11), Nineveh
113	end of 5th / begin. of 4th cent. BC (N. p. 56), Teima Oasis
116	n.d.
122	482 BC (N. p. 52), Saqqara
123	5th cent. BC (N. p. 22)[13], Memphis
125	5th cent. BC (N. p. 22), Abydos
126	same as above
127	same as above
128	same as above
130	same as above
132	same as above
134	5th cent. BC (N. p. 22), Akhmim
135	5th cent. BC (N. p. 22), Wadi es-Saba Rigaleh
136	same as above
138	*ca.* 475 (N. p. 37), Elephantine
140	Egypt
141	5th cent. BC (N. p. 42)[14], Egypt
142	early 5th cent. BC (N. p. 42), Egypt
154	2nd half of 5th cent. BC, Elephantine
155	same as above

[13] Cf. *KAI* 268 5th–4th cent. BC.

[14] Cf. Gibson's date: early 4th cent. BC (p. 120). *KAI* 269: 5th–4th cent. BC.

[6] ***LH*** (Bresciani and Kamil): from Hermopolis
late 6th or early 5th cent. BC (N. p. 16)[15]

[7] ***Krug*** (Lidzbarski): 5th cent. BC, Elephantine

[8] ***RES***

438	485 BC (N. p. 42), Syene
492	n.d.
961	Wadi es-Saba Rigaleh
1296	Elephantine
1372	5th–3rd cent. BC[16], Abydos
1373	same as above
1376	same as above
1787	Egypt
1788	Memphis
1789	Memphis
1791	Saqqara
1793	Elephantine
1810	436 BC, Saqqara.
1818	Memphis (?)
1819	Ma'sra (Eg)

[9] ***Saqqara*** (Segal): 5th cent. BC[17]

[10] ***TAÉ*** (Aimé-Giron): from Saqqara

2	7th cent. BC (N. p. 15)
5 – 86	middle or 3rd quarter of 5th cent. BC (N. p. 36)
86bis	1st half of 4th cent. BC (N. p. 43)
87	same as above
93–110	5th cent. BC (N. p. 22 n. 69)

15 J. Naveh, "The Palaeography of the Hermopolis Papyri", in *Israel Oriental Studies*, pp. 120ff; N. fig. 3. cf. the date of Bresciani and Kamil: middle of 5th cent. BC (*LH* p. 361).

16 Lidzbarski, *Eph* III, p. 96.

17 Naveh concluded that most of them belong to 5th cent. BC due to palaeographical criteria (*IEJ* 35, 1985, p. 212). Cf. Segal's date: 5th – 4th cent. BC (Saqqara p. 4). No. 30 is dated "year 34th" (according to Segal's reading). However, the text is so damaged that the date cannot be sure.

[11] **Other Works**

E. Bresciani, *Aegyptus*, 39 p. 4: n.d., El-Hibeh

——— *Frammenti di un Testo Aramaico*: 5th cent. BC, Saqqara

Degen-Müller-Röllig, *NEph*, II,

p. 10 (Papyrus Berol 23000): end of 5th or 4th cent. BC[18], Elephantine or Hermopolis

p. 67 (papyrus): 7th cent. BC

p. 75 (papyrus): late 6th or beginning of 5th cent. BC, Eleph.

Herr, *Seals* p. 30 (seal): 6th cent. BC

Lidzbarski, *Eph* III

p. 20 (ostracon): *ca.* 475 (N. p. 38), Eleph.

p. 107 (graffito): 5th cent. BC (N. p. 22), Abydos

p. 109 (graffito): 5th cent. BC (N. p. 22), Abydos

p. 112 (graffito): 5th cent. BC (N. p. 22), Abydos

p. 114 (graffito): 5th cent. BC (N. p. 22), Abysos

p. 122 (ostracon): n.d., Egypt

Porten C3.7: *ca* 475

Sefire I (*KAI* 222): 8th cent. BC

Sznycer, in *Homage à A. Dupont-Sommer* p. 186: 5th cent. BC, Hermopolis[19]

[12] **Journals**

Aìmé-Giron, *JA* 18 (1921) p. 61 (papyrus): 5th cent. BC, Saqq.

——— *AE* 23 (1923) p. 42 (on wall): 450–475 BC (N. p. 40f)[20], Sheikh Fadl

——— *ASAE* 26 (1926) p. 25 (ostracon): *ca.* 475 (N. p. 38), Elephantine.

——— *ASAE* 39 (1939) p. 352 (graffito): 5th–4th cent. BC, Wadi-el-Hûdi

——— *BIFAO* 38 (1939)

p. 38 (ostracon): late 4th–early 3rd cent. BC (N. p. 44), Edfu.

p. 42 (stela): 5th cent. BC, Saqq.

p. 58 (ostracon): mid 2nd cent. BC, Edfu

Bauer-Meissner, *SBPA* 1936 (papyrus): 515 BC (N. p. 16), Eleph.

Bresciani, *RSO* 35 (1960) p. 22 (papyrus): 2nd quarter of 5th cent. BC (N. p. 21), Padua

18 Naveh, *JAOS* 91, p. 379.

19 Porten, *Semitica* 33 p. 92.

20 Cf. Giron's date: mid 7th and 6th cent. BC.

Cowley, *PSBA* 25 (1903) p. 264 (ostracon): *ca.* 450, Eleph.
——— *PSBA* 37 (1915) p. 218 (papyrus): beginning of 3rd cent. BC (N. p. 44), Edfu
——— *JRAS* (1929) p. 109 (ostracon): *ca.* 475 (N. p. 38), Syene
A. Dupont-Sommer, *RES* 1941–45 p. 67 (ostracon): *ca.* 475 BC (N. p. 38), Elephantine
——— *Semitica,* 1 (1946) p. 44 (papyrus): 600 BC (N. p. 16), Saqq.
——— *ASAE* 48 (1948) p. 112A (ostracon): *ca.* 475 (N. p.38), Elephantine
——— *RSO* 32 (1957) p. 3 (ostracon): *ca.* 475 (N. p. 38), Elephantine
Kornfeld, *WZKM* 61 (1967) p. 11 (graffito): n.d., Syene
——— *AÖAW* 110 (1973) p. 133 (graffito): 330–300[21] Edfu
Marakten, *MDIK* 43 (1987) p. 170–172 (ostraca): 5th cent. BC, Elephantine
Porten, *Or* NS 57 (1989) p. 26 (papyrus): 5th cent. BC, Elephantine
Rabinowitz, *JNES*, 15 (1956) p. 2 (metal bowl): 5th entc .BC (N. p. 22), Tell el-Maskhûta
——— *JNES* 18 (1959) p. 154f. (metal bowl): 5th cent. BC (N. p. 22), Tell el-Maskhûta
Sayce, *PSBA* 26 (1904) p. 208 (graffito): Memphis
——— *PSBA* 30 (1908) p. 28f (graffito): Heshân
——— *PSBA* 33 (1911) p. 183 (ostracon): *ca.* 475 BC (N. p. 37), Elephantine
Teixidor, *Syria* 41 (1964) p. 286 (papyrus): 417 BC, Abydos
Torrey, *Numismatic Note* (graffito): 318 BC (N. p. 52), Damanhur

[21] Lipinski, *OLP* 6/7, p. 388.

B. INVENTORY OF EGYPTIAN PROPER NAMES AND LOANWORDS

[1] Personal Names

אגן ?

--- *ikn(.i)* 

G p.462; K p.121

[Aram] *APO* 75.2.15 (pl. 62)

[Eg] Ranke I.48.17 m. NK. cf. also 16 (m. MK)

The correspondence between Aram ג and Eg *k* needs further evidence (cf. פקרקפתח--- *p3-n-grg-ptḥ*) (see Chapter VI: alveolars). Though not attested as a PN, there is a Aram root אגן "bowl" (*DISO* p.3) and Heb אָגָן (KB p.11). Akk *akūnu* (*CAD* A 286; *AHw* I 30) "a kind of jar" is generally regarded as an Eg loanword (*ikn Wb* I.140; cf. Lambdin *Or* NS 22,1953, p. 363). Yet Burchardt considers that the word has a Semitic origin (Burchardt II, p. 10). Assy PN *a-gi-nu* also occurs (*APN* p.136). The identification is far from certain.

אופתשתו **

--- *ip(.t)-t(3)-šd(.t)* "Opet, the saviour"

[Aram] *Saqq* 1.3, 8

[Eg] cf. Ranke I.148.17 *mw.t-šd.t* 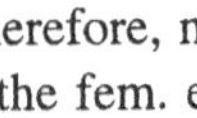 ; 370.13 *t3-šd.t-mw.t* f. Dyn 21f.

ʾIp.t, Goddess of Luxor, was pronounced [ope] in the Late Period. The final ו seems to contradict the Eg fem. ending *-t* which is normally realized as Aram י, though not necessarily so. The masc. form of the saviour is *p3-šd.w* (*Wb* IV.563. 10f), so the fem. form is *t3-šd.w.t*. The final ו, therefore, may be a counterpart of the Eg consonant *w*, protected by the fem. ending *-t*, or it may be a dialectal variant. Cf. Segal's *wpwty-št3* which is not attested.

אחא

--- *iḥ3* (< *ʿḥ3*) 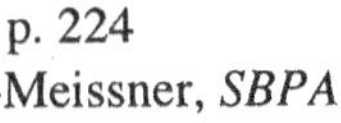 "Warrior"

K p.119; V 11 p. 224

[Aram] Bauer-Meissner, *SBPA*, 1936, 415.2; 16 אח[א]; 19 אח[א]

[Eg] Ranke I.44.7 m. NK or a short form of *iḥ3*-type (Ranke I.44.8–

16).

Equally possible is *i(ʿ)ḥ*  "moon" (Ranke I.12.13) and its hypocoristicon (Ranke I.12.14–13,10). However the Semitic root אח "brother" prevents us from confirming that this is Eg. The name can also be a hypocoristicon with the Semitic אח.

אחמן *

--- *i(ʿ)ḥ-mn* 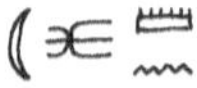 "The Moon is enduring"
V II p.225
[Aram] *Saqq* 105.5
[Eg] cf. DN + *mn.w* type of PN. *e.g.*, *ḥp-mn(w)* (Ranke I.237.15); *ḥr-mn(w)* (I.252.3); *ḫns.w-mn(w)* (I.271.5); *iʿḥ-ms-mn(w)* (I.13.2). Those names are all attested between NK and Gk.

A hybrid interpretation such as *אח-*mn(w)* "Min is a brother" is not entirely excluded though less likely.

אחטף

--- misreading of אחטב (corrected by Porten in his letter)
[Aram] ostracon: Sayce, *PSBA* 33 P.183.2.

אחמס **

--- *i(ʿ)ḥ-ms* 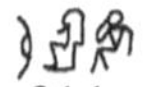 "The moon is born"
K p. 77; V p. 214
[Aram] ostracon: *APO* 76.4.6 (pl. 63)
[Eg] see Ph אחמס.

אחפפי

--- **iḥ(3)-pp.y* "Pepi is a warrior"
G p. 463; K p. 77; V II p. 214
[Aram] *AD* 4.4
[Eg] cf. *iḥ3*  (Ranke I.44.7 m. NK); *pp.y* (Ranke I.131.12 m./f. OK–NK); [Gk] cf. 'Απιας, 'Απιπῆς

3ḫ-pp.y "Pepi is beneficial" (for *3ḫ*, see Ranke I.2.21) is another possible reconstruction. The first element *3ḫ* is used from OK to the Late Period: *3ḫ.t-imn-ʾr.w* "Amun is effective against them" (Ranke I.3.10 m. Late) and *3ḫ-iʿḥ* (Ranke I.2.22 m. Dyn 19). A hybrid explanation is also possible *אח-*pp.y* "Pepi is a brother." Note that Vittmann suggests the alternative reading, *i.e.*, אחרפי, yet he gives no explanation of it. To change the reading to אחרפי (Vittmann) is unnecessary.

אחרחיב

--- misreading of אחרטיס

L p. 117; K p. 77; V II p. 214

[Aram] *AP* 73.16.

אחרטיס **

--- *i(ʿ)ḥ-(ii)r-di-s(w)* "It is the Moon who has given him"

S II p. 3; L p. 117; K p. 77

[Aram] *AP* 63.2, 73.16 אחרחיב (corrected to אחרטיס by Vittman p. 214, and Porten, C3.19:16); *Saqq.* 28a. 7; 41.9 אחרטיס; 43a.3 אחרטיס

[Eg] Ranke I.12.14 and 15 m./f. Late; *DemNB* I.57 (*iʿḥ-i.ir-ti-s*)

[Gk] cf. ʻΑρταϊς, ʻΑριτις (for *ḥr-i.ir-di-s(w)*) (*NB* p. 56, 49).

אחתבסתי

--- אחת-*b3st(.t)* "The sister of Bast"

G p. 460; K p. 40; Lìpinski, *Bibl. Or.* 31 p. 121; Teixidor, *Bulletin* p. 355 (no. 41)

[Aram] *AD* 11.1 אחתבסתי; 4 אחתבסתי

[Eg] see Ph אבסת

Cf. חתובסתי

The name has been explained as Semitic: Assy **aḫatu-bâstī* "The (divine) sister is my gurdian angel" (cf. masc. *aḫu-bâs/ští APN* p. 15; Driver *AD* p. 32, G., K. and Teixidor). However, E. Lìpiński (*Bibl.Or.* 31, p.121) points out the Eg theophoric element Bast, which is found in Ph PNs עבדבסת, עבדאבסת, עבדבסת. פאלאבסת. The identification is open to choice.

אטי

--- *idi*

G p. 494; K p. 119

[Aram] *LH* 4.3 and 6

[Eg] Ranke I.53.22 m. OK–MK, f. MK. For the similar names, see Ranke I.53.23ff, *id.i*, *id.y* etc. Yet these names are only attested until MK.

A short form of the name composed with the element *it(f)* such as *itf-wr, itf-ws-ir, itf-m3ʿ* etc. (Ranke I.50.18ff) is a possible explanation, yet Eg *t* is usually not represented by Aram ט.

אכי

--- *iky*

K p. 119

[Aram] graffito: *TAÉ* 93

[Eg] Ranke I.48.5 cf. Rank I.47.26–48.12 m. Late

Aimé-Gìron suggests אכי is Assy *ak-ki* (*APN* p. 266). Lycian Ακκα. Yet his affiliation חרזבד "Horus has bestowed" points out the possibility of an Eg name. Cf. Ug *aky* (Gröndahl p. 216), *ʾky* (Harding p. 63).

אמון *

--- *imn* "Amun"

[Aram] *AD* 5.3

[Eg] Ranke I.26.18 m. MK–Late cf. *DemNB* I.83; [Gk] 'Αμων, 'Αμμων, 'Αμωνιος, 'Αμωνιος, 'Αμῶνις (*NB* p.29)

Equally possible is a Semitic explanation אָמוֹן (2Kings 21:19, a king of Judah, *IPN* 228–9), which is derived from אמון "master workman" (?).

אמורטים **

--- *im(n-i)r-di-s(w)* "It is Amun who has given him"

S II p. 3; L p. 117; K p. 77

[Aram] *AP* 35.1; 6 אמו[רט]ים; *BP* 13.3 אמורטי[ס]

[Eg] Ranke I.26.24; II p. 243 m. Late–Gk; *DemNB* I.84 (*imn-i.ir-[ti-s]?*); [Gk] 'Αμορταῖος, 'Αμυρταῖος, 'Αμεναρτεῖς, 'Αμονορταϊσις, 'Αμορταϊς (*NB* p. 27); [NA] *a-mur-ṭí-še* (*APN* p. 23; Ranke *KM* p. 27)

As is shown in Gk forms, *n* of *imn* is assimilated into the following *r* (*nr* > *r*), likewise in Akk form.

[א]מחות

--- *i(i)-m-ḥt(p)* "Coming in peace"

K p. 77

[Aram] *AP* 69A.11 אמחות[(Porten's reading is [---]מחות B8.5.14);

69D [א]מחו[ת]
[Eg] Ranke I.9.2 m. OK-Gk; *DemNB* I.55; [Gk] Ἰμουθου, Ἰμουθης, Ἰμουτης, Ἰμουθης, Ἀμουθις (*NB* p. 27, 149)
Cf. ימחות, Ph ימחת
For the discussion of this name, see ימחות.

אסוטים *
--- *3s(.t)-(ii)r-di-s(.t)*  "It is Isis who has given her"
S II p. 4; L p. 117
[Aram] *AP* 66,12.2
[Eg] Ranke I.3.19 f. Late-Gk; [Gk] Ἐσορταΐς, Ἐσερταΐς (*NB* p. 108f)
Cf. אסטים
With respect to the loss of Eg *iir* which is usually represented by Aram ר, the following two explanations can be offered; (1) the misspelling of ו for ר (S, L and K, see אסרטים); (2) the progressive assimilation of *r* into [o]: [-sor-] > [-so-].

אסורי **
--- *3s(.t)-wr(.t)*  "Isis is great"
S III p. 347; L p. 117; G p. 475; K p. 77; V II p. 214
[Aram] *LH* 7.2; *AP* 43.2 and [13]
[Eg] Ranke I.4.1 f. NK-Gk; *DemNB* I.76; [Copt] ⲉⲥⲟⲩⲉⲣⲉ; [G Ἐσοῆρις, Ἐσουῆρις, Ἐσυῆρις (*NB* p.108f)
Equally possible is *ns-wr.t* "He/she who belongs to the great" (Ranke I.174.11 m. Gk, f. Late-Gk; [Gk] Εσοηρις; [Copt] ⲉⲥⲟⲩⲉⲣⲉ. The final י is a *mater lectionis*, representing the Eg fe ending.

אסחור **
--- *(n)s-ḥr(.w)*  "He belongs to Horus"
S I p. 1111; L p. 117; G p. 470; K p. 77
[Aram] *AP* 15.2, 17, 19, 21, 23, 24 [אס]חור, 26, 30, 37; 20.3, 6, 8, 20
[Eg] Ranke I.178.7; II p. 365 m./f. Late–Gk
Eg *ns* is always rendered as אס because of the assimilation of *n* to *s* (S I p. 1111).

אסחנום **

--- *(n)s-ẖnm(.w)*  "He belongs to Khnum"
S I p. 1099; L p. 117; K p. 77
[Aram] ostracon: *CIS* II,155A.2, 155B.5 אסרונפר (the latter was read as אסחנום by Vittmann, yet remains uncertain)
[Eg] Ranke I.179.1 m. Late

Notice Eg *ẖ* corresponds to Aram ח, not כ like Ph (see the later discussion [6] Spirantization).

אסטוֹמֹ[-]

--- see אספעמרא
K p. 77
[Aram] *CIS* II, 155A.3 (corrected to אספעמרא by B. Porten in his letter).

[א]סיפא

--- **3s(.t)-(m-)p* "Isis is in Buto"
[Aram] Lidzbarski, *Eph* III p. 25.6 סיפא (Porten read as [נתנ א]סיפא in his letter)
[Eg] cf. Ranke I.247.21 *ḥr-m-p* "Horus is in Buto"; I.249.4 *ḥr-n-p* m. Late.

The identification is uncertain. The final א is to be considered as a *mater lectionis*.

אסיתון *

--- *3s(.t)*-יתון "Isis has given"
Maraqten p. 70. 134
[Aram] ostracon: Naveh *'Atiqot*, 17 p. 119 no.10.2
[Eg] see Ph DN אס.

אסיתעא **

--- * *3s(.t)-t(3)-ʿ3(.t)* "Isis the great"
[Aram] *Saqq* 56.1]אסית̊, 2 אסית̊ע̊א, 3
[Eg] cf. *3s. t-wr.t* 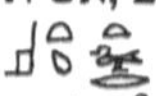 "Isis is great" (Ranke I.4.1 f. NK–Gk). For the second element, cf. *t3-ʿ3.t* (Ranke I.354. 13ff f. NK–Late)
Cf. Ph אסעא.

אסכישו *

--- short form of אסכשית (*ns-ḳ3y-šw.ty*)

L p. 117; G p. 470; K p. 77

[Aram] *AP* 2.19

[Eg] see אסכשית

The short form אסכש + a *mater lectionis* ו as a caritative ending.

אסכשית *

--- *(n)s-ḳ(3y)-š(w.)t(y)* 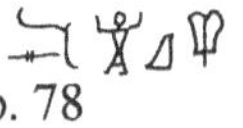 "He belongs to *ḳ3y-šw.ty*"

L p. 117; G p. 501; K p. 78

[Aram] *AP* 53.7

[Eg] Ranke I.179.8 m. Late–Gk, f. Late cf. *ns-p3-ḳ3y-šw.ty* (Ranke I.175.18)

The correspondence between Aram כ and Eg *ḳ* is unusual.

אסמן **

--- *(n)s-mn(.w)*  "He belongs to Min"

S I p. 1099; L p. 117; K p. 78

[Aram] ostracon: *CIS* II.138A.l

[Eg] Ranke I.176.12 m. Late–Gk; [Gk] 'Εσμῆνις, 'Εσμινῖς, Ζμῆνις, Ζμιν, Ζμινις, Σμῖνις (*NB* p. 108, 118, 388).

אסמת

--- see below אסמתשבם.

S I p. 1099; L p. 117; K p. 78; V II p. 215

[Aram] *CIS* II.155A.1.

אסמתשבם

--- **(n)s-md(w)-šps(y)* "He who belongs to the glorious Rod"

[Aram] *CIS* II.155A.l (corrected to אסמתשבם by Porten in his letter)

[Eg] cf. Ranke II.295.9 (m. Dyn 20, Late) *ns-p3-mdw-špsy* "He who belongs to the glorious rod"; I.175.1 (m. Late–Gk) *ns-p3-mdw*.

Though reconstructed, the type of the Eg name and the elements are well attested (see above). **3s(.t)-m-t(3)-šps(.t)* "Isis is the noble" is another possible solusion. The equation of ב with *p* is not impossible.

אספטנס֯ני

--- *(n)s-p(3)-d(i)-n(.i)-sn(.t)* "He belongs to him who has given me a sister"
[Aram] *CIS* II.155B.6 אספטח[-]ני (corrected here)
[Eg] For the type of *ns-p3-* see Ranke I.174.19–175.21. For the structure of the second half, see Ranke I.124.5 *p3-di-n.i-3s.t* "He whom Isis has given to me." Since *ns-* can be attached to any name in order to produce another name, this combination is possible.

אספטח[-]ני

--- see אספטנס֯ני
K p. 78; V II p. 215

אספמט **

--- Var. of אספמת (*ns-p3-mdw*)
S I p. 111; G p. 471; K p. 78
[Aram] *AP* 2.2 אס֯פ֯מ֯ט, 22 אספ[מט]; 3.3 אספ[מט]; 4.7
[Eg] see אספמת.

אספמת **

--- *(n)s-p(3)-md(w)* 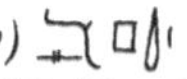 "He belongs to the (sacred) staff"
S I p. 1111; L p. 118; K p. 78
[Aram] *AP* 6.10; 8.7; graffito: *TAÉ* 98; ostracon: *CIS* II.155B.1 אספ֯מ֯ת; 155B.5 (corrected by Porten in his letter); Porten, *Or*.NS, 57 p. 26; *NEph* II,p. 75
[Eg] Ranke I.175.1; II p. 365; [Gk] 'Εσπμῆτις, 'Εσπμῆθις (*NB* p.108f); [Akk] *iš-pi-ma-a-ṭu* (*APN* p.105a)
Cf. אספמט

As the Gk form shows, Eg *d* of *md.w* changed into [mēt-], which is realized as מת in Aram. The Eg *d* also corresponds to Aram ט in אספמט under the influence of a preceding labial. There is no necessity to deal with אספמת and אספמט differently, as Lambdin proposes. Akk *ṭ* of *iš-pi-ma-a-ṭu* should be remembered here.

אספעמ֯ר֯א֯

--- **(n)s-p(3)-ʿ(3)-mrw.t* "He who belongs to *p(3)-ʿ(3)-mrw.t*"
[Aram] *CIS* II.155A.3 אסטום (corrected by B. Porten in his letter)
[Eg] For the last part of the name see Ranke I.57.21 *ʿ3-mrw.t* "Love

is great" (m. MK, Dyn 20).

אספשן *

--- *(n)s-p(3)-šn* "He belongs to the (sacred?) tree"

[Aram] *Saqq* 1.5

[Eg] for the element of *šn.w* see Ranke I.211.5 *nḫt-ḥr(.w)-n3-šn.w* "Strong is Horus of the trees" (m.Dyn 25); Ranke I.244.8 *ḥnw.t-šn.w* "Mistress of trees" (f. Dyn 20); Ranke I.422.13. Yet the element *šn.w* is always used in plural in these attested forms.

א֯ס֯ר֯ו֯נפ֯ר

--- see אספמת

S I p. 1099; L p. 118; K p. 78; V 11 p. 215

[Aram] *CIS* II.155B.5 (corrected to אספמת by B. Porten in his letter)

אסרחם (hybrid) *

--- *3s(.t)-*רחמ "Isis is gracious"

Maraqten p. 70. 134

[Aram] *CIS* II no. 43.2 clay tablet; Delaporte, *Épigraphe Araméens*, p. 44 no. 26.2

[Eg] see Aram DN אסי

The explanation of both Delaporte and Maraqten is "אסר (Assur) is gracious" with the supposition of the merger of אסר(ר)חם. However the solution above is a little more likely because it does not resort to such supposition.

אסרטים *

--- see אסוטים

S II p. 3; L p. 118; K p. 78; V II p. 215.

אסרשות **

--- *3s(.t)-ršw.t(y)*  "Isis is rejoicing"

S II p. 3; L p. 118; G p. 475; K p. 78

[Aram] *AP* 34.3

[Eg] Ranke I.4.10 f. Late–Gk; II, p. 336; *DemNB* I.79; [Gk] Ἐσερσῦθις, Ἐσερσῦς, Ἐσορσῦς (*NB* p. 108f)

Cf. אסרשת.

אסרשת **

--- Var. of אסרשות
G p. 475; K p. 78
[Aram] *LH* 1.3
[Eg] see אסרשות.

אסתח *

--- **(n)s-tḫ* "He belongs to (Thoth's) plummet"
G p. 470; K p. 78
[Aram] *AP* 22.81
[Eg] cf. *Wb* V.325.17

Kornfeld prefers *ns-(p)tḥ* (Ranke I.176.5). Although the dropping of the *p* of *ptḥ* is well attested in El-Amarna tablets (see Chapter IV: *Taḫmassi, Taḫmaya, Ḫiku(p)taḫ*) it is not usual in NW Semitic. I follow Grelot who suggests Eg *tḫ* , a synonym for Thoth. Many other possibilities should be remembered: **ns-t3-ḫy.t* (cf. Ranke I.366.21); **ns-t3-ḥwt* "He belongs the temple" (cf. Ranke I.110,1 *p3-n-ḥwt* "He who belongs to the the temple" m. NK); **3s.t-tḫy* "Isis is drunk" **ns-tḫw* (cf. *Wb* V.325.5).

אפו

--- see יפע
K p. 79; V p. 215.

אפה̊

--- *ỉpw, ỉpi* etc.
cf. K p. 501; K p. 79 אפו, אפע
[Aram] *AP* 24.37 אוה (corrected into אפה here, cf. *APO* אזה)
[Eg] cf. Ranke I.22.15 *ỉpi* m./f. OK–Late; Ranke I.22.22ff *ipy* etc. m./f. MK–Late.

אפע

--- see יפע

אפרי **

--- *ỉ(w.)f-r(r) (< *ỉw.f-r.ỉ)*  "He is against me"
[Aram] Jar: *APO* 82,15.1 (pl. 69)
[Eg] Ranke I.14.21; 17.10 m. Late; [Gk] cf. 'Απριος, 'Εποῦρις

(*NB* p. 42, 101)

רי- corresponds to Copt ЄРОΙ "for me", which is represented as an emphatic form of Eg preposition *r* (cf. *ḥr* > *ḥrr Wb* III.131).

בחי

--- **bḫ* "Buchis bull"

K p. 79

[Aram] Weil, *REJ* 65 p. 18.5

[Eg] cf. *DemNB* I.184 *p3-bḫ*; 364 *pa-bḫ*; *Wb* I.472.14 *bḫ* "Buchis"

[Gk] Βοῦχις (*NB* p.78)

MB *Ba-ḫu-ú, Ba-ḫe-e*, NA *Ba-ḫi-i* (*AHw* I.96b; cf. *APN* p. 50, derived from *baḫu* "meager, thin") suggest that בחי could be an Akk name.

ביכנא

--- **bik.n* "Our falcon"

[Aram] *Saqq* 40.1

[Eg] For *bik*, see Ranke I.93.18 and 19 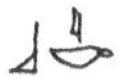 ,  . **p3-bik* and *t3-bik.t* are preserved in Gk forms Πβηκις, Τβηκις (Ranke II.279.8; II,324.23).

Segal considered that ביכנא was a variant of ביקן. Only if we accept that כ and ק are interchangable, is his solution possible.

בכרנף

--- *b(3)k-(n-)rn.f*  "The servant of his name"

K p. 79

[Aram] *RES* 1788

[Eg] Ranke I.91.11 and 17 (*b3k-rn.f*) m. Late; *DemNB* I.147 (*bk-rn.f*)

[Gk] Βοχορινῖς (*NB* p. 78); [NA] *Bu-kur-ni-ip* "a king of *Pahnuti*" (Assurb. I.105; Ranke, *KM* p. 27).

בלא *

--- *br*  "The blind"

G p. 468; K p. 79; V II p. 215

[Aram] *AP* 28.5

[Eg] Ranke I.97.27 m. Gk; *DemNB* I.143ff (*br, bl, bl.t, b13, bli*)

[Gk] Βελλῆς, Βελῆς, Βελᾶς, Βέλλιος (*NB* p. 73); [Copt] ΒΑΛΛЄ

(Crum p. 38a) cf. ⲡⲃⲁⲗⲉ; [Akk] *bēlā, bēl-a-a, Be-la-a* (*ANG* p. 113); [Pu] בלא (Benz, p. 89, 287, left unexplained)

The Eg name *br* / *bl* is attested well in Demotic documents. His mother תבא and his brother פטוסירי are Egyptians in *AP* 28. So בלא, a slave, is likely to be from an Eg family. Yet the Semitic derivation is still conceivable due to the Akk form, *bēlā* (hypocoristicon with "Baal").

בסא

--- *bs.y* 

L p. 118; G p. 468; K p. 79

[Aram] *TAÉ* 100a, b; 112a, b; *BP* 11.2, 15

[Eg] Ranke I.98.18f m. Late / f. NK; [Gk] Βεσᾶς, Βησᾶς, Βῆσα, Βησαῖς (*NB* p. 74f. *OAP* p. 79f)

Probably a shortened form of the name of which theophoric element is Bes. Equally possible is a Semitic explanation: *ba-sa-a* (*APN* p. 53a), cf. Heb *bēsay*, Amorite בסא (*APNMT* p. 177).

בסה

--- Var. of בסא (?)

K p. 79

[Aram] *LH* 8.11.

בשׂאה

--- *bš3w* 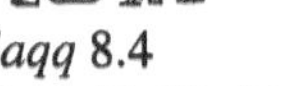

[Aram] *Saqq* 8.4

[Eg] Ranke I.98.22–24; see Ph בשא..

גלהב

--- *grhb* "The young of the Ibis"

G p. 471; K p. 79; V II p. 215

[Aram] *APO* 75.2. 15 (pl. 62)

[Eg] Ranke I.352.12 f.(?)Gk; Erichsen p. 587 *gl-hb, p3-gl-hb* ; [Gk] Καλῖβις (*NB* p. 160)

The final letter ב is uncertain. Grelot prefers ן rather than ב. Sachau read it as ו. Because of the attestated Eg name, ב is preferable. As for the meaning of the name, it is parallel with *gr-šr(ı)* "the young of the lad" (Ranke I.352.13; cf. Copt ⲥⲁⲗⲁϣⲓⲣⲉ

(Westendorf, *Koptisches Handwörterbuch.* p. 453).

הפרא ?

--- probabaly אבמא

K p. 79; V II p. 215

[Aram] *CIS* II.130; cf. the reading of *RES* 1368 אבמא, and the reading of Porten in his letter is [-]אבמא, which is a Semitic.

הריו **

--- *hr-ib* 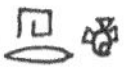 "Contented"

L p. 119; V II p. 223

[Aram] *AP* 74.5 הדיו (corrected to הריו by Lambdin and Vittmann)

[Eg] Ranke I.230.5 m. OK–Gk / f. Late–Gk; [Gk] ‘Ἐριευς; [Ph] הרב

Cf. Aram הריוטא

The final *b* of *hr-ib* was assimilated into the previous /w/ sound: *ib* *[iŭb] > [iŭw] > [iw]. For the discussions on vocalization of *ib*, see W. Albright (*JEA* 23 p. 203), and his review article on *Phonétique historique de l'Égyptien* (*JAOS* 66 p. 317). for the examples of the loss of *b*, see K. Sethe, *ZÄS* 50 p. 80–83, *e.g.*, *skb*, *sgb* > *skr*, *ski*; *msb* > *ms*. Cf. ‘Ἐριανουπις *hr-ib-inpw* with loss *b*.

הריוטא **

--- **hr-w(3)ḏ(.t)* "Uto is contented"

G p. 472; K p. 80; V II p.2 15

[Aram] *LH* 7.4

[Eg] cf. Ranke I.230.12 *hr-b3st.t* 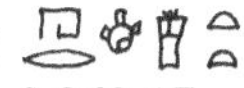 (m. Late); for *w3ḏ.t* "Uto (cobra-goddess)" see *Wb* I.268.17; cf. Gk Βουτω, Copt ПОΥΤО / ВОΥТО = *pr-w3ḏ.t*; Aram הריו

Ranke's reading *hr-ib* is more likely to be *hr*, for the *ib* is a determinative since NK, see *Wb* II.496.

וחפי *

--- **w(3)ḥ-(i)b* "(DN) is kindly"

[Aram] *AP* 74.1 פחפי (corrected here to וחפרי); *Saqq* 53.13]וחפ̊י

[Eg] cf. Ranke I.72.28ff

Probably a short form of *w3ḥ-ib-rꜥ*; the final י is a hypocoristic ending.

וחפרע **

--- *w(3)ḥ-(i)b-r*ᶜ  "Reᶜ is kindly"

L p. 119; G p. 496; K p. 80

[Aram] ostracon: *CIS* II.154.3 וחפרע, 7 וחפרע, (cf. Aimé-Giron, *BIFAO* 38 P.36); *AP* p. 317A.3 (Aimé-Giron, *JA* 18 p. 61); *TAÉ* 26.2 [וח]פרע, 29.2 [ו]חפרע, 30.1; *LH* 2.14, 3.5, 4.14; ostracon: Dupont-Sommer, *RSO*, 32 p. 403.3; *Saqq* 10.10

[Eg] see Ph וחפרע.

וחפרעמחי **

--- *w(3)ḥ-(i)b-r*ᶜ*-m-(3)ẖ.(t)*  "(King) *w(3)ḥ-(i)b-r*ᶜ is on the Horizon"

S II p. 5; L p. 119; G p. 496; K p. 80

[Aram] *AP* 26.1, 24 וחפרעמחי (cf. *APO* ʾ, *AP* י for ע); *AD* 3.4

[Eg] Ranke I.73.3; *DemNB* I.112.

[ו]חפרענח[ת] *

--- **w(3)ḥ-(i)b-r*ᶜ*-nẖt* "(King) *w(3)ḥ-(i)b-r*ᶜ is strong"

L p. 119; K p. 80

[Aram] *TAÉ* 69

[Eg] cf. Ranke I.209.22-212.19 for the compounds with *nẖt* as the first element, Ranke I.29.21 for *nẖt* as the second element: *imn-nẖt*, *3s-ir-nẖt* etc.

וחתרו *

--- **w(3)ḥ-t(3)-(n-)rw* "May she who belongs to the lion endure"

[Aram] Bordreuil, *Catalogue des sceaux*, p. 103 no. 135

[Eg] For the first element, see Ranke I.72.26ff. For the second part, see תרו. **W3ḥ-tri* "May the willow tree endure" may be another possibility (cf. Ranke I.158.2 *mr-tri.t*; *CDME* p. 306 *ṯrt* > *tr(t)*).

ונפר **

--- *wn(n)-(n)fr(.w)* 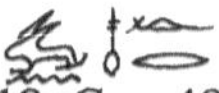 "(The) good exists"

S I p. 1108; L p. 119; G p. 483; K p. 80

[Aram] *AP* 24.36 ונפר, 66.10 ונפר[ן]

[Eg] Ranke I.79.19; I.xxi; II p. 349; *DemNB* I.118; [Gk]

'Ονvώφριος, 'Εννόφρι, 'Ονvόφριος, 'Ονvόφρις, 'Ονvώφρεις, 'Ονvῶφρις, 'Ονώφριος, 'Ονωφρις, 'Ονοφρι, 'Ονόφρις, 'Ονοβερ (*NB* p. 241f); [Copt] ΟΥⲀΝΟϤΡЄ, ΟΥЄΝΟΒΡ.

For some discussion of this name, see Gardiner, *JAOS* 56 p. 19O.

וצחור **

--- *wḏ(3)-ḥr*  "May Horus be prosperous"
[Aram] *AP* p. 317.2 וצחור[
[Eg] Ranke I.88.26 m. Late–Gk (many)
Cf. חריץ.

ורשנף **

--- *wrš-nf(r)*  "Good watcher"
S II p. 5; L p. 119; G p. 487; K p. 92
[Aram] *APO* 75.2.3 פרשנף (corrected to ורשנף by Lidzbarski)
[Eg] Ranke I.83.7; *DemNB* I.120; [Gk] 'Ορσενουφις, 'Ορσενούφιος, 'Ορσενουπις, 'Ορσενούφεις, 'Αρσενοῦπ, 'Αρσενουφις, 'Ωρσενοῦφις, Οὐερσενουφιος, Οὐερσενοῦφις, Οὐερσινουφιος, Οὐρσενοῦφις, Γορσενοῦφις (*NB* p. 244), Βαρσανουφιος (Crum p. 491a); [Copt] ΟΥЄΡϢЄΝΟΥΒЄ, ΒЄΡϢЄΝΟΥϤΙ (Crum p. 491a)

Grelot and Kornfeld, following the original publication פרשנף, reconstructed **pry-šri-(n-)inp.w* "Son of Anubis came out" (cf. Ranke I.133.18f). Other possibilities are; (1) a metathesis פרשנף > פשרנף (*p3-šri-(n-)inp.w* Ranke I.118.9 m. Gk); (2) **p3-rš(w)-nfr* (Ranke I.115.1). Yet the reading ורשנף is epigraphically more likely and this name is attested very well.

חור **

--- *ḥr(.w)*  "Horus"
S I p. 1109; L p. 119; G p. 475; K p. 80; Teixidor, *Bulletin*, p. 357
[Aram] *AP* 23.3, 24.8]חור, 13 [ור]ח, 16 [ר]חו, 38.4, 6, 8a, 8b, 53.7; *AD* 3.4 חור; *BP* 6.8, 9.10, 10.6; *Saqq* 69b.3 חור; stele: *CIS* II.122.1 (*KAI* 267); Porten, *Or* NS 57 p. 37 no. 10 col. 2.8, col. 3.4; Bauer-Meissner, *SBPA* 1936 p. 415.16; Bresciani, "Frammenti di un Testo Aramaico" B x+2; graffito: Kornfeld, *WZKM* 61 p. 11 no. 2606
[Eg] see Ph חר.

חורי **

--- *ḥr.y*  "He of Horus" (?)

G p. 475; K p. 81; V II p. 215

[Aram] *AP* 22.40, 79 [חוֹ[רי, 85, 23.9, 37.13, 15; *TAÉ* 25.6 [חור[י;
ostracon: *CIS* II.125; *NEph* I p. 10 (Pap.Berol 2300).1, 9

[Eg] Ranke I.251.17 m. NK–Late; [Gk] ʻΩρῖς (*NB* p. 497)

Grelot and Kornfeld proposed *ḥr-ii* "Horus has come", (Ranke I.245.21; Gk ʻΩρεῖς). However, as Vittmann observed, חר "Horus" in construct state is not realized as חור, but as חר (see the later discussion [3] Matres lectionis e) Notes on the Use of *matres lectionis*). Moreover, *ḥr.y* is a simpler solution and much more common in the period. The final *y* is an ending of a shortened form (Ranke II p. 146) or an adjectival form. A Semitic explanation is not impossible: חֹרִי (Gen 36:22). Yet this well-attested Eg name is more probable. Twice חורי is the father of an Egyptian (*AP* 23.9, *TAÉ* 25.6; probably *NEph* I p. 10.9).

חחר

--- *ḥ(.t)-ḥr(.w)* "Temple of Horus"(?)

[Aram] Porten *Or*.NS, 57 p. 26 [אס]פמת בר חחר[

[Eg] cf. Ranake I.235.6

Notice that the affiliation supports the Eg origin of the name. The name reconstracted [אס]פמת is fully attested in the line 12. Goddess *ḥ.t-ḥr.w* retains the feminie *-t* in Coptic ϩⲁⲑⲱⲣ, ⲁⲑⲱⲣ and in Aram חתחור (see the month name). However, the feminine ending of *-t* of the word *ḥ.t* dropped.

חיח

--- *ẖ(3)y-ḥ(r)* 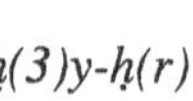 (meaning unknown)

L p. 119; G p. 474; K p. 114

[Aram] *BP* 3.23b

[Eg] Ranke I.262.8 m. Late

The identification was first made by Albright (*BP* p.164). Yet Grelot objected to it because a final א is usually expected for Eg *ḥr*, as חא (see צחא). Grelot prefers Iranian to Eg, because of its affiliation (son of אתרלי, a Caspian). He also sugests the possibility of a Hurrian name: *ẖai+ẖa* (*NPN* p. 212b); cf. Akk *ẖi-ẖi-e* (*APN* p. 88a) from Asia minor. Also Eg *ḥḥ* (Ranke I.254.8 cf. Copt ϩⲁϩ).

Therefore, the identification is open to choice.

חיף֯

--- *ḥ(3)p(y)* 

[Aram] *AP* 74.6 חנׄס֯ (= *CIS* II.148.6; corrected to חיף֯ by B. Porten C4.9.6)

[Eg] Ranke I.233.12 m. Late.

ח֯כ֯ונית

--- see חנונית

[Aram] *Saqq* 45a.5 (corrected to חנונית by Porten C3.18:5)

Though the first part of the name is partially damaged, the second part נית "Neith" is clear. So the name must be Eg. If the Segal's reading is correct, **ḥk3-m-ny.t* "the (god of) magic is Neith" is most probable. (cf. Ranke II.296.9 *ḥk3.ỉ-ny.t* "Neith is my magic")

חׄכנא

--- *ḥkn(.t)*  "Praised one"

S I p. 1100; K p. 81; V II p. 215

[Aram] *CIS* II.122B

[Eg] Ranke II.308.17 f. Late

There are many similar names attested in Ranke I.257.1 *ḥkn.ỉ*; 257.2 *ḥkn.y.t*; 257.3 *ḥkn.w*; II.308.16 *ḥkn* (all until MK). The exact identification is difficult. B. Porten suggested to me in his letter that this is probably not a PN. Due to the lack of the context, we cannot be sure whether it is or not.

חכרטיסו **

--- **ḥk(3)-(ỉ)r-dỉ-sw* "It is the (god) Magic who has given him"

S I p. 1100; L p. 119; K p. 8l

[Aram] ostracon: *CIS* II.138B.1 חברטיסן, 3 חברטי[ס]ן (corrected to חכרטיסו by Spiegelberg and confirmed by Degen, *NEph* I. p. 27)

[Eg] Ranke II.308.13 (reconstruction based on Aram)

Although the name is a reconstruction, it is certainly Eg. For the element *ḥk3*, see Ranke I.256.2ff. This type of name, DN + *ỉr-dỉ* + suffix, is very common.

חׄנׄונית *

--- **ḥnw(.t)-ny.t* “Mistress Neith”

[Aram] *Saqq* 45a.5

[Eg] For the first element *ḥnw.t* in the female personal names, see Ranke I.242.18–244.18. For the Goddes Neit, see *Wb* II.198.9.

This type of name became very common after NK. Notice that חנונית is a female name in the context. Though the above identification is most likely, the first two letters are too damaged to be read with certainty.

חנמו *

--- **ẖnm(.w)-iw* “Khnum came”

S II p. 5; L p. 120; G p. 457; K p. 81

[Aram] *AP* 53.5

[Eg] see DN + *iw* type, such as *imn-iw* (Ranke I.26.21; Gk ’Αμμευς), *ḥp-iw* (Ranke I.237.5; Aram חפיו), *ẖns.w-iw* (Ranke I.270,17)

If the final ו is a vowel letter, *ẖnm.w* (Ranke I.275.5 m./f. OK–MK) may stand for חנמו. Yet it is known that the final consonant ו has been lost in Eg, thus Gk χνουβις, χνουμ. Therefore, it is more likely that the final ו stands for the Eg *iw*. Spiegelberg, followed by Lambdin, interpreted it as *ẖnm-ʿ3*, which is impossible, because the Eg *‘ayn* does not lose its consonantal value. For Eg *iw* = Aram ו, see Ph חפיו.

חנמנתן (hybrid) **

--- *ẖnm(.w)*-נתן “Khnum has given”

K p. 50

[Aram] graffito: Sayce, *PSBA*, 30 p. 28f no.4

[Eg] see חנום.

חנ[ס]

--- *ḫns(.w)*  “Khons”

S I p. 1109; L p. 120; K p. 81; V II p. 215

[Aram] *AP* 74.6 חנׄסׄ (= *CIS* II.148.6; corrected to חיך by Porten C4.9.6); *CIS* II.132.1 חונת (חנס[–] by Lidzbarski *Eph* III, p. 109; yet B. Porten read it as [—]בר חנ.)

[Eg] Ranke I.270.16 m./f. MK–Late; [Gk] χῶνσις (*NB* p.48).

[-]ח̊ס̊ו̊ר̊ (?)
--- misreading of [--]ב[-]ח (Porten's reading, B8.4.20)
[Aram] *Saqq* 28a.8

חפי **
--- *ḥp.y* 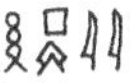 , *ḥp.w* 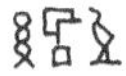 "Apis"
[Aram] *AP* 24.3 (Sachau's reading סחפי, corrected to חגי by B. Porten C3.14.3); *Saqq* 8.14 ח̊פי (Porten's reading is חפי[--] or נופי[--] B5.6.14); graffito:Torrey, *Numismatic Notes and Monographs*, no. 77 p. 9 (no. 6)
[Eg] Ranke I.238,6 m. MK–NK; 16 *ḥp.w* m./f. OK–Dyn 18; [Gk] Ἄπιος, Ἄππιος. For Eg *w*, see Ranke II p. 154b.

חפיאו **
--- Var. of חפיו
[Aram] *Saqq* 139.2 חפיאו[
[Eg] see Ph & Aram חפיו.

חפיו **
--- *ḥp-iw* "The Apis has come"
G p. 474; K p. 81
[Aram] Bauer and Meissner1 *SBPA*, 1936, 4/5.2 ח̊פיו
[Eg] see Ph חפיו.

חפימו
--- misreading of חפימן
L p. 120; K p. 81
[Aram] *AP* 73.16
[Eg] see חפימן (the final letter is fairly long, making it impossible for it to be ו).

חפימן **
--- *ḥp-mn*  "Apis is enduring"
S I p. 1100; L p. 120; K p. 81
[Aram] *TAÉ* 25.6; *AP* 73.16 חפימו (corrected to חפימן by Spiegelberg); *Saqq* 28b.5, 69b.6 ח̊פימן
[Eg] Ranke I.237.13 m. Late–Gk; [Pers] [m]*ḫa-pi-me-en-na* (*KM* p. 38)

Cf. חפמן, חפמו.

חפיענח

--- *ḥp-ʿnḫ(w)*  "May Apis live" or "Apis is alive"
L p. 120; K p. 81; V II p. 216
[Aram] *TAÉ* 87a. 10
[Eg] Ranke I.237.10 m. Late; [Gk] cf. 'Απέγχεις, "Απιγχις, 'Απίγχις (*NB* p. 43).

חפמן **

--- Var. of חפימן
[Aram] ostracon: *Saqq* VII.I
[Eg] see חפימן.

חר **

--- Var. of חור
K p. 122
[Aram] *TAÉ* 79.2; *Saqq* 50.6]חׄרׄ, 61b.2]-חׄר
[Eg] see חור.

חרבך **

--- **ḥr-b(i)k* "Horus, (the) Falcon"
[Aram] metal bowl: Rabinowitz, *JNES* 18 p. 154f
[Eg] cf. Ranke I.247.6 *ḥr-p3-bik* 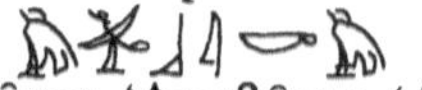 m. Gk
[Gk] (with the article *p3*) 'Αρφεβῆκις, 'Αρπβῆκις, 'Αρπβῆχις, 'Αρπεβηκις, 'Αρφεβεῖς, 'Ερφβηκις; (without *p3* **ḥr-bik*) 'Αρβῆκις, 'Αρβῆχις, 'Αρβῖχις, 'Ερβηκις, 'Ορβῆκ (*NB* p. 45)

The name חרבך cannot be "the servant of Horus" (Rabinowitz). If it were "the servant of Horus", the word order would be reversed: בכחר (*bik-ḥr*).

ח[רו]ט

--- Var. of חרוץ (?)
S I p. 1100; L p. 120; K p. 81; V II p. 216
[Aram] *AP* 73.10 שנות (according to *CIS* II.147B.10 the reading is חרוט, Yet cf. Porten's reading ח--ט C3.19.10); *APO* 75.1.col.i.12 חׄרוט (Porten's reading [-]דוע in his letter)
[Eg] see חרוץ

The reading of *AP* 73.10 is uncertain: it is impossible to read the first letter with certainty; the second letter could be either נ and ר; the final letter is clear; after ט is broken.

חרויץ **
--- *ḥr-wḏ(3)*  "Horus is prosperous"
K p. 51; V II p. 223
[Aram] *AP* 17.6, 24.5 (Sachau's reading זפרוׄת); *TAÉ* 87a. 13 חרׄוׄיׄץ; *LH* 1.3, 4, 6, 7, 8, 3.3, 5.5
[Eg] see Ph חרויץ
Considering the name to be Semitic, Kornfeld connected it with Akk *ḫurāṣu* "gold" (*AHw* 358a; *CAD* Ḫ 245b), which occurs in PN *ḫu-ra-ṣi* (*CAD* Ḫ 247a). However, Ph חרויץ and NA *ḫar-ma-ṣu*, *ḫa-ar-ma-ṣu* clearly indicate that the third letter ו should not be dismissed as a vowel letter. The names derived from Semitic root חרץ and this Eg name should be dealt with separately. For another example of conflation, J. Stark, p. 90a, Harris, p. 104 regarded Ph חרויץ as an error, resulting from the use of Aram spelling. Examples of Semitic names are *IPN* no. 523, *APN* p. 86b *ḫar-ru-ṣu*..

חרון **
--- *ḥr-wn*  "Horus exists"
[Aram] *Saqq* 190
[Eg] Ranke I.246.15; [Gk] cf. 'Αρων, 'Ααρων (*NB* p. 59).

חרוׄת
--- Var. of חרוט, חרויץ (?)
[Aram] *Saqq* 53.15 (The final ת is uncertain. Porten's reading is חרויׄץ, see above).

חרזבד (hybrid) **
--- *ḥr*-זבד "Horus has bestowed"
[Aram] graffito; *TAÉ* 93
[Eg] see חר.

חרחבי **
--- *ḥr-(m-)(3)ḫ-bi(.t)*  "Horus is in Chemmis"
S I p. 1101; L p. 120; K p. 81

[Aram] *AP* p. 317A.1; *TAÉ* 87b.6 חׄרׄחׄבׄי; seal: *CIS* II.140 (cf. Herr's reading: חורחבי)
[Eg] Ranke I.247. 15f; II p. 378 m. NK–Gk; [Gk] ʻΑρχῆβις, ʻΑρχῖβις, ʼΑρχίβιος, ʼΑρχιβειος, ʻΑρχῆμις (*NB*p. 58f)
Cf. Chemmis = χέμμις.

חרחת **
--- *ḥr-ḥt(p)*  "Horus is contented"
V II p. 225
[Aram] *Saqq* 11.5
[Eg] Ranke I.250.7, 8 m. OK–Late; [Gk] ʻΑρηότης, ʻΑρυώθης (*NB* p. 46)

Segal's suggestions *ḥr-m-ḥ3.t, ḥr-r-ḥ3.t, ḥr-ẖw.t* cannot explain the final ת, as he admitted. When the final *p* of *ḥtp* dropped, which is possible as with ימחות, ו would normally be expected between ח and ט. However the smaller development of *matres lectionis* in Saqqara could justify the identification. See the later discussion: [5] Matres lectionis, e) Notes on the use of *matres lectionis*.

חרי **
--- Var. of חורי
K p. 81
[Aram] graffito: *TAÉ* 109; graffito: *CIS* II.130 חרי
[Eg] see חורי

Another possible explanation is *ḥr.y*  (Ranke I.252.26 m. Late), which is much less common.

]חרין
--- *ḥr-in(y)*  "It is Horus who brings" (?)
[Aram] *Saqq* 159.1
[Eg] Ranke I.246.2 m. MK

Notice that there is no support from the context that it is a PN, and besides, the beginning is broken and *ḥr-iny* is not attested in the Late period.

חׄרכן
--- probably misreading of Lw סׄיכן (according to Porten, B8.6.1)
[Aram] *Saqq* 9.1

חרמחי **

--- *ḥr-m-(3)ḫ(.t)* "Horus is in the horizon"

L p. 120; K p. 81

[Aram] *TAÉ* 26.4, 11.1 חרמחי, 25.5 [י]חרמח

[Eg] Ranke I.247.17 m. Late–Gk; [Gk] ʽΑρμάχις (*NB* p. 50; *OAP* p. 50a).

חרמן **

--- *ḥr-mn(.w)* "Horus is Min?"

G p. 474; K p. 51; V II p. 223

[Aram] *AP* 12.2; 22.4

[Eg] Ranke I.248.19 m. OK–NK (often); [Gk] ʽΑρμενος, ʽΑρμῆνις, ʽΑρμῖνις (*NB* p. 51) cf. ʽΕρμῆνος, ʽΕρμινος, ʽΕρμῖνις (*NB* p. 105)

Vittmann reconstracted **ḥr-mn.w* "Horus is enduring," which is also possible, because DN + *mn.w* is a common type of name, *e.g.*, *imn-mn* (Ranke I.29.6 m. NK), *ḏḥwty-mn(.w)* (Ranke I.408.4 m. Gk) etc. Though *ḥr-mn.w* is most common, other possibilities should be noted: (1) *ḥr-mn(i.w)* (Ranke I.248.21 m./f. NK); (2) *ḥr(i)-mn(w)* (Ranke I.251.11 m. NK). Grelot and Kornfeld regard it as a Semitic name: the deity חרם to which נ is added. They suggested the נ represents the first letter of verb נתן. Though a Semitic explanation is supported by the affiliation, the abbreviation is not likely. Therefore, the Eg explanation is more satisfactory.

חרמעחר *

--- **ḥr-m(3)ʿ-ḫr(w)* "Horus is justified"

L p. 122; G p. 465; K p. 85; V II p. 217

[Aram] *AP* 72.6 (*CIS* II.136 עחר > חר by Sayce and Clermont-Ganneau, see *RES* 960; the reading עחר is corrected to חרמעחר by Porten C3.12.11)

[Eg] cf. *p3-di-ḥr-m3ʿ-ḫr(w)* (Ranke I.125.4 m. Late), also this type of name is attested in names such as *rʿ-m3ʿ-ḫrw* (Ranke 217.22 m. Late; II.373), *ptḥ-m-m3-ḫrw* (I.139.20 m. Late).

חרנופי **

--- *ḥr-nf(r)* "Beautiful Horus" or "Horus is beautiful"

S II p. 6; L p. 120; G p. 474; K p. 81

[Aram] *AP* 38.5; 24.6 צפר (corrected by Grelot to חרנופ[י])
[Eg] Ranke I.249.9 m. NK-Late; [Gk] ‘Αρνοῦφις (*NB* p. 52; *OAP* p. 506)
Cf. Heb חרנפר (*ḥr-nfr.w* 1 Chr 7:36).

חרנפת
--- *ḥr-(m-)nb-t(3.w)*  "Horus is the lord of the lands"
[Aram] *Saqq* 28b.1 חרנפת, 10 חרנפת
[Eg] Ranke I.248.2 m. MK

The Eg name is attested only in MK. The reconstruction *ḥr-n-p3-t3* "Horus of the land" may be possible; cf. *ṯ3y-ḥr-p3-t3* "Horus has seized the land" (Ranke I.388.5 m. Late–Gk), *p3-t3* (Ranke I.120.17 m. Late). See also Segal's reconstruction **ḥr-m-pd.ty* "Horus is bowman." The uncertain Aramaic text makes it impossible to identify the name with certainty.

חרסיס
--- *ḥr-s(3)-3s(.t)*  "Horus, son of Isis"
[Aram] *Saqq* 6.2 חרסיס, 3 חרסיס (Porten read it as חרסיסי B8.12:2, 3)
[Eg] Ranke I.250.13 m. NK–GK very common; [Gk] ‘Αρσιῆσις, ‘Αρσῆσις, ‘Αρσιἔσις, ‘Αρσιῦσις, ‘Ορσιῆσις, ‘Ωρσιήσιος (*NB* p. 244, 498).

Porten's reading חרסיסי enhanced the identification because of the final י, but since the document is much broken, the identification cannot be made with certainty.

חרפבך **
--- *ḥr-p(3)-b(i)k*  "Horus, the Falcon"
L p. 120; K p. 82
[Aram] *TAÉ* 87b.14
[Eg] Ranke I.247.6 m. GK; [Gk] ‘Αρφεβῆκις, ‘Αρπβηκις, ‘Αρπβῆχις, ‘Αρπεβηκις, ‘Αρφεβεῖχις, ‘Ερφβηχις (*NB* p. 53,5 107)
Cf. חרבך.

חרפנחס
--- **ḥr-p(3)-nḥs(y)* "Horus, the Nubian" (?)

K p. 82; V II p. 216
[Aram] *TAÉ* 32.3
[Eg] cf. Ranke I.113.13 *p3-nḥsy*  "The Nubian" (m. NK–Late); Heb פינחס

If the second letter is י, which is possible, the name must be *ḥy-p3-nḥsy*  "*ḥy* the Nubian" (Ranke II.304.20 m. NK).

חרפשת

--- **ḥr-p(3)-šd* "Horus, the deliverer"
[Aram] *Saqq* 61a.2
[Eg] cf. *p3-šd-ḥr* (?) "He whom Horus has delivered" (Ranke I.119.17 m. Dyn 20); see also *šd-ḥr* (Ranke I.331.1), and *ḏd-ḥr-p3-šd* (Ranke I.411.16 m. Gk) cf. 'Αρψατος (*NB* p. 59).

Notice the reading is quite uncertain.

חרתבא *

--- *ḥr-(n-)t(3)-b(w)i(3)* 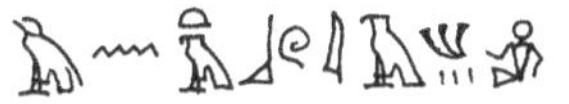 "Horus of the bush"
S I p. 1101; L p. 121; K p. 82; V p. 216
[Aram] ostracon: *CIS* II.138B.3
[Eg] Spiegelberg, *Rec.de Trav.* 25, 19 p. 194 Late; [Gk] 'Αρτβῶς (cf. Copt ⲂⲰ "bush") [Akk] cf. *ḫar-ti-bu-u*

Kornfeld prefers *ḥr-tb/tp* (Erichsen p. 321. cf. Heb חרטם). Yet this is an Eg title (*AEO* I.55*), not a PN. Vittmann, though he offered no identification, preferred to read it as חרמא. Yet the third letter is likely to be ט, rather than מ.

חשף

--- *ḫ(3y)-šb*  "Measuring value" (?)
G p. 501; K p. 122
[Aram] *APO* 75.29 (pl. 62)
[Eg] Ranke I.427.1 f. NK

It is perhaps possible to consider it as a short form of אלחשפו (Sachau). Kornfeld compares it with the Nuzi name *ḫašipa, ḫašipaya, ḫašipu* etc (*NPN* p. 57a–58b, 214f). Yet it may be an anachronism there.

חתובסתי

--- Var. of אחתבסתי

G p. 460; K p. 51 and 40

[Aram] *AD* 10. 3* ח̊ת̊ו̊ב̊ס̊ת̊י, 3 ח̊תובסתי, 4

[Eg] Ranke I.258.4 f. MK–Late

Cf. אחתבסתי.

טסתי **

--- *d(i.t)-sṯi(t)*  "Satis has given"

S I p. 1109; G p. 361f; K p. 82

[Aram] *AP* 22.83 טסתז (corrected by Spiegelberg and Porten, C3.15.86)

[Eg] Ranke I.397.14 f. Gk; cf. Gk Σατις for "Satis."

יחוט **

--- **iḥ(.t)-w(3)ḏ(.t)* "ʾIḥ.t (Hathor-cow) is prosperous"

L p. 121; K p. 82

[Aram] *TAÉ* 103

[Eg] cf. Ranke I.44.3–5 *iḥ.t-wr.t* "ʾ*Iḥ.t* is great" etc. For the second element, see Ranke I.22.7 *ip.t-w3ḏ.t* 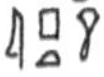 "*ip.t* is prosperous" (f. MK), Ranke I.5.8 *i-w3ḏ* (m. Late), Ranke I.49.6 *it-w3ḏ.t* (f. Dyn 12) etc.. Eg *w3ḏ* became *wt* in Demotic (Erichsen p. 104), ⲟⲩⲱⲧ in Copt (Černý p. 217). Less probable is *ii-ḥt(p)* (Ranke I.10.16), cf. Gk 'Αοῦτις, 'Αουτις (*NB* p. 37f), because of a change of ת > ט after ח.

ימחות **

--- *i(i)-m-ḥt(p)*  "Coming in peace"

[Aram] *Saqq* 10.4 ימ̊חות, 156.1 ימ̊ח̊ות; *TAÉ* 8 recto.3 ימחזת (corrected by Segal to ימחות)

[Eg] see Ph ימחות, Aram אמחות, יחות; [Gk] 'Αμούθις, 'Αμούτης (*NB* p. 27)

The loss of the final *p* of *ḥtp* is evident in Gk forms 'Αμενωθης, 'Αμενουθης (< *imn-ḥtp*; Ranke I.30.12; *DemNB* I.85; *NB* p. 24) and the month name *p3-n-imn-ḥtp*, which is represented by either [a]ⲡⲁⲣⲙϩⲁⲧⲡ or [b]ⲫⲁⲙⲉⲛⲱⲑ (Gk φαμενωθ). They show th final *p* was lost when the long [u] vowel came in between *ḥ* and *p*, like our example ימחות. One might try to compare the name with *imn-ḥtp* on the assumption that the Eg *n* of *imn* is assimilated, yet the Gk forms preclude it.

ינחרו *

--- *ir(.t)-n(.t)-ḥr-(i)r.w*  "The eye of Horus is set against them"

K p. 92; V II p. 216, 223

[Aram] *AD* 5.7 אנדרו (corrected to ינ[ח]רו by Vittmann); Frag.III.11.2 דו/ינחר

[Eg] Ranke I.42.11 m. Late–Gk; *DemNB* I.72f; [Gk] 'Ιναρως, 'Ιναρωοτος, 'Ιναρωτος.

Kornfeld considered it as *in-ḥr.t* (Onuris). However the first י and final ו contradict Onuris, though the ו is uncertain. Contrarily, the identification of Vittmann is strongly supported by the Gk forms.

יפע **

--- *i(w).f-ˁ(3)*  "He is great"

G p. 501; K p. 79; V II p. 215

[Aram] *AP* 53.6 (corrected to יפֿע by Porten C4.8.6); 24.4 [א]פ[ע]

[Eg] Ranke I.14.2 m. Late; *DemNB* I.59; [Gk] cf. 'Απου, ''Απων, 'Επῶς (*NB* p. 42f, 102)

ꜣIb(.y)-iˁ(.w) (Ranke I.19.4), suggested by Kornfeld, is only attested until MK, and we must assume that Eg *i* has been lost. The composition of an element *ip* and *ˁ3* (Grelot) is possible, though it is purely theoretical. As for *AP* 53.6, the reading is sure. Kornfeld's comment "Lesung unsicher, vielleicht --אפו" is unnecessary (Vittmann also questioned his reading). Grelot and Kornfeld read אפו in *AP* 24.4, yet no support is gained from the text itself.

כא

--- *k3*  "Soul"

G p. 476; K p. 115

[Aram] *AD* 5.4; *Saqq* כֿא

[Eg] Ranke I.338.15 m./f. MK–Late

The name is found in a list of Cilician slaves, making the Eg possibility doubtful. Grelot and Kornfeld compared it with *ka-a-a* (*NPN* p. 77b, 222a). Yet the Eg possibility is still open, if a Cilician slave could have an Eg PN.

כומן

--- see פומן
K p. 82; V II p. 216.

כיא

--- *k(3).ỉ(3)* 
L p. 121; G p. 476; K p. 120
[Aram] *AP* 2.19
[Eg] Ranke I.341.17-18 m./f. NK; [Gk] Καϊῆς (*NB* p. 157)
Cf. Aram כא

Other possible identifications (1) *kaia* (*APN* p. 289a), *kaia* (*NPN* p. 77b, 222a), *ky* (Gröndahl p. 277), make the exact identification impossible. Therefore Kornfeld considered that this is a lallname.

ככי

--- *kkỉ* 
G p. 476; K p. 120
[Aram] *LH* 7.2
[Eg] Ranke I.348.31–349.14 (esp. 4–6); [Gk] cf. Κακῆς, Κακῖς (*NB* p. 157)

Again other possible solutions, Hittite *kikki* (*NH* p. 569f), Nuzi *kak(k)* (*NPN* p. 222a), Ug *kky* (Gröndahl p. 395), make the identification difficult. Kornfeld classified it as a lallname.

כמ̊ן̇

--- *k(3)mn*  "Blind"
V II p. 216
[Aram] *NEph* I p. 11 recto 9 מ/ח̇כ (according to Porten, *Or* NS 57 p. 78)
[Eg] Ranke I.342.11 m. MK

Other possibilities, *km(.w).n.ỉ* "I finished" (Ranke I.345.10 m. MK) and *k3(.ỉ)-mn.ỉ* "My ka is enduring" (Ranke I.340.2 m. OK), are less likely, because they are only attested until MK.

כנ̇ופא̊

--- see כנופי

[Aram] *Saqq* 10.9 (corrected to כנופי by Porten B8.2.26).

כנופי **

--- *k(3.i)-nf(r)* "(My) ka is good"
S II p. 6; L p. 121; G p. 476; K p. 82
[Aram] *AP* 26.9, 21, 50.7; *Saqq* 10.9 (see above), 50.12 כ̇נ̇פ̇]
[Eg] see Ph כנפי.
**K3-nfr* "fine bull" is also possible (cf. *k3-nfr.w* Ranke I.338.6).

כסנו

--- see נסנו
K p. 83; V II p. 216.

כפא *

--- *kf3* "The trustworthy"
L p. 121; K p. 56
[Aram] *BP* 8.10
[Eg] Ranke I.344.15; for the meaning see *CDME* p. 285
Cf. כף
There is a Semitic root כפא as well as כף (*DISO* p. 125, BDB p. 495) כֵּף, "rock,"Κεφᾶς (NT, *NB* p. 173). So the identification is open to choice.

כשי **

--- *(i)kš* "The Nubian (the man from Kush)"
L p. 121; G p. 477; K p. 56
[Aram] *AP* 53.4 כשי, 23.8
[Eg] see Ph כשי
Kornfeld preferred to regard the name as Semitic. Yet the Greek forms, 'Εκυσις and Κοῦσις, seem to match the Eg bi-form, *ikš* and *kšy*.

לילו **

--- *ll* "Child"
S I p. 1112; L p. 121; G p. 477; K p. 83; V II p. 216
[Aram] *AP* 28.13
[Eg] Erichsen p. 262; Crum p. 141b PN ⲗⲉⲗⲟⲩ, ⲗⲓⲗⲟⲩ; Λιλοῦς, Λολοῦς, Λιλῶς, Λελους (*NB* p. 196) Cf. Ranke

I.224.23ff *rr*.

מֹחפרעֹ **

--- *m(n)-ḫp(r)-rʿ* 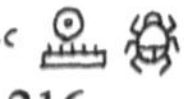 "*Ḫpr-rʿ* is established"

K p. 83; V II p. 216

[Aram] graffito: Aimé-Giron, *ASAE*, 39 p. 352

[Eg] Ranke I.150.14 m. NK

The loss of the Eg *n* would be supported by מחנית (*mnḥ-ny.t*). Though not attested, **mnḫ-ib-rʿ* is another good solution because the *mnḫ-ib*-type is common in the Late Period (see Ranke I.153.5–8 *mnḫ-ib-w3ḥ-ib-psmṯk* etc.), or, as Vittmann proposed, *mnḫ-p3-rʿ* is surely possible on the basis of the *mnḫ*-DN type, such as *mnḫ-rʿ*, *mnḫ-3s.t* etc. (Ranke I.153.11, 4, 9, 12). Therefore it is not necessary to regard it as a variant of וחפרע, as Kornfeld proposed.

מֹחנית[*

--- **m(n)ḫ-ny.t* "Neith is efficient"

[Aram] *APO* 83,15.1

[Eg] cf. Ranke I.153.9–11 *mnḫ* + DN type: *mnḫ-mw.t*, *mnḫ-imn*, *mnḫ-rʿ*

For מח = *mnḫ*, see מחפרע (*mn-ḫpr-rʿ* or *mnḫ-p3-rʿ*) and עחחפי (for *ʿnḫ-ḥpy* = ענחחפי). These three examples indicate that נ could be elided before ח.

ממה

--- *mm*  etc.

G p. 478; K p. 120

[Aram] *LH* 3.2, 10, 4.14

[Eg] Ranke I.149. 13ff m. MK / f.Late; Ranke II.184a; [Gk] cf. Μαμα, Μαμᾶς, Μαμμας, Μῖος (*NB* p. 204, 217); [Ph] cf. ממה; [Ug] cf. ממי (Gröndahl p. 285)

The various forms suggest that the name is either Semitic or Eg, possibly originating from a lallname (Kornfeld). Considering it to be Eg, Grelot suggested its connection with the Eg word *m3m3* "dom-palm" (*CDME* p. 103) which is possible (cf. other Eg names which are names of fruit, *e.g.*, *p3-ḏp[ḥ?]*, *t3-ḏpḥ* "the apple" Ranke I.420.3; 363.13, *prt* "the fruit" Ranke I.134.20, cf. Ranke II.180f).

מׄנׄחׄחנום
--- see צחחנום
S II p. 6; L p. 121; G p. 464; K p. 83
[Aram] *AP* 53.5 נחחנום[-] (Sachau and Spiegelberg מנחחנום; Grelot אוחחנום; yet Porten צחׄחנום C4.8.5).

מנחמן
--- see מרחמן
K p. 83
[Aram] *CIS* II.138A.2.

מסחנה
--- **msḥ-nh(.t)* "(The) Crocodile is protection"
[Aram] Porten, *Or* NS 57 p. 41.3
[Eg] for the first element *msḥ*, see Ranke I.164.14ff. However the second component *nh.t* is not attested as a PN. If the final ה is a *mater lectionis*, **msḥ-n.ỉ* "the Crocodile belongs to me" is possible.

מסטי
--- *ms(w).t(ỉ)*  etc.
K p. 83; V p. 217
[Aram] *AP* p. 318C.3
[Eg] cf. Ranke I.165.24 *msti*, 25 *mstw*; or *ms*-type names (Ranke I.164.19–165.4, 15).

Kornfeld compared the name with the element *msḏy* (Ranke II.293.20, Ranke I.165.28), yet the identification remains quite uncertain. The context does not support this as a PN: it could be a unit of measure, cf. *mstỉ* "basket (used as a measure)" (*Wb* II.151.6–7), which became *msd.t* (*Wb* II.152.14), phonetically corresponding to מסתי well. Vittmann, regarding it as a place name, suggested *msd* (Gauthier, *DG* III, 62). However a unit of measure is more probable in the context.

מפתח *
--- *m(r)-ptḥ* 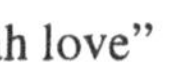 "May Ptah love"
K p. 59
[Aram] *AP* 22.83, 88, 106
[Eg] Ranke I.156.9 m./f. NK–Late

The Eg *mr* is represented by Copt ˢⲘⲈ, ᵇⲘⲈⲒ, yet ˢⲘⲈⲢⲈ-, ᵇⲘⲈⲚⲢⲈ- in combination, making the dropping of *r* less likely However already in the 13th cent. BC *mry-imn* occurs as *ma-a-i-*ⁱˡᵘA*-ma-na* without *r* (Ranke, *KM* p. 12). Hence מפתח could stand for *mr-ptḥ*. The Semitic root פתח prevents us from confirming the Eg possibility. B. Porten said in his letter that the name is a profane Semitic name.

מרחמן

--- **mr(y)-ḥmn* "Beloved of (goddes) *ḥmn*"

[Aram] *CIS* II.138A.2 מנחמן (corrected by B. Porten in his letter)

[Eg] For the name type *mry*-DN, see Ranke I.160.6ff.; For the divine element, see Ranke I.369.15 *t3-šry.t-n.t-ḥmn* (f. Gk).

נבס **

--- *nbs* "The *nbs*-tree"

G p. 483; K p. 83; V II p. 217

[Aram] *AP* 81.74

[Eg] Ranke I.193.1; II.p. 181a m. OK–MK. The element *nbs* occurs in NK (*Wb* II.245) in Copt ⲚⲞⲨⲂⲤ (Crum p. 222b) and is used in PNs, such as *t3-šri.t-(n.t-)p3-nbs* (Ranke I.368.18 f. Gk), Demot *ḏḥwty-(m-)p3-nbs* (Erichsen p. 215); [Gk] Νουψ (*NB* p. 235) cf.Πνουψ for *pr-nbs* (*Wb* II.246.1).

נֻפר

--- *nfr(.w)* "Beauty"

[Aram] *Saqq* 97b.2

[Eg] see Ph נפר.

נחמסאח **

--- **nḥm-s(w)-i(ʿ)ḥ* "The Moon has saved him"

L p. 121; K p. 83

[Aram] *AP* p. 317A.1

[Eg] cf. Ranke I.208, 10, 12–17 m./f. Late–Gk *nḥm* + obj. pron + DN type: *nḥm-s(.t)-3s.t*; *nḥm-s(w)-mw.t*; *nḥm-s(w)-mnṯ.w* etc.(cf. Vergote, *Gram. Copte* IIb, § 211). For אח = *iʿḥ* see Ph אחמס; [Gk] cf. Νουμισσιος, Νουμισσις (*NB* p. 237).

נחתחור **

--- *nḫt-ḥr(.w)*  "Horus is strong"

G p. 482; K p. 83

[Aram] *AD* 6.2, 7.1* נחתחור, 1, 8.1*, 1, 9.1*, 1, 10. 1* 1, 2 נחתחור, 4 נחתחור, 11.1*, 1, 12.1* נחתחור, 1, 3 [נח]תחור, 6, 13.1*, 1; *AD* Frag II A, 1–2 נחתחור, III 3.2 נחתחור, 4 נחת[חור]

[Eg] Ranke I.211.3 m. MK–Gk; [NA] cf. *Na-aḫ-ti-ḫu-ru-an-si-ni* (*nḫt-ḥr-n3-šnw* Ranke I.211.5; *KM* p. 30).

ניתרטיס **

--- *ny.t-(ii)r-di(.t)-s(.t)* 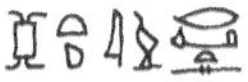 "It is Neith who has given her"

L p. 121; K p. 83

[Aram] *AP* p. 317A.3 ניתרטיס[

[Eg] Ranke I.181.26 f. Late.

נכי

--- *nky* 

G p. 501; K p. 123

[Aram] *LH* 4.3

[Eg] Ranke I.213.19 f. Dyn 18; [Gk] cf. Νόχις, Νόκις, Νοκιος, Νοῦχις, Νῶχις (*NB* p. 236f, 238)

Grelot prefers the identification as Eg, while Kornfeld doubts it. There is a Semitic root נכי "strike" (*DISO* p. 178; Heb נכה), as well as an Eg root *nk3* "to think about" (*CDME* p. 141). Neither are used in PN. The identification remains uncertain.

נכו **

--- *nk(3).w* 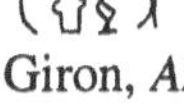 (meaning unknown)

[Aram] N. Giron, *AE* 23 p. 42; *AP* p. 317A.2 נפו (corrected to נכו by Porten C4.1:2)

[Eg] Ranke I.213.16 m. Late; [Gk] cf. Νεχω, Νεχως, Νεχους Νεχύς (*NB* p. 232); [Heb] נְכוֹ, נְכֹה; [LXX] Νεχαω; [NA] *ni-ik-ku-u / ni-ku-u* (Assurb. I 90, II 8; Ranke *KM* p. 31; *APN* p. 173b).

נכרסן

--- misreading of וכר/דסא (according to Porten C3.28:111)

G p. 482; K p. 84; V II p. 217

[Aram] *AP* 81.37 נכרם (restored by Harmatta in *DAÉ* p. 106)
[Eg] cf. Ranke I.180.10-28; II.296.1f *ny(.t)-k3*-DN type.

נסנו *

--- **n(3)-snw* "The brothers"
S II p. 6; L p. 121 K p. 83
[Aram] *APO* 87.4 (cf. Kornfeld's reading כסנו)
[Eg] cf. Ranke I.311.5 *sn.w*  (m./f. MK-NK);. [Copt] CNHΨ (pl.) > *NECNHΨ

Spiegelberg offered another proposal **wn.s-n-iw* "she is come" Eg *wn.s* became NECin Copt (Spiegelberg, *KHw* p. 73 NA/NE pers. sf. 3 m sg), *n-iw* is a late form of Eg *iw*, Copt NΣY, N̄NHY (Spiegelberg, *KHw* p. 72). However a *wn.s*-construction is not attested in Rake. So **n3-snw* is a little more possible. It seems to be unnecessary to change the reading to כסנו, as Kornfeld proposed.

נפו

--- see נכו
K p. 84; V II p. 217
[Aram] *AP* p. 317A.2.

נפנא

--- **nf(r)-(n-)n(.t)* "Good one belonging to Thebes"
G p. 482; K p. 84
[Aram] Cowley, *JRAS* (1929) p. 109
[Eg] cf. Ranke I.197.3 *nfr-n* (?) and Ranke I.202.11 *nfr.t-n-n.t* (fem)

It can possibly be reconstructed as **nfr-n.i*. However notice that the Eg name *nfr-n3* (Ranke I.193.23), proposed by Grelot and Kornfeld, has an alternative reading *ṯ3.w-n3*, so the latter is better avoided.

נפסי **

--- *nf(r)-(3)s(.t)* 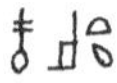 "Isis is beautiful"
L p. 121; K p. 84
[Aram] *TAÉ* 25.5 נפסי; 26.4
[Eg] Ranke I.194.3 f. Late; [Gk] cf. Νοῦψ(?).

נפעורת **

--- *n(3).f-ʿ(3)-rd* 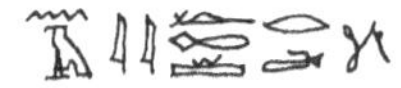 "His great ones are firm"

L p. 121; G p. 482; K p. 84

[Aram] *BP* 13.3, 4 נפעו[רת]

[Eg] Ranke I.170.18 m. Late; [Gk] Νεφορείτης, Νεφορίτης (*NB* p. 230)

The Coptic form ^{s}ⲞⲨⲢⲞⲦ for *rd* supports the identification of the last element ורת.

נפר

--- *nfr(.w)* "Beauty"

[Aram] *Saqq* 82a.4

[Eg] see Ph נפר.

נפראית **

--- *nfr(.t)-ii.t(i)* 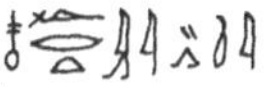 "The beautiful one is come"

[Aram] *Saqq* 7.2

[Eg] Ranke I.201.12 f. NK; [Gk] cf. Νοφερέτ (*NB* p. 237)

Nfr.t (Copt ⲚⲞϤⲢⲈ)-*ii*(Copt ⲈⲒ)-*ti*; the final ת reflects the old perfective ending.

נפרחונת

--- misreading of בר חנ[--] (by Porten in his letter)

K p. 84; V II p. 217

[Aram] *CIS* II.132.1.

נפרפון

--- **nf(r)-rpw* "An image is good"

[Aram] *Saqq* 176

[Eg] cf. Ranke I.364.22 *t3-rpw*

The reading נפרנף (*nfr-rnp.t* Ranke I.197.18 OK–Late) is possible.

נת

--- *n.t* 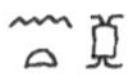 "Neith"

[Aram] Bordreuil, *Catalogue,* no. 139 (Porten commented in his letter that it is not a complete PN).

[Eg] *Wb* II.198; [Gk] Νηΐς.

סגרי

--- *sgry* .  "Silence"
G p. 490; K p. 123
[Aram] *AP* 22.61, 69
[Eg] Ranke I.321.12 m.NK; [Gk] Σγῆρις, Σγηρις (*NB* p. 366, 383)

Eg name is derived from *sgr* "silence" (*CDME* p. 252), which is commonly used in PN; *ỉỉ-m-sgr* (Ranke I.9.7 m. MK), *mr-sw-sgr.t* (Ranke I.157.21 f. NK), *mrr-sgr* (Ranke I.162.19 f. MK). However the root סגר is equally common in Semitic; Aram סגר "to deliver", Heb, Ph, Ug סגר "to shut" (cf Aram סכר; BDB p. 688b, Harris p. 126, *UT* 1738, cf. *DISO* p. 193), which are used in PN: Ug *sgr* (Gröndahl p. 256), *su-gu-ra* (*PNCP* p. 127), Therefore the identification is open to choice.

סומן

--- see ספמת
S I p. 1102; L p. 122; K p. 84; V II p. 217
[Aram] *CIS* II.154.5 (corrected to ספמת by Porten in his letter).

סחמרי *

--- **sẖm-r(3).ỉ* "My speech is powerful"
G p. 489; K p. 84; V II p. 217
[Aram] Cowley, *JRAS* 1929 p. 108.3
[Eg] cf. *sẖm-k3(.ỉ)* "my ka is powerful" (Ranke I.319.18 m. OK). The *sẖm* is a common element in Eg PNs, which is used from OK to the Late Period. The second element רי can be interpreted as *ỉri* "the belonging" (*Wb* I.105; Kornfeld); *ỉri* "the companion" (*CDME* p. 25; Grelot); *r3.ỉ* "my speefch" (*CDME* p. 145) etc..

ס̊י̊נ̊ר̊ה

--- corrected to באגרהא "for her wages" by Porten C3.28:89
G p. 490; K p. 84; V II p. 217
[Aram] *AP* 81.12 ס_גרה (Harmatta's reading סינרה in G p. 107).

סיפא

--- see אסיפא

סמשך *

--- *s-n-$m\underline{t}k$ "Man of mixed drink"

K p. 84

[Aram] *AD* 7.1

[Eg] cf. Ranke I.136.8; II p. 358 (*p3-s-n-m<u>t</u>k* ). See also *s-n*-type; *s-n-pt<u>h</u>*, *s-n-mn<u>t</u>.w* etc. (Ranke I.279.10–15), which occurs only in MK. The dropping of *p3* results from simple omission of the article rather than the survival of an old form.

סמתו **

--- *sm(3)-t(3).w(y)*  "He who united the two lands"

S I p. 1102; K p. 85

[Aram] *AP* 74.4

[Eg] Ranke I.296.10 m. Dyn19–Gk; [Gk] cf. Σεμθεῦς, Σεμθῶς, Σεμθῶϋς (*NB* p. 368f).

סנבנת **

--- **snb-n(y.)t* "May Neith be well"

[Aram] *Saqq* 28a.1

[Eg] cf. *snb*-DN type: *snb-imn* (Ranke I.312.18 f. Late); *snb-mn.w* (Ranke I.313.3 m. Dyn 18)

Segal proposed an Akk name "Sin, you have created" on the analogy of *sin-ibni* "Sin has created," without explaining the final ת (Akk would be *sin-tabni*). Eg *snb* is one of the most common elements of Eg PN and the goddess Neith occurs as either נית or נת. Therefore, an Eg name is most likely.

סענח **

--- *s(3.t)-ʿn<u>h</u>*  "The daughter of *ʿn<u>h</u>*"

[Aram] *Saqq* 8.9 (Porten B5.6:9)

[Eg] Ranke I.287.14 f. MK;

The fact that the name סענח is a female in the context makes the above identification more probable. Though the Eg name is attested only in the MK, each element of the name is very commonn throughout the Eg history. Therefore, it is more likely the Eg name has been preserved until the late period, and is now attested in Aram document.

ספמת

--- **sp-(n-)mw(.t)*
K p. 85; V II p. 217.
[Aram] *CIS* II.154.5
[Eg] Ranke I.296.4 f. MK. The same type of names are attested in the Late and Greek period (Ranke I.295.29, 296.5).

If Eg *ns* (*ny-sw* or *ny-sy*) became *s*, which usually appears as *ʾs* in Aramaic, *(n)s-n-p(r)-mw.t* "He/She belongs to the temple of Mut" (Ranke II.295.14 f. Dyn 26) is possible.

ספעמרא *

--- **(n)s-p(3)-ʿ(3)-mr(w.t)* "He who belongs to the great one of love"
L p. 122; G p. 501f; K p. 124
[Aram] *AP* 43.12
[Eg] cf. Ranke I.174.19 *ns-p3-ʿ3-ṯr*  "He who belongs to the great one of *Ṯr*." For the second element, cf. Ranke I.57.21 *ʿ3-mrw.t* "Love is great" or "greatness of love" m. MK–Dyn 20

For ס representing Eg *ns*, see ספמת / אספמת (*ns-p3-md.w*). The final א could be a *mater lectionis* reflecting an abstract noun ending. Kornfeld proposed two explanations: (1) Semitic ספא (*DISO* p. 196 "feed") + עמרא (which is compared with a deity עמרו). (2) Eg **s3-ip-ʿmr* "Son of Buto, the priest" or *s3-p3-ʿmr.y* "Son of priest *ʿmr*." However none of these are well grounded, as he admitted.

סשן **

--- *sšn*  "Lotus"
[Aram] *Saqq* 10. 8
[Eg] Ranke I.297.29ff m. MK; [Copt] ϣϣϣєn; [Heb] שׁשׁן

Porten suggested the possible reading of פסשן too. However the סשן is not used with the article *p3* in PNs. For a further discussion, see Heb שׁשׁן.

עבדאסי (hybrid) **

--- עבד*-3s(.t)* "The servant of Isis"
Maraqten p. 94
[Aram] ostracon: Naveh, *Tel Aviv* 6 (1979) no. 37.3 עבדאסי, no. 43 אבדאסי

[Eg] see Ph DN אס, cf. Aram עבדסי.

עבדחנס (hybrid) **

--- עבד-*ḫns(.w)* "The servant of Chons"

Maraqten p. 94

[Aram] seal: Lemairre, *Syria* 59 (1982) p. 115 no. 5

[Eg] *Wb* III.300.13–15

Though Maraqten left חנס unexplained, חנס is a normal realization of E god Chons (see Aram פטחונס).

[ע]בׄדחף (hybrid) *

--- עבד-*ḥp* "The servant of *Apis*"

K p. 65

[Aram] *AD* Frag. VII 3.2

[Eg] for Apis see *Wb* III.70; [Copt] [s]ϩⲁⲡⲉ, [b]ϩⲁⲡⲓ [Gk] 'Ἀπις.

עחפי **

--- Var. of ענחפי

G p. 465; K p. 85

[Aram] *AD* 2.2* עׄח֯ח֯פׄ֯י֯, 1, 2, 4, 3.1 עחחפ[י], 2, 3, 7, 12.2; *AD* Frag. IIA.8 עׄח֯[חפי], IXB.18 [עח]ח֯פׄ֯י֯, XI.5 [עח]ח֯פי, 12 [ע]חח[פי], XII.16 [ע]חח֯פׄ֯י֯; *Saqq* 189

[Eg] see ענחפי; [Gk] 'Αχοαπις (*NB* p. 69), 'Αχοαπιος (I.103), cf. 'Αγχαφις (*OAP* 18b)

For the elision of the נ of ענח, see Gk variants of the name. Another example is 'Αγχίριμφις and 'Αχορίμφις "May his name live" (I.102 cf. Ranke I.65.21; *NB* p. 69). For the elision of נ before ח, see מחנית and מחפרע.

עחמנוי *

--- *ʿnḫ-mr-wr* "May Mnevis live"

S I p. 1102; L p. 122; K p. 83; V II p. 217

[Aram] *TAÉ* 12 recto.2; *AP* 72.23 עחרנפי; (Aimé-Ciron, *TAÉ* p. 28, read as עחמנפי, yet Vittmann suggested עחמנוי, which is supported by Porten C3.12:34)

[Eg] Ranke I.64.16 m. Late; *DemNB* I.101

Cf. ענחמנוי.

עחמנפי
--- see עחמנוי.

עחר
--- see חרמעחר

עחרנפי
--- see עחמנפי
K p. 85; V II p. 218.

ע̊נחחב̊ס
--- see ענחחפי
S I p. 1102; L p. 122; K p. 85
[Aram] *AP* 73.9 (corrected to ענחחפי by Porten C3.19:9)

The first letter is not sure. The final ס is unusual. It is more likely that the fifth letter is פ. Hence I would suggest the reading ענחחפי, which already occurs in line 4. The fact that the father is פטאסי in each case strengthens my reading, which is supported by Porten.

ענחחפי **
--- *ʿnḫ-ḥp*  "May Apis live"
S I p. 1102; L p. 122; K p. 85
[Aram] *AP* 73.4, 9; *CIS* II.142
[Eg] Ranke I.65.25; II p. 347; I,103; [Gk] 'Αγχαφις (*OAP* p. 18b) cf. 'Αχοαπις, 'Αχοαπις.

ענחמנוי
--- Var. of עחמנוי (see above)
[Aram] *AP* 74.3, 4.

ענחמת̊
--- see ענחמנוי (corrected by Porten C4.9:3,4)
S I p. 1102; L p. 122; K p. 85; V II p. 218
[Aram] *AP* 74.4.

ענ̊חפמעי **
--- **ʿnḫ-p(3)-(n-)m(3)ʿ(.t)* "May *p3-m3ʿ.t* live"

K p. 85; V II p. 218
[Aram] ostracon: *Eph* III, p. 20.1
[Eg] cf. Ranke I.64.12 *ʿnḫ-m3ʿ.t-rʿ* "May the truth of Reʿ live" (m. Late). For *p3-n-m3ʿ.t* "He who belongs to the Truth" (Ranke I.108.3 m. Late–Gk), see Ranke I.108.3.

Vittmann's solution *ʿnḫ.f-n-m3ʿ.t* "He lives for the Truth" (cf. *ns-ʿnḫ.f-n-m3ʿ.t* Ranke I.174.5) is equally possible. However his alternative interpretation *ʿnḫ-p3-m3y* is impossible, because *p3-m3i* is פמי in Ph and פמוי in Aram (see פמי).

[ע]נחפרמנית
--- **ʿnḫ-p(3)-rm(ṯ)-(n-)ny.t* "May the man of Neith live"
[Aram] *AD* Frag VI,5.2 נחפרמנית[(there is no space between נח and פרמנית, though the name has been dealt with separately from נח)
[Eg] cf. *rmṯ-n-b3st.t* (Ranke I.222.19 f. Late). Notice the Eg *rmṯ* has lost the final *ṯ*, as shown in Copt [S]ⲣⲱⲙⲉ and [B]ⲣⲱⲙⲓ (*Wb* II.421) Though it is less likely, the name could be compared with *p3-rmnwti* "The shoulder" (Ranke II.282.13 m. Dyn 20) and I.222, 13ff esp. 16 *rmn.y-ʿnḫ(.w)* "*Rmn.y* lives" (m. MK). (for *rmn* see *CDME* p. 149).

עשה
--- *ʿš*  "The one who calls" (?)
G p. 466; K p. 85
[Aram] *LH* 4.3
[Eg] Ranke I.71.8 f. MK–Late; [Gk] cf. 'Ασᾶς (*NB* p. 60)

It can be a shortened form of a name whose first element is *ʿš3*  (Ranke I.71.11–19). At the same time, however, שעה is comparable with Aram root עשי "to do" (cf. Hebrew PN עשיאל 1Chr 4:35, and עשהאל 2 Sam 2:18 etc.). Therefore the explanation is open to choice.

עשחר **
--- **ʿš(3)-ḥr(w)* "Horus is rich"
L p. 122
[Aram] *Krug* 65
[Eg] cf. Ranke II.306.10 *ḥr(.w)-ʿš3*  , which could be read *ʿš3-ḥr.w* because of a graphic transposition with honorific intention (Gardiner, *EG*^{3}, § 57). See also Ranke I.71.11–19 where nine names

whose first element is *ʿš3* are attested, two in the Late, four in NK.

פאאני

--- (1) *p(3)-(n)-i͗(w)n(w)* 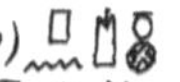 "He who belongs to Heliopolis"
--- (2) *p(3)-i͗(w)n.y* 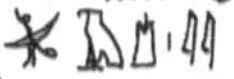 "The pillar"
--- (3) *p(3)-(n)-i͗(w)ny*  "He who belongs to Hermonthis"
[Aram] *Saqq* 67b.7
[Eg] (1) Ranke II.279.24/25 (m. NK)
(2) Ranke I.100.12 (m. Dyn 18)
(3) Ranke I.106.3 (m. NK).

פאוא

--- Var. of פוא
[Aram] *Saqq* 89.1
[Eg] see פוא
It seems that the first א functions as a *mater lectionis* as [a] vowel.

פאח **

--- *p(3)-(n-)i͗(ʿ)ḥ* 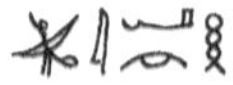 "He who belongs to the Moon"
[Aram] *Saqq* 53.15
[Eg] Ranke II.279.23 m. NK. Cf. *p3-i͗ḥy* "The Hathor child" (I.158).

פבא *

--- *p(3)-(n-)b3(.w)*  "He who belongs to souls" or "to might"
K p. 85
[Aram] Weill, *REJ* 65 p. 18.3
[Eg] Ranke I.107.7 m. Dyn 25; cf. *DemNB* I.363 (*pa-by*)
[Gk] cf. Πεβᾶς (*NB* p. 299); [Aram] cf. חבא.

פבי

--- (1) *p(3)-by*
(2) *p(3-n)-py* "He of Buto"(?)
K p. 89; V II p. 218
[Aram] *AP* 83.27 פי (in the list of Eg names) (corrected to פבי by Porten C3.27:28)

[Eg] (1) Ranke I.04.19 m. Dyn 26
(2) Ranke I.107.24, 25 m. Late
Cf. פיא cf. Gk Πάϊς, Φαῆς (*NB* p. 257, 327, 452).

פְּבְךְ
--- see פון
[Aram] *TAÉ* 87b.18.

פבן **
--- *p(3)-(n-)bn(r)*  "He who belongs to the date-palm"
K p. 86
[Aram] ostracon: Aimé-Giron, *BIFAO* 38 p. 38 no. 113.2
[Eg] Ranke I.104.24 m. NK; [Gk] Παβάνη (*NB* p. 252) cf. Copt ΒΝΝΕ "date-palm" (Crum p. 40a).

פְּגְרְבִי
--- **p(3)-gr(y)-(m)-p(.t)* "The pigeon in the sky"
[Aram] *Saqq* 60.7
[Eg] cf. *p3-gr*  (Ranke I.120.15 m. Late) and *gry-m-p.t*  (*Wb* V.181.2) cf. Copt [s]ϬΡΟΟΜΠΕ, [b]ϬΡΟΜΠΙ "pigeon"

Besides the uncertain reading, the correspondence between Aram ב and Eg *p* is questionable. A possible explanation is that voiceless *p* > voiced *b* after a labial *m*.

פּוֹא
--- see פפא
[Aram] *Saqq* 61b.1 (corrected to פפא by Porten B8.4:19).

פוחרב *
--- **p(3y).w-ḥr(y)-(i)b* "Their mediator"
K p. 86; V II p. 218
[Aram] *CIS* II.138B.4 פוחרך (corrected to פוחרב by Degen *NEph* I, p.27)
[Eg] cf. *p3-ḥr-ib*  "The mediator" (Ranke I.115.26 m. NK).

The initial פו may stand for the Eg article *p3* because of Heb

פוטיפר with ו as *mater lectionis*. Another possible reconstruction is **p3y-ḥr.t-ib* "Their desire" (for *ḥr.t ib* see *CDME* p. 195). **P3y-ʿ3-ẖrd* which Kornfeld proposed is much less likely because *ʿ3* is assumed to correspond to Aram ו.

]פומונ[

--- Var. of פומן

[Aram] *Saqq* 162

[Eg] see below

It is not probable that פומון is a variant of פמון (Segal), because of the second ו. However Eg *mnỉ* "to moor" fits the מון because of Copt ˢⲘⲞⲞⲚⲈ, ᵇⲘⲞⲚⲒ. Cf. פומן.

פומן **

--- *p(3)-w(ỉ3)-mn(ỉ.w)* 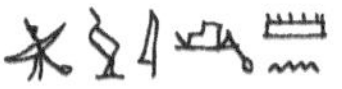 "The ship has moored"

K p. 86; V II p. 218

[Aram] ostracon: *CIS* II.138A.8 כומן (corrected to פומן by Degen *NEph* I.27)

[Eg] Ranke I.103.21 m. Late. Cf.]פומון[.

פומש

--- see פסמשך

K p. 86; V II p. 218.

פון

--- *p(3)-wn(w)* "The door keeper"

L p. 1122; K p. 86.

[Aram] *TAÉ* 87b.18.(corrected by Porten C3.26:36)

[Eg] Ranke I.103.25 m. Late (the name is very common in the Late period); The name is also comparable with *p3-n-wn* (Ranke I.106.26 m. Gk)

פונש **

--- *p(3)-wnš*  "The wolf"

S I p. 1103; L p. 123; G p. 488; K p. 86

[Aram] *AP* 71.11, 12

[Eg] Ranke I.104.3; II p.352; I,176 m. NK–Late; [Gk] Πουνσις, Πουῶνς, Φουνσις, Πονσις, Πουονς, Πουῶνσις, Φουνσις

(*NB* p. 342, 338, 468); [Copt] ⲠⲞⲨⲰⲚϢ
Cf. פמנש (?).

פוסי **
--- *p(3)-(n-)ws(r)* "He who belongs to the powerful one"
G p. 485; K p. 86; V II p. 218
[Aram] *AP* 12.7, 22.78, 79 פוסי
[Eg] *DemNB* I.361; cf. Ranke I.104.14 *p3-ws(r)-imn* (m. Dyn 21);
[Gk] Παϋσις, Πιϋσις, Φαϋσις (*NB* p.293)

That the final *r* has been lost is indicated in the Gk forms, a variant of Demotic form (*pa-wsy* *DemNB* I.361) and the PN *p3-ws(r)-imn* (see Černý, *LEG* § 1.9 the final *r* became *i*). **P3-w3s.t* (reconstructed by Grelot and Kornfeld) phonetically corresponds to פוסי, yet it is not attested.

פחא **
--- *p(3)-(n-)ḥ(r)* "He who belongs to the face"
K p. 86
[Aram] *BP* 8.12; Kornfeld, *AÖAW* 110 p. 133 no. 6 פנחס (corrected to פחא by Lipinski, *OLP*, 6/7 p. 382)
[Eg] Ranke I.110.6; *DemNB* I.401 (*pa-ḥr*); [Gk] Παως, Παᾶς, Παους, Πεως, Φαως, Φεως (*NB* p. 297, 274, 251, 323, 458
[Heb] פחא

Various similar names are attested: פחא, פחה, פחי, פחוי, תחא, תחה, תחוא, תחי. These identifications depend upon the interpretation of the final leter, which can be either a vowel letter or a consonant. If we consider them to be *matres lectionis*, the following identification would be possible on the basis of the corresponding Copt forms; (1) פחא (fem תחא) --- *p(3-n)-ḥ(r)* (cf. Copt ϨⲞ for *ḥr* "face") Gk Παως, Παους. Another name חא (*ḏd-ḥr*) confirmes that the Eg *ḥr* is חא in Aram. (2) פחה (fem תחה). If the final ה is a *mater lectionis* [ā/ē], as generally accepted, *p(3-n)-ḥ(3.t)* (cf. Copt ϨⲎ for *ḥ3.t* "front") is most probable; cf. Gk Παης. If the ה indicates [o], as תבה, פרעה, פחה is identical with *p3-n-ḥw.t.* (cf. Copt -ⲐⲰ in ⲚⲈⲂⲐⲰ for *ḥw.t* "temple") is more likely. (3) פחי (fem תחי): if the final י is used as a *mater lectionis* [ī/ē], the name is a variant of פחה. If the י is a consonant, this name can be a variant of פחוי.

פחה **

--- *p(3)-(n-)ḥ(3.t)* "He who belongs to the front"
S I p. 1103; L p. 123
[Aram] *AP* 72.11; 40.2; *TAÉ* 11.2; *Saqq* 192.1 פחה
[Eg] Ranke I.109.25 *p3-n-ḥ3.t*; I.115.11 *p3-ḥ3.t*; *DemNB* I.397;
[Gk]Παῆς, Πεῆς, Πιῆς, Φαῆς (*NB* p.255)
Cf. פחא, פחי; Akk *pa-ḫi-i* (*APN* p. 179a)

The interpretation depends upon which vowel is indicated by the final ה. Judging from the general assumption that ה indicates [ā/ē] vowels, I prefer to identify it with *p3-n-ḥ3.t* (cf. Copt ϩΗ for *ḥ3.t*). For further discussion see פחא.

פחו **

--- *p(3)-(n-)ḥ(w.t)* "He who belongs to the temple"
[Aram] *AP* 81.111 פחי (corrected to פחו here)
[Eg] Ranke I.110.3 m. NK

פחוי **

--- *p(3)-ḫy* "He who belongs to the height"
G p. 484; K p. 86; V II p. 218
[Aram] *APO* 75,2.15
[Eg] Ranke I.116.10; 1,404 m. NK–Late; [Gk] Παχ̓ϊς, Παχῶϊς (*NB* p. 295) cf. Copt ϢѠΙ for *ḫy* "height" (*Wb* III.237; Erichsen p. 349)

The identification *p3-n-ḥ(w).t* (Grelot, Kornfeld) cannot explain the final letter, because the Copt form of *ḥ(w).t* is ΘѠ. Copt ϢѠΙ (for *ḫy*) indicates that there is a long [ō] vowel between the two consonants *ḫ* and *y*, which is represented by the Aram ו and Gk ό/ῶ.

פחון

--- see פחור

פחור **

--- **p(3)-(n-)ḥr* "He who belongs to Horus"
[Aram] *Saqq* 53.17 פחון (corrected to פחור by Porten C4.3:17)
[Eg] cf. Ranke I.110.7 m. Gk; [Gk] Παϋρις, Παῶρ, Πεῶρ, Παῶρος, Πιϋρις, Φαϋρις (*NB* p. 294); [Copt] ΠΑϨѠΡ (Heuser, p. 17)

פחוֹרה
--- *p(3)-ḫr*  "The Syrian"
K p. 86
[Aram] Aimé-Giron, *BIFAO* 38 p. 58 no. 120.2 (Porten read it as פת/ח[-]ד/רה in the letter)
[Eg] Ranke I.116.17; *DemNB* I.210 m. NK–Dyn22ff; [MB] cf. *pa-ḫu-ra, pi-ḫu-ra, pu-ḫu-ur, pu-ḫu-ra, pu-ḫu-ri, pu-ḫu-ru* (Rake, *KM* p. 15, 17); [Gk] cf. Πχορις, Παχουρις
The whole reading is uncertain.

פחטב
--- corrected to וחבוב "and Ḥabub" by Porten in his letter
[Aram] ostracon: Aimé-Giron, *BIFAO*, 38 p. 58 no. 120.5

פחי *
--- Var. of פחוי
S I p. 112; L p. 123; G p. 484; K p. 86; V II p. 218
[Aram] *AP* 14.2,12, 51.4 פֿחי; *APO* 75.2.2, 13; *BP* 12.20; *TAÉ* 105a
[Eg] see פחוי, cf. פחה, תחי
If we consider the final י to be a vowel letter, a different identification is required, such as *p3-n-ḥ3.t* (see פחה). However we are not informed enough to distinguish consonants from vowel letters. Yet as for this identification, scholars unanimously agree that פחי is *p3-n-ḫy*, which is very common in Demotic texts, so as in Aram. For further discussion see פחו.

פחים **
--- *p(3)-ḫm*  "The ignorant"
S I p. 1103; L p. 123; K p. 87 V II p. 218
[Aram] *AP* 70.1
[Eg] Ranke I.419.17 m. NK; [Gk] Παχῆμις (*NB* p.294)
Due to the unknown value of the vowel between *ḫ* and *m*, the identification still leaves some room for doubt. In terms of the value of the vowel, *p3-ḫm* "the youth" (Erichsen p.359) gives a more satisfactory correspondence to פחים (Spiegelberg), because Copt form of *ḫm* is ϢΗΜ (Crum p. 563a). *P3-ḫm*, however, is not attested as a PN, though the element *ḫm* occurs in the PN *ḥr-p3-ḫm* (Gk ʻΑρπχιμις Erichsen p. 360). Kornfeld's suggestion *p3-ḥ3-imn*

(Ranke I.115.15) is not likely; no evidence of ימ for *imn* is known. Another suggestion **p3-ḫy-ym* (*CDME* p. 18; Erichsen p. 58) is not impossible, though not attested. Whichever the true correspondent of פחים is, the consonantal values are comparable.

פחיקצץ

--- **p(3)-ḫy-(r-)ḳ(3y)-d̲(3)d̲(3)* "He who ascends to the high head"
[Aram] Kornfeld, *AÖAW* 110, p.134 no.8 "He who high of front" (Ranke I.116.11); for קצץ, see *ḳ3y-d̲3d̲3* (Ranke I.429.21 m. NK).

It seems to be too long to be a PN. Another reconstruction is **p3-ḥr-ḳ3y-d̲3d̲3* "He who possesses the high head" (for the first element *p3-ḥr* see Ranke I.115.21–23). Yet the identification cannot be made sure.

פחנום **

--- *p(3)-(n-)ḫnm(.w)*  "He who belongs to Khnum"
K p. 87
[Aram] *BP* 11.2, 10, 15; *AP* 34.2 חנום (corrected to פחנום by Porten A4.4:4, *Aram Texts* p. 84); Bresciani, *RSO* 35 p. 22 I,verso.3; Porten, *Or* NS 57 p. 38 no. 23129.1
[Eg] Ranke I.110.17; II p. 353; *DemNB* I.408f m. NK–Gk; [Gk] Παχουβις, Παχνουμις, Παχνουμιος (*NB* p. 295)
Cf. פחנם.

פחנם **

--- Var. of פחנום
S II p. 7; L p. 123; G p. 484; K p. 87
[Aram] *AP* 23.5
[Eg] see פחנום.

פח̊נס̊

--- see month name פחנס

פחנתא

--- corrected to בחנתא "in/as the חנת" by Porten in his letter.
[Aram] Maraqten, *MDIK* 43 P. 170 no. 3.2

פחפי **

--- *p(3)-(n-)ḥp* 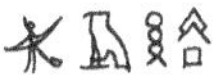 "He who belongs to Apis"

S I p. 1103; L p. 123; K p. 87

[Aram] *TAÉ* 87b.22 פ̇חפ̇י; *Saqq* 14.1 [י]פחפ̊; Porten, *Or* NS 57 p. 35 no. 23128.3

[Eg] Ranke II.280.23; *DemNB* I.400 m. Late; [Gk] Παάπης, Παάπεις, Παάπις, Παᾶφις, Πᾶπις, Πᾶφις (*NB* p. 251).

פחר̊ו

--- Var. of פחרי (?)

[Aram] *Saqq* 64b.11

[Eg] Ranke I.115.24 m. NK–Late

Perhaps *p3-ḥry* (Ranke I.115.25 m. NK) is equally possible. Yet it is impossible to identify the name with certainly, until the final value, represented by ו, is determined. *P3-n-ḥr* (Ranke I.110.7), suggested by Segal, is less likely, because after the ר no vowel is required.

פ̇חרי̊ **

--- *p(3)-ḥry*  "The overseers" or "He who belongs to the overseers"

G p. 486; K p. 87; V II p. 218

[Aram] *AP* 24.18

[Eg] Ranke I,115.24f m. NK–Late; [Gk] Πάρις, Παρεις (*NB* p. 280), φρι- (Griffith, *ZÄS* 46 p. 132–4); [Gk] cf. ρι- for *ḥry* (*Wb* III.141); [Copt] ϩⲣⲉ "over" (Spiegelgerg, *KHw* p. 242).

פטא *

--- Var. of פטי

[Aram] *Saqq* 41.9 פ̇ט̊א̊; 47.6]פ̇ט; 53.9]פט[; 14]פטא; 61b.3]פטא

[Eg] see פטי (a short form of *p3-di*-DN).

פטאא̊

---Var. of פטא, פטי (?)

[Aram] *Saqq* 11.4

[Eg] see פטי.

פטאח **

--- *p(3)-d(i)-i(ˁ)ḥ* 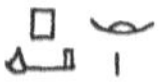 "He whom the Moon has given"

[Aram] *AP* 74.5 (Porten C4.9:5)

[Eg] Ranke I.121.21.

פטאס **

--- Var. of פטאסי

[Aram] Vattioni, *SF* no. 134 (cf. Herr, *Seals* p. 30 no. 48)

[Eg] see Ph פטאס.

פטאסי **

--- *p(3)-d(i)-3s(.t)* 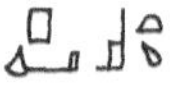 "He whom Isis has given"

S I p. 1103; L p. 123; G p. 486; K p. 87

[Aram] *BP* 9.10, 10.6; *AP* 14.11, 53.2, 73.4, 9, 74.5 פטאסׄי֯ 6 פטאסׄי֯, 83.3 [י]פטאס֯; *TAÉ* 27.1, 87b.5 פׄטׄאס֯י֯, 96a, b; *Saqq* 6.6, 19,4 [י]פׄטאס֯, 35.3 פׄטׄאסׄי֯ 38.9 פטא֯ס֯י֯, 61a.4 פׄטאסי֯; stela: Aimé-Giron, *BIFAO* 38 p. 42 no. 114 [י]פטאס; ostracon: Maraqten, *MDIK* 43 p. 170

[Eg] see Ph פטאסי snd פטאס; cf. also Aram פטיסי. This is a very common Eg name.

פטא֯ס֯ר֯

--- Var. of פטוסירי

[Aram] *Saqq* 68.6

[Eg] see פטוסירי

The letters are too faded to be read except the first two. The *aleph* of אסר (Osiris) is always elided when it is the second component of PN. Therefore, the reconstruction is also not likely.

פטבסתי

---Var. of פטובסת

[Aram] *TAÉ* 87a.10 [סתי]פׄטׄבׄ, 16 פטׄבׄסׄתׄי

[Eg] see Aram פטבסתי.

Note that the reading is uncertain.

פטואסי

--- see פטנאסי

K p. 87; V II p. 218

[Aram] *CIS* II.155B.4.

פטובסת *

--- *p(3)-d(i)-b(3)st(.t)* "He whom Bast has given"
[Aram] *Saqq* 61a.3 (cf. Porten's reading פטובסתי B8.4:10)
[Eg] Ranke I.123.5f; *DemNB* I.303 m. Late–Gk; [Gk] Πετουβάστος, Πετουβάστις, Πετοβάστις, Πετουβεστ(ις), Πετοβάσθις (*NB* p. 319f.), Πετθυβεστις (*DemNB* I.303).
Cf. פשובסתי; Heb GN פיבסת.

פטוסירי **

--- *p(3)-d(i)-(3)s-ir* "He whom Osiris has given"
S I p. 1103; L p. 123; G p. 486; K p. 87
[Aram] *AP* 28.4, 6, 8, 10, 11, 17
[Eg] Ranke I.123.1; II p. 356; *DemNB* I.298 m. Late-Gk; [Gk] Πετοσῖρις, Πετοσεῖρις, Πατουσῖρις, Πετωσῖρις, Πετυσίριος, Πετσειρις, Πετσιρις (*NB* p. 319); [Copt] ⲡⲁⲧⲟⲩⲥⲓⲣⲉ, ⲡⲉⲧⲥⲓⲣⲓ;
Cf. Aram פטוסרי, פטסרי, פטסורי, פטסרי.

פטוסרי **

--- Var. of פטוסירי
S I p. 1103; L p. 123; G p. 486; K p. 87
[Aram] *CIS* II.138A.4; *AD* 8.1; *TAÉ* 25.3 פטוסרי; *Saqq* 19.7, 41.7 פטוסרי, 92.1, 2 פקחסתי (corrected to פטוסרי here), 138.2 [פ]טוסרי; ostracon: Aimé-Giron, *ASAE* 26 p. 25; Porten, *Or.* NS 57 p. 35 no. 23128.7
[Eg] see פטוסירי.

פטחנום **

--- *p(3)-d(i)-ḫnm(.w)* "He whom Khnum has given"
S I p. 1103; L p. 123; G p. 486; K p. 87
[Aram] *CIS* II.155A.4 פטחנום; *AP* 6.17
[Eg] Ranke I.126.4; II p. 356; *DemNB* I.33.9; [Gk] Πετεχνοῦμις, Πετεχνόμις, Πατεχνούμιος, Πετεχνοῦφις, Πετεχνουβις, Πατεχνούμιος, Πατεχνοῦβις, Πατουχνάμ, Πετεχνόμις (*NB* p. 287, 317, 320)
Cf. Aram פטחנם.

פטחנם **

--- Var. of פטחנום

S II p. 7; L p. 123; G p. 486; K p. 87

[Aram] *AP* 23.9; *LH* 4.12, 15, 5.10; ostracon: Maraqten, *MDIK* 43, p. 170

[Eg] see פטחנום.

פטחרטיס **

--- *ptḥ-(i)r-di-s(w)* "It is Ptah who has given him"

G p. 48; K p. 88

[Aram] *LH* 4.11

[Eg] Ranke I.138.16 m. Late; [NA] *ip-ti-ḫar-ṭi-e-šu* (Assurb. I.103; Ranke, *KM* p. 29)

Notice, again, Aram ת > ט between a labial and ח (see פטחב).

פטחרפחרט **

--- *p(3)-d(i)-ḥr-p(3)-ẖrd* "He whom Harpokrates has given"

S I p. 1104; L p. 123; K p. 88

[Aram] *CIS* II.138A.7; *AP* 73.11; *Saqq* 142.1 [פט]חרפח[רט]; Bresciani, "Frammenti di un Testo Aramaico" B x+3 פטחרפחרט

[Eg] Ranke I.124.24; II p. 356; *DemNB* I.328 m. Late-Gk; [Gk] Πετεαρποκράτης, Πετεαρποχρατης, Πεταρποχράτης (*NB* p. 311)

Cf. Ph חרפכרט.

פטי **

--- *p(3)-di* "He whom (DN) has given"

S I p. 1104; L p. 128; K p. 88; V II p. 219

[Aram] *AP* 74.1; *TAÉ* 87b.10 פְּטִי; Sayce, *PSBA* 26 p. 207; ostracon: Maraqten, *MDIK* 43 p. 170

[Eg] Ranke I.121.17 Dyn 22–Gk; [Gk] Πετῆς, Πατῆς, Πατῆ, Πετέ, Πατε, Πιτῆς (*NB* p. 286f, 310, 318)

Cf. פטא

Perhaps the name is a shortened form of *p3-di*-DN.

פטיו

--- see פטסי

פטיה
--- *p(3)-d(i)-ih(y)* "He whom the Hathor-child has given"
[Aram] *Saqq* 52a.6
[Eg] cf. *p3-ti-ihy* (*DemNB* I.290) *ʾIḥy* "Hathor-child" occurs as *ihy* in Demotic (Erichsen p. 40).

פטיחר
--- *p(3)-di-ḥr*  "He whom Horus has given"
[Aram] *Saqq* 77a.1
[Eg] Ranke I.124.19; *DemNB* I.322f. m. Late-Gk; [Gk] Πετεῦρις, Πατεῦρις, Πατῶρ, Πετώριος (*NB* p. 317, 292, 322).

פטיסי
--- see פטאסי
K p. 88
[Aram] *AP* 53.2 (corrected to פטאסי by Porten C4.8:2)
The intervocalic *aleph* was elided *p3-di-3s.t* > [paṭi/ēsi], as Gk forms show the elision of *aleph*: Πετεῆσις, Πετῆσις, Πατεησις, Πατῆσις, Πατεισις, Πατισις. However Porten told me this is probably פטאסי.

פטמחו *
--- *p(3)-d(i)-mḥ (.t)*  "He whom (goddes) *Mḥ.t* has given"
[Aram] *NEph* I p. 10 no. 2300.1, 7, 9 [ו]פטמח (Naveh, *JAOS* 91 p. 379–382)
[Eg] Ranke I.123.20 m. Gk; *DemNB* I.315 m. Late; [Gk] cf. Πετεμῆχις (*NB* p. 313)
The final ו is troublesome, because the reflection of Eg fem. ending is י (cf. Copt ⲘϨⲎ, Ph מחי in פשמחי). However it is interesting that *mḥ.t* is written *mḥw.t* (cf. *Pamahu* EA 7.76). Yet the identification remains uncertain.

פטמיחוס **
--- *p(3)-d(i)-m(3)i-ḥs(3)*  "He whom (the god) Mihos has given"
[Aram] *Saqq* 28b.5 פטמיחר/דס (corrected to פטמיחוס here)
[Eg] Ranke I.123.15; [NA] cf. *pu-ṭu-um-ḫe-e-šu.*
For the מוי [moui] "lion", see Y. Muchiki, *JSS* 36 (1991) p. 7-10.

For *m3ỉ-ḥs3* "lion god", see *Wb* II.12.2–5.

פטמו[-]

--- see פטמון

K p. 88; V II p. 218

[Aram] *CIS* II.155B.2 (read as פטחור or פטמכבסא by Porten in the letter)

Note that the final ו, which is indistinct, is probably followed by one more letter. Therefore the most reasonable reconsturuction is פטמון.(*p3-dỉ-ỉmn*). The reading suggested by Vittmann is פטמן (the final נ instead of ו: *p3-dỉ-mn.w*). Yet Porten also suggested to me in his letter פטחור (*p3-dỉ-ḥr* Ranke I.124.18 m. Gk) or פטמכבסא (next line ?).

פטמון **

--- *p(3)-d(ỉ)-(ỉ)mn* 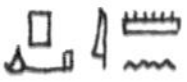 "He whom Amun has given"

S II p. 1104; L p. 124; K p. 88

[Aram] *CIS* II.126, II.155B.2 פטמו]; *LH* 7.3

[Eg] Ranke I.121.23; *DemNB* I.281 m. Dyn 21–Gk; [Gk] Πετεμούνιος, Πετεμοῦνις, Πεταμουνις, Πετεαμουνις, Πετεμοῦν, Πετεμῶν, Πεταμῶν (*NB* p. 314, 309); [NA] cf. *pu-ṭi-ma-a-ni[* (?) (Ranke, *KM* p. 37).

פטמן **

--- *p(3)-d(ỉ)-mn*  "He whom Min has given"

G p. 486; K p. 89

[Aram] Bauer-Meissner, *SBPA* (1936) p. 415.17

[Eg] Ranke I.123.18; II p. 356; *DemNB* I.310; [Gk] Πετεμεῖνις, Πατεμεῖνις, Πετεμῆνις, Πετεμῖν, Πετεμῖνις, Πατεμεῖνις, Πατεεμῖνις (*NB* p. 286, 313).

פטמ[ת]

--- *p(3)-d(ỉ)-m(w).t*  "He whom Mut has given"

G p. 486; K p. 89; V II p. 218

[Aram] *AP* 24.1 פ[ט]מ[ת] (Porten's reading[--]פטמ C3.14:1)

[Eg] Ranke I.123.17 m. Dyn 22–Late; [Gk] Πετεμοῦτις, Πτεμοῦτις (*NB* p. 314); [Copt] ⲠⲈⲦⲈⲘⲞⲨⲦ (Černý p. 350)

Though Porten corroborates the second letter, the last one is reconstructed.

פטנאסי **

--- *p(3)-d(i)-n(.i)-3s(.t)* "He whom Isis has given to me"
S I p. 1104; L p. 124; K p. 89
[Aram] *Eph* III p. 114; *CIS* II.155B.4 פטואסי (corrected to פטנאסי by Spiegelberg)
[Eg] Ranke I.124.5; II p. 356; *DemNB* I.315; [Gk] Πετενιῆσις (*NB* p. 314); [NB] *pa-ṭa-ni-*[ilu]*e-si-*ʾ (Ranke, *KM* p. 40).

פְּטנִי

--- *p(3)-d(i)-n.i* "He whom (god) has given to me"
[Aram] *Saqq* 91.4
[Eg] Ranke I.124.4 m. Late; [Gk] cf. Πατένιος, Πετενεῦς (*NB* p. 286, 314)

This is an apocopated form, such as פטנאסי (*p3-di-n.i-Isis*).

פטנפחת[ף] **

--- *p(3)-d(i)-nf(r)-ḥtp* "He whom *nfr-ḥtp* has given"
S I p. 1104; L p. 124; K p. 89
[Aram] *AP* 69.2
[Eg] Ranke I.124.12; II p. 356; *DemNB* I.318 m. Late–Gk; [Gk] Πετενεφώτης, Πετενηφώτης (*NB* p. 314). For *nfr-ḥtp* (Νεφερώτης) see Ranke I.198.14.

פטנתי̊

--- *p(3)-d(i)-nṯ(r)* "He whom the god has given"
G p. 486; K p. 89; V II p. 218
[Aram] *AP* 24.25 פטנתן (Grelot, p.273, read it as פטנתי; yet Porten, C3.14:21, suggested פטנתר, see below)
[Eg] Ranke I,124.14f; [Copt] ПЕТЕΝΟΥΤЕ (Heuser p. 27) cf. Copt [S]ΝΟΥΤЕ, [B]ΝΟΥϮ for *nṯr* "god" (the final *r* has been lost in the singular form)

Two more explanations were proposed by Kornfeld; (1) **p3-di-nw.t* (cf. *t3-di.t-nw.t* Ranke I.373.16), which could not explain the final תי, because Eg fem ending *-t* was dropped. (2) *p3-di-ny.t* (Ranke I.124.6; *DemNB* I.316), which could not explain the final י, because the Aram form of Neith (*ny.t*) is either נת or נית. Gk and

Copt forms also do not show any vowel after *-t*; ⲚⲒⲐ, ⲚⲈⲐ; ⲚⲎⲐ; cf. Heb אסנת. Therefore we agree with Grelot's explanation of *p3-di-nṯr* which is phonetically most reasonable, see above for Copt forms for *nṯr*.

פטנתר **

--- *p(3)-d(i)-nṯr(.w)* "He whom gods have given"

S I p. 1104; L I p. 124; K p. 89

[Aram] *AP* 66 no. 1; 83.23; 24.25 (according to Porten A4.6:24);*CIS* II.138B.8 [פ]טנתר

[Eg] Ranke I.124.15; II, p.356 m. Gk. For the uncertain reading of the Eg name, see Ranke I.124.22; 185.27. cf also Ranke I.124.2 *p3-di-n3-nṯr* Gk Πετενεντηρις (Eg article *n3* + *nṯr.w*); *DemNB* I.320 (*p3-ti-nṯr.wy* dual form of *nṯr*).

The fact that the *r* of *nṯr.w* is protected by the plural ending *w* is clearly indicated in the Copt forms; sg. [S]ⲚⲞⲨⲦⲈ, [B]ⲚⲞⲨϮ (Aram נתי in פטנתי), pl. ⲈⲚⲦⲎⲢ (Aram נתר) (Crum p. 230b).

פטסבק **

--- *p(3)-d(i)-sbk* "He whom Sobek has given"

S I p. 1105; L p. 93; K p. 89

[Aram] *AP* 73.12; Porten, *Or* NS 57 p. 41.4

[Eg] Ranke I.126.8; II p.356 m. Gk; *DemNB* I.340; [Gk] Πετασοῦχος, Πετεσόβχις, Πετεσῦβκις, Πετεσουχις, Πετεσοῦχος, Πετεσῶχις, Πετοσοῦχος, Πετοσοῦκος, Πετσώουκις (*NB* p. 310, 316f, 320f)

Eg *sbk* is expected to appear in Aram as סבך. The correspondence between Eg *k* and Aram ק is, however, conceivable, for the preceeding bilabial may influence the change /k/ > /q/. It is noteworthy that the intervocalic Eg *b* is eventually weakened in some Gk forms. (For the loss of Eg *b*, see K. Sethe "Der Name des Gottes Suchos" *ZÄS* 50 pp. 80–83.)

פטסורי

--- Error for פטסירי

[Aram] *AD* 8.5

[Eg] see פטוסירי.

פטסי **

--- Var. of פטאסי

L p. 124; G p. 486; K p. 89

[Aram] *CIS* II.154.6 (*BIFAO* 38 p. 37); *AP* 24.5; *TAÉ* 96c, 97a,b; *Saqq* 192.3 פטס̊י]

[Eg] see פטאסי.

פטסרי **

--- Var. of פטוסירי

S I p. 1103 פטאסרי (פטסרי!); followed by L p. 124; K p. 89

[Aram] *AD* 8.3; *CIS* II.113.9 פ̊ט̊ס̊ר̊י̊, 11, 21 פטסרי̊; *Eph* III p. 114

[Eg] see פטוסירי.

פ[ט]פתח

--- *p(3)-d(i)-pth̬*  "He whom Ptah has given"

[Aram] *CIS* II p.134 (Porten read it as פתח[?] in his letter)

[Eg] Ranke I.123.13, II p. 356 m. Late–Gk; *DemNB* I.309.

פטתום **

--- *p(3)-d(i)-(i)tm* 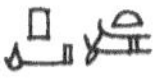 "He whom Atum has given"

S I p. 1105; L p. 124; K p. 89

[Aram] *AD* 73.15 פטתנם (according to the reading of *CIS* II.147.15)

[Eg] Ranke I.122.15, II p. 355 m. Gk; *DemNB* I.294; [Gk] Πετετυμις, Πετεθυμις (*NB* p. 317).

פטת̇וס̊]

--- **p(3)-d(i)-t(3)-wsr(.t)* "He whom the powerful goddess has given"

[Aram] *Saqq* 105.7

[Eg] cf. Ranke I.355.22 *t3-wsr.t* "the powerful goddess" as an epithet (*Wb* I.363.11f)

The final *r* of *wsr* should be protected by the feminine ending *-t*, but the text is broken. Another possibility is *w3s* "scepter" (*Wb* I.259) or *w3s.t* the name of the Theban nome (cf. פוסי). As for the Aram text, I would suggest פטתום (*p3-di-itm*), because the left downstroke of a *mem* seems to be traceable.

** פטתורי

--- **p(3)-d(i)-t(3)-wr(.t)* "He whom the great lady has given"
[Aram] *Saqq* 47.5
[Eg] cf. *t3-wr.t* 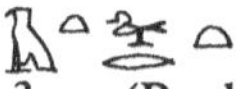 "the great lady" (Ranke I.355.13 f. MK–Late) and *p3-wr* (Ranke I.104.4; MB *pa-wi/e/a-ra* Ranke, *KM* p. 16)

Note Segal's reconstruction: **p3-di-t3-wry* "He whom Thoueris has given". Yet **t3-wry* is not attested in Ranke.

פי

--- see פבי
K p. 89; V II p. 218
[Aram] *AP* 83.27 פי (in the list of Eg names; corrected to פבי by Porten C3.27:28).

* פיא

--- *pi3* 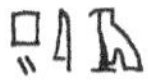
L p. 124; G p. 485; K p. 89; V II p. 219
[Aram] *AP* 14.1, 9, 12, 14
[Eg] Ranke I.129.23ff m. NK; [Gk] cf. Παϊῆς, Φαϊῆς, Πεϊῆς (*NB* p. 257, 453, 300)

The name is difficult to explain with certainty, because both י and א could be either a consonant or a vowel, though it is surely Egyptian.

* פיסן

--- *p(3)-sn* 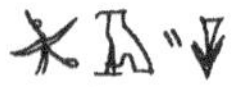 "The brother"
G p. 485; K p. 110
[Aram] *AP* 40.2; 37.9 (see *AP* p. 134)
[Eg] Ranke I.117.6 m. Dyn 20; cf. *t3-sn.t* (Ranke I.367.16 f. Gk); [Gk] cf. Πισων (*NB* p. 328)

For the י of פיסן see Chapter IV: [5] Notes on the Hebrew Vocalizations, a) Eg article *p3*. Phonetically **p3y.i-sn* "my brother " would be a better equation of פיסן (cf. Gk Πεισων *NB* p. 300), though it is not attested. The element *p3y.i-* occurs after NK (Ranke I.126.24–127.7, such as *p3y.i-nfr.w* "My beautiful one," *p3y.i-nḫt* "My strong one"). The second element *sn* is common in Eg PN (see Ranke I.117.6 *p3-sn* m. Dyn 20 etc.). It is conceivable that the name *p3y. i-sn* has been preserved in the Gk form Πεισων. However an Iranian explanation (*paesāna/ān) seems to be possible (Grelot, Kornfeld). The identification remains questionable.

פא/יתרשת

--- **p(3)-(n-)i(r).t-rš(i).t(i)* "He who belongs to the rejoicing"
[Aram] *Saqq* 122.2
[Eg] For the first part cf. *p3-n-ir.t* (Ranke I.106.13 m. Gk), and for the second cf. *3s.t-ršwty* "Isis rejoiced" (Ranke I.4.10). Copt ⲉⲓⲁ, ⲉⲓⲁⲧ "eye", derived from *ir.t* (Černý p. 44), shows that the *r* of *ir.t* was reduced. Since the Aram reading is not sure, it is impossible to identify it with certainty. Segal suggests that it is compounded with Luwian *piya* "give by".

פכ/נא

--- **p(3)-(n-)k(3) / p(3)-(n-)ni(w.t)* "He who belongs to ka / He who belongs to the city"
[Aram] Porten, *Or* NS 57 p. 26.9
[Eg] cf. *p3-n-k3-n-ḥ.t-nṯr* (Ranke I.111.11 m. Late).
For p*3-n-niw.t*  see Ranke I.108.20 m. NK–Gk. The short form *p3-n-n3* is also possible (cf. Ranke I.108.19.19)

* פכיף

--- *p(3)-k(3)p(.w)*  "The bird catcher"
S II p. 7; L p. 124; K p. 90
[Aram] *APO* 75,2.1, 10 (pl.62)
[Eg] Ranke I.120.5; II p.190 m. Late-Gk; *DemNB* I.278
[Gk] Φχωιφις, Πακειφῖς, Πακοῖβις (*NB* p. 258)
Spiegelberg mentioned that the *yodh* of פכיף shows up in the Gk form Φχωιφις. Yet the Copt form ϭⲱⲡⲉ (noun; Crum p. 825), ϭⲱⲡⲉ is derived from *k3p* (Černý p. 334, cf. Spiegelberg, *KHw* p. 291), does not support the *yodh*. As the two Gk forms Φχωιφις, Πακειφῖς suggest, the *k3p* may have bi-form [keif] and [koif]. The identification is still open to question.

פכמי

--- *p(3)-kmy*  "The bull" (?)
[Aram] *Saqq* 28a.3

[Eg] Ranke I.120.8 m. Gk; cf. *DemNB* I.279 (*p3-gm* "the calf"); [Gk] Πακαιμις, Πακαιμιος (*DemNB* I.279)

There are two alternatives: **p3-n-km.t* (!) "He who belongs to Egypt" is proposed by Segal. The feminine from *t3-(n.t-)km.t* (?) "The Egyptian" (?) is attested (Ranke I.363.7). When we consider Copt [S,A]ⲔⲎⲘⲈ, [B]ⲬⲎⲘⲒ for Eg *km.t*, it is possible (cf. Gk Πακαμις, Πακημις *NB* p. 257f). Yet the masc. form which he quoted as evidence, *p3-(n-)km* 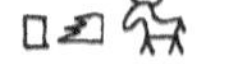 is perhaps "He who belongs to the bull" or "The bull." Demotic name *p3-gm* should be compared with this Eg name. Demotic *gm* (Copt ϬⲀⲘ) is a calf (*JEA* 58, pp. 36–310). Equally possible is *p3-k3my* 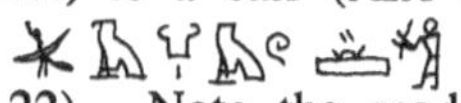 "the Gardener" (Ranke I.120.6 Dyn 22). Note the reading is uncertain.

פכעס *

--- **p(3)-(n-)k(3)-ʿs(.t)* "He who belongs to the ka of Astarte"

[Aram] *Saqq* 38.7

[Eg] For עס see *p3-di-ʿs.t* (?) (Ranke II.284.15 m. Late) and *k3-ʿsṯi.t* (Ranke I.338.27 m. Late). Since *k3-ʿsṯi.t* is attested, **p3-n-k3-ʿs.t* is no problem in the Late Period, if *ʿs.t* is a short form of *ʿsṯi* (= *'atrt*, Ashtarte, see *KRI* I.73.1), though there is no evidence for this (see Ranke II.284b n.1). J. D. Ray suggested the common name *p3-ḫ3ʿ-sw* (Ranke II. 282.24 m. Late), which is possible, if Aram כ represents Eg *ḫ*, as Ph כ.

פלוץ

--- **p(3)-rwḏ* "The strong"

G p. 487; K p. 90; V 11 p. 219

[Aram] *APO* 75,2.16

[Eg] cf. *rwḏ* 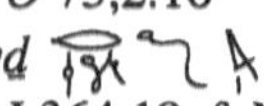 (Ranke I.221.12 m./f. OK–Gk) and *t3-rwḏ.t* (?) (Ranke I.364.19 f. NK). Also cf. Ranke I.361.14; 365.9; cf. Demotic *rḏ* = *lwḏ*, Copt [S]ⲞⲨⲢⲞⲦ, [B]ⲈⲢⲞⲨⲞⲦ for *rḏ*.; [Copt] ⲠⲖⲞⲨϪ; [Gk] cf. Πλοῦτ (*NB* p. 333)

The above information indicates not פלוץ but פלוט is the Aram form of *p(3)-rwḏ*, because the normal equation of Aram צ is Copt Ϫ and Eg *ḏ* which did not change into *d*, as Vittmann shows that the name was preserved in Copt ⲠⲖⲞⲨϪ. Therefore, the interpretati is still questionable, but no other explanation is at hand. So the Eg name may be preserved in Aram as פלוץ (cf. Copt ⲡⲗⲟⲩϫ Schiller, *Ten Coptic Legal Texts* no.1 1.4).

פמא

--- *p(3)-mi(w)* 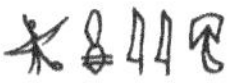 "The cat"
L p. 124; K p. 90
[Aram] *TAÉ* 86bis
[Eg] Ranke I.105.7; II p.353 m. Dyn 18–Late; *DemNB* I.187 (*p3-mi*); [Gk] Πεμαυς, Πεμαυτος (*NB* p. 303); [Copt] ⲡⲙⲁⲓ (Heuser, p. 23)

Kornfeld identified it with *p3-m3y* "The lion" (Ranke I.105.5). Yet we usually expect פמ[ו]י for *p3-m3y* (see Muchiki, *JSS* 35, p. 7–10 ; cf. Ranke II.283.7). Therefore, *p3-miw* is perhaps more likely. Spiegelberg prefered to read it as פמי, and identified it with *p3-m3y* of *TAÉ* p. 68. However, the text is damaged, it is impossible to determine the reading with certainty.

פמהן

--- *p(3)-(n-)mn (.w)*  "He who belongs to Min"
K p. 124
[Aram] *APO* 77.2, Innen 2
[Eg] see פמן

The identification is based upon the assumption that the ה of פמהן is a *mater lectionis* for [i] in the middle position, which is unique. Or **p3-mhn* "the milk jar" might be an other solution (see *mhn* < *mhr* "milk jar" *Wb* II.115.5–8.).

פמון **

--- *p(3)-(n-i)mn* 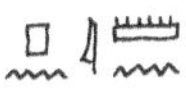 "He who belongs to Amun"
G p. 495; K p. 90
[Aram] *AD* 8.1-6; Saqq 43a.1 פַּמֹּון, 53.14, 47.3 פַּמֹּון
[Eg] Ranke I.106.8 m. NK–Gk; *DemNB* I.350 (*pa-imn*); [Gk] Παμμωνις, Παμουνις, Παμουνιος, Παμωνις, Φαμουνις, Φαμων (*NB* p. 39); [NA] *pa- mu-nu* (Ranke, *KM* p. 39). [Copt] ⲡⲁⲙⲟⲩⲛ.

פמט **

--- **p(3)-md(.w)* "The Staff" or *p(3)-(n-)md(.w)* "He who belongs to

the Staff" (the staff is a symbol of ruler)
G p. 486; K p. 90; V 11 p. 219
[Aram] *BP* 12.20; *AP* 44.5 [אספ]מט (corrected to [פ]מט by Porten B7.3:5, *Aram Texts* p.122)
[Eg] cf. *ns-p3-md.w* (Ranke I.175.1; II p.365 m. Late-Gk; Gk Aram אספמת); *p3-mdw-nḫt* "The Staff is strong" (Ranke I.105.16 m. NK); [Gk] Παμηθις, Παμιτης, Παμμιτος, Φαμειθης (*NB* p. 262f, 454) Πεμητος (*OAP* p. 247b).

פמן **
--- *p(3)-(n-)mn(.w)* "He who belongs to Min"
S I p. 1105; L p. 124; G p. 485; K p. 90
[Aram] *CIS* II.122.4; *AP* 74.3; Herr, *Seals* p. 30 no. 49 (AvEgad, *IEJ* 4 p. 238)
[Eg] Ranke I.108.8 m. Gk; *DemNB* I.369; [Gk] Πεμήνις, Παμῆνις, Πεμῆν, Φαμηνις, Παμῖν, Παμῖνις, Παμιν, Παμεῖν, Παμίνιος, Φαμίνιος, Φαμῖνις, Φεμῖνις, Πιμῖνι, Παμῖνος, Φαμινος, Φανηνις (*NB* p. 262f); [Copt] ⲡⲁⲙⲓ (cf. Copt [s]ⲙⲁⲉⲓⲛ, [b]ⲙⲏⲓⲛⲓ for Eg *mn.w*); [Ug] *pmn*
Cf. פמהן.

פמס
--- see פמסה.

פמסי **
--- *p(3)-ms* "The child"
L p. 124; G p. 485; K p. 90
[Aram] *AP* 44.5 [פמ]סי, 44.7
[Eg] Ranke I.105.11 m. NK. As an element of PN, *p3-ms* is attested until the Late Period (Ranke I.105.12–14; II.279.17 etc.); [Gk] Πμᾶσε (*NB* p. 334) cf. Copt [s]ⲙⲓⲥⲉ, [b]ⲙⲓⲥⲓ for Eg *ms*.

Copt ⲙⲓⲥⲉ seems to justify the final *yodh*. **P3-n-ms.t*, proposed by Grelot, is not attested, and even the element *ms.t* "mother" is quite rare (cf. Ranke I.29.11; 249.2 meaning is obscure.)

פמסה **
--- *p(3)-msḥ* "The crocodile"
--- *p(3)-(n-)msḥ* "He who belongs to the crocodile"

S I p. 1105; L p. 124; K p. 90
[Aram] *AP* 73.13 פמסא (cf. *CIS* II.147.13 פמסה̇)
[Eg] Ranke II.279.17 (cf. I.164.14) m. Late; *DemNB* I.191 m. Late; [Gk] Πεμψᾶς, Πεμψάϊς, Πεμσάϊς, Πεμσάεις, Πεμσᾶς, Πομσαϊς, Πομσάϊς (*NB* p. 304).

פמת **
--- **p(3)-(n-)m(w).t* "He who belongs to Mut"
S I p. 1105; L p. 124; G p. 485; K p. 91; V p. 219
[Aram] *AP* 22.69 פ̊מת, 72.4, 74.2 פ[מ]ת; Porten, *Or* NS 57 p. 47 no. 18.2
[Eg] see Ph פמת

As Vittmann pointed out, if we accept that אספמת is a variant of אספמט, there is no reason to reject פמת as a variant of פמט. Therefore, *p3-mdw* is also possible. However, since both are attested, we should seek the consistence of phonetic correspondence in our study.

פנא **
--- *p(3)-(n-)ni(w.t)*  "He who belongs to Thebes" (for the reading of *niw.t*, see GN נא)
G p. 485; K p. 91
[Aram] Bauer-Meissner, *SBPA* 1936, 415.16; *Saqq* 9.3
[Eg] Ranke I.108.20 m. NK–Gk; II.108.20; *DemNB* I.376 (*pa-n3*); [Gk] Πανᾶς, Πινᾶς (*NB* p. 265); [Copt] ⲡⲁⲛⲁ
Cf. פני; cf. Heb GN נא and Aram GN נא "Thebes."

פנ̊חס̊
--- see פחא
K p. 91; V 11 p. 220.

פני
--- Var. of פנא (?)
[Aram] *Saqq* 110.1
[Eg] see פנא.

פנס
--- *p(3)-ns(y)* 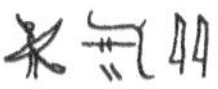 "He who belongs to (DN)"

[Aram] Porten C3.7Jr2:6, Ev2:17
[Eg] Ranke I.114.1 m. Dyn 22.

פנפתם **

--- **p(3)-(n-)nf(r)-tm* "He who belongs to Nefertem"
L p. 124f; K p. 91
[Aram] *TAÉ* 11. recto 5
[Eg] cf. the fem. form *t3-n.t-nfr-tm* (Ranke I.361.4 f. Late). DN *nft-tm* occurs in Late Eg male names (Ranke I.200.25–201.2).

פסא **

--- *p(3)-(n-)s3(w)* "He who belongs to Sais"
L p. 125; K p. 91
[Aram] *TAÉ* 87b.11
[Eg] Ranke I.110.20 m. Dyn26; *DemNB* I.413 (*pa-si*); [Gk] Πασᾶς, Πσᾶς, Πισᾶς, Πεσαϊς, Πεσαΐς, Φασᾶϊς (*NB* p. 285, 307, 327, 457); cf. Πεσάϋς, Πεσῶϋ; cf. other forms of Sais (GN) NA *sa-a-a* (Assurb I.90; II.16), Copt ^{s}ⲥⲁⲓ, ^{b}ⲥⲁ
Cf. פסו, פסי

Three similar names are attested, to which the above Gk forms correspond well; (1) Πασᾶς, Πεσᾶς, Πεσᾶς: פסא (the *aleph* is mater lectionis [a]); (2) Πεσαϋς, Πεσῶϋ: either פסא (the *aleph* is a consonant) or פסו (the *aleph* elided and the ו is *mater lectionis*); (3) Πεσαϊς, Πισαΐς: either פסא (the *aleph* is a consonant) or פסי (the *aleph* elided).

פסו

--- **p(3)-s(r)* "The ram"
L p. 125; G p. 486; K p. 124; V 11 p. 224; Zausich, *Enchoria* 13 p. 117
[Aram] *AP* 37.11, 83.24
[Eg] cf. *sr* (*Wb* III.462.7ff); Copt ^{s}ⲉⲥⲟⲟⲩ, ^{b}ⲉⲥⲱⲟⲩ, ^{f,a}ⲉⲥⲁⲩ; [Gk] Πεσου, Πεσόου, Πεσαϋς, Πεσωϋ (*NB* p. 307f)
Cf. תסו

J. D. Ray suggested that *sr* "ram" is for סו; the drop of the final *r* and the final vowel [u] are evident in the Coptic forms (see above) and the later writing of *sr* Late , Gk . Demotic names *pa-siw3*, *pa-sw3*, **pa-swr* may be more conceivable (*DemNB* I.413). Grelot proposed **p3-sw.t* "the wheat." However, wheat has never been attested as an element of PN, though the names of plants are common in Eg PNs (Ranke II.p. 180ff).

פסי *

--- *p(3)-(n-3)s(.t)*  "He who belongs to Isis"
L p. 125; K p. 91; V II p. 220
[Aram] *LH* 4.10, 11; *TAÉ* 28.2; 87b.10; 86 [bis], 108; *Saqq* 47.4
[Eg] Ranke I.105.21 m. Late; [Gk] Παῆσις, Παήσιος, Παῆσ Πεῆσις, Πιήσιος, Πιῆσις, Φαήσιος, Φαήσις (*NB* p. 2:
[Copt] ПАНСЄ

Kornfeld considered פסי as a variation of פסא, which is not impossible, if the final א and י are vowel letters indicating the same value. However, judging from the fact that Isis sometimes appears as סי in composite names, like נפסי (*nfr-3s.t*), פטסי (*p3-di-3s.t*), *p3-n-3s.t* is more likely. Also it could be the short form of *p3-n-3s-ir* (Ranke I.107.5 m. Dyn 21–Gk), *pa-si* (*DemNB* I.412). For *pa-si* as a variant of *p3-di-3s-ir* or *p3-n-3s-ir*, see de Meulenaere, *CdE* 38 p. 215. See also the discussion of פסא.

פסמי *

--- Short form of פסמשך
L p. 125; G p. 487; K p. 91
[Aram] *LH* 1.14, 2.4, 18, 3.1, 14, 4.13; *BP* 1.13; *NEph* II,75, recto.5; Porten, *Or* NS 57 p. 26
[Eg] see פסמשך; [Gk] Ψαμις, Ψσμες, Ψαμμις (*NB* p. 481; *OAP* p. 343b)

That פסמ is a short form of פסמשך is supported by the following PN פסמסנית, that is, פסמ(שך)-*s3-ny.t*. The addition of the hypocoristic morpheme י is common (*e.g.*, וחפי, פוסי) see *LH* p. 381. Spiegelberg (S II. p. 7) said that the king's name has been shortened to *Psam-*, which is attested in Gk form, though not attested in Eg.

פסמסנית **

--- *psm(ṯk)-s(3)-n.t* 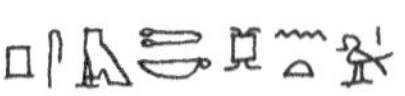 "Psammetich, son of Neith"
S II p. 7; L p.125; G p. 487; K p. 91; V II p. 220

[Aram] *AP* 26.1 [פסמסנית], 7
[Eg] cf. Ranke I.136.21; II, p.136; *DemNB* I.214 (*p3-s-n-mṯk-s3-ny.t*); [Ph] פסמסנית
Cf. פסמי (short form of *psmṯk*)

Grelot, followed by Kornfeld, prefers **p3-s3-n-s-ny.t* "the son of man of Neith." Yet the reduction *n* > *m* is left unexplained. Though there are certain cases where *n* became *m* in Copt, this adjectival *n* has been elided, showing no reflection in Aram, while the short form of *psmṯk* is preserved in Gk forms (see פסמי). Therefore, *psmṯk-s3-n.t* is more probable.

פסמשך **
--- *psmṯk*  (Libyan)
S I p. 1106; L p. 125; G p. 487; K p. 91
[Aram] *CIS* II.154.8 פומס (corrected to פסמשך by Aimé-Giron, *BIFAO* 38 p. 37); *AP* p. 317A.4 פסמשך֯, 74.2; *TAÉ* 2.1; *AD* 1.2 [פ]סמשך, 2.2 [פס]מ֯שך, 4 פסמ֯שך, 3.2* פסמש[ך], 1 [פס]מ֯שך, 3 פ֯ס֯[משך], 4, 7, 4.2* פ֯ס֯מ֯ש֯[ך], 1, 2, 3 פסמש֯[ך], 12.2 פ֯ס֯[מש]ך֯, 4; *AD* Fragment 1A.6, 3.6, 10.9; *Saqq* 28b.9, 45a. 2, 53.11; graffito:N.Aimé-Giron, *AE* 23 p. 41
[Eg] Ranke I.136.8 m. Late–Gk; *DemNB* I.212; [Gk] Ψαμμητιος, Ψαμματιχος (*NB* p. 481) [Akk] *pi-ša-me-el-ki, pu-sa-mis-ki, pi-ša-mi-iš-ši-k!, pi-sa-mi-is-ki* (see E. Edel, "Neue Deutungen" p. 36f)

The meaning of the name is *p3-s-(n-)mṯk* "the man of mixed drink." The *mṯk* stands for Copt ⲘⲞⲨϪϬ "be mixed." Cf. Heb מָסַךְ "mix", מֶסֶךְ "mixture" (Černý p. 101).

פסמשכמר **
--- *psmṯk-mr(y)*  "Psammetich, the beloved (of X)"
[Aram] *Saqq* 21.1 פסמשנמר (corrected here), 2 פסמשכ֯מ֯ר֯
[Eg] cf. *psmṯk-mry-ptḥ, psmṯk-mry-nt* (Ranke I.136.17–18 m. Late).
Hence פסמשכמר is a short form of *psmṯk-mry*-DN.

פסמשכחסי **
--- **psmṯk-ḥsy* "Psammetich is favoured"
G p. 487, K p. 92
[Aram] *AD* 3.3, 6 [פ]סמ[שכ]חסי
[Eg] For *ḥsy*, cf. *rᶜ-ms-sw-ḥst* "Ramesses is favoured," (Ranke

I.219.5) and *p3-ḥsy* (Ranke I.116.2).

פסמשכמ[חי]

--- *psmṯk-m-(3)ḫ(.t)*  "Psammetich is on the horizon"
L p. 125; K p. 92
[Aram] *TAÉ* 34.4
[Eg] Ranke I.136.11 m. Late; II p. 358; *DemNB* I.213

It was N. Aimé-Giron who reconstructed the final element חי (*3ḫ.t*). Yet פסמשכמר is equally possible. Only the first element פסמשך can be used for later analysis.

פסרי **

--- *p(3)-(n-3)s-(i)r* 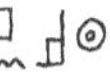 "He who belongs to Osiris"
[Aram] Metal bowl: Rabinowitz, *JNES* 18 p. 154f
[Eg] Ranke I.107.5 m. Dyn 21–Gk; *DemNB* I.360 (*pa-3sir*); [Gk] Παϋσεῖρις, Παϋσιρεις, Παϋσῖριος, Παϋσῖρις (*NB* p. 293, *DemNB* I.360).

פסתוקנס

--- **p(3)-sṯ(3)w-ḳns* "He who averts violence"
[Aram] *Saqq* 157.1
[Eg] cf. *sṯ3-it.t-bn.t* "Averts the Evil eye" (Ranke I.323.1), *sṯ3-t3-wt.t* "Averts the Thunderbolt" (Ranke I.323.5)

Segal noted that this reconstructed name is possibly a mythological reference to Thoth or Horus. Yet the element *ḳns* (*gns*! *Wb* IV.177.5–6) is never attested in PNs. *Gns* became ˢϭⲟⲛ̄ⲥ, ᵇϫⲟⲛ̄ⲥ in Copt (Černy; p. 332), which is always represented by טנס or צנס in Aram. Therefore the correspondence is also dubious.

פע̇נ̇ן̇

--- **p(3)-ʿn-n(.i)* "The beautiful one belongs to me"
[Aram] *Saqq* 69b.4
[Eg] cf. *p3-ʿn* "the beautiful one" (Ranke I.102.23 m. NK).

Notice the reading is quite uncertain.

פעצ[ב]

--- *p(3)-ʿ(3)-ṯb*  "The great of sandal"
K p. 92; V 11 p. 220

[Aram] *Saqq* 38.19]פעצ
[Eg] Ranke I.102.18 m. Late; cf. *p3-ʿḏb* (Ranke I.102.19)

Kornfeld corrected פעצב (*AP* 74.2) to פעצב, yet נ is much more likely. It is more probable that the second letter is ט rather than ע (cf. *CIS* II.148.2 נטצב).

פפא

--- *pp.i, ppy*
[Aram] *Saqq* 61b.1 (corrected to פפא by Porten B8.4:19).
[Eg] Ranke I.131.12 m./f. OK–NK; I.131.18 m./f. MK–NK (this name is extremely common since OK).

פפטעונית **

--- *p(3).f-ṯ(3w)-(m-)ʿ.w(y)-(n-)ny.t*  "His breath is in the hand of Keith"
S I p. 1112; L p. 125; K p. 92
[Aram] *AP* 2.2 [פפטעונית], 5.13, 6.10; 8.7
[Eg] Ranke I.128.2

The unique correspondence between Aram ט and Eg *ṯ* could be resolved through the Copt forms of *ṯ3w*, [S]ΤΗΥ, [B]ΘΗΟΥ, because Aram ט is always equated with Eg *d* > Copt Τ. The change ת > ט takes place between a labial and laryngeal, see the later discussion: [4] Notes on the Correspondences e) alveolars.

פפני

--- *p(3)-(n-)pn(w)*  "He who belongs to the mouse"
[Aram] *Saqq* 64b.13
[Eg] Ranke I.108.1 m. Dyn26; cf. I.133.6; [Gk] πιπιν (*NB* p. 343); [Ph] פפן

The reading, though the text is clear, is doubtful. It seem that the first and the second letters are not identical. I would rather read it as פחי, representing *p3-n-ḥ(w).t* (Ranke I.110.3 m. NK) see Aram פחי.

פקטנותי *

--- **p(3)-ḳd-nṯ(r)* "The builder of god"
Zauzich, *Enchoria* 13 p. 117
[Aram] *Saqq* 11.3
[Eg] cf. *p3-ḳd(w)*  "The builder" (Ranke I.120.2 m.

NK), *ptḥ-p3-ḳd* (II.287.13), *ỉmn-qd* (I.31.6; II.341).

P3-k3-tn-(n)wt(.t) "the high and exalted of birth" was proposed by Segal. Yet the representation of *t* by ט is questionable.

פקנותי

--- **p(3)-(n-)-k(3)-nṯ(r)* "He who belongs to the ka of god"

[Aram] *Saqq* 94.1

[Eg] cf. *p3-n-k3-ḥ.t-nṯr* (Ranke I.111.11 m. Late)

Another reconstruction **p3-ḳn-wḏ3* is proposed by Segal. Yet Eg *wḏ3* occurs as וט or וץ in Aram. The reading פקנותי is not likely. More likely is פינותי (*p3-n-nṯr* "the servant of god" or **p3.ỉ-nṯr* "my god" cf. Ranke I.126.24ff).

פקרקפתח

--- see GN פקרקפתח

פרו

--- *p(3)-(n-)rw*  "He who belongs to the lion"

[Aram] *Saqq* 57.7

[Eg] Ranke I.109.14 m. NK; [Gk] Παρου, Παρουα, παρους (*NB* p. 280)

The inscriptions on the papyrus are too faded to read with certainty. What is more, there is no indication from the context that this is a PN.

פרט

--- **p3-n-r(w)ḏ* "He who belongs to the strong one" (?)

[Aram] *Saqq* 28a. 6. 9 רט (corrected to פרט by Porten B8.4:18)

[Eg] cf. Ranke I.361.14 *t3-n.t-rwḏ* f. Late–Gk; 364.19 *t3-rwḏ.t(?)* f. NK; 365.9 *t3-rd(.t?)* f. Late–Gk

Cf. פתירות (*p3-ṯ3w-rwḏ.w*)and Ug *rt* .

פרמתי

--- see month name פרמתי

K p. 92; V II p. 220.

פרשנף

--- see ורשנף

K p. 92; V II p. 220.

פשובסתי **

--- *p(s)š-b(3)st(.t)* "Bastet divided"

G p. 485; K p. 92

[Aram] *AD* 3.4

[Eg] Ranke I.137.5, 6; II.208.2

Equally possible is *p3-šri-n-b3st.t* "the son of Bastet" (Rake I.118.15 m. Dyn 22–Gk; II.282.12 (see de Meulenaere, *RdE* 11 p. 79f.), if the *n* between *sri* and *b3st.t* was assimilated into a semi-vowel ו. However, the Gk forms Ψεοβαστις, Ψανουβαστις, Ψενοβασθις, Ψενουβαστεις (*NB* p. 481, 487f) do not lose the Therefore it seems more likely פשובסתי is identical with *psš-b3st.t*, because Eg Aram does not have n-assimilation (see Leander p. 13).

[פ]שמון

--- *p(s)š-(i)mn* "Amun divided"

[Aram] *Saqq* 129.1

[Eg] see פשובסתי

Again *p3-sri-n-imn* 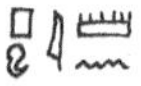 "the son of Amun" (Ranke I.118.8 m. Gk) is equally possible; cf. Gk Ψεναμουνις.

פשנפור **

--- *p(3)-š(ri)-n-p(3)-wr*  "The son of the great god"

G p. 487; K p. 92; cf. Spiegelberg, followed by Lambdin, put פשנך (S II p. 7; L p. 125)

[Aram] *APO* 75.2, 7

[Eg] Ranke I.118.16 m. Gk; II p. 355; *DemNB* I.234; [Gk] Ψενποῆρις, Πενπουῆρις, Ψενπουῆρ (*NB* p. 488)

Notice Eg *n* which is reflected in the Aram form, as well as the Gk form, while the Ph never shows it. This phenomenon may be connected with the fact that the assimilation in Eg Aram is uncommon (Leander section 3 m). For the loss of the Eg genitive *n*, see Černý, *LEG*. p. 5. The *n* may be protected by a labial *p*. Notice that *p3-šri-n-*type is represented by (1) - פש, (2) - פשר, (3) - פשנ, yet is never fully written like -פשרנ.

פשנפמוי **

--- *p(3)-š(ri)-n-p(3)-m(3)i* "The son of the Lion"

S II p. 8; L p. 125; G p. 487; K p. 93

[Aram] *APO* 75,2.8

[Eg] *DemNB* I.235 (*p3-šri-p3-m3y*); Ranks II.283.7 m. Late; [Gk] Ψενπμουις.

פשנפתח **

--- *p(3)-š(ri)-n-ptḥ*  "The son of Ptah"

K p. 93

[Aram] Sznycer, in *Hommages à André Dupont-Sommer*, p. 186.6

[Eg] Ranke I.118.18 m. Late; *DemNB* I.244 (*p3-šr-ptḥ*); [Gk] Ψενφθα, Ψενπταις (*NB* p. 485, 488).

פשנתסף

--- **p(3)-š(ri)-n-t(3)-sp(.t)* "The child of the nome"

V II p. 225

[Aram] *Saqq* 8.15

[Eg] cf. Rake I.117.2 (*p3-sp.t*)

The last פ is not visible. Vittmann, followed by Porten, reconstructed it as פשנתס[ו], which he interpreted as *p3-šr(i)-n-t(3)-(i)sw* (*DemNB* I.263). Yet it remains questionable due to the uncertain text.

פשתות *

--- **p(3)-šd-w(3)ḏ(y.t)* "He whom Uto has saved"

Zauzich, *Enchoria* 13 p. 117

[Aram] *Saqq* 54.5

[Eg] cf. Ranke I.119.15 m. Late *p3-šd-b3st.t*;

Though it is a reconstruction, the *p3-šd*-DN type of names is well attested. The equation of שת with *šd* is supported by the fact the *šd* became ϢΙΤЄ; Ϣ Ιϯ.

פת

--- *p(3)-(n-)t(3)* "He who belongs to the land"

[Aram] Bordreuil, *Catalogue des Sceaux*, p. 105 no. 137

[Eg] Ranke I.112.3; [Ph] cf. פתא; [Aram] פתא

Bordreuil considers the name to be Iranian, composed of פת

"protected" (see Ph פתא). Yet an Eg name is equally possible.

פתא

--- *p(3)-(n-)t3* 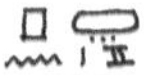 "He who belongs to the land"
[Aram] *Saqq* 6.1 פתא, 54.14 פתא
[Eg] see Ph פתא and Aram פת.

פתו **

--- *p(3)-(n-)t(3.)w(y)* 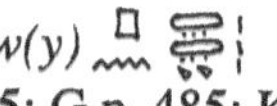 "He who belongs to the two lands"
S II p. 8; L p. 125; G p. 485; K p. 93; V II p. 220
[Aram] *APO* 75,2.1, 4, 5, 7, 10; *AP* 81.103 פתו, 106, 113, 114; *BP* 12.3, 33; *Saqq* 105.3
[Eg] Ranke I.112.4; 11 p. 354; Ranke I.253,13; *DemNB* I.420; [Gk] Πατοῦς, Πετους, Πτους (*NB* p. 290, 320, 350); [NA] cf. *pat-tu-ú* (Zadok, *GM* 26 p. 64).

P3-ṯ3w "the wind" (Spiegelberg) is less likely because Copt "wind" is [s]ⲦⲎⲨ, [b]ⲐⲎⲞⲨ.

פתום **

--- *p(3)-(n-)(i)tm* 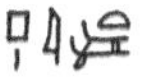 "He who belongs to Atum"
L p. 126
[Aram] *AP* 68 no 3.5
[Eg] *DemNB* I.355; cf. feminine form *t3-(n.t-)itm* (Ranke I.358.19 f. Late); [Gk] Παθυμις, Πατουμις, Πατυμις, Πατω (*DemNB* I.355, *NB* p. 289, 292); [Copt] ⲠⲀⲐⲀⲘ

Copt form of Eg god *itm* is ⲐⲰⲘ, ⲦⲰⲘ, rather than ⲐⲀⲘ, *e.g.*, [b]ⲠⲈⲐⲰⲘ, [a]ⲠⲈⲒⲐⲰⲘ (*pr-itm* "Pithom"), ϢⲈⲚⲈⲦⲰⲘ. The ו of פתום is a *mater lectionis*.

פתופעסת

--- **p(3)-t(3).w(y)-p(3)-ˁ(3)-st(y)*
K p. 93; V II p. 220
[Aram] *APO* 75,2.2
[Eg] see פתו. For פעסת cf. *ˁ3-sty* "Seth is great" (Ranke I.416.22 m. NK)

Perhaps two names are combined. Identification is very difficult. Kornfeld considers פעסת as a dialectic form of *B3st.t*, which Vittamnn supports by considering it as a wayward spelling. Yet there is no certain evidence. Another possibility is *p3-(n-)t3.wy-p3-n-ʿst(r.t)*, for Astart as *ʿst*, see Ranke II.284.15f.. Vittmann accepted the correspondence between Eg *d* and Aram ת, saying that it is an old prejudice that Eg *d* only correspond to Aram ט. Then he not only identified פתופעסת with *p3-di-b3st.t* but also identified the פת + DN type name as a *p3-di* type name such as פתחונס (*p3-di-ḫnsw*), פתחור (*p3-di-ḥr*) etc.. However, as shown later, it is not necessary to accept this correspondence (see also the discussion in פתחונס, for the case ת > ט between a labial and ח).

פתחוא **

--- *ptḥ-(m-)wi(3)* 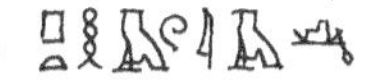 "Ptah is in the bark"

K p. 93; V II p. 221

[Aram] Sznycer, in *Hommages à André Dupont-Sommer* p. 186 פתחרא (corrected to פתחוא by Porten, *Semitica* 33 p. 94f)

[Eg] Ranke I.139.18 m. NK (many); Ranke noted that the name was also written without *m*.

Vittmann suggested a reading פתחפא and identified it as *p3-di-ḥp*. However, the fourth letter is most likely to be ו, as Porten noted. Phonetically ת = Eg *d* is not acceptable (see above), also Eg *ḥp* "Apis" is always realized as חפי in Aram, not חפא.

[-]פתחונס

--- *pt(ḥ)-ḫns(.w)* "Ptah is Khons"

K p. 93; V p. 220

[Aram] *AD* Frag IB.1 (corrected to [-]פתחונס by Porten in his letter)

[Eg] Ranke I.141.10 m. MK (the same type of name occure until NK: *ptḥ-sbk* Ranke I.141.14)

The name *ptḥ-ḫns*.w, proposed by Kornfeld, is based on the assumption that in Eg two different *hs* (*ḥ* & *ḫ*) were merged, which is not unconceivable. Considering that the name has another letter at the initial (Porten), Kornfeld's proposal may be the most likely, because the God Ptah can be either פתח or אפתח (hence [א]פתחונס) (see DN אפתח), while *p3-di-ḫns.w* as supported by Vittmann is impossible because of the representation of *d* by ת. Since the first letter is unknown, the identification cannot be sure. If it is an Eg article, *p3-n-pt(r)-ḫns* is also possible. cf. *t3-n.t-ptr-imn* "She who belongs to *ptr-imn*" (Ranke I.430.20, II.405 f. Dyn 22).

פתחור **

--- *ptḥ-wr*  "Ptah is great"

S III p. 347; L p. 126; G p. 488; K p. 93; V II p. 220

[Aram] *APO* 75,2.11

[Eg] Ranke I.139.6 m. OK–Late

Vittmann preferred *p3-di-ḥr*, because this Eg name frequently occurs and is much more common in the Late Period. However, since the correspondence between Eg *d* and Aram ת has not been confirmed and the name *ptḥ-wr* is attested, there is no need to suppose a new correspondence here.

פתחנופי **

--- *ptḥ-nf(r)*  "Ptah is good"

[Aram] *Saqq* 4.2, 3 פתחנופי

[Eg] Ranke I.140.14 m./f. MK–Late.

[פת]חׄנסׄ

--- Var. of פתחונס

V II p. 221.

[Aram] *AD* Frag III,15

[Eg] see פתחונס.

פתחקׄי

--- **ptḥ-k̟(3)i͗* "Ptah is exalted"

[Aram] *Saqq* 87.4 (cf. Porten's reading תחק[-] C3.23:4).

[Eg] cf. DN + *k̟3i͗* type name: *k̟3i͗-ptḥ* (Rake II.319.28 m. OK), *k̟3i͗-i͗mn* (Ranke I.332.6 m. Dyn 22), *k̟3i͗-i͗n-ḥr.t* (Ranke I.332.7 m. Late)

The reading is quite uncertain. Especially the final י is hopelessly faded.

פתחרא

--- see פתחוא

K p. 93; V II p. 221.

פתחרות

--- see פתירות

K p. 93; V II p. 221.

פתי

--- *p(3)-ṯ(3w)*  "The wind"

--- *p(3)-(n-)ṯ(3w)* "He who belongs to the wind"

K p. 93; V. II p. 221

[Aram] *CIS* II.116.1

[Eg] Ranke I.121.7 m. NK; cf. *p3-ṯ3w* (Ranke I.419.29 m. Late)

Cf. פתו (*p3-n-ṯ3.wy*)

The identification *p3-ṯ3w* is much more likey than *p3-ṯ3y* (Kornfeld) on the basis of Copt forms of *ṯ3y* and *ṯ3w* : [s]ΤΗΥ, [b]ΘΗΟΥ for *ṯ3w*. The former is rendered in Aram טו / תו. Notice the Semitic root פתי adj. "simple", פתה verb "be simple."

פתירות **

--- **p(3)-ṯ(3w)-rwḏ(.w)* "The strong wind"

K p.9 3; V II p. 221

[Aram] *AP* 69.10; *Saqq* 74.4 פתיר]

[Eg] see פתי; cf. *p3-ṯ3w-nḫt.w* "The wind is strong" (Ranke I.420.1).

פתמעי **

--- **p(3)-(n-)t(3)-m(3)ʿ(.t)* "He who belongs to the Truth"

[Aram] *Saqq* 38.8

[Eg] cf. *p3-n-m3ʿ.t* 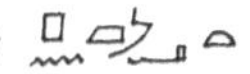 "He who belongs to Truth" (Ranke I.108.3 m. Late-Gk). *M3ʿ.t* is used with the feminine article in Ranke II.325.27 *t3-(n.t-)m3ʿ.t*.

פתמרו **

--- **p(3)-(n-)t(3)-mrw(.t)* "He who belongs to the beloved"

[Aram] *Saqq* 63.2

[Eg] cf. *p3-n-mrw* 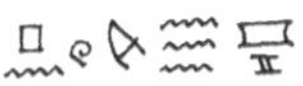 (Ranke I.108.13 m. NK). The feminine occurs in Ranke II.28.16 *p3-n-mrw.t* (m. NK).

פתנוטא *

--- **p(3)-(n-)ṯn(i)-wḏ3(.w)* "The Thinite is prosperous"

[Aram] *Saqq* 111.2

[Eg] cf. *p3-n-ṯni*  "The Thinite"; [Gk] πατινις; [Copt] ΠΑΤΙΝΕ (Ranke I.112.8).

פתנק

--- **p(3)-ṯn(ỉ)-k(3)* "The exalted of ka"

[Aram] *Saqq* 8.1 (yet Porten, B5.6:1, reads it as ב/והפתח)

[Eg] cf. *wsr-ṯnỉ* (Ranke I.86.19), *ḏd.t-ṯnỉ* (Ranke I.403.20)

Segal's *p3-tnr-k3* "The strong of ka" is theoretically possible, yet note that *tnr* is probably a foreign word, being read as *tl* (Ranke I.120.26 *p3-tnr / p3-tl*). The Aram text is quite uncertain.

פתענח **

--- **p(3)-(n-)t(3)-ʿnḫ(.ỉ)* "He who belongs to my life"

G p. 488; K p. 93; V II p. 221

[Aram] *APO* 75,2.12

[Eg] cf. *t3-ʿnḫ.ỉ* (Ranke I.354.24)

Eg *ṯ* which became ϫ in Copt ([S]ⲉϫⲱ, [B]ⲉⲥⲟⲩ for *ṯ3y*) does n correspond to Aram ת. Therefore **p3-ṯ3y-ʿnḫ.w* "The child lives" (Grelot, Kornfeld) is unlikely. However, **p3-ṯ3w-ʿnḫ* "The breath of life" is not impossible, because *ṯ3w* is ⲧⲏⲩ in Copt, though an additional letter is usually expected to occur in Aram spellings, like תי (cf. Ranke I.121.7–10; see פתי). If we assume the contraction between Eg *ḥ* and *ʿ*, *ptḥ-ʿnḫ*.w is possible (Ranke I.138.20 m. OK–NK many).

פתפי

--- **p(3)-(n-)t(3)-(ỉ)p(w)* "He who belongs to *t3-ỉpw*"

G p. 488; K p. 93

[Aram] *AP*'81.102

[Eg] cf. *t3-(n.t-)ỉpw* "She who belongs to Ekhmim" (Ranke I.358.3 f. NK)

Cf. Grelot's *p3-tpy* "The headman." However *tpy* is not used in PNs.

פתר *

--- *p(3)-tr(ỉ)*  "The respected"

[Aram] *Saqq* 64b.14

[Eg] Ranke II.283.25 m. Dyn 20

The letters of the Aram text are unusual.

פ̊ת̊שׁת̊

--- *p(3)-(n-)t(3)-šd(.t)* "He who belongs to *t3-šd.t*"
[Aram] *Saqq* 66a. 5, 3
[Eg] cf. *t3-šd.t-ʿnḳ.t, t3-šd.t-mw.t, t3-šd.t-ḫns. w* (Ranke I.370.12-14 f. Late)

Text no. 66 of *Saqq* is too faded to allow a reliable reading.

פתת

--- *p(3)-t(w)t*  "The agreeable"
G p. 486; K p. 94
[Aram] *APO* 75,2.5
[Eg] Ranke I.121.11 m. Late; [Gk] Πατοτη (*NB* p. 289)

Two identifications have been proposed; (1) **p3-ṯt* (reconstructed through Copt ⲡϫⲁϫ "The sparrow" Ranke II.184), (2) *p3-ḏ3-ḏ3* "The head" (Ranke I.126.22; Copt ⲡϫⲱϫ). However, Copt ϫ corresponds to Aram צ, not ת. Instead Eg *ṯwt* became *twt* from MK (*Wb* V.360); cf. Ranke I.120.24 *p3-twtw* and *DemNB* I.344. The meaning of Eg *twt* is not clear. It seems that the two words *twt* were not distinguishable in appearance. Yet in Copt two different readings testify that there were differences in reading (1) ˢⲦⲰⲦ, ᵇⲐⲰⲦ "be agreeable" (2) ˢⲦⲞⲨⲰⲦ, ᵇⲐⲞⲨⲰⲦ "statue" (both are mixed in *CDME* p. 295). As the latter shows a consonant in the middle, we prefer the former.

צחא **

--- *ḏ(d)-ḥ(r)*  "The face speaks"
G p. 490f, K p. 94
[Aram] *AP* 15.2 [צחא], 18.4, 20.3, 20, 24.6, 32, 37.14 [א]צח̊, 38.4 צח̊א, 6 צח̊א, 41.1 [א]צח, 9 [צחא], 67.no. 17, 72.4, 76.1 צ̊ח̊א̊, 2, 3, 83.2, 22, 25, 30 צח̊א; *TAÉ* 5.8, 34.3 צחא, 35.1 צח̊א; *CIS* II.138B.1; *Saqq* 6.6, 8.2, 28a.5, 53.18 צחא̊], 19 צח], 52b.13 [א]צח̊, 132.3 צחא
Metal vessel: Rabinowitz, *JNES* 15 p. 2.B
[Eg] see Ph צחא

This frequently occurring name is to be identified with the well-attested Eg name *ḏd-ḥr* rather than Semitic צחא which is rarely attested.

צח

--- see צחא

[Aram] *Saqq* 53.19]צח (צחא occurs in the previous line).

צׄחׄנום **

--- **d(ḏ)-ḥ(r)-ẖnm(w)* "*ḏd-ḥr* Khnum"

[Aram] *AP* 53.5 נחנום[-] (corrected by Porten C4.8:5)

[Eg] cf. Ranke I.411.12 (m./f. Late–Gk, many) *ḏd-ḥr*; I.411.13–16 (m. Gk).

צחפמו

--- see Ph צחפמו (letters are Ph, language is Aram)

K p. 94.

צׄמׯחׯוׯ *

--- **ḏ(d)-mḥ(y.t)* "The North speaks"

V II p. 225

[Aram] *Saqq* 8.2 (Porten, B5.6:2, reads it as [-]חׯ[-]הנ)

[Eg] cf. *ḏd-mḥ.y-iw.s-ʿnḫ* (Ranke I.411.5), *ḏd-mḥy.t-iw.f-ʿnḫ* (Ranke II.334.16 m. Late); Since this long form is attested, the existence of *ḏd-mḥy.t* is beyond doubt; cf. *ḏd-3s.t: ḏd-3s.t-iw.s-ʿnḫ; ḏd-b3st.t: ḏd-b3st. iw.s-ʿnḫ; ḏd-mw.t: ḏd-mw.t-iw.s-ʿnḫ* etc. (Ranke I.409.1–412.9). For מחו = *mḥy.t*, see פחמחו and cf. EA *Pamaḫu (p3-n-mḥy.t)* see Chapter V.

Another possible identification is *ṯ3y-mḥ.t-im.w*. Eg *-im.w* is usually transcribed as מו in Aram. Yet a contraction מו > ו is reasonably assumed, because מ and ו are interchangable (cf. תמת > תות). Yet the Aram text is not clear enough to give a definite identificaion.

צׄנא

--- *ṯn, ṯni, ṯn3* 

[Aram] *Saqq* 47.2

[Eg] Ranke I.391.13–18 until NK

Segal compares the name with Eg *ṯnr / tnr* (Ranke I.381.18). However the *ṯ*, which became *t* (cf. ) is not comparable with Aram צ.

קמוחפי

--- *gm.w-ḥp* 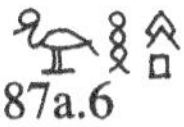 "They found the Apis"

[Aram] *TAÉ* 87a.6

[Eg] Ranke I.351.6 m. Late; [Gk] Κομοᾶπις (NB p. 180)

The reading is almost all reconstructions, making the identification impossible.

קנחנתי

--- see Lw קנחנתי

L p. 126; K p. 94; V II p. 221

[Aram] *BP* 9.9; 10.5; (Vittmann and Porten deny that this is a PN.)

קנפי

--- Var. of כנופי

[Aram] *Saqq* 17.1

[Eg] see כנופי

Segal considered קנפי as a variant of כנופי on the basis of the assumption that ק is interchangable with כ (*Saqq* p. 12). As for the examples of PN which are quoted as evidence, their readings are not clear enough to prove it: קנפי and קנפ]. Aram קנ can stand for a very common element of Eg PN, *ḳn*. Therefore, the other possiblities **ḳn-p.t* "The sky is strong", **ḳn-ip.t* "*ip.t* is strong" etc. may not be excluded (cf. Ranke I.334.17ff).

רחמרע

--- see וחפרע

[Aram] *AP* 5.19 רחמרע (corrected to וחפרע by Porten B2.1:19, cf. *CIS* II.154.7).

רט

--- see פרט

[-]רנף

--- *rnp(.w)* or *-rn.f*

[Aram] *Saqq* 8.5 (Porten B5.6:5)

[Eg] cf. Ranke I.237.16 *ḥr-rnp(.w)*: I.197.18 *nfr-rnp.t,* or Ranke I.91.11f *b3k-(n-)rn.*

The name element רנף can only be explained by Eg *rnpy*

"young" or *rn.f* "his name", both of which were used as a name element until the Late period. Since the name is incomplete due to the broken document, the name identification is impossible.

רנפנפרי **

--- *rnp(.t)-nfr(.t)* 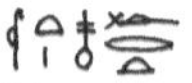 "Beautiful year"
K p. 94; V II p. 221
[Aram] *BP* 1.12 דנונרי (corrected by Porten B3.2:12; *Aram. Texts* p. 36)
[Eg] Ranke I.224.11 m. OK / f. OK–Gk esp. common in Late

Kornfeld's interpretation *rn.f-nfr* "His name is beautiful" (Ranke I.223.15) does not explain the final רי-, because the masculine singular form of Eg *nfr* always occurs without the final *r* in Aram, *e.g.* נפ / נפי, Copt ^{s}ⲚⲞⲨϤⲈ, ^{b}ⲚⲞⲨϤⲈ. Yet the feminine form preserves the final *r* with the protection of the feminine ending *t*.

רעיא *

--- *r*ʿ*.i3* 
[Aram] *AP* 22.86
[Eg] Ranke I.220.7 m./f. NK; [EA] cf. *Peya, Pieya*
Cf. רעיה (possibly a variant)

Kornfeld considered it as a Semitic name, arguing there is a Semitic root רעי (*DISO* p. 201), to which the Aram determinative was added, meaning "The companion." However, this name is not attested. In the Palmyrene inscriptions רעא, which Stark regards as a hypocoristicon without DN, occurs. Hence this could be a hypocoristicon רע(ו)יה.

רעויה

--- *r*ʿ*-(m-)wi(3)*  "Reʿ is in the sacred bark"
K p. 71
[Aram] *AP* 8.33, 9.21, 22.118, 23.10
[Eg] Ranke I.217.15 m. NK

Equally possible is a Semitic solution. The final יה can be a theophoric element. cf. *rəʿûʾēl* (Ex 2:18 etc.), likewise רעויה "YH is friend."

רעיה

--- $r^{c}.i(y)$

K p. 71

[Aram] *LH* 1.1, 2.16, 3.3; *AP* 34.3 רעיה (corrected here)

[Eg] Ranke I.220.8, 9 m./f. NK (the name occurred in the Late Period, K. A. Kitchen, *TIP* § 126); [Akk] *rēʾû* (Borger, *JNES* 19 p. 53); [Gk] cf. Ῥεᾶς.

Cf. רעיא

A Semitic explanation, which we considered in the entry of רעויה, is possible.

שד/רנהיב

--- see שרנהיב

שחפימו **

--- *ṯ(3y)-ḥp-im.w*  "Apis can seize them"

S I p. 1106; S II p. 9; L p. 126; K p. 94

[Aram] *AP* 73.10, 13

[Eg] see Ph צחפמו

It is remarkable that the spelling of this name differs between Aram and Ph. The possible explanations are (1) dialectical (^{s}ϫⲓ; ^{b}ϭⲓ for Eg *ṯ3y*) or (2) the different phonetic value between Ph צ and Aram ש. As for the former, we should remember that both שחפימוis and צחפמו occur in Eephantine in the fifth century. We also have Ph צכנסמו (*ṯ3y-ẖns.w-im.w*). Therefore, the latter explanation is more acceptable.

שחפמו **

--- Var. of שחפימו

K p. 94

[Aram] *CIS* II 138A.5 שחומו (corrected to שחפמו by Degen, *NEph* 196 I, p. 27)

[Eg] see שהפימו.

שמו **

--- *ṯ(3y)-(i)m.w*

S II p. 9; G p. 492; K p. 94

[Aram] *AP* 26.8, 21; *Saqq* 28a.1, 61b.3 שׁמו

[Eg] see Pu שמו.

שמחר (hybrid) **

--- שמ-*ḥr* "The name of Horus"
[Aram] Sayce, *PSBA* 30 p. 28f no. 5
[Eg] see חר.

שׁנוט]

--- **š(ri)-n-w(3)ḏ(.t)* "Son of Uto"
K p. 94
[Aram] *AP* 73.10 (cf. *CIS* II. 147B.10 חׄרוט, Porten's reading חׄ--ט C3.19:10)
[Eg] cf. *t3-(n.t-)w3ḏy.t*  "She of Uto junior" (Ranke I.359.4 f. Late).*šri.t-n.t-3s.t* "Daughter of Isis" (Ranke II.319.6 f. Late); [Gk] cf. Σενοῦθ, Σενοῦθε, Σενούθης (*NB* p. 373)

וט perhaps corresponds to *w3ḏy.t* "Uto", so **šri.t-n-w3ḏy.t* "Daughter of Uto" is theoretically possible.

שפנית **

--- **šp-(n-)ny.t* "Gift of Neith"
G p. 493; K p. 95; V II p. 221
[Aram] *LH* 7.3
[Eg] cf. the *šp-n*-DN type of PNs: *šp-n-3s.t* 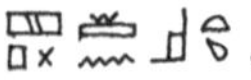, *šp-n-b3st.t* etc. (Ranke I.325.17ff f. Late-Gk); *t3-n.t-šp-n-nt* (Ranke I.363.4 f. Late).

שפתׄם

--- **šp-(n-i)tm* "The gift of Atum"
[Aram] *Saqq* 29.4
[Eg] cf. *šp-n*-DN type (see שפנית); [Gk] cf. Σεπτουμις (*NB* p. 379).

For תם for *itm*, see פטתום, פתום. Yet the reading is uncertain.

שׁרׄנהיב **

--- **šr(i.t)-(n-)n(3-)hb(.w)* "The daughter of the Ibises"
[Aram] *Saqq* 6.4 שר/דנהיב (Porten's reding שׁדׄנהיב)
[Eg] cf. *t3-šri.t (-n.t-n3?-)hb(.w)*  "The daughter of the Ibises" (Ranke I.369.5 f. Late), *t3-n.t-n3-hb.w*

(Ranke I.360.20 f. Late).

The *(p3)-šri-n*-type is represented either by (פ)ש or (פ)שנ, yet never fully transliterated as (פ)שרנ. Though the ר in this name could be protected by the feminine ending, it seems that in Aamaic both ר and נ were not retained at the same time. Therefore, **šrỉ-n-hb.w* is impossible. However the נ can be explained differently, *i.e.*, Ibis is often written with the Eg *n3*, like *p3-dỉ-n3-hb.w* (Ranke I.124.3), *t3-(n.t-)n3-hb.w* (Ranke I.360.20), *t3-n-n3-hb.w* (Ranke I.386.30). So the נ of נהיב is not the Eg genitive but the plural article. Notice that the reading שדנהיב (**šd-n3-hb.w* "The Ibises rescue" cf. *šd-ptḥ* (Ranke I.330.22 m. OK–NK; *šd-ḥr* Ranke I.331.1 m. Dyn 21 etc.) is also possible. However the equation of Eg *d* with Aram ד is not usual. Therefore, I prefer to read it as שרנהיב.

תֿאיס

--- *t(3)-(n.t-)(3)s(.t)*  "She who belongs to Isis"

[Aram] *Saqq* 54.13

[Eg] Ranke I.357.20 f. NK–Gk; [Gk] Ταησις (*NB* p. 405) cf. Copt *3s.t* is ^{s}HCE, ^{b}HCI

If the reading is correct, is it certainly an Eg name.

* תבא

--- **t(3)-(n.t-)b3(.w)* "She who belongs to the souls / might (?)"

S I p. 1107; L p. 127; G p. 493; K p. 95; V II p. 221

[Aram] *APO* 75,col.ii.3; *AP* 28.4, 5, 12, 73.8, 81.11 תבֿא; *TAÉ* 78.3; *CIS* II.141.1; *Saqq* 3.6 תבאֿ, 61b.1 תבֿאֿ

[Eg] cf. *p3-(n-)b3.w* 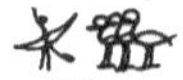 (Ranke I.107.7 m. Dyn 25)

[Gk] Ταβᾶς , Τεβᾶς (*NB* p. 425, *OAP* p. 304b)

A few other possibilities, though less likely, are *t3-bỉ* (Ranke I.356.9, Lambdin and Vittmann) and *t3-bỉ3* (Ranke I.356.II, Spiegelberg), **t3-(n.t-)b3* (cf. *t3-n.t-b3-ʿnḫ(.t)* Ranke II.325.17, Grelot and Kornfeld).

תבה

--- Var. of תבא

[Aram] *Saqq* 43b,ii.3

[Eg] see תבא.

תבי

--- *t(3)-bi* 

L p. 127; G p. 493; K p. 95; V II p. 222

[Aram] *TAÉ* 87a. 11; *LH* 2.5, 7, 5.1, 6.1

[Eg] Ranke I.356.9 f. Gk; [Gk] Ταβῆς, Θαβῆς, Τεβῆς, Ταβι, Ταβει (*NB* p. 404).

The meaning of *bi* is uncertain; it may represent *b3* "soul": *b3* "soul" > Demot *by* > Copt ⲂⲀⲒ (Černý p.20).

תהרקא **

--- *thrk* 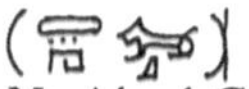

[Aram] N. Aimé-Giron, *AE* 23 p. 38–43 (*Sheikh Fadl* 5.5, 6a, 6b, 8.6, 11.11)

[Egl Gauthier, *LR* IV, 23f. (Eg king Dyn 25); [Heb] תרהקה (notice a metathesis of ה and ר; see K. A. Kitchen, *TIP* § 421 n.136)

[NA] *Tarqû* ; [Gk] Θαρακα (LXX).

תוא

--- **t(3)-(n.t-)wi(3)* "She who belongs to the boat"

S II p. 10; L p. 127; K p. 125; V II p. 224

[Aram] *APO* 75,2.4

[Eg] cf. *p3-wi3*  "(He who belongs to) the boat" (Ranke I.103.20) f./m. NK–Late

Cf. תויא

Equally possible is **t3-w3.t* "The way" (Ranke I.355.5 f. NK–Gk). If תוא is the same as תויא, as Spiegelberg considered, **t3-wi3* is perhaps a better identification. If the final *aleph* is *mater lectionis*, *t3-w3* (Ranke I.376.16 f. NK) is also possible. Yet as Eg *wi3* is usually realized as Aram וא, *t3-n.t-wi3* is most likely (see פתחוא etc.).

תובא *

--- *t(3)-(n.t-)wb3* "She who belongs to the open court"

L p. 127; K p. 95

[Aram] *TAÉ* 87a. 12

[Eg] cf. *t3-n.t-p3-wb3* "She who belongs to the open court" (Ranke I.359.18 f. Dyn 20)

Another possible solution is **t3w.b3* "their ba," *t3-bi* and *twbi*

(m. MK) are not closely comparable.

תוי

--- Var. of תוא or תויא
K p. 125; V II p. 224
[Aram] *TAÉ* 92.

תויא *

--- **twi3* (meaning unknown; could be *t3-wi3* "She who belongs to a boat")
S II p. 10; L p. 127; G p. 494; K p. 125
[Aram] *AP* 63.2; *BP* 12.20
[Eg] Ranke I.379.6 m./f. NK (esp. feminine form is common)
[Gk] cf. Θαΰῆς, Θαΰΐς, Ταΰῆς, Τεΰῆς, Θαΰϊς (*NB* p. 129f)
Cf. תוא.

תורא *

--- *t(3)-wr(.t)* "The great lady"
[Aram] *TAÉ* 87a.12]תורא
[Eg] Ranke I.355.13 f. NK–Late.

תות

--- misreading of תמת
K p. 95
[Aram] *BP* 4.25

תחא **

--- *t(3)-ḥ(r)* 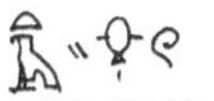 "The face"
L p. 127; K p. 95; V II p .222
[Aram] *TAÉ* 87a.8; *BP* 8.3; *Saqq* 61b.2
[Eg] Ranke I.366.1 f. Gk; [Gk] Ταῶς, Θαῶς, Τεῶς, Θεῶς (*NB* p. 424, 433); cf. Copt ϩⲟ for Eg *ḥr*

Another possibility is *t3-n.t-ḥ(w.t)* "She who belongs to the temple" (Ranke I.361. 22 f. Gk); cf. Copt ϩⲱ for Eg *ḥw.t* (Crum 651b). See the discussion in פחו.

תחבס *

--- *t(3)-ḫ(3)bs*  "The starry sky" or "She who belongs to the star"
S I p. 1107; L p. 127; K p. 95
[Aram] *CIS* II 142; *Saqq* 28a.4
[Eg] Ranke I.366.14 f. Late.

תׄחׄהׄ

--- **t(3)-(n.t-)ḥ(3.t)* "She who belongs to one who is in front"
[Aram] *Saqq* 4.3
[Eg] cf. *p(3)-n(-)ḥ(3.t)* (Ranke I.109.25); see the discussion in פחו).

תחוא

--- a short form of *t3-n.t-ḥw.t*
L p. 127; G p. 493; K p. 95; V II p. 222
Aram] *BP* 8.3
[Eg] see Aram תחא and פחו

The alternative of תחא or תחוא depends upon the interpretation of the ו between ח and א. If we admit that the ו is a consonant, this name is the same as Ph תחוא, the identification of which is not clear. If we understand, however, the ו as a *mater lectionis*, the name is either a variant of תחא (*t3-ḥr*), and in that case we must admit that the final *aleph* functions as a consonant to close the final syllable, or a shortened form of which the first element is *t3-n-ḥw.t*, such as *t3-n.t-ḥw.t-ʿ3.t* etc. See the discussion in פחו.

תחותמעו **

--- *ḏḥwt(y)-m(3)ʿ.w* 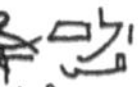 "Thoth is true / the guide or navigator"
[Aram] *Saqq* 28a.6 תחותׄמׄעו, 53.10 תחותמׄ], 10
[Eg] Ranke I.408.3 m. Gk; [Gk] Θοτομοῦς, Θοτομμοῦς (*NB* p. 142).

The morpheme of the Eg old perfective is retained as ו.

תחי *

--- *t(3)-(n.t-)ḫy* 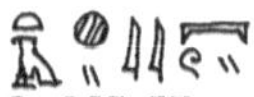
[Aram] Porten, *Or* NS 57 p. 38.5
[Eg] Ranke I.366.17 f. NK–Late; [Gk] Ταχοϊ, Ταχόϊς, Ταχόϊ
Cf. פחי, פחוי. See the discussion of פחו.

תחנא *
--- *t(3)-ḥn(w.t)* "The lady"
[Aram] *AP* 74.1
[Eg] Ranke I.365.19 f. MK–Gk.

תחנום **
--- *t(3)-(n.t-)ẖnm(.w)* 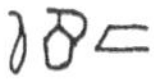 "She who belongs to Khnum"
L p. 127; G p. 493; K p. 95
[Aram] *AP* 39.2, 65.7 תחנום
[Eg] Ranke II.326.5 f. Late; [Gk] Ταχνοῦμ, Ταχνοῦβις, Ταχνουμις (*NB* p. 423)
Cf. פחנום.

תחפי **
--- *t(3)-(n.t-)ḥp*  "She who belongs to Apis"
S I p. 1107; L p. 127; G p. 493; K p .95
[Aram] *CIS* II.141.1; *Saqq* 54.6 תחפי
[Eg] Ranke I.362.6 f. Late [Gk] Ταάπις, Ταάπεις (*NB* p. 402).

תחפרי **
--- **t(3)-(n.t-)ḫpry* "She who belongs to Khepre"
L p. 127; G p .493; K p. 95
[Aram] APO 75,2.9
[Eg] cf. *š3ʿ-ḫpry* (Ranke I.324.21 f. Late cf. Gk Σαχπῆρις), *t3-š3ʿ-n-ḫpr* (Ranke I.367.20).

תחרת **
--- **t(3)-ẖrd(.t)* "The child (female)"
V II p.225
[Aram] *Saqq* 66a. 12 תחרת, 66b.1 תחרת, 7 תחרת
[Eg] cf. *p3-ẖrd*  (Ranke I.116.24 m. Dyn18-Late; *DemNB* I.211; cf. Gk Ταχράτις *NB* p. 423)
Cf. חרט in חרפחרט.

תטוסרי **
--- *t(3)-d(i.t)-(3)s-(i)r* 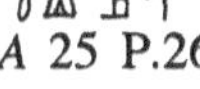 "She whom Osiris has given"
[Aram] Cowley, *PSBA* 25 P.264B.3; *Saqq* 8.1; 28b.6, 68.2]תטוס, 138.2 [פ/ת]טוסרי

[Eg] Ranke I.373.1 f. Late–Gk; [Gk] τεοσῖρις, Τατουσῖρις (*NB* p.416, 431)
Cf. תטסרי, פטוסיר etc.

תטחרור **
--- **t(3)-d(i.t)-ḥr-wr(.t)* "She whom Horus, the elder, has given"
[Aram] Porten, *Or* NS 57 p.38.2
[Eg] *DemNB* I.324; Ranke I.124.21; [Gk] Πετεαροῆρις, Πετεαρουῆρις, Πετεαροήρης, Πετεαρουήριος, Πεταποῆρις, Πεταρουῆρις (*NB* p. 311); cf. *t3-di.t-ḥr.w-p3-wr* "She whom Horus, the elder, has given" (Ranke II.328.17 f. Late).

ת[טחר]פחרט
--- *t(3)-d(i.t)-ḥr-p(3)-ẖrd* "She whom Harpokrates has given"
[Aram] Porten C3.8IVfrag.a.6
[Eg] Ranke I.374.7 f. Gk.

תטחרפי *
--- *t(3)-d(i.t)-ḥr-(n-)p*  "She whom Horus of Buto has given"
[Aram] *AP* p. 317 A.2 תטחרפע (corrected to תטחרפי] by Porten C4.1:2)
[Eg] Ranke I.374.9 f. Late; cf. masc form *p3-di-ḥr-n-p* (I.125.8).

תטחרפֿע
--- corrected to תטחרפי by Porten (cf. Vittmann's reading תטחרפ)
L p. 127; K p. 96; V II p. 222.

תטסרי **
--- Var. of תטוסרי
K p. 96
[Aram] *LH* 2.17
[Eg] see תטוסרי.

תמא
--- *t(3)-(n.t-)mi(w)* 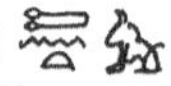 "She who belongs to the cat"
S I p. 1107; K p. 96
[Aram] *RES* 1788, 1300.4 תמ[א]

[Eg] Ranke I.360.8 (for the reading see n.2); [Gk] Τεμᾶς
Cf. Aram פמא, Ph פמי

תמאי (Spiegelberg, Kornfeld), which may not be a PN, could not be a lion; For some discussion, see Y. Muchiki, *JSS* 36 (1991) pp. 7-10. Porten said it is more likely to be Semitic.
cf. פמת

תמין **
--- *t(3)-(n.t-)mn(.w)*  "She who belongs to Min"
L p. 143; K p. 96
[Aram] *TAÉ* 103
[Eg] Ranke I.360.13 f. NK-Gk; [Gk] Θαμῆνις, Θαμῖνις, Θαμῖνις, Θαμεινις, Θαμῆνις, Ταμῖνις, Ταμῖε, Ταμῖν, Ταμειν, Τεμινις (*NB* p. 127)
Cf. פמן.

תמ̊סי[
--- *t(3)-ms*  "The girl"
[Aram] *Saqq* 56.1
[Eg] see תמס.

תמת **
--- *t(3)-(n.t-)m(w.)t*  "She who belongs to Mut"
L p. 127; G p. 493; K p. 96; V II p. 222
[Aram] *BP* 2.3, 4, 7, 8, 9, 11, 12, 13, 14, 16, 4.2, 6, 25 תות (corrected to תמת by Porten B3.5:25), 6.3 תמ̊[ת]
[Eg] Ranke I.360.10 f. NK–Late; [Gk] Ταμούθης, Ταμοϋθις, Ταμοϋτις, Ταμύθης, Ταμύτις (*NB* p.409f).

As Vittmann proposed, *t3-mtr* "She who belongs to the staff" is possible. For the discussion on this problem, see פמת.

תנופי **
--- **t(3)-(n.t)-nf(r)* "She who belongs to the good one"
G p. 493; K p. 96
[Aram] *TAÉ* 64
[Eg] cf. *p3-n-nfr* (?) 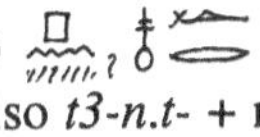 (Ranke I.109.4); *t3-n.t-nfr.w* (?) (Ranke I.361.5). Also *t3-n.t-* + masc. noun type, such as *t3-n.t-nht* "She who belongs to the strong one." [Gk] Τανοῦφις (*NB* p. 412).

Perhaps it is better to avoid *t3-nfr.t* "the Beauty" (Ranke I.364.1), because the final *r* of *nfr* is usually protected.

תנית **

--- **t(3)-(n.t-)ny.t* "She who belongs to Neith"

[Aram] *Saqq* 30b.3

[Eg] cf. *p3-n-ny.t* "He who belongs to Neith" (Ranke I.108.21 m. NK-Late); [Copt] ⲦⲀⲚϨⲐ (Heuser p. 61).

תׄנׄפׄי

--- Var. of תנופי

G p. 494; K p. 96

[Aram] *APO* 75.1.9

[Eg] see תנופי

Kornfeld tried to distinguish תנפי from תנופי on the basis of two Gk forms as follows; תנפי = *ṯ3-nfr* (Ranke I.387.9) Gk Φανοῦφις; תנופי = *t3-nfr* Gk Τανοῦφις. However, Eg *ṯ* which became ^{s}ϫ , ^{b}ϭ in Copt normally corresponds to צ or ש. Besides Gk τ and θ often occur in parallel (see תמס, תנופי).

תׄנׄר

--- **t(3)-nr(.t)* "The vulture"

[Aram] *Saqq* 52b.i.7

[Eg] cf. *s3-nr.t* "Son of Vulture" (Ranke II.312.13)

The reading is not certain. Segal's reading:]ילׄד/תׄנׄר/ר, yet more probably לפתׄנׄר.

תנרי

--- Var. of תנר

[Aram] *TAÉ* 87a.9

[Eg] see תנרי.

תסא

--- *t(3)-s3(w)* "The guardian"

[Aram] Cowley 81.27

[Eg] Ranke I.367.10

Other possible solusions are *ts* (Ranke I.383.6-8 f. NK), *t3-n.t-s3i* (Ranke I.363.1 f. Dyn 22), whose meanings are unknown.

תסו *

--- see תסרי

תסי *

--- *t(3)-(n.t-)(3)s(.t)* "She who belongs to Isis"

[Aram] *Saqq* 28a.4, 7 (Porten B8.4:16, 8.4.:19)

[Eg] Ranke I.357.20 f. NK-Gk (many); [Gk] ταησις.

Isis is normally represented by אסי. Yet the first *aleph* could be elided (see פסי).

תסרִי *

--- *t(3)-(n.t)-(3)s-(i)r* "She who belongs to Osiris"

[Aram] *Saqq* 9.8

[Eg] Ranke I.359.7 f. Late; [Gk] Ταϋσῖρις (*NB* p.422); [Copt] ⲦⲁⲨⲤⲒⲢⲁ

Cf. פסרי

Another possible solusion is **t3-n.t-sry* (cf. Ranke I.419.18 *p3-sry* m. NK.).

תפחי

--- **t(3)-(n.t-)p(3)-ẖy* "She who belongs to *p3-ẖy*"

S I p. 1112; K p. 96; V 11 p. 222

[Aram] N.Aimé-Giron, *BIFAO* 38 p. 38 no. 113.2

[Eg] cf. *p3-ẖy* (Ranke I.116.10 m. NK), *t3-ẖy* (Ranke I.366.17 f. NK–Late)

Cf. פחי, Gk Παταχόις (*p3-n-t3-ẖy*).

תפחנום **

--- **t(3)-(n.t-)p(3)-(n-)ẖnm(.w)* "She who belongs to *p3-n-ẖnm.w*"

K p. 96

[Aram] *APO* 87.4

[Eg] cf. *p3-n-ẖnm.w* "He who belongs to Khnum" (Ranke I.110.17 m. NK-Gk; Gk Παχνουμις); see פחנום. For the name formation *t3-n.t-p3-*, see Ranke I.359.16-360.3.

ת[--]פחרט

--- see תטחרפחרט

[Aram] Porten C3.8.IVfrag.a.6

תפממת

--- Dittography for תפמת

K p. 96

[Aram] *BP* 12.33

[Eg] see תפמת. From the context there is no doubt that תפממת is a dittographic spelling for תפמת.

תפמת **

--- **t(3)-(n.t-)p(3)-(n-)m(w).t* "She who belongs to *p3-n-mw.t*"

L p. 127; G p.494; K p.96; V II p.222

[Aram] *LH* 1.5, 10; *BP* 5.2, 11, 18, 12.1, 3, 11, 24, 35

[Eg] cf. **p3-(n-)mw.t* (Ranke II.280.13), *t3-(n.t-)mw.t* (Ranke I.360.10); see also פמת

Albright, followed by Grelot, explained as **t3-n.t-pr-mw.t* "She who belongs to the temple of Mut" (*BP* p. 180). As the second element is attested in Ranke II.295.14 *ns-n-pr-mw.t* (Dyn 26), it is not impossible. However, the type of *p3-n*-DN is much more common in the Late period. Therefore, it is more likely פמת is **p3-n-mw.t* (see פמת). Then **t3-n.t-p3-mw.t* is more acceptable. Equally possible is **t3-n.t-p3-mdw* "She who belongs to *p3-mdw*" (see אספמת). However Erichsen's explanation **t3-p3-mty* is not supported by attestation of its element.

תרו *

--- *trw (t3-n.t-rw)*  "She who belongs to the lion"

G p. 494; K p. 97; V II p. 222

[Aram] *LH* 5.1, 10, 6.8]תרו

[Eg] Ranke I.382.12 f. NK; [Gk] cf. Ταλέ, Ταλεῖς, ταλῆς, Θαλῆς, Ταλῖς (*NB* p.407). Eg *rw* is ⲗⲉ in Copt (?) (*Wb* II.403).

If the value of the *rw* is /l/ as in Gk and Copt, the identification is only acceptable with the assumption that the -*rw* is a dialectal form. Vittmann's solution **ta-rr=w* (cf. *pa-rr=w* "He who belongs to the pig" *DemNB* I.389) is less likely, because the second *r* is not lost (Copt ⲣⲓⲣ Crum 299a).

תרוח

--- *t(3)-rḫ(.t)*  "The knowledge"

G p. 494; K p. 97; V II p. 222

[Aram] *AP* 16.3 תר[וח], 5, 9
[Eg] Ranke I.365.5 f. NK; II 396; [Gk] Ταρόου, Ταρωοῦς;
Cf. Copt [b]ⲣⲱϣ, [b]ⲣⲁϣ- for Eg *rḫ* (Černý p. 142). Cf. *p3-n-rḫ.t* (Ranke I.109.20), *t3-rḫ.t-ʿn* (Ranke I.430.25), *p3-rḫ-nw* (Ranke I.419.11)

Grelot and Kornfeld explained it as **tnr-wḫ*, **ṯr-wḫ*, which are not attested, although their elements occur. Vittmann rejected their explanations and doubted that this is an Eg name. Yet *t3-rḫ.t* is unquestionablly comparable, and the ו of רוח is supported by the Copt word (see above). Judging from the fact that the name is a judge, Porten say in his letter, he may not be an Egyptian.

תרט **
--- *t(3)-r(w)d* 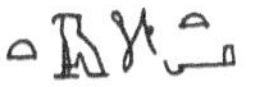 or *t(3)-(n.t-)r(w)d* "The strong"
L p. 127; K p. 97; V II p. 222
[Aram] *TAÉ* 87b.4 תׄרׄט, 15, 19
[Eg] Ranke I.364.19 f. NK or Ranke I.361.14 f. Late–Gk; *t3-rd* (Ranke I.365.9 f. Late–Gk) is the same as above; [Gk] Ταρόουτ (*NB* p. 417); cf. Copt ⲟⲩⲣⲟⲧ, [b]ⲉⲣⲟⲩⲟⲧ, dual [s]ⲣⲟⲟⲩⲧ, [b]ⲣⲱⲟⲩⲧ.

תרי
--- *t(3)-r(.t)* 
[Aram] *TAÉ* 87a.11
[Eg] Ranke I.364.13 f. Dyn 20; or Ranke I.6–8 *try*.

תשי
--- *t(3)-(n.t-)š(3)*  "She who belongs to Destiny"
G p. 494; K p. 97; V II p. 223
[Aram] *LH* 1.11, 2.1, 18, 3.9, 4.3
[Eg] Ranke I.367.19 (*t3-s3*); [Gk] cf. Τασαΐς, Τασοΐς (*NB* p. 417, 419); cf. Demot *šy* "Destiny" (Erichsen p. 485).

תשפׄוׄא
--- **t(3)-š(ri.t)-(n.t-)p(3)-wi(3)* "The daughter of *p3-wi3*"
[Aram] *APO* 75,l.ii.6 (pl.62)
[Eg] cf. *t3-šri.t-n.t-p3-wr*  (Ranke I.368.16 f. Late–Gk); for *p3-wi3* see Ranke I.103.20 m. MK–Late).

תת

--- *t(w)t*  "Statue" (?)

K p. 120

[Aram] *BP* 4.24

[Eg] Ranke I.379.15 and 16; 383.23 m. Gk /f. NK; [Gk] Τοτοῆς, Τοτῆς (*NB* p. 442).

This could be a shortened form of a Babylonian name like *Bel-tat-tan-nu-bul-lit-su* "Bel keep alive him whom you gave" (*BP* p. 175). See Eilers, *Iranische Beamtennamen* p. 35, 121. Other possibilities are *Ta-ti-i* (*APN* p. 231b), תת (Gröndahl p. 421). It could also be a lallname as Kornfeld pointed out.

תתו

--- Var. of תת

[Aram] *AP* 81.24

[Eg] see תת.

תתף **

--- **t(3)-(n.t-)t(3)-p(.t)* "She who belongs to the heaven"

[Aram] Porten, *Or* NS 57 p. 38 1.3

[Eg] cf. *iy-m-t3-p.t* 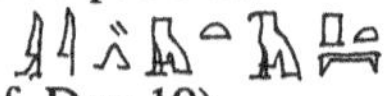 "She comes from the heaven" (Ranke I.9.8 f. Dyn 19).

[2] Divine Names

אוסרי **

--- Var. of אסרי

S I p. 1108; L p. 117

[Aram] stele: *CIS* II.122.2; 141.1, 3; 142; graffito: 130; *Eph* III p. 104 א[ו]סר[י], p. 113, p. 114

[Eg] see אסרי.

אוסי[רי]

--- Var. of אסרי

[Aram] Teixidor, *Syria* 41 p. 286

[Eg] see אסרי, Ph אסר.

אוסריחפי **

--- *3s-(i)r-ḥp*  "The dead Apis"

S I p. 1108; L p. 118

[Aram] stele: *CIS* II.123.1/2, 3/4 אוסח!ריחפי (The ח is a scribal error, *KAI* 268)

[Eg] *Wb* III.70.3; for the dead Apis see *LÄ*, V.870b; [Gk] 'Οσορᾶπις, 'Οσερᾶπις, Σεραπις, Σεραπις; [Copt] ⲥⲉⲣⲁⲡⲓⲥ in ⲫⲙⲁ ⲙⲡⲓⲥⲉⲣⲁⲡⲓⲥ.

אסי **

--- *3s(.t)* 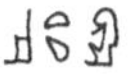 "Isis"

S I p. 1108; L p. 117

[Aram] *AP* 72.16 אסי; *CIS* II.135

[Eg] see Ph אס

In Aram the divine name is never written as אס without the final י, except פטאס in late 8th–early 7th cent. BC..

אסרי **

--- *3s-(i)r*  "Osiris"

S I p. 1108; L p. 117

[Aram] *Eph* III, p. 107 no. 38, p. 112 no. 55, p. 109 no. 46; *CIS* II.127 (corrected to אסרי in *RES* 608)

[Eg] see Ph אסר, Aram אוסרי, וסרי, אוסי[רי].

אפתו

--- misreading of אפתח (see below)

אפתח **

--- *ptḥ* "Ptah"

[Aram] *AP* 72.15 אפתו (corrected to אפתח by Porten C3.12:26)

לנקיה קדם אפתח אלהא רבא קלבי 1

לנקיה קדם אסי אלהתא קלבי 1

"For libation before אפתח the great god: 1 *qbly*.

for libation before אסי the goddess: 1 *qbly*."

[Eg] *Wb* I.565.9

The first א of אפתח can be considered as a prosthetic *aleph*, representing a vowel [i] (cf. Assy *Iptiḫarṭešu* = *ptḥ-ir-di-sw* Ranke I.138.17). It seems that nothing can be fit better than the god Ptah

וסרי **
--- Var. of אוסרי
[Aram] stele: *RES* 1788
[Eg] see אסרי
The initial *aleph* is elided (cf. אוסרי), as happens in composite names (such as פטוסרי). However notice that וסרי is preceded by the preposition ל. Cf. לחמלך for לאחמלך (Herr, *Seals* no. 146), לחתובסתי for אחתבסתי.

חנוב **
--- Var. of חנום
S I p. 1109; L p. 119
[Aram] *AP* 27.3, 8; 30.5
[Eg] see חנום; [Gk] cf. Χνουβις (*NB* p. 477).

חנום **
--- *ḫnm(.w)*  "Khnum"
S I p. 1109; L p. 119
[Aram] *AP* 38.7; *BP* 3.8, 4.10, 6.8 [חנו]ם, 9.10, 10.6, 16,H חנום
[Eg] *Wb* III.381; [Gk] Χνουμις, Χνουβις; [Copt] ⲭⲛⲟⲩⲭ.

חנם **
--- see חנום (above)
[Aram] ostracon: Aimé-Giron, *ASAE*, 26 p. 25 (1.B.3).

חר **
--- *ḥr*  "Horus"
S I p. 1109; L p. 119
[Aram] graffito: *CIS* II.136 עחר (corrected to חר by Sayce, *Rec.de Trav.* 17 p. 164, and Clermont-Ganneau *RES* 960); graffito: *RES* 961
[Eg] *Wb* III.122; [Copt] ϩⲱⲣ, ϫⲁⲣ-; [Gk] 'Ωρος, 'Αρ-.

פתח **
--- *ptḥ*  "Ptah"
S I p. 1109; L p. 126
[Aram] *AP* 11.2; *LH* 1.2, 2.2, 3.2, 4.2
[Eg] see Ph פתח

Cf. אפחה.

סתי **

--- *sti(.t)* 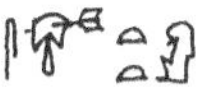 "Satis"

S 1 p. 1109

[Aram] *AP* 14.5; *Saqq* 35.5 °סתי, 181.3 סתי̊

[Eg] *Wb* IV.348.7 (Satis is a goddess of the 1st Cataract); [Gk] Σάτις.

תחות *

--- *ḏḥwty*  "Thoth"

S I p. 1109

[Aram] *AP* 69.10 תחות[(cf. Porten's reading מחות)

[Eg] *Wb* V.606; [Gk] Θωθ, Θωυθ; [Copt] cf. month names [s]ⲑⲟⲟⲩⲧ, [b]ⲑⲱⲟⲩⲧ

From the context תחות could be a PN (see Ranke I.407.13 m. MK Gk).

[3] Geographical Names

אבוט **

--- *3bḏ(w)* 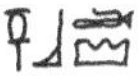 "Abydos"

[Aram] *AP* 38.3, 64.26 אבוט

[Eg] Montet, Géographie II,102; *Wb* I.9; [Copt] ⲁⲃⲱⲧ, ⲉⲃⲱⲧ.

אבוד **

--- Var. of אבוט

[Aram] Teixidor, *Syria* 41 p. 286

[Eg] see אבוט.

אפי **

--- *ip(.t)* 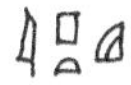 "Luxor"

[Aram] *LH* 5.10, 6.11, 7.5

[Eg] *Wb* I.67; [Copt] [s]ⲁⲡⲉ.

במרשרי

--- unknown GN

[Aram] *LH* 5.6.

חסתמח

--- *ḫ(3)s(w)-t(3)-mḥ(w)*
[Aram] *CIS* II.122A.1 כל 2 זי חסתמח קרבתא (corrected by Porten in his letter : כל 2 זי חסתמח קריתא)
[Eg] For תמח "the lower Egypt", see Montet I.5; *Wb* II.123.12ff. For חס, see *ḫ3sw* (Montet I.53)

חתהרבא

--- **ḥ(.t)-t(3-)hr(.t)-(i)b*
Zauzich, *Enchoria* 13 p. 117
[Aram] *Saqq* 103.2
Zausich changed Segal's original interpretation חתה רבא "great חתה" to חתהרבא which he interpreted as *ḥ.t-t3-ḥr-ib* "Athribis." However Eg *ḥ* represented by Aram ה is not likely. Though it is a reconstruction **ḥ.t-t3-hr-ib* is more likely, if this is a place name.

טבה **

--- *ḏb(3)*  "Edfu"
[Aram] *AP* 81.45 טבֹה; Cowley, *PSBA* 37 p. 218
[Eg] *Wb* V.562.1; Montet, *Géographie* II, p. 31; [Copt] ⲧⲃⲱ, ⲑⲃⲱ
Notice that the final ה indicates the /o/ vowel.

טמאסר

--- misreading of תמאסר (see below)

יב **

--- *3b(w)* 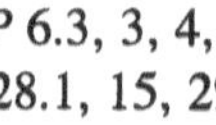 "Elephantine"
S I p. 1109; L p. 128
[Aram] *AP* 6.3, 3, 4, 7.1 [י]ב, 2, 8.2, 10.2, 3, 20.1, 2, 25.1, 2, 27.3, 5 יֹב, 5, 11, 28.1, 15, 29.1, 30.1, 5, 6, 7, 8, 13, 22, 25, 31.7, 12, 22, 24, 32.4, 33.6, 9, 34.6, 35.2, 43.1 [יב], 2, 65 no. 6 י[ב], 66 no. 6י[ב], 68 no. 2 [יב], no. 4; *BP* 1.2, 2.2, 3.4, 25, 4.2, 4, 5.2, 16, 6.2 [יב], 7.2, 9.2, 23, 10.17, 11. l0b, 12.2, 3, 4, 32, 14.2; Bresciani, *RSO* 35 p. 18 (I:Verso.1); ostracon: Dupont-Sommer, *RES* 1941–45 p. 67
[Eg] *Wb* I.7; Montet, Géographie II p. 15; [Copt] ⲓⲏⲃ, ⲓⲉⲃ
[Demot] *yb* (Erichsen p. 49); [Gk] 'Iηβ

Demot, Gk and Copt forms indicate that the internal change *3* > *y* took place at the initial position.

מאר/ד

--- *m(r)-(w)r* "The Great Channel"
[Aram] *Saqq* 4.8
[Eg] Montet, *Géographie* II p. 214

Segal compared the name with *mr-wr* Fayoum with the assumption that the final *r* of *mr* had been lost. However, the *w* of *wr* cannot be lost (cf. PN פתחור etc). The identification is unlikely.

מיע *

--- *m(3)ᶜ* "river bank"
[Aram] *AP* 75.2, 4
[Eg] cf. Montet, *Géographie* I p. 109; Gauthier III. p. 1-2.

מנפי **

--- *m(n)-nf(r)* "Memphis"
L p. 128
[Aram] *AP* 37.11, 42.7, 11 מ֯נ֯פ֯י֯, 13 [מנפי], 83.2; TAÉ 10 verso.3 מ֯נ֯פ֯י֯; *Saqq* 24.7 מ֯נ֯פ֯י֯, 30a. 1, 73.1; Bresciani, *RSO* 35 p. 18 (I recto:x+3)
[Eg] see Ph מנף.

מפי **

--- Var. of מנפי
[Aram] *LH* 2.3; *Saqq* 63.5 מ֯פ֯י֯, 136.2 מ֯פי (GN?); [Eg] see מנפי, Ph מנף.

נא **

--- *ni(w.t)* "Thebes"
[Aram] *AP* 24.18, 36, 34.3 [נא], 4, 37.6, 68.11,rev
[Eg] *Wb* II.210.6; [Heb] נא; [NA] *Ni-ʾi* (Assurb I,88.109 etc); [Gk] Ναυ(κρατις), (Ψουσεν)νῆ(ς), (Πα)να(ς); [Copt] ᴬⲚⲈ, ˢⲚⲎ

Edel, in "Nuew Deutungen Keilschriftlicher Umschreibungen ägyptischer Wörter", pp. 18–20, transliterates Thebes as *nʾ.t*, whose *aleph* can be any weak consonant: *3*, *i* or *w*, and discussed each case. Our study reveals that Thebes is most likely to be *ni.t* because of the common equation of Aram א and Eg *i*; *n3.t* also is not impossible, yet *nw.t* is impossible (see the discussion in Ug *PNI*).

נפא

--- *nb(.y.t)* 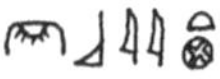 "Kom Ombo"

L p. 128

[Aram] *AP* 7.4 נפא, 20.4 (GN?)

[Eg] *Wb* II.242.4f; Montet, *Géographie*, II p. 25; [Copt] ^{s,b}ⲘⲂⲰ, ^{so}ⲚⲂⲰ, ⲚⲂⲞⲨ; [Gk] Ὄμβος; [Lat] Ombos

In neither attestation (*AP* 7.4, 20.4) does the context guarantee that נפא is a GN. Various other forms indicate that the second radical is ב, rather than פ. So the identification is unlikely.

סון **

--- *swn(.t)* 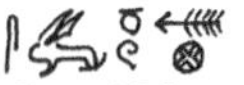 "Syene (Aswan)"

S I p. 1110; L p.128

[Aram] *TAÉ* 99.2; *BP* 2.2, 3.2, 7.2, 8.1, 2, 3, 11.1, 2, 3, 10b, 12; *AP* 3.9, 5.2, 2, 6.17, 8.28, 9.16, 13.2, 3, 14.2, 3, 3, 12, 15.2, 16.6, 7, 25.3, 4, 28.2, 29.2, 2, 30.7, 41.5, 45.1 ס̊[ון], 2, 9 [סו]ן, 56.2; *LH* 1.9, 14, 2.1, 18, 3.1, 14, 4.6, 15, 5.3; *RES* 438.2; Cowley, *PSBA* 25 p.264 (A.4); *CIS* II,138B.7; *APO* 77,2 innen 2, 78,2 innen 3

[Eg] *Wb* IV.68.3ff; Gauthier, *DG*, VII.17-18; [Copt] ^{s,b}ⲤⲞⲨⲀⲚ, ^{s}ⲤⲞⲨⲎⲚ (Griffith-Crowfoot, *JEA* 20 p. 8); [Gk] Συήνη; [Heb] סון, סונה; [Arab] *ʾswn*

פחפמיע

--- **p(r)-ḥp(y)-m(3)ʿ(.t)* "The house of true Apis"

[Aram] *AP* 75.3

[Eg] cf. *p(r)-ḥp(y)* (Gauthier II p. 111); For the י of מיע, cf. Copt ^{s}ⲘⲈ, ^{b}ⲘⲎⲒ. The place name is not attested in an Eg document.

פילה

--- *p(3)-i(w)-r(ḳ)* "Philae"

[Aram] *Saqq* 43a.4

[Eg] *Wb* I.47.9; Montet, Géographie, II, p.21; [Gk] Πιλακ, Φιλή, Φιλαῖ; [Copt] ^{s}ⲠⲒⲖⲀⲔ, ⲠⲒⲖⲀⲔϨ (Černý p. 348)

It seems that the lack of the final *ḳ* is justified by Gk forms, yet the other forms keep the final consonant. If we assume that there were bi-forms in its pronounciation retained in the Gk forms, the identification could be acceptable, yet at the moment it is very doubtful.

פסחמי **

--- *p(r)-sẖm.t* "Persekhmet"

[Aram] *Saqq* 28b.3

[Eg] cf. Gauthier, II.130; Montet, *Géographie*, II, 143, for *sẖm.t*, cf. Coptic ⲤⲀⲬⲘⲒ

Porten pointed out that this is a GN, Persekhmet (B8.4:4).

פְּפְּרֵם *

--- **p(3)-(n-)p(3)-rm(ṯ)* "Papremis"

Ray, *GM* 45 p. 58-61

[Aram] *AD* 12.6

[Eg] Bresciani, *Studi e Orientali*, 21 p.299-303. The Eg form is reconstructed through Gk form (Herodotus, II.59.63).

For the lack of the final *ṯ*, see the late spelling *rm*, and Copt [s,a]ⲢⲰⲘⲒ etc. (*rmṯ* > *rmt* > *rm*). Two other etymological identifications have been proposed (see *LÄ* IV p. 666): (1) Černý, (*Archiv Orientalni* 20 p. 86-89) reconstruced **p3-(n-)p3-rmṯ-mḥyt* on the basis of the same type of PN: *p3-rmṯ* + a geographical indication, such as **p3-rmṯ-i3bty* (Πρεμειβτε), **p3-rmṯ-rsy* (Ππουρησις)(?), **p3-rmṯ-3bdw* (Πρεμ-εβηθος). Yet **p3-rmṯ-mḥyt* is too long for Παπρημις, even if we assume the merger of double *m*. (2) Altenmüller (*JEOL* 18 p. 271–279) put forward **p3-(n-)p3-rmwy*. Yet the dual ending *-wy*, which is transcribed as ו in Aram, is not represented in the Gk form.

פקרקפתח **

--- **p(3)-grg-ptḥ*

S I p. 1106; L p. 125; K p. 92

[Aram] *AP* 75.4

[Eg] cf. Montet, *Géographie* II, 213 *[p3]-grg*, *Wb* V 188.15 *grg-ptḥ -ḥtp* (village name); Gauthier, II. 138 *pr-grg-ḥr, p3-grg-ḥr*; Ranke II.281.11 *p(3)-grg-ptḥ* ;

This identification is most likely. Notice that the correspondence between Aram ק and Eg *g*. Gk Πακερκεῆσις (**p3-n-grg-3s.t*

Ranke II.281.11), Copt ⲔⲈⲢⲔⲈⲤⲞⲨⲬⲞⲤ (**grg.t-sbk*) Gk Κερκεσουχος (Vycichl, p. 86) indicate the phonetic change /g/ > /k/ in Eg.

צעני **

--- *ḏꜥn(.t)* + gentilic י "a man of Zoan"
Porten C lvii
[Aram] *AP* 71.32 (Porten C1.2:25)
[Eg] see Heb צען.

תחמוצן

--- *t(3)-ḥ(w.t)-wḏ-n(ꜣ.t)* (?) "The house of the settlement of the town"
[Aram] *Saqq* 27.1, 4

תחמוצן is used with prep. ב, showing good possibility of being GN. The first two letters תח probably represent the common Eg GN form *t3-ḥw.t-*. The remaining element is difficult to explain.

תמאסר

--- **dm(i-n)-3s-(i)r* "The city of Osiris"
L p. 128
[Aram] *AP* 81.40
[Eg] for *dmi* "town, quarter, vicinity" see *CDME* p. 313; Copt ^{s}ϯⲘⲈ, ^{b}ϯⲘⲒ.

It is not impossible that אסר represents *3s-ir* "Osiris," as the Ph form of Osiris is אסר, which still preserves the first *aleph*.

תמנחור *

--- *(p3)-dm(i.t)-n-ḥr* "The city of Horus"
[Aram] *Saqq* 33b
[Eg] Montet, *Géographie* I p. 53; Gauthier, *DG* VI.94.1; Gardiner, *AEO* II.160.

תשטרס *

--- **t(3)-šd(y.t)-rs(.t)* "The southern province"
S p. 1110; L p. 128
[Aram] *AP* 24.39 תשטרס, 43 תש[טרס], 27.9
[Eg] *CDMF* p. 274 *šdy.t* "plot"; p. 153 *rsy* "southern"
Cf. פתרוס "The southern land."

[4] Loan Words

אחו ** "plant, vegetable"

--- *3ẖ(.y)*

[Aram] *Sefire* I.A.29, 32

[Eg] see Heb Lw אחו.

א°טשרי *

--- *id-šri* "small garment"

[Aram] *Saqq* 19.5 /// /// °טשרי זי בכצת שנת "small garment that is for the portion of the year 6"

[Eg] cf. *Wb* V.475.9-13

The identification is based on the assumption of **idr* < *dr* "dress, garment" (*Wb* V.475.9–13), in which the *aleph* is for a prothetic vowel. For *šri* "small" see *Wb* IV.524; cf. Copt [B]ϣⲓⲣⲓ, [S]ϣⲓⲣⲉ. Segal identified איטשרי as Eg red barley *it-ds]r* (*Wb* I.142.15) on the assumption that the final *t* was assimilated into the *d* of *dšr*. However, the second letter י (*mater lectionis* ?) of איטשרי seems to contradict Copt forms ⲉⲓⲱⲧ, ⲉⲓⲟⲩⲧ, ⲓⲱⲧ (Crum p. 87a), indicating [ō/ū]. The second component שרי is also comparable with Eg *šr.t* "a kind of grain" (*Wb* IV.524). Therefore the identification cannot be confirmed, and the reading remains uncertain.

אפסי *

--- *ips* "a part of a ship"

[Aram] *AP* 26.12

[Eg] *Wb* I.69.15; see Glanville, *ZÄS* 68 p. 15f.

אר *

--- *ir(w.t)* "a kind of tree"

[Aram] AP 26.10 (The context ארז ואר חדתן "new cedar and אר" shows it is probably a name of a tree.)

[Eg] *Wb* I.114

The word *irw.t* "a part of ship", which is only different in determinative from the above *irw.t*, suggests that the word in question was used for shipbuilding. There is an Akk word *eʾru*, which is a native hardwood used primarilly for making sticks (*CAD* E 318ff). But there is no indication that *eʾru* was used for shipbuilding.

דרי **

--- *ḏry(.t)* 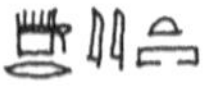 "room, dwelling"

[Aram] *BP* 9.3 (Porten B3.10:3) דרירסי "southern room"

[Eg] *Wb* V.600.7ff

cf. תרי רסי "southern side" *BP* 10.3

The word דרי is not likely to be a variation of תרי "side," because the ת of תרי is Eg article *t3*, which is never represented by Aram ד. Eg *ḏry.t* "room" is much more likely.

הירא

--- *ḫr* < *ḫyr* + Aram א

L p. 129

[Aram] *BP* 1.3, 5, 9; *AP* 68.6 יהיבא (corrected to הירא by Kraeling p. 135). It is clear that the context refers to a building or an object of some sort: כספ קלו בדמי הירא זי לכ זי "5 shekels as the price of היר of yours."

[Eg] Erichsen, p. 388, 377 "street" "house"; [Copt] ϩιⲣ (Crum p. 696b)

Aram ה does not represent Eg *ḫ*. There is an Eg word *hr* "a kind of furniture" (*Wb* II.498.5), which is phonologically much more likely.

הן ** "a liquid measure"

--- *hn(w)* "hin"

[Aram] *RES* 1791.[1], 2, 3, 4, 5

[Eg] see Heb Lw הין.

זרת "a span"

--- *ḏr.t* "hand, span"

[Aram] *AP* 36.3

[Eg] see Heb Lw זרת.

חותמ **

--- Var. of חתמ

[Aram] *AP* 76.1

[Heb] see חתמ, Heb Lw חתמ.

חלא *

--- *ḥr(y.t)* 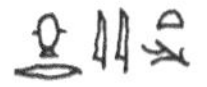 "a part of a boat" + Aram א

[Aram] *AP* 26.12, 12, [15], 20. The context refers to a part of boat: עקי חלא אמן שתן "the wood of חלא, 60 cubits"

[Eg] *Wb* III.148.20; Glanville (*ZÄS* 68 p. 35) suggests "gunwale", see also D. Jones, *Glossary*, p. 177 no. 110.

חסי **

--- *ḥsy*  "favourite one"

S I p. 1110; L p. 130

[Aram] Stele: *CIS* II.141.4

[Eg] *Wb* III.156 "an epithet of the blessed dead"

[Copt] ϩⲁⲥⲓⲉ, ⲉⲥⲓⲉ; [Gk] ‘ασιης, εσιης.

חתם ** "seal"

--- *ẖtm* "seal"

[Aram] *AP* 21.9 (as a verb), 76.1 חותמ; *AD* p. 2 n. 2

[Eg] see Heb Lw חתמ;

Cf. חותמ.

חתפי **

--- *ḥtp(.t)* 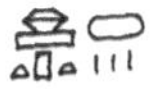 "offering"

S I p. 1111; L p. 130

[Aram] stone vessel: *CIS* II.123.1

חתפי לקרבת בנת לאוסרי חפי עבד אביטב בר בנת "offering for the approach of בנת to Osiris-Apis has אביטב, son of בנת, made"

[Eg] *Wb* III.183; [Ug] *ḥtp* (*RS* 24:266.V° 15).

טף

--- *dp(.w)* 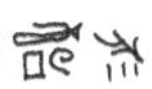 "a part of the mast"

[Aram] *AP* 26.10 ארז ואר חדתן טפ אמן עשרה "New cedar and אר; טפ 10 cubits"

[Eg] *Wb* V.447; Jones, *Glossary* p. 194, 185

An alternative solution suggested by Cowley is Baby. *adappu* "(wooden) board" (*CAD* D p. 106; *adappu AHw* I p. 106). However Copt ⲧⲟⲡ "keel" (Crum p. 422) which is attested once may be comparable. The identification is open to choice.

מנחה **

--- *mnḫ(.t)*  "(The) excellent one"

S I p. 1111; L p. 130

[Aram] stele: *CIS* II,142 ענחפי בר תחבס מנחה זי אוסרי אלהא

"*ʿnḫ-ḥpy*, son of *t3-ḫ3bs*, the excellent one of Osiris the god"

[Eg] *Wb* II.86.18 or 84ff.; [Gk] Μεγχῆς.

From the context *פמנחה (cf. תמנחא) is normally expected, if this is a masc. form, qualifing ענחפי. Yet the final ה is not easy to explain. Possibly it is the final vowel of masc. form.

מסטי *

--- *msd(.t)* 

[Aram] *AP* p. 318 c.3

[Eg] *Wb* II.152.14 probably from *msti* "basket (used as a measure)" (*Wb* II.151.6–7).

נמעתי *

--- *n(b)-m(3)ʿty* "The lord of two justices" (title)

[Aram] *CIS* II.141.4

[Eg] *Wb* II.21 *m3.ty* (Copt ⲘⲎⲦ)

KAI (III p. 319) suggests that נמעתי is a misspelling of נעמתי "my lovely one." Grelot (*Semitica* 17 p. 73–75) considered that the first נ is the Eg preposition *n*, to which is added Eg *m3ʿ.t* "sun bark" (Wb II.25.11f). Yet Couroyer (*Sernitica* 20 p. 17–20) criticized Grelot's explanation on two grounds; the use of the Eg prep. *n* which is hardly used in Aram texts, and the doubtful explanation of the ending *-t*. His explanation is *nb-m3ʿty* > *nm-m3ʿty*) נמעתי, which is much more likely. The assimilation of *b* of *nb* before *m* is evident in the El-Amarna tablets (see Chapter V: *Nimmḫuprreya* etc.). The loss of *b* of *nb* is also attested in Ph PN פטבנטט (*p3-di-b3-nb-ḏd.t*), and Akk GM *binṭēṭi* (*b3-nb-ḏd*) (Ranke, *KM* p. 46). The likelihood that this is an Eg title is strong.

נפרת

--- *nfr.t* (?)

[Aram] *AP* 14.3; Joüon, Mélanges de l'Universite Saint-Joseph, XVIII, 62 (Beyrouth) סון נפרת "Syene, the beauty" or a name of a quarter of Syene.

[Eg] for *nfr.t*, see *Wb* II 258f. ;

The final ה cannot be explained , because the fem. ending dropped in Eg. This may not be a place name. Portten tentatively translated it as "litigation." (Porten B2.8.3; 8.9.5)

סונכן **

--- *swn(.t)*-כנ "Syenians"

[Aram] *AP* 24.33, 33.6, 67 no. 3

[Eg] see GN סון; כן is a Persian suffix for gentilic (Sachau).

סי **

--- *s(3)w* "beam"

Porten C xlv

[Aram] Porten C3.7Gr3:24, C3.7Fr2:25, C3.7Dv3:3

[Eg] *Wb* III.419.14–17; [Copt] [s,b] ⲥⲟⲓ, [b]ⲥⲁⲓ, [a]ⲥⲁ

Since Dyn 19, *s3w* is written as *s3y* (*Wb* III.419).

סיכן **

--- **s(3)w*-כנ "Saites"

[Aram] *Saqq* 9.1, 5 חרכן (corrected to ס̇יכ̇ן by Porten B8.6:1,5)

[Eg] For *s3w* "Sais" *Wb* III.420.1; [Copt] [b]ⲥⲁⲓ; [Assy] [alu]*să-a-a* (Assurb I.90; II.16)

Though the Semitic root סכן is attested in Akk, Ug, and Heb, the *yodh* cannot be explained. B. Porten pointed out that סיכן is "Saites"(B8.6:1, 5). כן is a Persian gentilic (see above).

סעבל

--- **s*ʿ*(3)-bl* "outer plank"

[Aram] *AP* 26.11, 26

[Eg] *s*ʿ*3* "board-plank of ship"(*Wb* IV.43.1 OK–Gk); *bnr(bl)* "outside" (*Wb* I.461.1ff. since Dyn 18) Copt ⲃⲟⲗ (Černý p. 22).

פחטמוני **

--- **p(3)-ẖt-mni* "The mooring post (port stake of mooring)"

[Aram] *ẖt* "wood, log" (*Wb* III.389. 10ff. [s.,b]ϣⲉ, [f]ϣⲏ, [a]ⳉⲉ; *mni.t* "mooring post" (*Wb* II.72.12 cf. [s]ⲙⲟⲟⲛⲉ, ⲁⲙⲟⲛⲓ(Černý p. 84).

Two things should be noted; (1) the equation between Eg *t* and Aram ט can be justified, because Aram ט is caught by a labial and a laryngeal (see [4] Notes on the Corresnondences e) alveolars). (2) The *t* of *ḫt* was eventually elided as shown in Copt forms (see above). However the *t* is not a fem. ending, so it can be retained. Another Eg word *ḫd(r)*  "a part of boat" (?) (Jones, *Glossary*, p. 183 no. 129; Glanville, *ZÄS* 68 p. 35) might be comparable, though its meaning is obscure. The second part מוני corresponds well to *mni.t* "mooring post" whose Copt form is ⲙⲟⲟⲛⲉ.

פיק

--- *p(3)-(w)g* "the tray"

[Aram] *BP* 2.6, 7.18; *AP* 15.16 פק (Porten B3.3:6; 3.8:18; 2.6:16)

[Eg] *Wb* I.376.7f

Porten gives it the translation "tray." The nearest solusion is Eg *wq* "tray." For the equation of ק with Eg *g* , see Lw פקרקפתח.

* פלשני

--- *p(3)-(i)m(y)-(r-)šn* 

[Aram] *Saqq* 70.3 [פלשני]

[Eg] *Wb* IV.496.13 cf. Copt ⲗⲁϣⲁⲛⲉ (Černý p. 75), Gk λεσῶνι or λασᾶνι.

If this is a title, the equation is very good. Yet it is impossible to be sure from the context.

פסחנס

--- *p(3)-sḫ-ns(w)* "The royal scribe"

[Aram] *Saqq* 52b.9 (the whole text is very uncertain)

[Eg] For *sḫ* "scribe" see *Wb* III.474.

According to Segal the word פסחנס is a place name because the word is affixed by a preposition בּ, and followed by קרׄתׄא "the city." However both elements are quite doubtful. Only the final element חנס "Khons" suggests that פסחנס, if the reading is correct, is an Eg.

** פסחמצנותי

--- *p(3)-sḫ-mḏ(3.t)-nṯ(r)* "The scribe of the god's book(s)"

[Aram] *Saqq* 6.4

[Eg] cf. *sš md3.t nṯr* (*Wb* II.188.3) "the scribe of the god's book(s)"

The word, followed by PN שרנהיב, seems to be a title, as Segal points out. The first three letters fit Eg *p3-sẖ* "the scribe" (Copt ⲥⲁϩ *Wb* III.474). The final נותי can stand for Eg *nṯr* "god". This leaves מצ, with *mḏ* as the simplest Eg equivalent, perhaps a residual form from *mḏ(3.t)* "book(s)."

פערער *

--- *p(3)-ʿrʿr* "prow" (?)

[Aram] *AP* 26.12 פחטמוני לפערער חד לאמן תרין "the mooring post for פערער, one of 20 cubits"

[Eg] *Wb* I.210.5

It is suggested that the word *ʿrʿr* is a part of ship in *Wb* I.210.5: *ʿrʿr* "substantive (in zusammenhang mit der Erneuerung der Götterbarken genannt)", because of the position of the mooring post, "prow" (Porten A6.2:12, p. 99) is a reasonable guess.

פק **

--- *pg(3)* "piece of wood"

Porten C xlix

[Aram] Porten C3.7Jv1:24, Fv2:18, Fv3:14, Gv2:23, Dv3:1

[Eg] *Wb* I.563.6; [Copt] ⲡⲱϭⲉ Černý p.133, Crum 286a; [Demot] *pk* (Erichsen p. 141.3)

פרעה **

--- *pr-ʿ(3)* "Pharaoh"

[Aram] N. Aimé-Giron, *AE* 23 p. 42 no. 5, 8, 9); A. Dupont-Sommer, *Semitica* 1 p. 44 (3x).

[Eg] *Wb* I.513 *pr-ʿ3* "great house"; [Copt] ⲡⲣⲣⲟ, ⲡⲟⲩⲣⲟ; [Gk] Φαραώ; [Heb] פרעה; [Akk] *pirʾn.*

קב **

--- *ḳb(.y)* "a kind of jar (as a measure of capacity)"

[Aram] *AP* 45.8; ostracon: *Eph* III p. 122; Cowley, *PSBA* 37 p. 222; ostracon: Aimé-Giron, *ASAE* 26 p. 29 (III A.2); ostracon: Dupont-Sommer, *ASAE* 48 p. 112A.2

[Eg] *Wb* V.25 (*ḳby* is used as a measure of beer) since MK; [Copt]

[b]ⲕⲏⲃⲓ, ⲕⲁⲃⲓ (Černý) p. 52; Vycichl p. 71); [Gk] καβος; [Heb] see קב (about 1.3 littre in Heb).

קלבי **

--- *ḳlby* "a kind of wine"

[Aram] *AP* 72.2, 3, 8, 10, 13, 15, 16, 17, 19; in pl. קלבין *AP* 72.3, 4, 5, 14

[Eg] Demot *ḳlby* (as *ḳlby kmy* a kind of Eg wine) (Erichsen p. 546)

[Copt] cf. ϭⲗⲙⲁⲓ, ϭⲁⲗⲙⲁ etc. "jar, vase"; [Gk] καλπη.

קלול **

--- *krr* "vessel"

[Aram] *AP* 72.3 קלול, 5, 6 קלול, 7, 9, 10 קל[ול], 11 קלול, 12 [קלו]ל

[Eg] *Wb* V.135.8; [Copt] ⲕⲉⲗⲱⲗ "pitcher, jar" (Crum p. 104)

Černý (p. 56) suggests a Semitic origin quoting Arab *qulla* "earthernware pot," Aram קלל. However, the vowels of the Arab form clearly differ from Copt ⲕⲉⲗⲱⲗ, which perfectly correspond to Aram קלול. A little difficult is the correspondence between Aram ק and Eg *k* (cf. פטסבק, for interchange of Eg *k* and *ḳ*, see W. Ward, *JNES* 16 p. 200f.).

קנחנתי **

--- *ḳnḥ(.t)-nṯr* "the chapel of god"

[Aram] *BP* 9.9; 10.5 עליא לה בית קנחנתי "above it the house of קנחנתי (the chapel of god)"

[Eg] Erichsen p. 541, *ḳnḥ* "shrine;" *Wb* II.358 *nṯr* "god"

Vittmann and Porten (B3.10:5; *Aramaic Texts*, II p.89) denied that this is a PN. They interpreted it as a building *ḳnḥ(.t)-nṯr* which phonetically corresponds to קנחנתי very well.

קפא

--- *g(i)f* "ape"

[Aram] Ahikar 117

[Eg] see Heb קוף.

רסי **

--- *rsy* "southern"

Couroyer, *RB* 61 p. 252; Kutscher, *JAOS* 74 p. 237; Porten, *Aram*

Texts p. 62
[Aram] *BP* 10.3 דסי (corrected to רסי by Couroyer, Kutscher and Porten B3.11:3)
הו תרי רסי "That is the southern side"
[Eg] *Wb* II.452; Erichsen p. 254; [Copt] ⲢⲎⲤ (Crum p. 299b, Černý p. 193).

שושן ** "lily"
--- *sš(š)n* "lily"
[Aram] Bresciani, *Aegyptus* 39 p. 4 1.3 שושנן (pl.)
[Eg] see Heb Lw שושן, and Heb PN ששן.

שים **
--- *šm(y.t)* 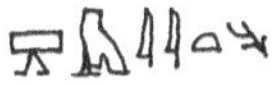 "pole"
[Aram] *AP* 26.10, 19
[Eg] *Wb* IV.467.11; [Copt] ϢⲘⲞⲨ (Černý p. 244; Vycihl p. 262).

שנטא **
--- *šnḏ(y.t)*  "kilt, apron" + Aram א
Couroyer, *RB* 61 p. 559
[Aram] *BP* 7.11
[Eg] *Wb* IV.522; [Copt] ˢϢ̄ⲚⲦⲰ, ᵇϢⲈⲚⲦⲰ (Černý p. 247); [Demo] *šnt* (Erichsen p. 516); [Gk] cf. σινδων

Kraeling (*BP* p. 211) compared Baby. *šintiu*, described in a word list as *šipatu* "wool" (see *AHw* 123. 9b). Yet Eg etymology (Couroyer) *šnḏy.t* is much more likely and the context supports it. The final *aleph* is either an Aram determinative or a vowel letter for /o/.

שף **
--- *š(s)p* "palm (= four fingers)"
[Aram] *BP* 17.3, 4, 5 שף 1 ס 3 "1 palm, 3 s(eah)"
[Eg] *Wb* IV.535.3ff since OK; [Copt] ϢⲞⲠ (Černý p. 248).

Porten's interpretation in the letter: (ש(ערם) פ(רסם "barley, (so many) peras." So the identification is open to choice.

שש ** "alabaster"
--- *šš* "alabaster"

Ginsberg, *JAOS* 74 p. 159; Kutcher, *JAOS* 74 p. 236
[Aram] *BP*7.18
[Eg] see Heb שש.

שש **
--- *šś* "linen"
[Aram] Bresciani, *Aegyptus* 39 p. 4 1.3
[Eg] see Heb Lw שש.

תחית **
--- *t(3)-ẖ(3)t(y)* 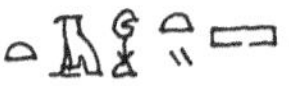 "the courtyard"
Couroyer *RB* 61 p. 252; Kutscher, *JAOS* 74.237
[Aram] *BP* 6.13, 9.4, 13, 15
[Eg] *Wb* III.222.5; [Demot] *ẖy.t* (Erichsen p. 377); [Copt] ϩⲁⲉⲓⲧ (Černý p. 298)

The context indicates that this is an Eg word: ופלג תרבצא הו פלג תחית מצד(ר!)ית "and half the court, that is the Eg תחית" Notice Gardiner's suggestion *h3y.t* (*AEO* II p. 210*) does not correspond to תחית phonetically.

תמא **
--- *dmỉ*  "precinct"
[Aram] *BP* 4.10 ··· מועה שמש לה תמא זי חנום אלהא "East of it (temple) is the תמא of Khnum the god ···"
[Eg] *Wb* V.455; [Copt] ^{s}ϯⲙⲉ, ^{b}ϯⲙⲓ.

Erichsen and Polotsky (*BP* p. 160), followed by Ginsberg (*JAOS* 74 p. 154) connected it with Demot *tmỉ* "town" (Erichsen p. 632, used as "*tmỉ* of god"). The meaning is not "town", but rather "precinct, quarter" (*CDME* p. 313). B. Couroyer (*RB* 61 p. 253) points out that the תמי/א stands for a construction, judging from the context, and puts foward a solution: feminine article *t3* + *m3y.t* (*Wb* II.12). Yet this Eg word is poorly attested, only once at the Saite period. The context shows that תמא is not necessarily a construction.

תמואנתי *
--- *t(3)-mỉ(.t)-nṯ(r)* "the way of god"
[Aram] *BP* 9.9 אגרא זי הנפנא זי בנהו מצריא הו תמואנתי "the wall

of the הנפנא, which the Egyptian built, that is תמואנתי"
[Eg] Erichsen p. 152.3; for *mi.t* see also *Wb* II.41.13-15

Couroyer explained תמואנתי as d*mi-nṯr* (*RB* 61 p. 557f). But this cannot resolve the ו of תמואנתי, because the Copt form of *dmỉ* is ^{s}ⲦⲘⲈ, ^{b}ϯⲘⲒ, pl *dmi.w* ⲦⲘⲈ (*Wb* V.455).

תמי **
--- Var. of תמא
[Aram] *BP* 3.8
[Eg] see תמא (it is evident from the context that תמי is a variant of תמא).

תמיס **
--- *tms(w)* 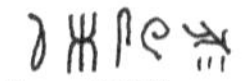 "panelling of fore- and aft- lookouts," "deck-planking (?)"
[Aram] *AP* 26.13, 20
[Eg] Jones, *Glossary* p. 194 no. 181; Glanville, *ZÄS* 68, p. 36.

תמנחא **
--- *t(3)-mnẖ(.t)*  "the excellent one"
[Aram] *CIS* II.141.1
[Eg] *Wb* II.86.18; Eg fem. article *t3* + *mnẖ.t* "excellent." The final *aleph* is an Aram determinative, rather than a vowel sign.

תסהרא **
--- *t(3)-shr(.t)* "the ship"
Porten C liv
[Aram] *AP* 71.10 תסהדא (corrected to תסהרא by Porten C1.2:1)
[Eg] *Wb* IV.209.1 *shry.t* "ship."

תרי **
--- *t(3)-rỉ(.t)*  "the side"
Couroyer, *RB* 61 p. 252; Kutscher, *JAOS* 74 p. 235; Ginsberg, *JAOS* 74 p. 158
[Aram] *BP* 4.3, 4.6, 9.4, 9.11, 10.3, 10.6, 12.13, 21.
[Eg] *Wb* II.400; Erichsen p. 241 *ri.t* "side, room." Cf. Copt ⲢⲒ (Černý, p. 134, compared with *rryt* (*rwy.t*) "official room" *Wb* II.407,13-14; *ry.t* "room" *Wb* II.400.2 is another possible etymology

of Copt ⲣⲓ, see Vycichl p. 171a).

The meaning "the side" is more suitable in the contexts in which the word תרי occurs.

[5] Month Names

תחות **

--- *ḏḥwt(y)* "the 1st month of *3ḫt*-season"

S I p. 1110; L p. 128

[Aram] *AP* 6.1, 10 1, 11.8, 25.1, 81.122; *BP* 11.1, 12.1, 10; Cowley, *PSBA* 25 p. 205; *Saqq* 24.3, 5 תחות, 128.2; Teixidor, *Syria* 41 p. 285.

[Eg] *Wb* V.606; [Copt] [s]ⲑⲟⲟⲩⲧ, [b]ⲑⲱⲟⲩⲧ (Černý p. 206, Crum p. 462a); [Gk] θωύθ; [Arab] *twt*.

פאפי **

--- *p(3)-(n-)ip(.t)* "the 2nd month of *3ḫt*-season"

S I p. 1110; L p. 128

[Aram] *AP* 2.1, 7.1 פאפי, 37.15, 43.1 פא[פי], 72.1, 2

[Eg] *Wb* I.68.6; [Copt] [s]ⲡⲁⲁⲡⲉ, ⲡⲟⲟⲡⲉ, [b]ⲡⲁⲟⲡⲓ (Černý p. 126; Crum p. 266f); [Gk] Φαωφι; [Arab] *pʾp*.

חתחור **

--- *ḥ.t-ḥr* "the 3rd month of *3ḫt*-season"

S I p. 1110; L p. 128

[Aram] *AP* 8.1; *TAÉ* 5.1 חתחור; *Saqq* 30a.1 חתחור, 117b.1 חתח[

[Eg] *Wb* III.5.12; [Copt] ϩⲁⲑⲱⲣ, [b]ⲁⲑⲱⲣ (Černý p. 303, Crum p. 728a); [Gk] ʻΑθυρ, ʻΑθῆρ; [Arab] *htwr*.

כיחך **

--- *k(3)-ḥ(r)-k(3)* "the 4th month of *3ḫt*-season"

S I p. 1110; L p. 129

[Aram] *AP* 72.18 כיחך; *TAÉ* 10a.3 כיחך, 7 [כ]יחך, 11 recto.3, 13 recto.5 כיחך, 14 verso.2 [כי]חך; *BP* 10.1

[Eg] *Wb* V,93.2; [Copt] [s]ⲕⲟⲓⲁϩⲕ, ⲭⲟⲓⲁϩⲕ, ⲕⲓⲁϩⲕ, [b]ⲭⲟⲓⲁⲕ; [Gk] Χοιάκ; [Arab] *kyhk*.

תעובי **

--- *t(3)-ʿ(3)b(.t)* 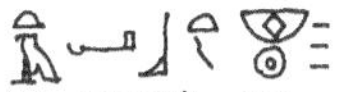 "the 1st month of *prt*-season"

[Aram] *AP* 42.14 תֿעובי, 67 no.1, 68 no.11, 83.1 תעבי; *BP* 14.1 תֿעֿוֹבי; *TAÉ* 12a.1 [תעו]בֿי; *Saqq* 22.3

[Eg] Černý p. 181; cf. *Wb* I.167.10 *ʿ3bt* "offering"; [Copt] ˢⲧⲱⲃⲉ, ᵇⲧⲱⲃⲓ (Crum p. 397b); [Gk] τῦβι; [Arab] *ṭwb*.

מחיר **

--- *mḫyr* 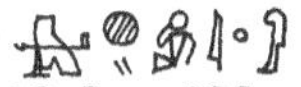 "the 2nd month of *prt*-season"

S I p. 1110; L p..129

[Aram] *AP* 24.34 [מ]חיר, 35 מ[חיר], 44 מֿחיר; votive stele: *RES* 438.3; *Saqq* 6.2 מֿחֿיֿרֿ

[Eg] *Wb* II.131,14; Lesko I.237; [Copt] ˢ·ᵇⲙϣⲓⲣ, ⲙⲉⲭⲓⲣ (Crum 206a; Černý p. 96); [Gk] Μεχειρ; [Arab] *ʾmṯyr*.

מחר **

--- Var. of מחיר

[Aram] Bauer-Meissner, *SBPA* 1936 p. 415

[Eg] see מחיר.

פמנחתף **

--- *p(3)-(n-)(i)mn-ḥtp*  "the 3rd month of *prt*-season"

L p. 129

[Aram] *AP* 22.1, 121, 35.1 [פמנ]חתף, 50.3 [פ]מֿנחֿתֿף; BP 1.1 פמנ[ח]תף, 5.1 פמנחתפ

[Eg] *Wb* I.493; Černý p. 128; [Copt] ˢⲡⲁⲣⲙϩⲁⲧⲡ, ᵇⲫⲁⲙⲉⲛ (Crum p. 269a); [Gk] Φαμενωθ; [Arab] *brmht*.

פרמותי **

--- *p(3)-(n-)rnnwt(.t)* 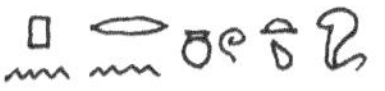 "the 4th month of *prt*-season"

L p. 129

[Aram] *AP* 35.6 פֿרמֿתי; *BP* 2.1, 6.1; *TAÉ* 87a.3 פֿרֿמֿ[תי]

[Eg] Černý p. 128; *Wb* II.437; [Copt] ˢⲡⲁⲣⲙⲟⲩⲧⲉ, ᵇⲫⲁⲙⲟ (Crum p. 269a); [Gk] Φαρμουθ; [Arab] *brmwd*.Cf. Demo *rmwt*.t (Erichsen p. 247); *rn.t, rnn.t* (Erichsen p. 250).

Notice the change *nn* > *m* which is evident in the Copt, Gk,

Demot, and Arab.

פחנס **

--- *p(3)-(n-)ḫns(.w)*  "the 1st month of *šmw*-season"
S I p. 1110; L p. 129
[Aram] *AP* 5.1, 14.1, 29.5, 35.8 [פ]חנס, 50.2 [פ]חנ̊ס̊ (? חחי?); Aimé-Giron, *ASAE* 39 p. 357 no. 124.7.8
[Eg] *Wb* III.300.15; [Copt] [s]ⲡⲁϣⲟⲛⲥ, [b]ⲡⲁϭⲱⲛ (Črerný p. 131, Crum p. 279a); [Gk] Παχων; [Arab] *bṯns*.

פאוני **

--- *p(3)-(n-)in(.t)*  "the 2nd month of *šmw*-season"
S I p. 1110; L p. 129
[Aram] *AP* 20.1 פא[וני], 76.3 [פ]אוני; *BP* 3.1, 8.1
[Eg] Lesko I.172; Černý p. 126; cf. *Wb* I.93; [Copt] ⲡⲁⲱⲛⲉ, ⲡⲁⲱⲛⲓ (Crum p. 263); [Gk] Παῦνι; [Arab] *bwwn*.

אפף **

--- *ip(i)p* 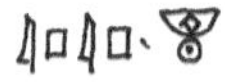 "the 3rd month of *šmw*-season"
S I p. 1110; L p. 129
[Aram] *AP* 1.1, 15.1, 63.15; *BP* 4.1, 7.1, 13.3 [א]פף, 8; *APO* 67,2.13 [א]פ̊ף̊ ; *TAÉ* 8 recto.I, 8 verso.1
[Eg] *Wb* I.69.4; Černý p. 37; [Copt] [s]ⲉⲡⲉⲡ, ⲉⲡⲉⲓⲫ, ⲉⲡⲏⲫ, [b]ⲉⲡⲏⲡ (Crum p. 57b); [Gk] 'Επεφ, 'Επῖφι; [Arab] *ʾbyb*.

מסורע **

--- *msw(.t)-rʿ* 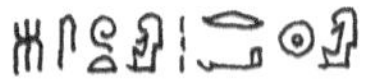 the 4th month of *šmw*-season
S I p. 1110; L p. 129
[Aram] *AP* 8.1, 9.1 [מסור]ע, 13.1, 29.1, 63.16 מ̊ס̊ו̊ר̊ע̊; *BP* 9.1
[Eg] *Wb* II.141.13; [Copt] ⲙⲉⲥⲟⲣⲏ (Černý p. 91; Crum p. 186b); [Gk] Μεσορή; [Arab] *msry*.

C. ANALYSIS OF PHONOLOGICAL CORRESPONDENCES

[1] Aram : Eg Phonetic Correspondences

Aram א: Eg *3* (late 8th - *ca.* mid. 4th cent. BC)
PN = אסיתעא, אסרסות, פטאס, פטאסי etc. (8 x); DN = אוסריחפי, אוסרי etc. (4 x); GN = אבוד, אבוט; Lw = אחו

Aram א : Eg *i* (late 6th – *ca.*375)
PN = אופתשתו, אחמס, חפיאו etc. (13 x); DN = אבדאמן; GN = אפי, אן; Lw = אף, פאוני, פאפי, תמא

Aram א : Ee lost *r* (5th – 4th cent.BC)[1]
PN = פחא, צחא, תחא

Aram א : Eg lost *n* (515 – *ca.*400)[2]
PN = אסחור, אסחנומ, אסמת, etc (6 x)

Aram א : Eg ø (5th – early 4th cent.BC)[3]
PN = תהרקא, הריוטא; Lw = תמנחא, שנטא, תסהרא

Aram ב : Eg *b* (5th – early 3rd cent.BC)
PN = בכרנף, חרבך, פטסבק, שרנהיב, (10 x); GN = אבוד, טבה, etc (4 x); Lw = קב, תעובי, קלבי

Aram ב : Eg *m* (late 5th cent.BC)
DN = חנוב[4]

Aram ד : Eg *ḏ* (> /d/) (417 –404 BC)
GN = אבוד (from Abydos; cf. אבוט); Lw = דרי

Aram ה : Eg *h* (late 6th – 5th cent.BC)
PN = הריו, הריוטא, שרנהיב, תהרא; Lw = הן, תסהרא

Aram ה : Eg ø (6th–beginning of 3rd cent.BC; PN from early 5th cent.BC)

(1) *mater lectionis* final (see below [5] *Matres lectionis*)

---

1. This correspondence is restricted to Eg *ḥr* "face" whose *r* is lost. The final א functions either as a syllable-closeing *aleph* or as a *mater lectionis* indicating [o].

2 This correspondence results from the loss of the initial *n* of *ns*: "nach dem abfall des *n* übrig bleibende *s* sich mit dem folgenden consonanten zu einer Doppel-konsonanz verbindet, vor der ein prostheticum trill" (Spiegelberg I, p. 1096).

3 The א in תהרקא and הריוטא is possibly a *mater lectionis*. The א of תמנחא, שנטא and תסהרא is most likely to be the Aram determinative (see the later discussion [5] *Matres Lectionis*).

4 חנוב, a variant of *ḥnwm* (*ẖnm.w*), results from a dissimilation of /m/after the long vowel [u]; cf. Gk Χνουμις, Χνουβις (Moscati, § 8.8 $m > b$).

(2) unknown: Lw = מנחה

Aram ו : Eg *w* (515 – early 3rd cent.BC)

PN = אסורי, וחפרע, ונפר, חפיו, etc. (36 x); DN = אוסרי, אוסריחפי, וסרי, תחות; GN = סון; Lw = מסורע, פרמותי, תחות[5]

Aram ו : Eg *b* (5th – early 4th cent.BC)

PN = הריו[6]

Aram ו : Eg ø (5th – end of 4th cent.BC)

(1) *matre lectionis* (see below [5] *Matres Lectionis*)

PN = אופתשתו, אמורטים, אסחור etc.(25 x); DN = חנוב, חנום; GM= אבוד, אבוט; Lw = חתחור, פאוני, פחטמוני, etc. (6 x)

(2) unknown

PN = אופתשתו; Lw = אחו

Aram ח : Eg *ḥ* (late 6th – early 3rd cent. BC)

PN = אחמס, אחרטים, חפאיו, חרבך,etc.(54 x); DN = אוסריחפי, תחות, etc. (7 x); Lw = חסי, כיחך, etc. (9 x)

Aram ח : Eg *ẖ* (8th – 4th cent.BC)

PN = וחפרעמחי, חרחבי, עחחפי, etc. (15 x); Lw = אחו, תמנחא,חתם, etc. (8 x)

Aram ח : Eg *ẖ* (late 6th – 5th cent.BC)

PN = אסחנום, פטחרפחרט, תחרת, etc. (9 x); DN = חנוב, חנום, חנמנתן, חנם; Lw = פסחמצנותי

Aram ט : Eg *d* (late 8th – 4th cent.BC)

PN = אחרטים, אמורטים, פטאסי, etc. (33 x)

Aram ט : Eg *ḏ* (>/d/) (late 6th – beginning. of 3rd cent. BC)

PN = הריוטא, תרט; GN = אבוט, טבה; Lw = פחטמוני

Aram ט : Eg *ṯ* (471 – 460 BC)

PN = פפטעונית

Aram י : Eg *i* (late 6th – 4th cent. BC)

PN = אחרטים, חכרטיסו, יחות, etc. (12 x); Lw = פחטמוני, תמי, תרי[7]

Aram י : Eg *y* (late 6th – 4th cent.BC)

PN = חורי, חפי, פפטעונית; תנית, etc. (10 x); Lw = חסי, מחיר, קלבי, רסי

---

5 Some of them are *matres lectionis*, such as אסרשות, נכו, סון (see below [5] *Matres Lectionis*).

6 Assimilation of *b* to the previous vowel [u] (see below [4] Notes on the Correspondences, b) Semivowels.)

7 The י functions as a vowel letter (only ימחות suggests the possibility of י being a consonant).

It is most likely the י is a vowel letter (see [5] *Matres Lectionis*).

Aram י : Eg lost fem. *t* (late 6th – *ca*.375)

PN = אסורי, אסיתעא, חרמחי, etc. (17 x); DN = אסי; GN = אפי;
Lw = חתפי, פאוני, פרמותי, etc. (5 x)
The י is a reflection of Eg fem. ending -*t*, which became [i]. Therefore the י is a *mater lectionis*.

Aram י : Eg lost *r* (late 6th – 399)[8]

PN = אפרי, חרנופי, כנופי, etc. (6 x); GN = מנפי, מפי; Lw = פסחמצנותי

Aram י : Eg *3* (5th cent. BC)

PN = פתירות; GN = יב[9]

Aram י : Eg ø

(1) *mater lectionis* (see also י : *i*, י : *y*, י : lost fem *t*, י : lost *r*)
PN = חפיאו, חפיו, לילו, שרנהיב, etc. (20 x); DN = אוסרי, וסרי, etc. (4 x); Lw = כיחך, שים, תחית, תמיס
(2) Gentilic
PN = כשי

Aram כ : Eg *k* (6th – mid 4th cent. BC)

PN = בכרנף, חכרטיסו, חרבך, כנופי, etc. (9 x); Lw = כיחך

Aram ל : Eg (Demotic) *l* (5th – 375. BC)

PN = לילו; Lw = קלבי

Aram ל : Eg *r* (*ca*. 375)

Lw = קלול

Aram מ : Eg *m* (6th – 4th cent. BC)

PN = אחמס, מחפרע, פחנום; etc.(52 x); DN = עבדאמן, חנום, חנם;
GN = מנפי, מפי; Lw = חסתמח, חתם, מחיר, etc. (13 x)

Aram מ : Eg *n* (2nd half of 5th cent. BC)

Lw = פרמותי[10]

Aram נ : Eg *n* (6th – 4th cent. BC)

PN = אסחנום, אסמן, נחמסאח, נכו, etc.(52 x); DN = עבדאמן, חנוב, etc. (6 x); GN = מנפי, נא, סון, צעני; Lw = הן, מנחה, פחנס, etc. (10 x)

---

8 The י represents Eg final *t*, which changed into /i/. Therefore, the י is a *mater lectionis*.

9 As a result of Eg change *3* > *y* : *ṯ3w* > (Copt ^{s}THY) > Aram תי; *3bw* > Demot *yb* > (Copt IHB, Gk Ἰηβ) > Aram יב.

10 The change *nn* > *m* took place in Eg, being demonstrated in Copt ⲠⲀⲢⲘⲞⲨⲦ Gk Φαρμοῦθ. The change occurs in Demot *rn(n).t* > *rmw.t* "the harvest goddess" (Erichsen p.250, 247).

Aram ס : Eg *s* (late 8th – middle 4th cent. BC)
PN = אחמס, אסורי, סמתו, etc. (46 x); DN = אוסרי, אוסריחפי, סתי, etc. (6x); GN= סון; Lw = חסי, חסתמח, פחנס, etc. (9 x)

Arm ע : Eg ʿ (6th – 4th cent. BC)
PN = אסיתעא, יפע, עחחפי, etc. (15 x); GN = צעני; Lw = מסורע, תעובי, פרעה

Aram פ : Eg *p* (late 8th – early 3rd cent. BC)
PN = אופתשתו, אספמט, פטנפחתף, etc. (89 x); DN = אוסריחפי, פתח; GN = אפי; Lw = אפף, חתפי, פחנס, etc. (11 x).

Aram פ : Eg *f* (late 6th – 4th cent. BC)
PN = יפע, אפרי, ונפר, etc. (16 x); GN = מפי, מנפי

Aram פ : Eg *b* (late 6th – 5th cent. BC)
PN = וחפרעמחי, וחפרע

Aram צ : Eg *ḏ* (late 6th – early 4th cent. BC)
PN = וצחור, חרוץ, צחא; GN = צעני; Lw = פסחמצנותי

Aram ק : Eg *ḳ* (5th – beg. of 3rd cent. BC)
PN = תהרקא; Lw = קב, קלבי, קנחנתי

Aram ק : Eg *k* (late 5th – early 4th cent. BC)
PN = פטסבק; Lw = קלול

Aram ק : Eg *g* (> /k/) (late 5th cent. BC)
PN = פקרקפתח; Lw = פק

Aram ר : Eg *r* (6th – 5th cent. BC)
PN = אחרטים, אסחור, רנפנפרי, etc. (57 x); DN = אוסרי, אוסריחפי, אסרי, etc. (7 x); Lw = חתחור, מחיר, תרי, etc. (8 x)

Aram ש : Eg *š* (late 6th – 4th cent. BC)
PN = אופתשתו, אסרשות, ששן, etc. (14 x); Lw = שים, שנטא, שף, שש.

Aram ש : Eg *s* > /š/ (420 BC)
Lw = שש

Aram ש : Eg *ṯ* (6th – 5th cent. BC)
PN = פסמשך, פסמשכחסי, פסמשכמר, שחפימו, שמו.

Aram ת : Eg *t* (late 6th – early 3rd cent. BC)
PN = אופתשתו, אסמת, נחתחור etc. (47 x); DN = פתח, תחות; Lw = חסתמח, חתחור, תחות, etc. (13 x)

Aram ת : Eg *ṯ* (> /t/) (449 – *ca.*400)
PN = טסתי, פטנתי, פטנתר, פתירות; DN = סתי; Lw = קנחנתי

Aram ת : Eg *d* (> /t/) (late 6th – 399)
PN = אופתשתו, אספמת, נפעורת, תחרת; Lw = תמא, תמי

Aram ת : Eg *ḏ* (> /d/> /t/) (5th cent. BC)
PN = פתירות, תחותמעו; DN = תחות; Lw = תחות.

[2] Eg : Aram Phonetic Correspondences

Eg *3* : Aram א (late 8th – *ca.* mid – 4th cent. BC)
: Aram י (5th cent. BC)
: Aram ø (passim)
Eg *ỉ* : Aram א (late 6th – *ca.*375 BC)
Eg *ỉ* : Aram י (late 6th – 4th cent. BC)
: Aram ø (late 6th – bed. of 4th cent. BC)
(1) Fall of Eg *ỉ*
PN = אחרטיס, פמון, פסרי, etc. (44 x); DN = אוסרי, אוסריחפי, etc. (4 x); Lw = אפף, חסתמח, פמנחתף
(2) Eg prothetic *aleph*
PN = כשי
Eg *y* : Aram י (late 6th – 4th cent. BC)
: Aram ø (8th – 4th cent. BC)
PN = אסרשות, סמתו, פתו, etc.(9 x); DN = תחות; GN = אבוט, מנפי, נא, סון; Lw = אחו, חסתמח, קב, etc. (7 x)
Eg *ʿ* : Aram ע (late 6th – *ca.* 300)
: Aram ø (5th cent. BC)
PN = אחמס, אחרטיס[11], פטאח
Eg *w* : Aram ו (515 – early 3rd cent. BC)
: Aram ø (passim)
PN = אחרטיס, אפע, ונפר, etc .; DN = אוסרי, חנום, etc.; GN = אבוט, etc.; Lw = חסתמח, etc.[12]
Eg *b* : Aram ב (5th – mid 4th cent. BC)
: Aram פ (late 6th – 5th cent. BC)
: Aram ו (5th – early 4th cent. BC)
Eg *p* : Aram פ (late 8th – early 3rd cent. BC)

11 The *ʿayn* of *iʿḥ* has been lost (see Ph אחמס).

12 The Eg *w*, mostly at the final position, was reduced to a vowel, already in NK. The loss of Eg *w* occurs in the following cases; (1) proper names (*e.g.*, *ḥr.w*, *mw.t*, *niw.t*, *3bdw*); (2) words (*e.g.*, *mdw*, *ỉw*, *ṯ3w*); (3) pronominal suffix *sw*, *sw.t*> Aram ס, however, sometimes סו); (4) Eg old perfective ending (e.g., *nfr.w*: the ending is sometimes realized as ו, אסרושת; cf. אסרת).

: Aram ø (5th cent. BC)[13]
PN = חרחת, ימחות
Eg *f* : Aram פ (late 7th – 4th cent. BC)
Eg *m* : Aram מ (6th – 4th cent. BC)
: Aram ב (late 5th cent. BC)
: Aram ø (471 – 460 BC)
PN = חרחבי, פפטעונית; Lw = פתחוא[14]
Eg *n* : Aram נ (6th – 4th cent. BC)
: Aram א (515 – *ca.* 4O0 BC)
: Aram ø
(1) Assimilation of Eg genitive *n* or *n.t* (psssim)[15]
PN = בכרנף, ענחפמעי, פאח, etc.; Lw = פאפי, פחנס, פמנחתף
(2) Other assimilations in Eg
PN = אמורטיס (*imn-ir-di-sw*), ונפר (*wnn-nfr*); GN = מנפי (*mn-nfr*)
(3) Assimilation in Aram
PN = עחפי, מחפרע (see below [7] N-Assimilation); GN = מפי
Eg *r* : Aram ר (late 6th – 4th cent. BC)
: Aram י (late 6th – 399 BC)
: Aram א (5th – 4th cent. BC)
: Aram ø (5th – end of 4th cent. BC)
(1) The Eg final *r*, which is usually represented by Aram י;
PN = ורשנף, נפסי, פטנפחתף, פנפתם; Lw = קנחנתי
(2) The Eg final *r*, which is usually represented by Aram א, restricted to *ḥr* (face-sign).
Lw = כיחך (*k3-ḥr-k3*)
(3) Eg word *šri* > ש
PN = פשנפור, פשנפמוי
Eg *l* : Aram ל (5th – 375 BC)
Eg *h* : Aram ה (late 6th – early 4th cent. BC)
Eg *ḥ* : Aram ח (late 6th – early 3rd cent. BC)
Eg *ḫ* : Aram ח (515 – 4th cent. BC)
Eg *ẖ* : Aram ח (late 6th – 5th cent. BC)
Eg *s* : Aram ס (late 8th – mid 4th cent. BC)
Eg *s* > /š/ : Aram ש (420 BC)

---

13 The example is restricted to Eg *ḥtp* > *ḥt* in Aram חת or חות, see Ph ימחת, Aram אמחות, ימחות.

14 Here the Eg preposition *m* has been lost.

15 The *n* rarely remains before a bilabial פ, *e.g.*, פשנפור, פשנפמוי, פשנפתח.

Eg *š* : Aram ש (late 6th – 4th cent. BC)
Eg *ḳ* : Aram ק (5th – beg. of 3rd cent. BC)
Eg *k* : Aram כ (6th – mid 4th cent. BC)
: Aram ק (late 5th – *ca.* 375)
Eg *g* : Aram ק (late 5th cent. BC)
Eg *t* : Aram ת (late 6th – early 3rd cent. BC)
: Aram ט (late 6th – early 3rd cent. BC)
: Aram י (late 6th – *ca.* 375)
: Aram ø (passim)[16]
Eg *ṯ* : Aram ש (6th – early 4th cent. BC)
: Aram ט (471 BC)
: Aram ת (5th – 4th cent. BC)
Eg *d* : Aram ט (late 8th – 4th cent. BC)
: Aram ת (525 – 399 BC)
: Aram ø (5th – *ca.*375 BC)[17]
Eg *ḏ* : Aram צ (late 6th – *ca.*375 BC)
: Aram ת (5th cent. BC)
: Aram ט (late 6th – beg. of 3rd cent. BC)
: Aram ד (417 BC)

16 Because Eg fem. ending *t* has been lost.
17 Note the change *d* > *t* > ø (*dd* > *ḏ* : צ).

[3] Table of Correspondences

	Aram	primary	secondary	Eg	primary	secondary
glottal stops	א	*3 ỉ*	*r^1 n^2* ø	*3*	א	י ø
				ỉ	א	י ø
	ע	ʿ		ʿ	ע	ø
semi vowel	י	*y ỉ*	*t r 3*	*y*	י	ø
	ו	ø		*w*	ו	ø
labials	ב	*b*	*m*	*b*	ב	פ ו
	פ	*p f*	*b*	*p*	פ	ø
				f	פ	
nasals	מ	*m*	*n(n)*	*m*	מ	ב ø
	נ	*n*		*n*	נ	א ø
latrals	ל	*l r*		*l*	ל	
trill	ר	*r*		*r*	ר	י א ø
sibilants	ס	*s*		*s*	ס	ש
	ש	*š ṯ*	*s*	*š*	ש	
	צ	*ḏ*				
pharyngals & laryngals	ה	*h*	ø	*h*	ה	
	ח	*ḥ ḫ ẖ*		*ḥ*	ח	
				ḫ	ח	
				ẖ	ח	
velars	ק	*ḳ k*	*g*	*ḳ*	ק	
	כ	*k*		*k*	כ ק	
	ג	-		*g*		ק
alveolars	ת	*t*	*ṯ d ḏ*	*t*	ת	ט י ø
	ד	-	*ḏ*	*ṯ*	ש	ת ט
				d	ט	ת ø
	ט	*d*	*t ṯ ḏ*	*ḏ*	צ	ט ת ד

*The above arrangement is based on the Eg alphabeticl order, not phonology.

Notes

1. In the case of *ḥr* "face".
2. In the case of *ns*.
3. *Mater lectionis*, Aram determinative or a syllable closing *aleph*.
4. Eg fem. ending *t*.
5. Eg final *r* > /i/.
6. The secondary change.
7. When ט is caught between a labial and laryngal.
8. when Eg *d* is located at the initial or final position.
9. When Eg *ḏ* which became /d/ comes at the initial or final position.
10. Dialectal in Abydos.
11. When ט is caught between a bilabial and a laryngal.
12. When Eg *ḏ* became /d/.

[4] Notes on the Correspondences

a) Glottal Stops

No Eg *3* is represented by Aram א except in DNs Isis and Osiris, and GN אבוט "Abydos". The survival of Eg *3* in the medial position can only be observed in the PNs composed of Isis, *e.g.*, פטאסי, פטנאסי etc. The Gk forms of פטאסי indicate that there were two different readings of the name; Πετεῆσις (פטאסי) with the *aleph* and Πετῆσις (פטיסי) with elision of the *aleph*.

Eg *3* well corresponds to Aram א in the initial position: אסי, אבוט, אוסרי. Osiris is rendered as אסרי, אוסרי, אוסי[רי], (once וסרי preceded by a preposition ל), and אסר in DN (אסרונפר, אסרתיס). Though the א of אסרי is elided in the medial position (such as פטסרי), it seemes that the א of אסרי is still functioning at least at the initial position, as a consonant of which the Eg counterpart has long since dissapeared. Osiris should be transliterated as *3s-ir* (see the discussion in Ph).

The correspondence between Eg *3* and Aram א in the final position is suggested by two PNs אסיתעא (**3s.t-t3-ʿ3.t*) and פסא (*p3-n-s3w*). However the possibility that they are *matres lectionis* is more likely.

For the correspondence between Eg *3* and Aram י, see above [1] Aram : Eg Correspondences.

Eg *i* is realized in Aram as (1) א, (2) י, and (3) א + a vowel letter. The nature of the double pronounciations of the Eg *i* is revealed as follows;

(1) Eg *i* : Aram י, *e.g.*, *i(i)-m-ḥt(p)* --- ימחות (cf. Ph ימחת)

(2) Eg *i* : Aram א or י, *e.g.*, *dmi* --- תמי, תמא (Lw)

(3) Eg *i* : Aram או, *e.g.*, *ip.t-t3-šd.t* --- אופתשתו

(4) Eg *i* : Aram אי, *e.g.*, *nfr.t-i(i).ti* --- נפראית

(5) Eg *i* : Aram או, *e.g.*, *p3-n-in.t* --- פאוני

As shown above, the pronunciation of Eg *i* is either [ʾi] or [ʾo/u]. The majority of Eg *i* have no correspondence, because Eg *i* was reduced to a vowel which is represented by either י or ø in Aram.

However the *aleph* pronunciation of Eg *i* is well preserved in any position. The correspondence between Eg *i* and Aram א is more normal than that between Eg *3* : Aram א which is restricted to "Isis," "Osiris" and "Abydos."

e.g., at the initial: אחמס, etc.

at the medial: חפיאו, נחמסאת etc.

at the final: תמא, פנא

Eg *i* at the beginning of words is commonly preserved as a consonantal *aleph*, e.g., *ip.t* > אופ, *iʿḥ* > אח, *imn* > אמו, אמן (cf. מון), (however, *ib* > יו, *itm* > תום, *ir* > ר, *im* > מ, *im3ḫw* > מח, *ip* > פ).

At the middle position the *i* is either preserved or elided, *e.g.*, *niw.t* > נא, *miw* > מא (however, *bik* > בך).

At the end Eg *i* is realized as either י (*mater lectionis*) or ø, *e.g.*, *di* > ט or טי, *bi.t* > בי, *m3i* > מוי, *šri* > ש etc.

As for the final *aleph*, there are certain difficulties, see below [5] *Matres Lectionis*.

b) Semi-Vowels

Eg *y* and *w* correspond to Aram י and ו respectively. It is difficult to say that Eg *y* and Aram י correspond to each other as a consonants, because this correspondence is restricted to the final position, except DN נית (which is realized as נת) and Lw מחית (which occurs as מחר). However there are many examples where Aram ו represents a consonantal value of Eg *w*;

e.g., At the initial: ורשנף ,ונפר ,וחפרע, etc.
At the medial: פונש ,חרוץ ,אסורי, etc.
At the final: פתו ,סמתו ,חנמו, etc.

Aram ו also stands for *b* (for this *b*, see הריו).

c) Pharyngals and Laryngals (Eg *h*s)

In contrast to the varied correspondences in Ph, it is striking that the three Eg hard *h*s are represented in Aram by ח without exception (see below [6] Spirantization)

d) Velars

Among velars the correspondences seem to be inconsistent. The real problem is that Aram ק represents three Eg velars: *ḳ, k, g*. The correspondence between Eg *ḳ* and Aram ק is naturally supported. Yet Eg *g* also corresponds to Aram ק in פק (= *pg3*; and probably in פקרקפתח = **pr-n-grg-ptḥ*). Eg *g* was usually prepalatalized[18] . Yet there are some Eg *g* which remain velar without being prepalatalized, and so are realized as Copt ⲕ (*e.g.*, *g3g3* :ⲕⲁⲕ ; *g3š* : ⲕⲁϣ etc.)[19]. The fact that Eg *pg3* took the same course of phonetic change is demonstrated in the Demotic *pk*. The *grg* of **Pr-grg-ptḥ* is also presented in the Gk form Πακερκεησις (**p3-n-grg-3s.t*) and the Copt form ⲕⲉⲣⲕⲉⲥⲟⲩⲭⲟⲥ (*grg.t-sbk*; Gk Κερκεσουχος). Therefore, it is not surprising that there is no correspondence with Aram ג.

The majority of Eg *k* are represented by Aram כ. However there are two cases in which Eg *k* is represented by Aram ק: פטסבק and קלול. Eg *k* can be rarely represented by Aram ק at the final and initial position.[20]

18 *Phonétique*, p. 40; W. H. Worrell, p. 27f.

19 *Ibid*, p. 41.Vergote,

20 For interchange of Eg *k* and *ḳ*, see W. Ward, *JNES* 16 (1957), p. 200f.

e) Alveolars

Eg *t* corresponds to Aram ת. When it is the fem ending, the *t* is realized either as י (as a vowel letter) or ø. There are three instances in which Eg *t* corresponds to Aram ט instead of ת;

e.g., פחטמוני (*p3-ẖt-mnỉ.t*)
פטחרטיס (*ptḥ-ỉr-dỉ-sw*)

Characteristically, the טs are caught between a labial and a laryngal (ח). Therefore, the secondary change in Aram ת > ט has taken place in this particular phonetic condition. The variation of מפטח and מפתח should be remembered here, whatever the identification is. This change is an Aram feature.

Eg *ṯ* is realized as Aram ת, ט and ש. Eg *ṯ* corresponds to Aram ת, because many Eg *ṯ*s became /t/ in the course of phonetic history. However, there is an exception in which Eg *ṯ* > *t* is represented by Aram ט, *e.i.*, פפטעונית. Here again the /t/ is caught between a labial and a laryngal (ʿ) and became /ṭ/. Therefore, we can suppose the secondary change Aram /ṯ/ > /t/ > /ṭ/. The primary correspondence of Eg *ṯ* (as /ṯ/, not /t/) is, therefore, to Aram ש[21]

Eg *d* corresponds mostly to Aram ט and rarely to Aram ת. The fact that Eg *d* usually does not correspond to Aram ת exhibits the existence of a phonetic difference beween Eg *d* and *t*, though
they are not distinguishable in Copt (both became Ⲧ[22]). Scribes prefer Aram ט to ת and ד for Eg *d*. The correspondence of Eg *d* to Aram ת is

---

[21] S. Segert observes that the emphatic ט is dissimilated to ת before ק in עתיק (< עטיק) and considers Heb *ʿattîq* as a loanword from Aram (*Altaramäische Grammatik* § 3.7.2.2.1; cf. BDB p. 801b). However, עטק is only attested in Eg Aramaic, the root "to pass" occurs in Ug (*UT* 19.1938), Akk *etēqu* "to pass" and Arab *ʿatīq* "old, ancient" (Aram אתיק is a passive form), making it impossible that עטיק is original. Also there is no reason to suppose Heb *ʿattîq* is an Aram loanword. It is more likely that ת is dissimilated to ט after a laryngal (עתיק > עטיק), as our observation shows the change of ת > ט.

Another example of the change ת > ט has been observed in שחט (< שחת), since Dupont-Sommer (*Les Inscriptions Araméennes de Sefiré*, p. 47), followed by Fitzmyer, *The Aramaic Inscriptions of Sefire*, p. 50, saying that שחט for שחת is due to the partial assimilation of ט to ת. Phonetically the change could be supported by our observation. Notice Degen's objection that שחט and שחת are independent words (*AAG* § 20, p. 41, Anm. II and n. 39).

Cf. Gesenius, § 54b.

For Ug *d* > *ṭ* under the influence of the emphatics, see *UT* 5.24.

[22] J. Vergote, *op.cit.* p. 28.

due to a secondary change, because they are restricted to the initial and final position;

e.g., at the initial: תמא, תמי

at the end: אספמת, נפעורת, אופתשתו, תחרת

Eg *ḏ* corresponds to either צ or ט (therefore, to ת, see above), exceptionally to ד. Eg *ḏ* has a double realization in Copt, namely, ⲧ and ϫ[23]. Some of the Eg *ḏ*s remain unchanged, realized as Copt ϫ, Aram צ; some of the Eg *ḏ*s, changed into Eg *d*, are represented by Copt ⲧ, Aram ט (see above). It is shown again that Aram ט can be replaced by Aram ת at the initial and final positions (see above);

e.g., at the end: פתירות --- *p3-ṯ3w-rwḏ(w)*

at the initial: תחותמעו --- *ḏḥwty-m3ˁ.w*

תחות --- *ḏḥwty*

f) Labials

Eg *b* is almost always represented by Aram ב, yet it is represented once by פ, once by ו. The correspondence Eg *b* and Aram פ is only realized in the name וחפרע, וחפרעמחי. All other forms of this name indicate the change *b* > *p* before ר, which took place in Eg before the name was recorded by Aram scribes.

For the correspondence between Eg *b* and Aram ו, see the discusion in חפיו.

Eg *p* is realized as Aram פ, once as ב at the final position, once dropped in *ḥtp* (see Eg *p* : Aram ø).

Eg *f*, for which Aram had no symbol, is realized by Aram פ, rather than the voiced ב. Only if Aram ב had been aspirated [b] >[v], might the ב have stood for Eg *f*.

g) Nasals

Aram מ and נ stand for Eg *m* and *n* respectively. The only exception is פרמותי in which Aram מ represents Eg *n* as a result of Eg change *nn* > *m* (see פרמותי).

DN *ḫnm.w* is realized by either חנום or חנוב. The Gk variant Χνουμισς and Χουβις indicate that this is not a question of Aram :

[23] J. Vergote, *Ibid.*, p. 28.

Eg correspondence, but Eg double values of *ẖnm.w*. Probably Eg *m* was dissimilated into *b* after [ū].

h) Sibilants

The correspondence of Aram ש to both Eg *š* and *ṯ* is in accordance with the fact that PS interdental **ṯ* is written with ש in OA (cf. with ס in the Fakhariya inscription), with ת in BA[24], assuming Eg *ṯ* was interdental at this period.

In the Ph section, we have observed that Eg *ṯ* corresponds to Ph צ, when Eg *ṯ* became Copt ϫ. However, it is clear enough that Eg *ṯ* (Copt ϫ) which is represented by צ in Ph., was never realized as צ in Aram. Aram ש is the usual counterpart of Eg *ṯ* (Copt ϫ).

e.g., Ph צ : Eg *ṯ* צחפמו (*ṯ3y-ḥp-imw*),
צכנסמו (*ṯ3y-ẖns.w-imw*)
Aram ש : Eg *ṯ* שחפימו (*ṯ3y-ḥp-im.w*)
שחפמו (*ṯ3y-ḥp-im.w*)

Therefore, we could conclude that there is a certain difference in phonetic value between Ph צ and Aram ש. Ph צ corresponds to Eg *ṯ*, to which Aram ש also corresponds.[25]

[5] Matres Lectionis

The *mater lectionis* is fully developed to designate Eg vowels as follows;

a) *Yodh*

(1) medial [ī]
PN = חפימן, פחים, נפראית, שרנהיב etc.; DN = אוסריחפי etc.; Lw = כיחך, שים, תחית etc.

(2) final [ī]
PN = אפרי, חרנופי, פטוסרי etc.; DN = אוסריחפי, אסי, אסרי etc.;

24 Degen, *AAG* p. 33; Segert, *op. cit.* § 3.2.6.1.

25 Ph שמו could be Eg *ṯ3y-im.w* (cf. Aram שמו). Then it could be said that Ph ש corresponds to Eg *ṯ*. Yet the identification cannot be confirmed.

GN = מנפי, אפי; Lw = תמי, פחטמוני etc.

b) *Waw*

(1) medial [ō / ū]

PN = אופתשתו, חרנופי, פשנפמו, etc.; DN = חנוב; GN = אבוט, אבוד; Lw = תעובי ,פחטמונית ,חתחור, etc.

(2) final [ō / ū] ?

In contrast to the frequent occurrence of ו as medial *mater lectionis*, the ו hardly appears as *mater lectionis* at the final position. The possibility of the ו as final *mater lectionis* is poorly suggested by PN נכו and לילו. The ו of נכו, however, more likely to be a consonant due to the Eg spelling *nk3.w* (and Heb variant נכו and נכה). The ו of לילו may also have a consonant value due to Copt ⲗⲉⲗⲟⲩ, ⲗⲓⲗⲟⲩ. The absence of ו as a *mater lectionis* at the end of words could be connected with the use of ה as a *mater lectionis* indicating [o].

c) *He*

(1) final [o / ō]

GN = תבה (Copt ⲧⲃⲱ); Lw = פרעה

PN פחה and Lw מנחה suggest that the ה is used as a *mater lectionis* though their phonetic value is not determinable.

d) *Aleph*

The א as a *mater lectionis* is uncommon and its phonetic value is not stabilized. Though it is difficult to distinguish א consonant from א *mater lectionis*, the following reveal that א is used as *mater lectionis* at the final position.

(1) final [i / ī]

Lw = תמא

The double realizations of Eg word *dmi* as Aram תמי and תמא present evidence to indicate that the א is used as *mater lectionis*, because, as we have observed, Eg *i* at the final position no longer preserved the *aleph* pronunciation. Therefore, the final י and א here are interchangable, functioning as *mater lectionis*.

(2) final [o / ō]
PN = הריוטא

(3) final [a / ā]
PN = תהרקא (cf. Heb *tirhaqāh*)

However, it is doubtful that Aram א is used as *mater lectionis* in the following; (1) PN = אסיתעא and פסא: though א could be interpreted as *mater lectionis*, the final א could also correspond to Eg *3*, preserved by Eg *t* and *w* (**3s.t-t3-ʿ3.t, p3-s3w*). The Ph אסעא (*3s.t-ʿ3.t*) indicates that the final א could be a consonant. (2) PN = פנא, תמא, GN = נא : their final אs could be either *matres lectionis* or realization of Eg *i* (*p3-n-niw.t, t3-n.t-miw, niw.t*). (3) PN = פחא, צחא and תחא: the final אs indicate a final short vowel [o], if they are used as *matres lectionis*. However, the Ph form צחא also has the final א, making it a syllable closing consonants. (4) Lw = תמנחא and שנטא: Both אs are most likely to be the Aram determinative.

In sum, medial and final [i / ī] are indicated by י, medial [ō / ū] by ו, final [o / ō] by ה, any final vowel by א. י and ו are predominantly used as *mater lectionis*.[26]

e) Notes on the use of *matres lectionis*

(1) *matres lectionis* in words or divine names which occupy the final position in PNs, never occur when such words or divine names occur in initial position. This seem to indicate that the use of *matres lectionis* is influenced by the position of accent.

(a) *nfr* : נפ in initial / נופי in final
At the initial: פנפחם פטנפחתף, נפרעית, נפסי
At the final: תנופי, פתהנופי, כנופי, חרנופי

(b) *ḥr* : חר in initial / חור in final
At the initial: חרמן, חרמחי, חרחבי, חרון, חרוץ, חרבך, חרנופי
At the final: פטחור, נחתחור, אסחור

26 Cf. in BA [ī] and [ê] are indicated by י, medial [ū] or [ô] by ו, final [ā] [ê] or [ē] by ה, final [ā] or [ê] and [ô] by א (Rosenthal, *BA* § 5). In OA [ū] by ו, [ī] by י, [ā] [ê] by ה (Degen, *AAG* § 6).

(c) *imn* : מן in initial / מון in final
At the initial: פמנחתף[27]
At the final: פטמון, פמון
(d) *m3i* : מי in initial / מוי in final
At the initial: פטמיחום
At the final: פשנפמוי
(e) *di* : ט in initial / טי in final
At the initial: פטאסי, פטוסירי, פטמן etc.
At the final: אחרטים, אמורטים, חכרטיסו, פטי, פתחרטים

The fact is that נפ, חר, חת, מנ, מי and ט can be the second elements, because scribes were not forced to use *matres lectionis*, though they are customary. Yet the fact that נופי, חור, חות, מון, מוי, טי can not be the first component indicates that scribes were forced to write them without *matres lectionis*.. Hence it is most likely that *matres lectionis* are used in the accented syllable. This means that. Eg usually had an accent at the final position in the Late Period.

(2) In Saqqara there are some indications that *matres lectionis* were less developed;

e.g. חור --- חר in Saqqara
חרחות --- חרחת in Saqqara
נית --- נת in Saqqara
Cf. אסרשות --- אסרשת in Hermopolois

However, unique in Saqqara is that the use of *matres lectionis* with א as אי, או;

e.g. אופתשתו (cf. אפי), נפראית, אוסרי, תאים

(3) Date of common use of *matres lectionis*

We are not in a position to determine the date of origin of *matres lectionis*. However, there are slight indications that uses of *matres lectionis* became much more common between 7th and 6th cent. BC in Aramaic. There is a seal containing the Eg name פטאס. In Aram, however, the theophoric element (Isis) is never written as אס without the final *mater lectionis* י when Isis is the last component of personal names, or used independently. However this seal (late 8th – early 7th cent. BC) bears -אס, which occurs in Phoenician twice. The names in *LH*, belonging to the end of 6th or early 5th cent. BC, tend to show that

27 Cf אמורטים; *imn* occurs in the initial position, a *mater lectionis* is used, instead the consonant *n* dropped.

matres lectionis were less developed in Hermopolis (see above). In this connection, we may infer that the Saqqara documents show an earlier form of writing in terms of *matres lectionis.*

[6] Spirantization[28]

The problems of the double pronunciation of the */bgdkpt/* have been extensively discussed for more than half a century, especially since P. Kahle, along the lines of traditional German scholarship, ascribed it to the innovations of the Masoretes between the 8th and 9th century, as a result of the influence of Syriac. The range of the question is threefold;

1) The date of the origin: from 10th cent. BC to 8th cent. AD.

2) The direction of influence: (i) from Akk to Aram, (ii) from Hurrian to Semitic[29] , (iii) from Aram to Heb.

3) The character of the pronunciation: phonemic or allophonic.

In the following, only evidence which others have proposed will be discussed. Convenient summaries and bibliographies are found in E. E. Knudsen's "Spirantization of Velars in Akkadian" (*Lišān mitḫurti*, pp. 150f).

a) Phoenician Evidence[30]

(1) Latin transliteration of Punic: *Poenulus* of Plautus[31] *ca.*200 BC.

(a) Latin *th* corresponds to Pu ת in both initial and postvocalic; *e.g.*, *thuulech* (=תהלך) 934, *ysthyalm* (אשתאלם) 931, *yth* (את) 930, 935, *alonuth* (אלונות) 930.

(b) Latin *ch* corresponds to Pu כ in both initial and postvocalic; *e.g.*, *chy* (כי) 931, *chil* (כל) 935, *chon* (כן) 935; *aelichot* (ה-הליכות) 937, *anechi* (אנכי) 995.

28 For this section, see Y. Muchiki, "Spirantization in Fifth-century B.C. North-West semitic," *JNES* 53 (1994) pp. 125–130.

29 E. A. Speiser, "Progress in the Study of the Hurrian Language," *BASOR* 74 (1939) pp. 4–7.

30 Spirantization took place in Ph accoring to Harris, *Development*, § 42. Yet Friedrich and Röllig are more cautious, *PPG*² § 38.

31 H. Sznycer, *Les Passages Puniques*, p. 108, 114, 147f (cf. § 38).

(c) Latin *ph* corresponds to Pu פ in initial; *e.g.*, *pho* (פה) 932.

(d) Latin *f* corresponds to Pu פ in initial; e.g., *liful* (לפעל) 935, *rufe* (רפא) 1006.

The above evidence does not prove non-existence of the spirantization in Punic. The inconsistent correspondences of Latin *th* and *ch* simply indicate the inadequate nature of Latin consonants to reflect the spirantization, as is now commonly recognized by many scholars (see below). We should pay more attention to the fact that Latin *ph* is used for an initial פ and Latin *f* for postvocalic פ.

(2) NPu ב represents /w/ in NPu transliteration of Numidian proper names (§ 38);

(a) יובזעלען (Latin iuzale) *KAI* 117.2 (NPu-Latin bilingual text 1st cent. AD; cf. תענברע (Latin *thanubra*)

(b) תבגג (Numidian *tbgg* *[Tuwga(g)] modern Thugga) *KAI* 101.1 (Numidic-Punic bilingual text, 139/8 BC)

(c) זבג (*CIS* I.499.4, 676.3), זיבק (*CIS* I.569.4), זיוג (*CIS* I.341.4; 460.4) for [zīwag] 4th – 2nd cent BC

The above examples are in favour of the spirantization of Punic ב after a vowel. However, it is not legitimate to ascribe Pu ב representing [w] only to the spirantization, because interchanges among the bilabial consonants including *w* are fairly common in Semitic[32].

(3) Pu ב for מ (§ 55) 4th – 2nd cent. BC;

(a) intervocalic: שמע > שבע, חמן > חבן

(b) non-intervocalic: עבדאשמן > עבדאשבן

(c) initial: מגן > בגן

It is self-evident that the chnage of מ > ב is not necessarily due to postvocalic spirantization[33], because it took place even in the initial position.

Therefore, though there are some indications that the spirantization was operative in Punic (*ca*. 200 BC), none of them is conclusive.

[32] Moscati, § 8.8; for Eg example see Ph הרב, Aram פטסבק, הריו, also Sethe, *ZÄS* 50 p. 80–83.

[33] Cf. *UT* 5.33.

b) Hebrew Evidence[34]

(1) ב for פ: *ca.* 598 or 587[35]

(a) נבש for נפש

(b) והבקדם for והפקידם

It is more likely that aspirated /b/ corresponds to labial /w/ rather than voiced labial /p/. The interchange of ב for פ is not necessarily due to the spirantization of ב. It already occurred in the second millennium[36].

(2) Late Babylonian transliteration of West semitic DN מלך in mid 5th cent. BC[37].

(a) *[d]Mil-ḫi-ta-ri-bi (BE* IX 42.3)

(b) *Nu-ú-ḫi-[d]Mil-ḫi* (*BE* IX 47.19)

(c) *[d]Mil-ḫi-AD.ŠEŠ* (*BE* X 75.5)

(d) *Ab-di-[d]Mil-ḫi* (*UMBS* II 1.226.19)

The validity of the evidence, NW Sem כ[ḵ]: LB *ḫ*, was denyed by Knudsen[38], because of a conditioned spirantization of Akkadian velar stops.

(3) ב for ו in the Biblical Hebrew;

(a) *parhar* (1Chr 26:18) for **parwār* in pl. *parwārîm* (2K 23:11).

Notice that the *b* is preceded not by a vowel, but a resonant. Though spirantization is a possible explanation, again a bilabial example much reduces the value of the evidence. The accent shift *parbár* > *parwārím* may have effect upon the change of consonantal value /b/ > /w/.

---

34 The spirantization in Hebrew has been in doubt because of Greek and Latin transliterations. For the claim that the double realization is due to Syriac influence, see Bergsträsser, *HG* § 6 m; H. Bauer and P. Leander, *Hist. Gram*, § 19 c; Kahle, *The Cairo Geniza*, p. 103–106; G. Beer - A. Meyer, *HG*[2], § 8.2, 13.2; G. Garbini, *Il semitica di nord-ovest*, pp. 26, 39. For evidence of the inadequacies of Greek and Latin transliteration, see E. Y. Kutscher, *JSS* 10 (1965) pp. 24ff; J. Barr, *JSS* 12 (1967) pp. 9ff; E. Brønno, *JSS* 13 (1968) pp. 195ff; G. Dalman, *Grammatik des jüdisch-palästinischen Atamäisch* (1960) p. 65. Also see Harris. *Development*, § 42.

35 Aharoni, *BASOR* 197 (1970) p. 20 n. 13.

36 Moscati, § 8.8; *UT* 5.28. For an oscillation of *b* and *p*, see M. Weippert, The Settlement of the Israelite Tribes in Palestine, p. 74ff.

37 A. Goetze, *JAOS* 59 (1939) p. 452 and n. 74; H. Zimmern, *KAT*[3] p. 471.

38 *Lišān mitḫurti*, p. 151.

(4) The Yemenite, a modern tradition, has preserved the double pronunciation of post vocalic /*bgdkpt*/[39] .

There no definitte evidence that spirantization took place in Hebrew except for the reading of the Masoretic *dagesh forte* and the Yemenite pronunciation.

c) Aramaic Evidence[40]

(1) The merging of the Proto-Semitic *d*, *t* and *ṭ* with their spirantized counterparts *ḏ ṯ*, and *ṭ̱*[41]

S. Kaufman says "once one accepts the inescapable conclusion that OA --- used the graphemes for the sibilants to represent the Proto-Semitic spirants for which the Canaanite alphabet had no symbols, it is obvious that a spirantized pronunciation of the stops could not have occured in OA, for if spirantization had occurred, *d*, *t*, and *ṭ* would have been confused with the corresponding spirants, still separate graphemes, in the orthography." However, this confusion took place in the period 700 - 400 BC. Therefore, in Imperial Aram spirantization systematically developed. Though this observation is certainly possible, it is not legitimate to ascribe this confusion only to spirantization in this lack of external evidence. The merging of consonantal value is always possible in the course of the history of any language. The relation between spirantization and the merging cannot be sufficient evidence of the existence of spirantization in Imperial Aramaic

(2) Akk transliteration of Persian PNs by Aram speakers[42].

(a) *U-ak-sa-tar* for *Uvakhšatra* Gk Κυαξάρης (*APN* 238a).

(b) *U-ma-ku-iš-tar* for *Uvakhšatara* Gk Κυάξαρης (*APN* 240a)

Here Persian postvocalic /ḫ̮/ was transliterated as Akk *k* [k].

---

39 Kutscher, "Yemenite Hebrew and Ancient Pronunciation," *JSS* 11 (1966) pp. 220ff.

40 Spirantization was not operative in OA: H. Schaeder, *Iranische Beiträge*, I p. 44; S. Kaufman, *The Akk Influences on Aram*, p.117. Spirantization already existed in OA; Segert, *Altaramäish Grammatik,* § 3.7.7.6.2 (?): Brockelman, *GVG* § 78. Spirantization was operative in Imperial Aramaic: Leander, § l; Kutscher, "Aramaic" p. 374 (in *Hebrew and Aramaic Studies*, p. 117).

41 Bergsträsser, *Introduction*, § 4/1.11 and n. c.

42 Kutscher, "Aramaic" p. 374; W. Eilers, *Iranische Beamtennamen*, p. 70.

Kutscher, following Eilers, assumes that as Akkadian by then was a dead language, the inscriptions were written by Aramaic speaking scribes who "superimposed on the Akkadian their Aramaic pronunciation." Though Aramaic-speaking scribes are probable, the fact remains that we do not know for sure. Moreover, we are now well informed on the alternation of Akk *ḫ* and כ. Therefore, the above argument is not sufficient.

(3) Arabic transliteration of Biblical GNs at the time of the Arab Conquest.[43]

(a) Arab *ḫ* : Sem כ [ḵ] (Arab *mḫmˀs* for מכמס)
(b) Arab *ḏ* : Sem ד [ḏ] (Arab *drˁ*, *ˀdrˁ* for אדרעי)
(c) Arab *s* : Sem ת [ṯ] (Arab *ˁṭˀrws* for עטרות)

It is evident that spirantization existed at the time of the Arab Conquest.

(4) it is well known that the Late Aramaic spirantization was operative.

The existence of spirantization in Aram, esp. since Imperial Aramaic, has never been doubted. However, external evidence has never proved it until the Arabic transliterations reflect it, and the Late Aramaic demonstrates it. As for the Biblical Aramaic, if we accept the Masoretic points, spirantization was operative on the same principle as Biblical Hebrew. Yet we could assume that spirantized reading in BA was introduced under the influence of Biblical Hebrew. Therefore, we conclude, with Moscati,[44] that "there is no certain proof that it pre-dates the Christian era", except perhaps in Punic.

d) New Evidence

With this lack of evidence for spirantization, our consonantal correspondences of Eg to Ph and Aram seem to afford evidence that spirantizations of Eg laryngals (*ḥ*, *ḫ* and *ẖ*) between Ph and Aram are significant. Their correspondences are as follows;

Eg	*h*	*ḥ*	*ḫ*	*ẖ*
Ph	ה	ח	ח/כ	כ
Aram	ה	ח	ח	ח

43 Kutscher, *JSS* 10 (1965) p. 27f.
44 Moscati, § 8.10.

There was a clear distinction in phonetic value between Eg *h* / *ḥ* and *ẖ* / *ḫ*, which was preserved until Coptic [45]. Eg *h* and *ḥ*, which are always realized in Copt as either ϩ or ø, were much weaker than Eg *ẖ* and *ḫ*. For example, the Greek forms of Eg names containing Eg *h* and *ḥ* often have no phonetic counterpart. On the contrary, Eg *ẖ* and *ḫ* are usually realized in Gk as either κ or χ, though the normal realization of Eg *ẖ* and *ḫ* in Semitic is still ח (cf. in Arab *ḫ*), not כ[46]. Therefore, it is normal for Eg *ḥ* to correspond to Ph and Aram ח and Eg *ẖ* and *ḫ* to Aram ח as above.

However, it is characteristic that Eg *ẖ* corresponds to Ph ח twice, at the same time to Ph כ four times, and Eg *ḫ* to Ph כ twice. These peculiar correspondences could only be explained either by the Eg velarization of *ẖ* and *ḫ* or by the spirantization of Ph כ. The former is not only not known to us, but also contradicts the fact Eg *ḥ*, *ẖ* and *ḫ* are all represented by Aram ח. Therefore, the spirantization of Ph כ seems to be most probable explanation of this correspondence. Furthermore, when we examine the condition of the spirantization, *i.e.*, postvocalic or not, it becomes more probable;

(1) Eg *ẖ* in initial corresponds to Ph ח:
e.g., חתם (*ẖtm*) 9/8th cent. BC – 53 AD

(2) Eg *ẖ* after a consonant corresponds to Ph ח:
e.g., ענחפמס (*ʿnẖ-p3-ms*) 5th cent. BC

The non-existence of a vowel before Eg *ẖ* is indicated by Gk ’Αγχα- and ’Αχο- for Eg *ʿnẖ*- and the fact that נ of ענח is assimilated as עח (see ענחחפי, עחחפי).

(3) Postvocalic Eg *ẖ* and *ḫ* correspond to Ph כ:

(a) פטכנס (*p3-di-ẖns.w*) 5th cent. BC

The existence of a vowel before Eg *ẖ* (Ph כ) is shown in Gk Πετεχωνς (cf. NB *Pa-aṭ-ḫa-an-si* showing vowel syncope, cf. *paṭa'ēsi'* : *paṭ'ēsi'*)

(b) צכנסמו (*ṯ3y-ẖns.w-ỉm.w*) 5th cent. BC

The vowel before Eg *ẖ* (Ph כ) is disclosed in Copt ϫⲓ and ϭⲓ for Eg *ṯ3y*.

(c) אמננך (*imn-nẖ*)

We can safely assume that there is a vowel before כ, because the the second נ opens a syllable.

(d) חרפכרט (*ḥr-p3-ẖrd*) 5/4th cent. BC and 4th/2nd cent. BC

45 J. Vergote, *Phonétique*, pp. 64–67.
46 *Ibid.*, p. 65.

The vowel preceding כ (Eg *ẖ*) is evident in Gk ʻΑρποκρατης, ʻΑρποχρατης. cf. Aram פטחרפחרט (*p3-ḥr-p3-ẖrd*).

(e) פּוסך (*p3-wsḫ*)

For Eg *wsḫ* cf. Copt ⲟⲩⲱϣⲥ̄ (metathesis, cf. Arab *wasiʿa* "be wide"). Notice the reading is difficult.

The above PNs consistently indicate that Eg *ḫ* and *ẖ* correspond to Ph כ when the condition of the spirantization, *i.e.*, postvocalic, is satisfied. Since Ph כ was spirantized after vowel: /k/ > /k̲/, Ph כ was able to represent Eg *ḫ* and *ẖ*. On the other hand, Eg *ḫ* which is not preceded by a vowel or in the initial position is represented by Ph ח. Therefore, we can conclude that the spirantization was operative in 5th cent. BC in Phoenician.

On the contrary, when we turn to the Aram documents and examine the thirty-seven Eg proper names and loan words (attestation 81 times) containing Eg *ḫ* and *ẖ*, we are led to the opposite conclusion, because every Eg *ḫ* and *ẖ*, whether preceded by a vowel or not, is exclusively represented by Aram ח;

(1) Eg *ḫ* after a consonant (= Aram ח):

e.g., ענחחפי (*ʿnḫ-ḥpy*) cf. Ph ענחפמס

(2) Eg *ḫ* and *ẖ* after a vowel (= Aram ח):

e.g., פחנס (*p3-ẖns*); cf. Ph פטכנס (see above)

פטחרפחרת (*p3-di-ḥr-p3-ẖrd*); cf. Ph חרפכרת

This striking fact displayed in 81 examples seems to be sufficient evidence to indicate that the spirantization was not operative in Aram. If spirantization was operative, we could expect the correspondence between Eg *ḫ* / *ẖ* and Aram כ, as shown in Ph as well as the late Aram and Arab: *mḫmʾs* for מכמס (see above). With respect to the date, the 81 examples cover a considerable length of time as follows;

(1) פטחנם (*p3-di-ẖnm.w*) : late 6th cent. BC, Hermopolis

(2) נחתחור (*nḫt-ḥr*) : 5th cent. BC, outside Eg

(3) פחוי (*p3-ḫy*) : end of 4th cent. BC, Elephantine

These examples tell us that the spirantization did not take place during the currency of imperial Aramaic.

Once we accept the inescapable conclusions that the spirantization was operative in Ph, but not in Imperial Aramaic[47], it seems more reasonable to assume that the spirantization first took place in Ph and was introduced to Heb under the influence of Ph. Yet in Aram it did not become operative until Middle Aram (300 BC - 200 AD). As for the Biblical Aram, we could assume the influence of the Heb pronunciation upon it.

[7] N-Assimilation

As Leander justly observed that "die Assimilation des *n* an einen folgenden kons. ist nur selten durchgefuhrt worden," Aram scribes seem to be sensitive to [n] sound.

a) Eg *ʿnẖ-* > עח in *AD* (9 x) and Saqq (עחחפי)
However Eg *ʿnẖ* > ענח in Elephantine (ענחחפי, ענחפמעי, ענחמחֹ).
b) PN *mn-nfr* > מפי in Hermopolis
However מנפי in Elephantine, Saqqara and Padua
c) Eg *mn* > מ in Wâdi el-Hûdi (מחפרע)
However the usual realization is מנ (see above)
d) DN *ỉmn-* > אמו in Elephantine (אמורטים)

This assimilation may not result from the usage of Aram scribes, because some Gk forms and the Akk form lack the *n* (see אמורטים). Probably the intervocalic *n* was merged with vowels *[ʾamu/onorṭa/eis] > *[ʾamu/orṭa/eis].

The sensitivity to the /n/ sound in Eg Aram may be best expressed in the PNs of *p3-šrỉ-n*-type. The *n* (Eg genitive) occurs before פ three times: פשנפור (Eleph.), פשנפמוי (Eleph.), פשנפתח (Saqq.). Cf. פשובסתי (*AD*), פשתות (Saqq.), also Ph פשמחי.

---

47 Maybe we can add one more observation as an evidence of spirantization in Ph; the different realizations of Eg PN *hr-ib* between Ph and Aram, *i.e.*, Ph הרב and Aram הריו. As I have discussed in the entry הריו, the final Eg *b* of *hr-ib* was partially assimilated into the previous vowel: *[ıub] > *[ıuw] > יו. However, in Ph the ב still stands for Eg *b* which was assimilated as [w]. This is possible only when Ph ב is spirantized. while in Aram the ב, a plosive, did not bear that sound value, hence, the Aramaic rendering of Eg *hr-ib* is הריו. Therefore, we could conclude that Ph הרב suggests the spirantization of ב in Ph (Eg *b* [ḇ] = Ph ב [ḇ], Aram ו).

III

EGYPTIAN PROPER NAMES AND LOANWORDS IN HEBREW

Various attempts at the identification of Eg elements in the Old Testament have been made since the last century. The first organized study appeared when W. Spiegelberg collected his independent essays and published the monograph *Aegyptologische Randglossen zum Allen Testamemt* (1904; see a review by J. H. Breasted, *AJSL* 21 1905 pp.247–250). Most of his discussions are still valuable. A half century later (1952) T. Lambdin throughly dealt with Eg elements in the Old Testament in the first chapter of his Ph.D. dissertation. It is obvious that his main concern was with Eg loan words. His extensive discussion of 45 possible Eg loan words was published in *JAOS* 73 (1952) pp.145–155. This remains as a standard work on Eg loan words in the Old Testament today. Eg loan words were re-examined by M. Ellenbogen, *Foreign Words in the Old Testament: Their origin and Etymology* (1962). Mostly following Lambdin, he added 6 more possibilities to Lambdin's list following identifications included in KB[1] and eliminated 20 loan words from it. As far as Eg loan words are concerned there was little progress in his reexamination. Therefore there is room for further advances in the identification of Eg loan words. Even though Eg proper names are always discussed in commentaries, Bible dictionaries and independent articles, there has been no systematic treatment of their identifications. In the following will be treated all Eg proper names found not only in the Old Testament, but also in all Hebrew documents including seals.

References are cited in each inventory; for the references

concerning Eg elements in the Joseph story, see the inventory of אברך.

A. HEBREW DOCUMENTS: DATES AND PROVENANCES

Y. Aharoni, *Arad Inscriptions*, no. 54, 12 (ostracon): end of 8th cent. BC[1] , Arad
N. Avigad, *Michmanim*, 4 no. 6 (seal): 8th cent. BC, n.p.
———. *Hebrew Bullae*, pp. 68, 69: 7h–6th cent.BC, Burnt Archive
A. Lemaire, *Semitica*, 30 (1980) p. 19–20 (ostracon): late 8th–7th cent. BC, Aroer (Negev)
Anonymous, *IEJ*, 12 (1912) p. 146 (amphora): n.d., En-Gedi
F. Vattioni, *SE* I (*Biblica* 50) no. 148: n.d., near Jerusalem
———. *SE* II (*Augustinianum* 11) no. 267: n.d., Judea.

1 A. Lemaire, *Inscriptions Hébraiques*, vol. 1, p. 201.

B. INVENTORY OF EGYPTIAN PROPER NAMES AND LOANWORDS

[1] Personal Names

אוא

--- *iwi* 

[Heb] Yadin, *Hazor*, II p.70]אוא; [Ammonite] Vattioni, *SE* I no. 194

[Eg] Ranke I.16.10 m. MK–NK. There are many similar names attested (see Ranke I.16.9–23, e.g., *iwi, iwy*)

The name is more likely to be Semitic as Hammond (*BASOR* 160 p. 39) compared it with the Midianite King *'Ewî* (Num 31:8), to which the hypocoristic termination *aleph*, which is relatively common in Ammonite (Jackson, *Ammonite Lang* p. 89), was attached.

אחימות (hybrid) *

--- אחי-*mw.t* "Brother of Mut"

[Heb] 1Chr 6:10 (25)

[Eg] *mw.t* (*Wb* II.54) is one of the commonest elements in Eg PNs.

The name could be interpreted as a pure Eg name: *3ḫ-mw.t* (Ranke I.2.24) "Mut is glorious." The name also could be interpreted as a pure Semitic "Brother of Death." Yet the fact that אחימות was born in Egypt leads us to be inclined to think it Eg. For מות see ענמות.

אחירע (hybrid)

--- אחי-*rʿ* "Brother of Reʿ"

[Heb] Num 1:15, 2:29, 7:78, 83, 10:27

[Eg] for Eg god *rʿ* see *Wb* II.401

There is a Heb noun רַע "evil" (from root רעע). Yet a divine name is more probable. While a Semitic explanation is possible, the root רע "evil" is not used in PNs (cf. *IPN* p.236). Heb *rēʿa*, though its vocalisation differs from אחירע, could be an alternative.

אסיר *

--- *3s-ỉr(.w)*  "Osiris"

IPN p. 63 n. 2; Avigad, *IEJ* 4 p. 238

[Heb] Ex 6:24, 1Chr 6:7(22), 8(23), 22(37)

[Eg] Ranke I.85.5 m. Dyn. 18.

The bearers of this name were probably born in Egypt. Therefore an Eg name is likely. Another Eg explanation is *ỉsr*, *ỉsr.w* (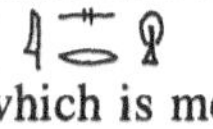) "Tamarisk" (Ranke I.46.22–25; II.246.14 m. OK–MK), which is more common (cf. Copt ⲞⲤⲒ, Demot *ỉsr*). However אסר is also a common. Semitic root meaning "bind", of which derivations are *ʾāsîr* and *ʾassîr* "prisoner." Therefore, the identification is open to choice, although the root אסר is not otherwise found in Heb PNs.

אסנה *

--- **(n)s-n(w.t)* "He who belongs to Nut"

IPN p. 63

[Heb] Ezr 2:50

[Eg] For a goddess Nut as a theophoric element, cf. *ỉnb-m-nw.t* (Ranke I.191.2 f. Dyn. 18), *t3-dỉ.t-nw.t* (Ranke I.373.16 f. Late), *ʿnḫ-nw.t* (Ranke II.271.10 m. Late).

Noth admitted that the name is Eg, probably because of the absence of a proper Semitic etymology. If אסנה is an Eg name, it is most likely to be identified with **ns-nw.t*.

אסנת **

--- **(n)s-n(y).t* "She who belongs to Neith"

L p. 56; For other references see Lw אברך

[Heb] Gen 41:45, 50, 46:20 (wife of Joseph)

[Eg] cf. *ns* + DN type names (Ranke I.173.17ff m./f. OK–Gk; cf. Aram אסחור, אסחנום, אסמן, אסמת, אספמט, אספמתetc.). Though *n(y)-s(w/y)*-DN is one of the most common type of Eg PNs after NK, this type of name occurs even in OK and MK (Ranke I.174.13, 15, 16, 173.3, 13, 176.5, 14, 15, 177.16, 23 etc.); [LXX] 'Ασεννεθ, 'Ασενεθ.

Possible is K. Kitchen's reconstruction, based on an attested form, **ỉw.s-n.ṯ* "She belongs to you" (cf. *ỉw.f-n.t* "He belongs to you (?)" Ranke I.14.12; *ỉw.f-n.ỉ* "He belongs to me") which often occurs in MK (Kitchen, *NBD* p. 94). However genitival adjective *n* plus the suffix of 2nd masc. sg. hardly appears in Eg PNs. The above *iw.f-n.t,* which is only example in which the 2nd masc. sg. suffix is used, can be interpreted as "He shall belong to Neith" (Ranke did not give the meaning to the name), whose identification with this name has been suggested by Vergote, following Spiegelberg (*Joseph en Égypte* p. 148f). *iw.f-(n-)D*N type is a common type of name in NK–Late (Ranke I.13–18). Therefore, this explanation is equally possible.

אשׂראל (hybrid)
--- *3s-ir-*אל "Osiris is god"
[Heb] 1Chr 4:16
[Eg] see Ph אסר
The fragmentary genealogy in which the name appears makes it impossible to date it. Phonetically the Eg identification is possible (cf. שׂכיות = *śk.tw*). The absence of the Heb root אשׂר perhaps indicates a foreign name, unless a misspelling took place as follows: אסראל > אשׂראל (root אסר "to bind", yet could still be *3s-ir-*אל). If Heb אסיר is Eg name *3s-ir.w*, as I discussed before, אשׂראל is less likely to be identified with Osiris.

אשׂראלי (hybrid)
--- Var. of אשׂריאל (?)
[Heb] Num 26:31b
[Eg] see אשׂראל, אסיר.

אשׂראלה (hybrid)
--- Var. of אשׂראל (?)
[Heb] 1Chr 25:2, 14
[Eg] see above.

אשׂריאל (hybrid)
--- Var. of אשׂראל
[Heb] Num 26:31a, Josh 17:2, 1Chr 7:14 (son of Manash)
[Eg] see above and Ph אסר
That the bearer of this name was born in Eg strengthens the Eg explanation (for the root אשׂר, see אשׂראל). The י of -אשׂרי corresponds to the Aram form אסרי "Osiris." Therefore, the Eg

theophoric element is most likely.

בנחור (hybrid)

--- בן-*ḥr(.w)* "Son of Horus"
[Heb] 1Kings 4:8
[Eg] see חור; [LXX] Βεὲν υἱος Ὦρ.

בסי

--- *bs.y* 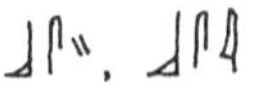
[Heb] Neh 7:52 (= Ezr 2:49); seal: Vattioni, *SE* I no. 245
[Eg] Ranke I.98.18f m. Late; [Akk] cf. *bi-i-sa-a* (*ANP* 64b; Tallqvist considers that the name is Aram). Cf. Aram בסא

The meaning of Aram בסי is unknown, "negligent" (?) (*DISO* p. 39). Noth considered it the short form of בְּסוֹדְיָה (*IPN* p.152). In the absence of a proper Sem etymology, Eg is likewise possible.

בתיה

--- *b(i).ty(.t)*  "Queen"
KB[3] p.160
[Heb] 1Chr 4:18 (daughter of Pharaoh, Bithia)
[Eg] *Wb* I.435.16–18 Gk (cf. *by.ty* "King" since Pyr.)

Other similar names are also attested: *bity* (f. Dyn 12), *bity.i* (?) (f. MK), *bti* (f. MK–Dyn. 18) Ranke I.93.21, 22, 99.5, 7. However, phonetically *bi.ty.t* best fits Heb בתיה. Therefore, if the Heb פרעה in 1Chr 4:18 really designates an Eg King, the identification is most probable.

הראל (hybrid)

--- *hr*-אל "אל is pleasing"
[Heb] Ezr 43:15 (Qere *ʾărîʾēl*)
[Eg] cf. *hr* + DN type names (Ranke I.230.20f. Late)
Cf. Ph הרבעל, Heb הריהו

The Semitic interpretation "Mountain of El" is not impossible. See הריהו.

הריהו (hybrid)

--- *hr*-יהו "YHW is pleasing"
[Heb] seal: Vattioni, *SE* III p. 238 no. 273

[Eg] cf. *hr-b3st.t* (Ranke I.230.20f); *Wb* II.496.6ff *hr* "pleasing" Copt ^{s}ϩⲣⲣⲉ, ^{b}ϩⲉⲣⲓ

Both father הריהו and son עניהו have possible Eg element *hr* "please" and *ʿn* "beautiful" both of which are common in Eg PNs, to which the same theophoric element יהו is attached. However Semitic explanations are also possible; see הראל and עניהו.

חור *

--- *ḥr(.w)* "Horus"

[Heb] Ex 17:10, 12, 24:14, 31:2 (35:30), 38:22, 1Chr 2:19, 20, 50, 4:1, 4; 2Chr 1:5; Num 31:8, Josh 13:21; Neh 3:9

[Eg] see Aram חור, Ph חר; [LXX] Ὥρ

Though admitting the possibility of the Eg name *ḥr.w*, Noth identified חור and חורי with Akk *ḫūru* "child" (*IPN* p. 220 no. 1). However the origin of these names is Egypt.

חורי **

--- *ḥr.y* "He of Horus" (?)

[Heb] Num 13:5

[Eg] see Aram חורי and above; [LXX] Σουρὶ.

חפני *

--- *ḥfn(r)* "Tadpole"

IPN p.63

[Heb] 1Sam 1:3, 2:34, 4:4, 11, 17

[Eg] Ranke I.239.13 m. MK; [LXX] Φινεες

Though the occurrence of the name is restricted to the first four chapters of 1Sam, that his brother has Eg name פינחס strengthens the Eg explanation. However the root חפן "hollow of hand" (Aram חפני), which is not used in PNs, leaves the identification open to choice.

חפרע **

--- *(w3)ḥ-(i)b-rʿ*

[Heb] Jer 44:30 (Eg king of Dyn 26 , Apries 589–570)

[Eg] see Ph וחפרע; [LXX] Ουαφρη.

חרחור

--- *ḥr(y)-ḥr*  "Horus who is higher"

[Heb] Ezr 2:51; Neh 7:53

[Eg] Ranke I.253,10 m. Dyn. 20 / f. NK

BDB considered that the name was a reduplicated noun deriving from a root חרר "to be free." However, the Eg explanation is equally possible (cf. Copt ϩⲣⲉ for *ḥry* Černý p. 292).

חרחס

--- **ḥr-ḥs(.w)* "Horus is praised"

[Heb] 2Kings 22:14 (= 2Chr 34:22 חסרה; many MSS חרחס

[Eg] cf. *ḥs* + DN type names: *ḥs-b3st.t*  "Bastet is praised", *ḥs-ptḥ*, *ḥs-rʿ* (Ranke I.254.16, 18, 20)

Though DN + *ḥs.w* (old perfective) is not common (cf. *ỉmn-nb-ḥs.w* Ranke I.29.16), the possibility of an Eg interpretation should be noted, because of the lack of a Semitic explanation. However the text is uncertain. No Eg interpretation of the alternative reading חרחס appears possible.

חרנפר **

--- **ḥr-nfr(.w)* "Horus is good"

IPN p. 64

[Heb] 1Chr 1:36

[Eg] cf. *ḥr-nfr* (Ranke I.249.9 m. MK–Gk) and DN-*nfr*; [LXX] Αναρφαρ

Note the Copt verb form, ^{S}ⲚⲞⲨϤⲢ, ⲚⲈϤⲢ-, ^{B}ⲚⲞϤⲈⲢ, "be good." Vocalization of *nefer* took analogy from *qatl*: *[nafr-] > *[nefr] > [nefer].

ירחע

--- **ỉr(t)-ḥʿ(ỉ)* "Eye of rejoicing"

[Heb] 1Chr 2:34

[Eg] cf. *ỉr(.t?)-ḥr*  "Eye of Horus" (Ranke I.42.13 m. MK, *ỉr.t-n(.t)-ḥr-ỉrw.w*(Ranke I.42.11 Ιναρως; Copt ⲉⲓⲉⲣ- for eye)

The context indicates that ירחע is an Eg servant, and as רחע has no cognate in Semitic, the possibility of an Eg name is most likely. However we must acknowledge that the identification is hypothetical as the name is not found in Egyptian.

ירימות (hybrid) *

--- ירי-*mw.t* "Mut has thrown"

[Heb] 1Chr 7:7, 8 *y*^{e}*rēôt*, 12:6(5), 24:30, 25:4, 27:19; 2Chr 11:18, 31:13; seal: Vattioni, *SE* III p. 245 no. 361.

[Eg] For מות for *mw.t*, see ענמות

Cf. ירמות

This name belongs to the group of יר(י) + DN type names, *e.g.*, יריאל, יריהו. יר(י) is derived from the root ירה (Ug *yrw*) "to throw, shoot," and מות is Eg goddess Mut (see the discussion in ענמות). If the root derived from a root **yrm*, the second י of ירימות cannot be explained (KB^3 p. 419). The fact that Jeremoth in 1Chr 7:7 was born in Egypt makes it likely that an Eg element entered this name.

ירמות *

--- Var. of ירימות

[Heb] 1Chr 8:14 (brother of ששק), 23:23, 25:22, Ezr 10:26, 27

[Eg] see ירימות

Notice that Jeremoth in 1Chr 7:8, who is different from the Jeremoth in the previous verse, was also born in Egypt. Both are grandsons of Benjamin. (see Albright, *BASOR* 125 p. 25ff. and *JAOS* 42 p. 320f.).

כוש **

--- *kš*  "The Nubian"

[Heb] Gen 10:6,7; 2K 19:9; 1Chr 1:8, 9; Est 1:1, 8:9; Job 28:19, Ps 68:32, 87:4; Is 11:11, 18:1, 20:3, 4, 5, 37:9, 43:3, 45:14; Jer 46:9; Ezek 29:10, 30:4, 5, 9, 38:5, Nah 3:9; Zeph 3:10

[Eg] see Ph כשי.

כושי **

--- gentilic of כוש

[Heb] Num 12:1; 2Sam 18:21, 22, 23, 31, 32; 2Chr 12:3, 14:8, 14:11, 12, 16:8, 21:16; Jer 13:23, 38:7, 10, 12, 39:16; Dan 11:43; Amos 9:7; Zeph 2:12

[Eg] see כוש, Ph כשי.

מיאמן **

--- *m(r)y-imn* 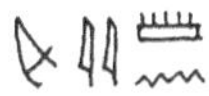 "The beloved of Amun"

[Heb] seal: Vattioni, *SE* III no.437; Avigad, *Hebrew Bullae* no.87, 89 [מ]יאמן

[Eg] Ranke I.160.6 m. NK; [Gk] Μιαμμουν; [MB] *ma-a-i-*[ilu]*a-ma-na* (Ranke, *KM* p. 12)

The MB form indicates that the Eg *r* has been lost (perhaps assimilated to *y*). Therefore, the name perfectly fits a common Eg name *mry-imn*. The names of the *mry* + DN type are among the most common from OK to Late (Ranke I.160.1–162.1). Avigad's interpretation: מי "who" + אמן "faithful" > "Who is of truth" is not impossible. However, Micaiah which he quoted is not really comparable: מי "who", כ "like", יה "divine name". The Eg explanation seems much more likely. Another Eg identification is noteworthy, i.e., *m3y-imn*  "Amun is a lion" (Ranke I.144.2 m. NK), which is less common.

מראל

--- *mr(y)*-אל "The beloved of אל"

[Ammonite] seal: Vattioni, *SE* I no. 194 אוא בן מראל (Jackson, "Ammonite PNs" no. 66)

[Eg] cf. *mry* + DN type names (*mry-imn, mry-b3st.t, mry-ptḥ, mry-r*ʿ Ranke I.160.1ff m./f. OK–NK).

As previously discussed in מיאמן, Eg *mry* became *my*. Therefore, it seem to be unlikely that Heb מר stands for Eg *mry*. However, there is some reason to assume that the *r* might be still preserved as a bi-form. Prof. K. Kitchen drew my attention to the peculiar writing of the word *mry* in the inscriptions of Ramesses IX and XI, that is, *mrr* (*KRI* V.481.14; VI.456.4; 706.3, 4; 734.9 etc.). Prof. Kitchen suggested that the extra *r* may be added to indicate the pronounciation [r], which is not indicated in the normal writing  *mr(r)*. If this is the case, מראל and others (מרבעל, מרמות, מרימות) could be Eg names or Sem names containing Eg element. Semitic explanations, however, should not be excluded; (1) Aram מר "lord," (2) Ug *mr* "to strengthen, bless" (common element of Ug PNs, see Gröndahl, p. 159f), (3) Ug *mr* "to drive away", Hebrew מְרָיָה is undoubtedly comparable, whatever its interpretation is. Hence the identification is open to choice.

מרבעל

--- *mr(y)-bꜥr*  "The beloved of Ba'al"
[Heb] Samaria Ostracon 2:7 (Reisner, *HES* p. 233 no. 2)
[Eg] Ranke I.160.12 m. Dyn. 19; for מר, see מראל.

מרים

--- *mry(.t)* + מ "The beloved"
Gardiner, *JAOS* 56 p.195
[Heb] Ex 15:20, 21; Deut 12:1, 4, 5, 10, 15, 20:1, 24:9, 26:59; Mic 6:4; 1Chr 5:29 (a sister of Aaron). 1Chr 4:17 (a Judahite)
[Eg] Ranke I.161.14; [Gk] Μαριαμ, Μαιων (1Chr 4:17) (LXX)

For the discussion on the Eg *mry*/*mry.t* and Semitic מר, see the entry מראל. Gardiner made the comment: "Nevertheless there is one way in which the old pronounciation *Marye* can be saved for an etymology of Mary, Mariam, Miriam." He supposed a possible connection of Miriam with the Egyptian goddess and priestesses who were called *Mrt*. However he left unexplained the afformative מ, which is usually added to masculine names, such as גרסם, מלכם, עמלם (Gesenius, § 85t). Another Eg explanation is *mr-ib* "Heart desires" (Ranke I.155.17 m./f.(?) OK–Late) with a slight phonetic change *b* > /*m*/ (cf. Lw חרטם). Thus Eg identifications are still open to question. If we admit a pagan element in the name, the interpretaion "Yamm is the lord" might be possible.

מרימות

--- *mr(.t)-mw.t* 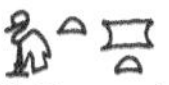 "The beloved of Mut"
[Heb] Bordreuil-Lemaire, *Semitica* 32 p. 29f.; Aharoni, *Arad Inscriptions* p. 85 (ostracon no.50)
[Eg] Ranke I.158.24 f. Dyn. 18; cf.*mri-mw.t* (Ranke I.159.26 m. Late)

Again both מרי and מות can be Semitic. Then four interpretations are possible as follows; (1) Eg *mr.t-mw.t* (above), (2) hybrid מרי-*mw.t* (for מרי see מראל), (3) hybrid *mry*-מות (for מות see ענמות), (4) Semitic מרי-מות. In the inventory of ענמות, I concluded that the Semitic god Mawet "Death" is unlikely, therefore, the first two explanations are more probable.

מרמות

--- Var. of מרימות

[Heb] Neh 3:4, 21, 10:6, 12:3; Ezr 8:33, 10:36

[Eg] see מרימות.

מריב בעל

--- *mr-ib*-בעל "The beloved of the heart of Baal"

[Heb] 1Chr 8:34, 9:40a

[Eg] cf. *mr-ib-ptḥ* 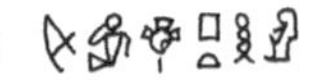 (Ranke I.155.18; II.361 m. Dyn. 26); *mr-ib* (Ranke I.155.17 m. OK / f. Late)

As there seems to be no satisfactory Semitic explanation of this name, this Eg solution is a good possibility. For מר, see מראל.

מריבעל

--- Var. of מריבבעל

[Heb] 1Chr 9:40b

[Eg] see מריבבעל.

מררי

--- *mrr.y*  , *mrr.i*  "The beloved" (?)

L p. 55

[Heb] Gen 46:11; Ex 6:19; Num 3:20 etc. (39x)

[Eg] *mrr.y* (Ranke I.162.24 m./f. MK, I.162.22 m./f. OK–MK); [LXX] Μεραρ(ε)ι, Μεραρει.

The fact that Merari was born in Egypt strengthens the possibility that the name is Eg. The Eg name *mrr.i/y* is common until MK. It is conceivable that a good Eg name has been preserved in Hebrew.

A Semitic explanation is likewise possible; Pu PNs מרר, מררבעל, ימרר (Benz p. 354) indicate that the root מרר is used in PNs, whatever their etymology is. Benz, followed by KB³, compared מרר with Ug *mrr* (UT 19.1556 "strengthen"), cf. Noth compared it with Arab *mirratum* (*IPN* p. 225 n. 9).

משה ?

--- *ms* "(The) child"

Gardiner, *JAOS* 56 p. 192ff (with doubt); Griffith, *JNES* 12 p. 225ff.

[Heb] passim

[Eg] Ranke I.164.18

A considerable number of discussions have been made on the etymology of Moses. The decisive point is on the correspondence between Eg *ś* and Heb שׁ. As has been shown, there is no conclusive evidence of the representation of Eg *ś* by NW Semitic *š*, when Eg names or words were borrowed and transliterated by NW Semitic (see below [4] Notes on the Correspondences e) sibilants). Even the same Eg word *ms* in GN רעמסס (*rᶜ-ms-s*) is transliterated as מס in the same period. Furthermore, the Heb root משה "to draw" is to be prefered and the meaning of the root best fits the context with a word-play. Therefore, an Eg origin for the name is very doubtful. J. Griffiths, in his lengthy article devoted to this name, found support for the corresondence between Eg *ś* and Heb שׁ only in the cases of Egypto-Semitic cognates. Then he strangely made a distinction between "names which are transliterated from Eg into Heb or vice versa for a temporal purpose and those which find a permanent place in the second language and hence get a chance to develop." Then he said that the case of Moses should be compared with those of Egypto-Semitic cognates which show the equation of Eg *ś* to Heb שׁ. However, there is no evidence of the "development" of *משה > משה. It is normal that, once borrowed, the consonants of the word do not undergo secondary change, cf. פנחס (borrowed for a permanent purpose!), Lw קסת etc. Therefore, at the moment, in the absence of clear evidence of the correspondence between Eg *ś* and Heb שׁ, the name is most likely to be of Semitic origin.

משעא

--- **mšᶜ* "March"

[Ammonite] seal: Vattioni, *SE* I no. 114

[Eg] cf. *mšᶜ-nfr (?)* 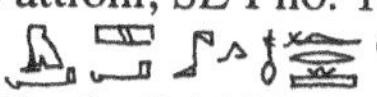 "Good march," *mšᶜ-sbk* (?) "Splendid march" (Ranke I.166.2 f. Dyn. 20; I.166.3 m. Dyn 21)

The name could be a hypocoristicon of the above Eg names. Likewise possible is a derivation from Semitic root ישע "to deliver", cf. Heb מישע "deliverance" (king of Moab), מֵישָׁע son of Caleb. The final א is a hypocoristic ending.

* נבי

--- *nb.y*  "He who belongs to the lords" (?)

[Heb] seal: Vattioni, *SE* III no. 343 and 433
[Eg] Ranke I.187.5 m. Dyn 6 and NK. Cf. other similar names *nb* (Ranke I.183.1 m./f. OK, NK), *nb.i, nb.w, nb.t* (Ranke I.187.4, 6, 7, 17).

Eg *nb* with its fem. form *nb.t* is one of the most common elements of Eg PNs used from OK to Gk.

נכה **
--- Var. of נכו
[Heb] 2K 23:29, 33, 34, 35
[Eg] see Aram נכו.

נכו **
--- *nk(3).w*  (Necho II, Eg king of Dyn 26)
[Heb] Jer 46:2; 2Chr 35:20, 22, 36:4
[Eg] see Aram נכו.

סוא
--- Abbr. of *w(3)s(3)rkn(i)* 
Kitchen, *TIP*[2] pp. 372–4, 551, 582–3
[Heb] 2K 17:4 *Ketib* סיא
[Eg] Gauthier, *LR* III p. 399f Osorkon, Eg king of Dyn 22
[Gk] Σωα, Σηγωρ, Σωβα (LXX)

As Ramesses was abbreviated as *sese*, it is possible that Osorkon was shortened as סוא representing *-s(3)r-*. Osorkon is perhaps the only Eg king who supported Israel at that time. For the impossibilities of other identifications: *sib'e turtan, shabako*, Eg *ṯ3* (vizier), and Tefnakht, see K. Kitchen, *TIP*[2] pp. 372–374. 551, 582–3.

עמיחור (hybrid)
--- עמי-*ḥr* "My kinsman is Horus"
[Heb] 2Sam 13:37 (*Qere* *ʿammîhûd* "My kinsman is majesty") (a Geshurite)
[Eg] see Ph חר

With a slight change of the reading of the Masora Text [hūr] > [hōr] (cf. שפחור, בנחור), the hybrid name is likely. However, חור could be explained as a word derived from a root חרר "be free," such as חר "noble." As for the name formation, cf. עמיאל, עמהוד, עמינדב.

עניהו

--- ʿn-יהו "יהו is beautiful"

[Heb] seal: Vattioni, *SE* III no. 273

[Eg] for ʿn + DN type names, see Ranke I.61.11ff: *ʿn-b3stt*, *ʿn-mw.t* etc.

Eg *ʿn* is one of the most common elements of Eg PNs used from OK to Gk. Therefore, the hybrid name is possible. However, Heb root ענה, though used in only one PN עֲנָיָה, leaves the identification open to choice. On Ug *ʿnil* (*UT* 1066.3) Gordon commented that *ʿn* may be the masculine counterpart of goddess *ʿnt*, without citing evidence. It should be kept in mind that ען often occurs with Semitic theophoric elements; Heb עניהו, Ph ענבעל, ענכתבעל, Ammonite ענאל, making it more likely to be Semitic (cf. ענמות).

ענמות

--- *ʿn-mw.t*  "Mut is beautiful"

[Ammonite] seal: Vattioni, *SE* I no. 116 (maidservant of דבלכס)

[Eg] Ranke I.61.18 f. NK. For *ʿn* + DN type name, see עניהו.

Albright, "Notes on Ammonite History" *Miscellanea Biblica B. Ubach* p. 4, followed by G. Landes, *BA* 24 p. 82f., and Jackson, Ammonite Lang p. 81f., considered that ענמות was related to the Thamudic, Safaitic, and Arabic name group, Ghânim or Ghânimat or Ghanîmat. There are ancient Arabic names *ʿnm, ʿnmt, ǵnm, gnmt* (Harding, p. 445, 458), deriving from *ǵnm* "booty" "to take as booty" (Biella p. 396; Beeston p. 54), and a Palmyrene name ענמו "successful, noble", derived from Arab *ǵānim* (Stark p. 106). However all these similar names cannot explain the ו of ענמות. Jackson thinks that it is possibly a *mater lectionis* indicating [ū] of a fem. ending [-ut]. Yet that is very unlikely. As J. Tigay discussed in *You shall Have no Other Gods*, p. 66 n. 12, judging from the fact that each of the מות- names can be paralleled by others in which a theophoric element appears in place of מות-, *e.g.*, אחיח(ו), יריאל, מרי(ב)בעל, עזגד, it seems to be more likely that the מות is a deity. Hence he identified the מות with the Semitic god Mawet "Death." The possibility that מות is a deity is strengthened by another fact that initial element -ענ is often followed by a theophoric element, *e.g.*, Ph ענבעל, ענבתבעל, Heb ענידהו (for the discussion on ענ, see ענידהו). However, as far as the identification of the מות is concerned the god Mawet is not likely, because its existence is not certain outside Ug literature, and its occurrence in PNs is doubtful. As the Eg goddess Mut is one of the most common theophoric elements. I am inclined to think that is an Eg name. However, as ענ could be a Semitic root, the identification is open to choice as follows;

(1) pure Eg: *ʿn-mw.t* (see above)

(2) hybrid with Eg goddess: ענ-*mw.t* "Mut has answered" or "Mut has returned"

(3) hybrid with Sem goddess: *ʿn*-מות "Mot is beautiful"

(4) pure Semitic: ענ-מות "Mot has answered."

ענמש *

--- *ʿn-m-š*  "The beautiful one is on the lake"

Lemaire, *Inscriptions Heb.*, p. 54

[Heb] Samaria Ostracon no. 24 (Reisner, *HES*, I p. 235)

[Eg] Ranke I.61.15 f. NK

Reisner noted that ענמש is apparently Eg (p. 235). Albright, "The Evolution of the West-Semitic Divinity 'AN- 'ANAT- 'ATTÂ" *AJSL* 41 p. 83f, half admitted Reisner's note and identified it as 'Anemôs(e) for 'Anat-mâsey "born of 'Anat" on the assumption that the fem. ending *-t* of 'Anat dropped. However, there is no evidence that the Semitic ending *-t* dropped as the Eg ending did. What is more, the equation of Semitic שׁ with Eg *s* is questionable. Lemaire's interpretation *ʿn-m-š* is much more likely. One may wonder wether the Semitic form of *ʿn-m-š* is ענמסי, because the Copt form of *š* "cistern" is ϢΗΙ. However, as the *š* is usually represented by שׁ in Heb (see שׁיחור, שׁחר), the Copt from is perhaps a result of the later development.

פוטיאל ** (hybrid)

--- *p(3)-di*-אל "He whom אל has given"

[Heb] Ex 6:25

[Eg] cf. *p3-di*-DN type names (Ranke I.121.18ff m. NK–Gk); [LXX] Φουτιηλ.

פוטיפר

--- *p(3)-di-p(3)-(i)r(y)* "He whom the companion has given"
L p. 56
[Heb] Gen 37:36, 39.1
[Eg] For *p3-iry*  see Ranke I.101.17f (m. NK often); see also Ranke I.354.3, *DemNB* 1. 352 *pa-iry*, Copt ⲡⲁϩⲣ (ᵇⲎⲢ "companion, love" for *iry* Černý, p. 42). Also *p3-di-iry* is attested in Demotic (*DemNB* I.287); [Gk] Πετεφρης (LXX).

The name has been considered to be identical with פוטיפרע. However, it is not likely that the strong consonant *ʿayn* dropped. If this is the case, *p3-di-p3-iry* is most probable. However, it is fair to note that this type of name usually takes a theophoric element after *p3-di-*, though not exclusively; see Ranke II.328.20 *t3-di-ry* (?) and *DemNB* I.287 *p3-ti-iry*. Unfortunately the meanings of Eg *ry* (a sort of plant ?) and *iry* (short form of *iry-ḥms-nfr* ?) are not certain. Other names which have nontheophoric elements are *DemNB* I.295 *p3-ti-ʿš3-ihy* "He whom the Kingdom has given", *DemNB* I.309 *p3-ti-pp* "He whom (PN) *pp* has given", *DemNB* I.342 *p3-ti-sn-snw* "He whom two brothers have given."

פוטיפרע **

--- *p(3)-di-p(3)-rʿ* 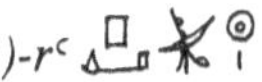 "He whom Reʿ has given"
L p. 56
[Heb] Gen 41:45, 50, 46:20
[Eg] Ranke II.356 m. Dyn 22(?)–Late (cf. I.123.11); *DemNB* I.529; [Gk] Πετεφρης (LXX), Πετεπρης.

פועה

--- *p(3)-ʿ(3)* 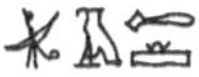 "The great"
[Heb] Ex 1:15
[Eg] Ranke I.102.11 m./f. NK; [LXX] Φουα

פועה is a Heb midwife, Eg *p3-ʿ3*, though a male form, was used as a female name as well. פועה, however, can be explained by Ug PN *pǵt* "girl" (< *pǵy* "a boy" *UT* 2083, 2081). The identification is open to choice.

פחא **

--- *p(3)-(n-)ḥ(r)*  "He who belongs to the face"

[Heb] seal: Avigad, *Michmanim* 4 p. 10 (no. 6)
[Eg] see Aram פחא.

פט **

--- *p(3)-d(i)* "He whom (DN) has given"
[Moabite] seal: Vattioni, *SE* II no. 267
[Eg] see Aram פטי.

פטיהו (hybrid) **

--- *p(3)-di-*יהו "He whom יהו has given"
[Heb] amphora: *IEJ* 12 p. 146
[Eg] cf. *p3-di*-DN type names (Ranke I.121.18ff.).

פינחס **

--- *p(3)-nḥs(y)*  "The Nubian"
Gardiner, *JAOS* 56 p. 191f.; L p. 54
[Heb] Ex 6:25; Num 25:7 (17x); 1Sam 1:3 פנחס, 2:34, 4:4, 11, 17, 19, 14:3; Ezr 8:33
[Eg] Ranke I.113.13 m. NK–Late; II. 354; *DemNB* I.194 (*p3-nḥs*); [Gk] Φ(ε)ινεες (LXX); [Copt] ⲡⲁⲛⲉϩ ⲁⲥ (Heuser p. 16); [Aram] cf. חֿרפנחס

P3-nḥsy as a PN is common in Egypt. One who is called "The Nubian" is not necessarily a Nubian. The word Nubian signifies something like "blacky", perhaps because his skin is a little darker. The use of כש "Kushu (Nubian)" as Heb PN can be comparable.

פכמת

--- **p(3)-(n-)k(3)-(n-)m(w.)t* "He who belongs to the ka of Nut"
[Heb] Jar: *Lachish Inscription* 29 (Ussishkin, *Tel Aviv* 5 pp. 85-88)
[Eg] cf. *p3-n-k3-n-ḥ.t* "He who belongs to the ka of temple" (Ranke I.111.11 m. Late)

Another suggestion is **p3-kmt(.y)*; cf. *kmt.y* , *kmt.w*, *kmt.t* etc. (Ranke I.345.22ff m./f. MK). Though all belong to MK, it is conceivable that the names occur with the article in NK.

פסמי *

--- short form of *psm(ṯk)*
[Ammonite] ostracon: Heshbon 5.4 (Jackson, *Ammonite Lang* p. 55

no. 5.4)

[Eg] see Aram פסמי; [Gk] Ψαμις, Ψαμες, Ψαμμις

For the Ammonite hypocoristic ending *-y*, see Jackson, "Ammonite PNs" p. 518 (*e.g.*, חגי, פלטי etc.).

פפי **

--- *pp*

[Heb] ostracon: Aharoni, *Arad Inscriptions* p. 96 no. 72

[Eg] Ranke I.131.8 m. MK / Late

Identical consonants in the first two positions are excluded in Semitic. Therefore, a Semitic explanation is impossible. On the other hand, Eg does not have such a restriction and there are Eg names which commonly have *p* in the first two positions, *e.g.*, *pp* (above), *ppi* (Ranke I.131.12 m. OK–NK / f. OK–MK), *ppy* (131.18 m./f. MK–NK). Cf. also the divine element of *p3-di-pp* (Ranke I.123.12 m. Late–Gk). Other possible explanations which are less likely are *p3-n-p* ,*p3-n-py* (Ranke I.107.12 m. Dyn 22f.; 107.24, 25 m. Late).

פרע *

--- *p(3)-(n-)rʿ* "He who belongs to Reʿ"

[Heb] seal: Vattioni, *SE* I no. 126

[Eg] Ranke I.109.13 m. NK

There is a Heb root פרע "let someone loose" (cf. Ug *prʿ*), which is not used in PN. Therefore פרע is likely to be an Eg name.

פשחור **

--- **p(s)š-ḥr* "Horus shares" or "Share of Horus"

[Heb] Jer 20:1, 2, 3a, 3b, 6, 21:1, 38:1a, 1b; Ezr 2:38, 10:22; Neh 10:4, 10:22, 11:12, 7:41

[Eg] cf. *psš-mw.t* (Ranke I.137.5 m. Late), *psš-mn.w* (Ranke I.137.6 m. MK).

Another possibility is *p3-šri-(n-)ḥr* (Ranke I.119.3 Ψενυρις) "The son of Horus." This type of name is much more common than the *psš* + DN type in the Late period. However, the Gk form indicates that Eg *n* is retained though the N-assimilation is quite possible in Hebrew. Therefore, *psš* + DN is a little more probable. Cf. Ph פש- type and Aram פש- and פשן- type. Cf. פשחר.

פשחר **

--- Var. of פשחור

[Heb] ostracon: Aharoni, *Arad Inscriptions* p. 86 no. 54; ostracon: Lemaire, *Semitica* 30 p. 20 no. 2; seal: Vattioni, *SE* I no. 148 and 152; Avigad, *Hebrew Bullae* p. 97. no. 151, p. 98 no. 152, p. 107 no. 183

[Eg] see פשחור.

צחא **

--- *ḏ(d)-ḥ(r)*  "Face speaks"

IPN p. 63

[Heb] Neh 7:46

[Eg] see Ph צחא; [Gk] Σηὰ (LXX)

KB[3], comparing it with Aram צחא, accepts that Heb צחא is also an Eg name. However, its meaning cannot be "Horus/face speaks" as KB[3] say, but only "Face speaks," because the Eg *r* of Horus was never lost. צחא can hardly be derived from any Heb root. So it is most likely that the name is Eg.

ציחא **

--- Var. of צחא

[Heb] Ezr 2:43

[Eg] see צחא; [Gk] Σουθια (LXX).

צפנתפענח

--- **ḏf(3.i)-nṯ(r), p(3)-ʿnḫ* "My provision is god, the living one"

[Heb] Gen 41:45

[Eg] cf. *ḏf3(.i)-ḥʿpy* 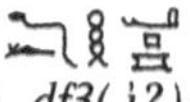 "My provision is the Nile" (Ranke I.406.16 m./f. MK), *ḏf3(.i?)-k3(.i?)* "My provision is my ka" (?) (Ranke I.406.18 f. OK)

Steindorff's interpretation (*ZÄS* 30 p. 50–52) has been widely accepted (*e.g.*, D. Redford, *A Study of the Biblical story of Joseph* p. 230; A. Schulman, *SAK* 2 p. 235–243), that is, **ḏd-p3-nṯr-iw.f-ʿnḫ* "The god said, let him live" (cf. *ḏd-imn-iw.f-ʿnḫ* "Amun said, let him live" Ranke I.409.23 m. Late). However, (1) phonetically, an *aleph* is normally required between ת and פ, because *iw.f* is normally represented by אפ (see Aram PN אפע = *iw.f-ʿ3*, אפרי = *iw.f-rr*), though it is conceivable that the *aleph* is elided; (2)

semantically, the meaning of the name is inappropriate in the context.

K. Kitchen has proposed (*NBD*[2] p. 1273) another solution with consonantal metathesis: *צתנפ > צפנת, because the sequence of צת is alien to Heb speakers. His interpretation is (Joseph) *ḏd-n.f-ʾIp-ʿnḫ* "Joseph is called 'Ip'nkh," which is a common name in the MK and Hyksos periods (cf. Ranke I.22.16). However, (l) phonetically, the *aleph* of 'Ip'nkh is not reflected in the name; (2) the interpretation is based upon a metathesis for euphony in Hebrew.

A large number of suggestions has been produced as follows[2]. Yet each one is either (1) semantically inappropriate, (2) phonetically incorrect (3) or not attested;

(1) A. Harkavy (1870): *ḏf3-nḏ-p3-ʿnḫ* "Food, protection of the life." The name form is not attested; נת cannot stand for Eg *nḏ*.

(2) A. Wiedemann: *p3-snṯ-n-p3-ʿnḫ* "The foundation of the life." The name form and the element *snṯ* are not attested; a metathesis (צפ > פצ) is assumed; צ can hardly represent Eg *s*.

(3) J. Krall (1888): *ḏ(d)-mnṯ.w-iw.f-ʿnḫ* "Mont said may he live." Though the form of name is attested well, a shift of a consonantal value (/m/ > /p/) is presupposed; the *aleph* of *iw.f* dropped.

(4) J. Lieblein (1898): *ḏf3-nty-p3-ʿnḫ* "He who gives the provision of the life." Though phonetically the name corresponds to the Heb form, the type of name is not attested.

(5) É. Naville (1903): *ṯs-n.t-p(r)-ʿnḫ* "The head of the school of learning, of the sacred college." Eg *ṯs* cannot be represented by Heb צפ, neither *n.t* by Heb נת. The form is also unknown.

(6) E. Mahler (1907): *ḏf3-n-t3, p3-di-ʿnḫ* "Provision of the land, Life-giver." The name type of *ḏf3-n-t3* is not attested, *di* has no correspondence in צפנתפענח.

(7) W. F. Albright (1918): *p3-snṯ-(n-)p3-ʿnḫ* "The sustainer of Life." A metathesis is assumed, *i.e.*, צפ > פצ (cf. the Gk form); Heb צ does not represent Eg *s*; no parallel is found.

(8) R. Engelbach (1924): *ḏd.w-n.f-p3-ʿnḫ* "One called him, (Joseph is) 'the living one'." The interpretaion is assumed with a metathesis, *i.e.*, *-צתנפ > -צנפת (cf. K. Kitchen's *ḏd-n.f-ip-ʿnḫ*).

---

2 See Vergote, *Joseph en Égypte* p. 151f. There are nine interpretations listed, and Vergote's interpretation p. 145. (cf. Kitchen's review *JEA* 47 p.161). For two more interpretations, see Redford, *A Study of the Biblical Story of Joseph* p. 230 n. 2, and A. R.Schulman, *SAK* 2 pp. 235–243.

(9) H. Lutz (1945): *(i.t)-(ḫ)p(r)-n-t(3-ḫ.t-n)-p3-ꜥnḫ* "To procure the way of life" has no phonetic correspondence at all.

(10) J. Vergote (1959): *p3-s-nty-ꜥm.f-n3-iḫ(.t)* "The man who knows the matter." The whole interpretation depends upon the Gk form Ψονθομιφανήχ. No parallel from of the name is found in attested Eg PNs.

(11) Leibovitch (1964): *ḏf3-n-t3wy, p3-ꜥnḫ* "Sustainer of the two lands, the living one." The form *ḏf3-n-* is not attested. Eg dual ending *-wy* cannot be elided, cf. Aram PN סמתו (*sm3-t3.wy*), פתו (*p3-n-t3.wy*).

The solution proposed here *ḏf(3.i)-nṯ(r), p(3)-ꜥnḫ* is phoneticlly perfect, the name form is attested, and the meaning fits the context.

שושא *

--- *šš*  , *šš.i*  (untranslatable)

[Heb] 1Chr 18:16

[Eg] Ranke I.330.2 m. Dyn 26; [Gk] Σουσα (LXX)

Cf. other forms שיא, שישא

שושא, שיא (2Sam 20:25), שישא (1K 4:3) and שריה (2Sam 8:17) designate the same person, *i.e.*, the scribe of King David. שריה is most likely to be the adopted Hebrew name of a foreign official. Therefore, several attempts have been made to identify it as a foreign name; (1) a Babylonian name: *šamšu* (B. Stab, J. Marquart, etc. see *RB* 72 p. 384). (2) a Hurrian name: a hypocoristicon of *šewi-šarri* (B. Maisler, *RB* 72 p. 384); *šešwe*, *šešwiya* > **šewše*, **šeyša* (K. Kitchen, *VTS* 40 p. 114). (3) an Eg name: *šš*, *šš.i*, *šš.y*, *šš.w* (de Vaux, *RB* 48 p. 398f); **s3wy-s3i* "His is satisfaction" (K. Kitchen see above); *s(ḫ)š(ꜥt)* "secretary" (A. Cody, *RB* 72 p. 387ff; supported by T. Mettinger, *Solomonic State Officials*, pp. 25–34). If the final *aleph* is a *mater lectionis*, *šamšu* for שושא is possible, though שישא cannot be explained. If the hypocoristicon of *šewi-šarri* is attested as *šewiša*, Maisler's solution is acceptable. If a metathesis took place, a Hurrian *šešwe*, *šešwiya* is probable. If both the ו / י and the *aleph* of שו / שיא are vowel letters, Eg *šš*, *šš.i*, *šš.y*, *šš.w* is likely. However, Eg *s3wy-s3i* requires an unusual correspondence between Eg *s* and Heb שׁ, and Eg *sḫ šꜥt* makes the inconceivable assumption that the Eg *ḫ* dropped and the Eg ꜥ was reduced to *aleph*. Therefore, both are unlikely. Considering that

Heb ו and י, when they are vowel letters, appear alternatively, esp. between שׁ and שׁ, e.g., שׁושׁק, שׁישׁק; שׁושׁן, שׁישׁן, we could assume the ו and י of שׁישׁא and שׁושׁא are also vowel letters. It is true that the MT dealt with the ו as a consonant (note the י as a vowel letter), yet the Masoretes rarely failed to recognize a vowel letter and vocalized it as consonant (*e.g.*, *ʾāwen* = *ʾôn*! "On") when they did not know the etymology. Therefore, the Eg solution of de Vaux is certainly possible. This type of name occurs from OK to Dyn 26 (see Ranke I.330.1–5).

שׁושׁק **

--- Var. of שׁישׁק

[Heb] 1K 14:25 (Qere שׁישׁק)

[Eg] see שׁישׁק, cf. שׁשׁק; [Gk] Σουσακιμ (LXX).

שׁישׁק **

--- *šš(n)ḳ* 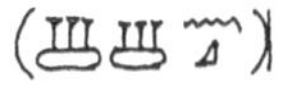 Shoshenq I (*ca.* 945–924)

[Heb] 1K 11:40; 2Chr 12:2, 5, 7, 9

[Eg] Gauthier, *LR* III, pt. 2 p. 307 (Eg king of Dyn 22); [Gk] Σουσακιμ (LXX)

Cf. שׁושׁק, שׁשׁק

The NA form *su-si-in-ḳu* suggests that שׁושׁק reflects the original vocalization. K. Kitchen notes that Manetho's Σεσωγχωσις probably shows metathesis and that the omission of *n* of שׁישׁק reflects its common omission in Eg throughout the Libyan period (*TIP*² p. 73 n. 356).

שׁענף

--- **š(3)ʿ-nf(r)* "Beautiful beginning"

[Heb] seal: Vattioni, *SE* III no. 343 and 433

[Eg] cf. *š3ʿ* (Ranke I.324.20 f. Dyn 18), *š3ʿ-ḫpry* (Ranke I.324.21 f. Late)

In the absence of a Semitic explanation, an Eg identification deserves to be considered.

שׁשׁן **

--- *sšn* 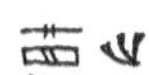 "Lily"

Gardiner, *JAOS* 56 p. 189f

[Heb] 1Chr 2:31, 34, 35 (cf. Apocrypha, Book of Daniel v. 2 etc.שושנה)
[Eg] Ranke I.297.29 m. MK; [Copt] ϢⲰϢⲈⲚ; [Gk] Σωσ (LXX); [Aram] ששן
Cf. Heb Lw שושן "lily"

The original spelling of Eg lily was *sššn* (*Wb* III.487 OK–MK), it then took a bi-form *sšn* (*Wb* III.485 since MK) and *ššn* (cf. Copt ϢⲈϢⲈⲚ), which is now inscriptionally confirmed (K. Kitchen, *VA* p. 29–31). Therefore Heb ששן corresponds to Eg *ššn*, not *sšn*. Note that the Heb loan word שושן (*šûšan*) shows a different vocalization of PN ששן (*šēšan*), behind which a change of vocalization [ū] > [ē] took place (see below [5] Notes on the Hebrew Vocalizations c) Other Vowel Changes).

* ששק

--- *šš(n)ḳ* 
IPN p. 64
[Heb] 1Chr 8:14, 25 brother of ירמות
[Eg] Ranke I.330.6 m. Late–Gk
Cf. שושק

ששק, relating to the fall of Gath (1Chr 8:13), most likely belongs to David's time. Since the Libyans had already settled in the Delta in Dyn 21 (1069–945 BC; K. Kitchen, *TIP* p. 244f.), it is conceivable that the Libyan name *ššnḳ* entered Heb at that period. In the absence of a Heb cognate, an Eg name is more than likely.

תחפניס

--- **t(3)-(n.t-)ḥ(.t)-p(3)-ns(w)* "She who belongs to the house of the king"
Stricker, *AO* 15 pp. 11 – 12; Grdseloff, *Revue de l'Histoire Juive en Egypte* I pp. 69 – 99; Albright, *BASOR* 140 p. 32
[Heb] 1K 11:19, 20, 20 תחפנס
[Eg] cf. *t3-n.t-ḥ(w).t* "She who belongs to the temple", *t3(-n.t?)-ḥ(w).t-ʿ3.t* "She who belongs to the great house" (Ranke I.361.22f). For a *mater lectionis* י, cf. Copt ϨⲚⲎⲤ (*Ḥ.t-nn-nsw* "Henes").

Two more interpretations have been put forward; (1) Gredseloff: **t3-ḥm.t-p3-ns(w)* "Royal wife." The title rather than PN is preferable to the context where תחפנים is followed by a title "queen." Since we know that there is a vowel after the *m* (cf. Copt ϩⲓⲙⲉ for *ḥm.t*), the assimilation is rather unusual. (2) Albright: **t3-ḥn.t-p3/pr-nsw* "She whom the king / palace protects." Although an assimilation of *n* to *p* is assumed, it is more likely, because of Copt ϩⲱⲛ, ϩⲟⲛ- for *ḥn.t* "to protect."

תרהקה **
--- *thrḳ* 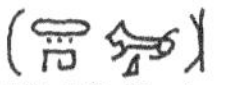
[Heb] 2K 19:9 (= Is 37:9) (Eg king (690–664 BC) of Dyn 25)
[Eg] see Aram תהרקא (Notice a metathesis of ה and ר).

[2] <u>Divine Names</u>

אמון **
--- *imn* "Amun"
[Heb] Nah 3:8, Jer 46:25
[Eg] see Ph אמן.

חף
--- *ḥp*  "Apis"
[Heb] Jer 46:15 אביריך לא עמד // מדוע נס חף "Why did Apis flee? // Your bull did not stand ?" Cf. LXX Διὰ τι ἔφυγεν ἀπὸ σου ὁ 'Απις
[Eg] *Wb* III.70; Ph and Aram חפי

Interpretation of חף as "Apis" in this context, following LXX, (accepted by modern tranlations *NEB*, *JB*, see J. Bright, *Jeremiah* p. 303) is preferable, though it is impossible to make a final judgment, because Heb root סחף "prostrate" exists and so MT נסחף could be correct.

[3] <u>Geographical Names</u>

און **
--- *iwn(w)*  "Heliopolis"
[Heb] Gen 41:50; Ezek 30:17 אָוֶן·

[Eg] *Wb* I.54; Montet, *Géographie* I p. 156; Gauthier, *DG* I p. 54; Gardiner, *AEO* II 145*; [Ph] אן; [Copt] ⲱⲛ; [Gk] Ων; [NA] *u2-nu* (Parpola, *NAT* p. 368); [Baby] *āna* (del Monte-Tischler, *Die Orts- und Gewässdernamen der hethitischen Texte* p. 15).

אן **

--- Var. of און

[Heb] Gen 41:45, 46:20

[Eg] see און.

אתם

--- *ỉtm* (?)

[Heb] Ex 13:20; Num 33:6, 7, 8; [LXX] 'οθομ, 'οθωμ

Phonetically the most natural correspondence is *ỉtm* "Atum." K. Kitchen orally suggested **ỉw-(ỉ)tm* "the island of Atum" which is also possible, though both are pure reconstructions. Though often proposed, *ḫtm* is impossible phonetically.

חנס **

--- **ḥ(w.t-nnỉ)-ns(w)* "Heracleopolis parva"

Spiegelberg, *ÄRAT* p. 36–38

[Heb] Is 30:4

Although חנס is commonly identified with Eg *ḥ(w.t-nn)-nsw* "Heracleopolis" (Gauthier, *DG* IV p. 86; Montet, *Géographie* II p. 187; *AEO* II p. 113f.), Heracleopolis in UE seems to be a strange parallel with Tanis in the context Is 30:4. Therefore, Spiegelberg proposed **Ḥ(w.t-nnỉ)-nsw* "Heracleopolis parva" in the Delta (cf. *ḫi-ni-in-ši* Assurb. I.95; Ανυσις Herodotus II 166). K. Kitchen also furnished a simple solution *ḥ(w.t)-nsw* "The palace," because there was a palace in Tanis (*NBD*[1] p. 504).

מי נפתוח *

--- *mr(y)-n-ptḥ* (in *n3-ḫnm.t-mr.n-ptḥ* 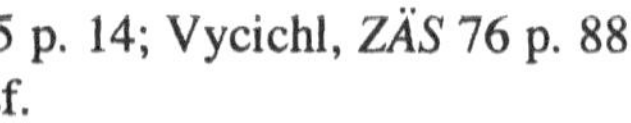 "The wells of Merneptah")

Calice, *OLZ* 6 p. 224; Stricker, *AO* 15 p. 14; Vycichl, *ZÄS* 76 p. 88; Aharoni, *The Land of the Bible* p. 172f.

[Heb] Josh 15:9; 18:15

[Eg] Anastasi III, vs. 6.4; Wolf, *ZÄS* 65 p. 41f; Caminos, p. 111,

says “name of watering station in Palestine” (p. 554).
Cf. Hittite PN ^{m}*Mar-ni-ip-taḫ* (Laroche no. 765)

It seems to be identical with modern Lifta (Abel, II p. 398; Aharoni p. 111 and 382), about 5 km, west of Jerusalem.

מף **

--- Var. of נף
[Heb] Hos 9:6
[Eg] see Heb נף

Probably the middle נ (cf. Aram מנפי) was assimilated into the following a labial פ (cf. Aram מפי); see the later discusion p. 296-297.

נא **

--- *ni(w.t)* “Thebes”
[Heb] Jer 46:25; Ezek 30:14, 15, 16; Nah 3:8
[Eg] see Aram נא.

נף **

--- *m(n-n)f(r)* “Memphis”
[Heb] Is 19:13, Jer 2:16, 44:1, 46:14, 19; Ezek 30:13, 16
[Eg] *Wb* II 63.6–7 Montet, *Géographie* I p. 29; Gauthier, *DG* III p. 38f.; Gardiner, *AEO* II p. 122*; [Ph] מנף; [Aram] נפי, מנפי; [Heb] מף; [Copt] ^{s}MN̄ϤЄ, MNBЄ, ^{b}MЄMϤI etc.; [Gk] μεμφις; [Akk] *me-em-pi* (S. Parpola, *NAT* p. 246); [Baby] *mempi* (Zadok, *GNNLB* p. 228)

The change מ > ן is not usual though conceivable (see the later discussion [4] Notes on the Correspondeces d) Nasals).

נפתח (in נפתחים)*

--- **n(3)-p(3)-(i)dḥ(w)* “Those of the Delta”
Spiegelberg, *OLZ* 9 pp. 276–9; Kitchen, *NBD* p. 865
[Heb] Gen 10:13 (= 1Chr 1:11)
[Eg] cf. *Wb* I.155.8 *n3-idḥw* “those of the delta land”

From the context, the designation of Lower Egypt by נפתח, being followed by פתרוס (Upper Egypt), is likely. Therefore, Brugsch (*Wb* VI p. 633) and Erman emend the text to (נ)פתמחי to fit

Eg *p3-t3-mḥw* "Lower Egypt." However Spiegelberg, without resorting to an emendation, proposed another possibility **n3-p3-idḥ(w)*, which is more likely. Spiegelberg, followed by Ranke, *KM* p. 31, also compared it with NA *nathu* (Assurb. I 92 and 97) and Gk Ναθω (Herodotus II 165). However these designate a city *n3y-t3-ḥwt* (Montet, *Géographie* I p. 169) in the Delta.

סונה **

--- *swn(.t)* 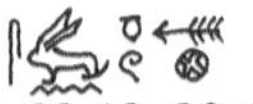 "Syene" (modern Aswan)

[Heb] Ezek 29:10, 30:6

[Eg] see Aram GN סון.

סין **

--- *sin* 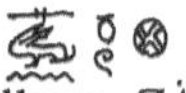 "Pelusium" (modern Tell el-Farama)

Spiegelberg, *ZÄS* 49 p. 81ff; Kitchen, *TIP* p. 377 n. 877

[Heb] Ezek 30:15, 16

[LXX] Σαΐν; [NA] *ṣi-ʾi-nu* (Assurb. I 91, 134; cf. Ranke, *KM* p. 34)

Streck (Assurb. p. 10 n. 3) suggests that *ṣi-ʾi-nu* is identical with *ṣa-ʾa-nu* "Tanis." However the context indicates that these cities are different from each other. Despite the variation in sibilant *ṣi-ʾi-nu* is most likely to be Pelusium (see Kitchen above).

סינים **

--- Var. of סונים "Syenites"

[Heb] Is 49:12

[Eg] see סונה; also the later discussion in [5] Notes on Hebrew Vocalization c) Other Vowel Changes.

סכת ?

--- *ṯkw*  (modern Tell el-Maskuta)

Brugsch, *ZÄS* 13 p. 8; Naville, *The Store-city of Pithom* p. 23; Redford, *VT* 13 p. 404f.; Helck, *VT* 15 p. 35f.; Aharoni, p. 179

[Heb] Ex 12:37 (with locative ה), 13:20; Num 33:5, 6

[Eg] Gauthier, *DG* VI p. 83; Montet, *Géographie* I p. 213

Since Brugsch identified סכת with *ṯkw*, the identification has been generally accepted by scholars, except Gardiner "The Geography of the Exodus" p. 213 and his followers (Peet, *Eg and the Old Testament* p. 139; Caminos, p. 256). The reason why

Gardiner denied it is that he mistakenly identified Raamsses with Pelusium (Gardiner, *JEA* 5 p. 270). The location of *ṯkw* and the identification of *ṯkw* with סכת is almost certain by now. However, a philological question still remains, that is, the representation of Eg *ṯ* by Heb ס. No scholar has ever doubted since Brugsch that Heb borrowed *ṯkw* as סכ, to which a Heb ending ת was added. Yet the facts that Eg *ṯ* is not represented by Heb ס, and Heb ס is normally represented by Eg *ṯ* when Eg borrows from Semitic (Burchardt, p. 147; Albright, *VESO* p. 65) lead us to conclude that Eg *ṯkw* was derived from Semitic סכת. This conclusion more easily explains the loss of the final *t* in Eg, because Eg *t* ending was lost in NK. The fact that *ṯkw* first occurs under Ramesses II (*e.g. Hyksos and Israelite Citis*, 1906, pl. 31, bottom right; E. Naville, *The Story City of Pitom*, 4th ed., 1903, p. 4, pl. 3A and probably 3C etc.) also strengthen this conclusion. What is more, Heb סכת occurs as another GN, and the root סכה "booth", derived from סכך "cover, isolate," is well attested, and designates a military camp in 2 Sam 11:11. Contrarily Eg *ṯkw* is meaningless in Eg. Therefore, it is conceivable that Semitic people named this place as a temporary shelter or a camp site, when they arrrived in Egypt, then the name entered Eg as **ṯkwt* > *ṯkw* (cf. 𓏏𓅱 /tu/ as the regular ending of the Canaanite feminine ending in Eg transcription in Dyn 18, Burchardt, § 133).

פיבסת **

--- *p(r)-b(3)st(.t)* "Bubastis" (modern Tell Basta)

[Neb] Ezek 30:17

[Eg] Gauthier, *DG* II p. 75; Montet, *Géographie* I p. 173; [Gk] Βουβαστις, Βουβαστος; [Copt] ⲡⲟⲩⲃⲁⲥⲧⲉ, ⲡⲟⲩⲃⲁⲥⲧ.

Notice the vowel change Heb [pî-] > [p/bū-] (see the later discussion [5] Notes on the Hebrew Vocalizations, c) Other Vowel Changes).

פיהחירת ?

[Heb] Ex 14:2, 9; Dt 33:7

Several attempts have been made to identify the name with Eg names: *i.e.*, *pr-ḥwt-ḥr* (Gardiner, "The Geography of the Exodus" p. 213; Albright, *BASOR* 109 p. 16), *p3-ḫrw(m)* (Saft El Henne;

Cazelles, *RB* 62 p. 350ff.). However none of these correspond phonetically to (פי)החירת. A Semitic explanation is perhaps more persuasive. Since פיהחירת occurs without פי in Num 33:8, it is acceptable that פי means "mouth" and the real place name is החירת. The ה could be an article with which חירת, derived from root חרר "hole", was combined, meaning "the mouth of the canal." If this Heb form entered Egypt, perhaps it was spelled as **p3-ḥrt* > *p3-ḥr*, which might be comparable with Eg *p3-ḥr* in Anastasi III.2.9 (Caminos p. 74, 78f).

פתם **

--- *p(r)-(i)tm* 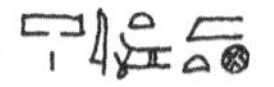 (probably modern Tell el-Rataba)
Bietak, "Cooment on the Exodus"; Kitchen, "Raamses, Succoth and Pithom" (forthcoming)
[Heb] Ex 1:11
[Eg] Gauthier, *DG* II p. 59; Montet, *Géographie* I p. 215; [Gk] πεθωμ (LXX), πάτουμου (Herodotus II 158); [Copt] ⲡⲉⲑⲱⲙ

Philologically no doubt has ever been cast upon the identification: the *r* of *pr* lost its consonantal value, becoming [i], with which the *i* of *itm* was merged. However, the actual location has been long discussed. Though the localization is beyond the range of the scope of the present study, it is much more likely that Pithom is to be located in Tell el-Rataba (M. Bietak, above p. 168f.) than being identical with *ṯkw* which is located in Tell el-Maskuta by most scholars, because Tell el-Rataba is a city of Raamses II, in which a temple of Atum existed (*PM* IV p. 55; Petrie, *Hyksos and Israelite Cities* p. 30f and pl. 30). This identification (*i.e.*,separation of Pithom from Succoth of *ṯkw*) makes it easy to explain why Pithom was never mentioned, while *ṯkw* (סכת) is always mentioned in the route of the Exodus in the OT. Succoth was on the route, while Pithom was too far West to be the route taken.

פתרוס **

--- **p(3)-t(3)-rs(y)* "The southern land" (i.e., Upper Egypt)
[Heb] Is 11:11, Jer 44:1, 15; Ezek 29:14, 30:14
[Eg] Inscriptionally this name is not attested, yet it occurs as *pa-tu-ri-si* in a NA inscription of Esarhaddon (Ranke, *KM* p. 31; Parpola, *NAT* p. 276) in the context "king of Egypt, *paturesi* and Cush."

Therefore, the identification is beyond doubt. The *mater lectionis* ו of רוס suggests a different vocalization from the NA form *-risi*, and Copt -ⲣⲏⲥ (Vycichl, p. 178). Therefore, it is most probable that Eg *p3-t3-rsy* entered Hebrew before Eg [ŭ́] in a closed accented syllable became [ĕ́] (*e.g.*, *pûya* > ⲡⲏⲓ, Albright, *Rec. de Trav.* 40 p. 66f.; Sethe, *ZDMC* 77 p. 207; Osing "Lautsystem" *LÄ* III p. 948).

פתרסים **

--- gent. of פתרוס

[Heb] Gen 10:14; 1Chr 1:12

[Eg] see פתרוס.

צען **

--- *ḏ*ʿ*n(.t)* "Tanis" (modern San el-Hagar)

[Heb] Num 13:22; Is 19:11, 13, 30:4; Ps 78:12, 43; Ezek 30:14

[Eg] Gauthier, *DG* VI p. 111; Montet, *Géographie* I p. 192ff.; [Gk] Τᾶνις; [Copt] ˢϫⲁⲁⲛⲉ, ᵇϫⲁⲛⲏ, ϫⲁⲛⲓ; [Demot] *ḏ*ʿ*ny*; [NA] *ṣa-*ʾ*a-nu* (Assurb I 96, 134; Ranke, *KM* p. 34); [Arab] *ṣān*.

רעמסס **

--- *(pr-)r*ʿ*mss* (area of Avaris, modern Tell el-Dab'a)

Bietak, *Tell el -Dab'a* II; *Avaris and Piramesse*

[Heb] Gen 47:11; Ex 1:11 *ra*ʿ*amsēs*, Ex 12:37; Num 33:3, 5

[Eg] Gauthier, *DG* III p. 129; Montet, *Géographie* I p. 194; [Gk] ʽραμεσσῆ (LXX)

The location of Rameses is firmly established by Bietak (see above), at a tell about 20 km south of Tanis.

שׁיחור **

--- *š-ḥr* "The lake of Horus"

Gardiner, *JEA* 5 p. 251f.

[Heb] Is 23:3 שׁחר; Jer 2:18 שׁחר; 1Chr 13:5 שׁיחור; Josh 13:3 השׁיחור

[Eg] *Wb* IV.397.4; Gauthier, *DG* V p. 124f.; Montet, *Géographie* I p. 200

Shihor is a branch of the Nile in NE of the Delta, between Tell el-Dab'a and Pelusium.

תחפנחס **

--- **t(3)-ḥ(.t)-p(3)-nḥs(y)* "The mansion of the Nubian" (modern Tell Defneh)

Cledat, *BIFAO* 23 p. 40ff.

[Heb] Jer 2:16 תחפנס 43:7, 8, 9, 44:1, 46:14; Eze 30:18

[Eg] This GN is not attested inscriptionally; [Gk] Δαφνη (Herodotus II 30),Ταφναι, Ταφνη (LXX); [Ph] תחפנחס

Cf. PN פנחס (*p3-nḥsy* "the Nubian").

[4] Loan Words

אברך

--- *ỉb-r.k* "attention!"

Spiegelberg, *OLZ* 15 pp. 317–321 (cf. review by Breasted, *AJSL* 21 p. 24); Ungnad, *ZAW* 41 p. 206; Lambdin, p. 146; *Vergote, Joseph en Égypte* p. 135–141 (cf. review by Kitchen, *JEA* 47 p. 162; Couroyer, *RB* 66 p. 591f); Croatto, *VT* 16 p. 113–115, Redford, *Joseph* p. 226ff (cf. review by Kitchen, *Or. An.* 12 pp. 233–242); Lipinski, *ZAH* 1 p. 61f; Ellenbogen p. 3ff.

[Heb] Gen 41:43

Spiegelberg's solution seems to be fit the context, if the word is an exclamation. Breasted questioned it because the pl. *tn* instead of the sg. *k* would be expected. However, it is not a problem if we think that the exclamation was made as if to an individual. Another possibility, proposed by Brugsch (?), Vergote, followed by Redford, is Eg imperative prothetic *aleph ỉ* + Sem Lw *brk* "to pay homage." However, if the word is a designation of a title, Sum Lw provides *abarakku* "steward, minister" (*AHw* 3b, *CAD* Al 32), proposed by Ungnad, Croatto, and Lipinski. However, judging from the context, an Eg solution is more probable. Ellenbogen tried to compare the word Eg *b3k*, however, there is no phonological basis. The first two Eg solutions seem to remain most likely.

אביון ? "poor"

--- *bin* 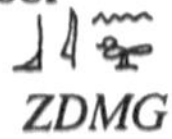 "evil"

Eman, *ZDMG* 46 p. 109; Calice no. 590; Lambdin p. 145f.; Ellenbogen p.1

[Heb] Deut 15:4 (total 61x)
[Eg] *Wb* I442f; [Copt] ^{b}ⲂⲰⲚ, ^{s}ⲂⲰⲰⲚ "bad"; cf. ⲈⲂⲒⲎⲚ "poor"; [Demot] *bin* "bad"; cf. *3byn* "poor"; [Ug] *abyn* (Aist p. 18; *UT* 19.24) "poor"

There has been a general agreement that Heb אביון is an Eg loan word. However, Eg *bin* does not mean "poor" which Heb אביון always designates. Therefore, we cannot confirm that אביון is an Eg loanword unless we assume that the meaning was changed when the word *bin* was borrowed. When we consider the other related words, the following conclusion is drawn;

	Eg	Ug	Heb	Demot	Copt
"poor"	-	*abyn*	*ʾbyn*	*3byn*	ⲈⲂⲒⲎⲚ
"bad"	*bin*	-	-	*bin*	ⲂⲰⲰⲚ

Therefore, it is more reasonable to assume either that the Eg and Sem words were cognates which developed differently from each other (*i.e.*, **bin* > *abyn*; **bin* > *bin*) or that there were no connections at all. In the latter case, the word אביון was derived from a root *אבי, as BDB classified it under the entry *אבה, followed by Ward (see Ug Lw *abyn*), to which is added the afformative *-ôn* (Gesenius § 85u). Then in the Late Period the Sem word was borrowed by Eg as Demotic *3by*, Copt ⲈⲂⲒⲎⲚ. Erman supposed that the Heb אביון was derived from ⲈⲂⲒⲎⲚ. However, the occurrence of Ug *abyn* in the late second millennium BC makes it unlikely.

אבנט * "girdle, sash"
--- *bnd*  "wrap up"
Stricker, *AO* 15 p. 10; Calice no. 594; Lambdin p. 146; Ellenbogen p. 2
[Heb] Ex 28:4, 39, 40, 29:9; Lev 8:7, 13, 16:4, Is 22:21
[Eg] *Wb* I.465 NK–Gk; [Gk] cf. αβανηθ (Josephus, *Anti.* III vii 2), βυνητος "an Eg garment" (Liddell & Scott p. 333b)

If אבנט is an Eg loan word, it is probably derived from a passive participle of Eg *bnd*. The Gk form βυνητος (see above) , if derived from Eg *bnd*, indicates that a noun form of *bnd* existed.

אח * "brazier for heating a room"

--- *ʿḫ* "brazier as an instrument for burning offering"

Müller, *OLZ* 3 p. 51; Calice no. 401; Lambdin p. 146; Ellenbogen p. 21

[Heb] Jer 36:22, 23

[Eg] *Wb* I.223.13–16 Saite–Gk; [Copt] ⲁϣ "furnace, oven"; [Demot] *ʿḫ*

There is no indication that Eg *ʿḫ* became *ʾḫ* in the historical course of the Eg language (cf. Demot *ʿḫ*; against Ellenbogen). However, it is possible that Eg *'ayn* became *aleph* before *ḫ* Osing, *SAK* 8 pp. 217–221). It is also not impossible to assume that the dissimilation *'ayn* > *aleph* took place in Heb, when the word was borrowed, because *'ayn* and *aleph* are incompatible in the first two consonants in Hebrew (cf. J. Greenberg, "The Patterning of root morphemes in Semitic" *Word* 6 p. 164, 169, for the case of verb root).

אחו ** "grass, reed"

--- *3ḫ(y)* "plant"

Spiegelberg, *Rec. de Trav* 24 p. 180–182; Lambdin p. 146

[Heb] Gen 41:2, 18; Job 8:11; Hos 13:15

[Eg] *Wb* I.18.8 NK; cf. *3ḫ3ḫ* (I.18.16ff since NK); *i3ḫ.y* "become flooded" (I.33.2 *Pry*); *w3ḫy* (*w* dropped in early period) "become flooded, be green" (I.258.13ff. Pyr–Gk); Demot *3ḫ.t* "flood season"; Copt ᵇⲁϩⲓ, ⲁϫⲓ derived from Gk ἄχει LXX (Černý p. 17). It is not surprising in Egypt that the word *3ḫ.y* "plant, green grass" originated from the word *w3ḫy* "become flooded," because the green pasture land was the result of the annual inundation; [Ug] *ʾaḫ* "meadow"; [Aram] אחוה.

Lambdin notes that the final ו of אחו points to a very early borrowing, when the final *-w* of the Eg word was still pronounced. The Ug form Indicates later borrowing because of the absence of the Eg w.

אחלמה ** (the name of a precious stone)

--- *ḫnm(.t)* "reddish jasper"

Brugsch, *Wb* p. 1100; Erman, *ZDMG* 46 p. 116; Lambdin p. 147; Ellenbogen p. 22

[Heb] Ex 28:19, 39:12

As far as the equation between Eg *n* and Heb *l* is concerned, it has been known that some Eg *ns* were actually pronounced as [l], *e.g.*, Eg *nšm.t* (לשם); *ns* (= Copt ^{s,b}ⲗⲁⲥ, ^{a,f}ⲗⲉⲥ, Demot *ls*). Especially interesting is that the change /*n*/ > /*l*/ is often observed between *ḫ*/*ḥ* and *m*, *e.g.*, *ḫnm* "smell" = Copt ϣωλⲙ (Černý p. 241), *ḥnmnm* "become entangled" = ϩⲗⲟⲙⲗⲙ, *ḫnmt* "spring" = ϩⲁⲗⲙⲉ, ^{s}ϩⲟⲛⲃⲉ (Černý p. 280). The above examples are strong enough to justify the case of *ḫnm.t*.

As for the identification of this precious stone, Harris says "it is quite apparent that *ḥnmt* is to be interpreted as red jasper and the glass and faience imitations frequently substituted for it" (p. 124). The traditional translation "amethyst" should be corrected.

אטון **

--- *idm(i)* "red linen"

Spiegelberg, *ZVS* 41 p. 130; Lambdin p. 147

[Heb] Prov 7:16 אטון מצרים "Egyptian linen"

[Eg] *Wb* I.153.15–16 since OK; [Demot] *itm.t* / *itmi*; [Gk] οθονη, οθονιον "fine linen" (Liddell and Scott 1200b)

A dissimilation *m* > *n* could be supported by the Gk form. cf. preposition *m* > *n* (Copt ⲛ-).

אי "coast, region"

--- *iw* "island"

Brugsch, *Wb* p. 29; Erman, *ZDMG* 46 p. 107; Calice no.481; Lambdin p. 147

[Heb] Gen 10:5; mostly Is, Jer, Eze (36 x)

[Eg] *Wb* I.47.4ff. since MK; [Copt] -^{b}ⲓ- in ⲡⲓⲗⲁⲕϩ "Philae"; [Ph/Pu] אי (*DISO* p. 12)

It is possible that אי is an early borrowing from Eg *iw*. However, the correspondence between י and ו prevents us from determining whether it is an Eg-Sem cognate or an Eg loanwoard. That Eg *iw* became *i* is suported by Copt ⲓ in ⲡⲓⲗⲁⲕϩ, and *ʾI-sa-ḫy-ra* (= Isḫara) (*VESO* p. 35).

איפה ** "ephah"

--- *ip(.t)* "measure for corn and fruit"

Brugsch, *Wb* p. 49; Erman, *ZDMG* 46 p. 107; Sethe *ZÄS* 62 p. 61; Lambdin p. 147; Ellenbogen p. 26.
[Heb] *Wb* I.67 since Dyn 18; [Copt] ^{s}ⲟⲓⲡⲉ, ^{b}ⲱⲓⲡⲓ, ^{f}ⲁⲓⲡⲓ (Černý p. 121); [Gk] οἰφί (LXX)

There has been no doubt that איפה is an Eg word. The vocalic change of *ip.t* is **apyat* (James, *Hekanakhte* p. 65f) > *aypat* (= Heb איפה) > Copt ⲟⲓⲡⲉ.

בוץ ? "byssus"
--- *w(3)d(.t)* "a green coloured material for clothing"
Spiegelberg, *ZVS* 41 p. 128f.; Lambdin p. 147f. (with doubt)
[Heb] Est 1:6, 8:15, Eze 27:16, 1Chr 4:21, 15:27, 2Chr 2:13, 3:14, 5:12
[Eg] *Wb* I.268.10–12 since Pyr; [Ph] ב(ו)ץ; [Syria] בוצא; [Old S. Arab] *bazz*; [Eth] bīsōs; [Gk] βυσσος; [NA/NB] būṣu (earliest occurrence in a text of Shalmaneser III *ca.* 850 BC)

We have to note the fact that בוץ only occurs in 6th cent. BC and later documents, in which period Eg *ḏ* became *d* which does not correspond to Heb צ. The correspondence between Eg *w* and Heb ב is also unlikely. So the borrowing from Eg is very doubtful. A. Hurvitz, after observing the usage of שש and בוץ in the Bible, and their distribution in non-Hebrew sources, concluded that בוץ is of northern origin and entered biblical Hebrew not before the 6th cent. BC ("The Usage of שש and בוץ in the Bible and its implication for the date of P" *HTR* 60 pp. 117–21). Then בוץ replaced שש due to the increased post-exilic contact with the Northeast. He points out (pp. 119f) that Ezekiel distinguishes explicitly between the בוץ imported to Tyre from Aram or Edom (Ez 27:16) and the שש imported from Egypt (Ez 27:7). Cf. also Est 8:15, Gen 41:42.

בהט "a costly stone"
--- *(i)bht(y)* "a type of stone from Nubia"
Lambdin p. 147 (with doubt)
[Heb] Est 1:6
[Eg] *Wb* I.64.1; Harris, *Lex. Stud.* p. 96f.

Harris notes that *ibhty* is undoubtedly identical with Eg *bht* (not in *Wb*) which has the same meaning. So the absence of Eg *i* in the Hebrew form is not a problem. However the correspondence between Eg *t* and Heb ט makes the identification very doubtful. Furthermore, the meaning of *ỉbhty* is uncertain.

בחן "tested"

--- *bḫn(.w)*  "dark hard stone for monuments"

Lambdin p. 148; Ellenbogen p. 48

[Heb] Is 28:16 cf. Eze 21:18 (13) בחן (?)

[Eg] *Wb* I.471.1–5 since MK; Harris, *Lex. Stud.* p. 78

According to Lambdin, Sethe, assuming the *bḫn.w* is used as a touchstone, points out the Eg origin of Heb בחן. He asserts that the meaning "touchstone" fits well in the context (Is 28:16). However, the Heb root בחן "to test" is well attested (cf. Aram בחן) and בחן is a qutl-form with the second laryngal. There seems to be no necessity to change the meaning of the word in the context. Therefore, it is unnecessary to suppose that בחן is an Eg loanword.

בחן * "watch-tower"

--- *bḫn(.t)*  "gate building, pylon tower"

Brugsch, *Wb* p. 414; Erman, *ZDMG* 46 p. 110; Lambdin p. 148f

[Heb] Is 32:14 cf. *בחין (Is 23:13)

[Eg] *Wb* I.471.9–11 since NK

Because of the lack of any Heb etymological explanation, it is possible that the word בחן was borrowed from Eg *bḫn.t*.

בחין * "siege tower (?)"

--- Var. of בחן

[Heb] Is 23:13 *Qere* בחוניו

[Eg] see בחן.

גמא ** "rush"

--- *gmy*  "rush, material for mat and basket"

Loret, *Rec.de Trav.* 13 p. 201; Keimer, *OLZ* 30 p. 145–154; Lambdin p. 194; Ellenbogen p. 56; Spiegelberg, *KHW* p. 40; Černý p. 57

[Heb] Ex 2:3, Is 18:2, 35:7, Job 8:11

[Eg] *Wb* V.170.5 since NK; [Copt] s,bⲕⲁⲙ (Černý p. 57); [Demot] *ḳm* (Erichsen p. 537.3); [Aram] גמא

It has been acknowledged since V. Loret that Heb and Aram גמא

is an Eg loanword. The word is hardly derived from Heb root גמא "to swallow." Lambdin casts a serious doubt as to whether the word is an Eg loanword; because he identified גמא with Eg *ḳm3* (*Wb* V.37.14–16; since Dyn 21), the phonetic problem (Eg *ḳ* = Heb ג) arose. However *ḳm3* is identical with *gmy* (Keimer, above; accepted by Černý p. 57), because *ḳm3* occurs in perfect parallel with *gmy*. There may be bi-forms, one of which was borrowed by Semitic, and survived until the Late period (Is 18:2). On the contrary, the form *gmy* fell out of use in Eg (no Demot equivalent), only *ḳm3* survived as Copt ⲔⲀⲘ.

דיו ? "ink"
--- *ry(.t)*  "colour of the writing and drawing"
Lambdin p. 149
[Heb] Jer 36:18
[Eg] *Wb* II.399 since MK; [Aram] דיותא; [Arab] *dawā*

Lambdin assumes that Heb דיו is a graphic error for ריו. The identification is possible simply because there are no other explanations known. However, we would also have to assume that the Aram, Syria and Arab forms derived from a manuscript of Jeremiah in which the graphic error occurred.

הדם ? "footstool"
--- *hdm(.w)*  "footstool"
Brugsch, *Wb* p. 912; Erman, *ZDMG* 46 p. 114; Burchardt no. 669; Albright, *VESO* p. 52; Ellenbogen p. 66
[Heb] Is 66:1; Ps 99:5, 110:1, 132:7; Lam 2:1; 1Chr 28:2
[Eg] *Wb* II.505.17–19 since Dyn 18; [Ug] *hdm*

Ellenbogen suggests that the word הדם is derived from Eg *hdm.w*. However, the Eg sylllabic writing indicates that the word was borrowed in Eg as **hadmu* (*Wb* II.505; Albright, "The Furniture of El in Canaanite Mythology" *BASOR* 91 p. 42; K. Kuhlmann, Der Thron im Alten Ägypten p. 14f). C. Gordon has a further comment on this word, "the fact that Heb הדום has no Semitic etymology, while Eg *hdm.w* is not attested before the 18th Dyn, suggests that the word is East Mediterranean" without any specification (*UT* 19.751).

הובן (in הובנים, Qere הבנים) ** "ebony"

--- *hbn(y)* "ebony"

Brugsch, *Wb* p. 896; Erman, *ZDMG* 46 p. 114; Lambdin p. 149; Ellenbogen p. 63

[Heb] Ezek 27:15

[Eg] *Wb* II.487.7–12 since Pyr; [Gk] ἔβενο (LXX εἰσαγομενοι); [Latin] *ebenus;* [Ug] *hbn.*

הין ** "hin"

--- *hn(w)* "a vessel, liquid measure"

Brugsch, *Wb* p. 901; Erman, *ZDMG* 46 p. 114; Lambdin p. 149; Ellenbogen p.68

[Heb] Ex 29:40, Lev 23:13; Num 15:4 (total 22 x)

[Eg] *Wb* II.493.2f since Pyr; [Copt] ϩⲓⲛ (Černý p. 285); [Demot] *hn*; [Gk] εἶν (LXX); [EA] *hi-na* (14.III.62); [Aram] הן; [Ug] *hn* (*UT* 19.785)

This Eg loan word is identical in function with, but different in value from Eg *hnw*. Eg *hnw* is about 0.5 litre (Gardiner, *EG*^{3} p. 199), while Heb הין about 4 litres.

זרת "a span (as a measure)"

--- *ḏr.t* "hand"

Bondi, ZÄS 32 p. 132; Sethe, *Verbum* p. 183; Calice no. 946; Lambdin p.149f

[Heb] Ex 28:16, 39:9; 1Sam 16:4, Is 40:12, Eze 43:3

[Eg] *Wb* V.580.3ff.; [Copt] sⲧⲱⲣⲉ, bⲧⲱⲣⲓ, fⲧⲱⲗⲓ, sⲧⲟⲟⲧ´, bⲧⲟⲧ´ [Aram] זרת (*DISO* p. 80); [Syria] זרתא; [Ug] *drt* (*UT* 710)

If this is an Eg loanword, as Lambdin pointed out, the borrowing must have taken place in a very early period (end of 3rd millennium to early 2nd millennium), because *ḏ* of *ḏr.t* became *d* which cannot be represented by Heb ז, and the *t* of *ḏr.t*, which is represented by Heb ת, was lost quite early. Ug *drt* reflects the period after Eg *ḏ* became *d*, before the final *t* was lost. The fact that the root זרת has no Semitic etymology favours the Eg origin, though we cannot be sure.

חניך (in חניכיו) ? "the trained, retainers"

--- *ḥnk* "the trustful"

Yahuda, *Language* p. 291; Albright, *AfO* 6 p. 221; *BASOR* 94 p. 24

n. 87; Lambdin p. 150
[Heb] Gen 14:14
[Eg] *Wb* III.118; cf. *mḥnk* (II.129.7–8 since OK); [Aram] חנך (vb), חנכה (noun) (*DISO* p. 92)

As opposed to Yahuda, Albright regarded Heb חניך as an Eg loanword. He advocated that חניך, as well as *ḫa-na-ku-u-ka* (*Taanach letters* no. 6.8, *CAD* H 76b) is unquestionably connected with Eg *ḥnk/mḥnk* (*AfO* 6 p. 221). However, later he changed his view, and doubted the identification, because he admitted that the reading of Eg *ḥnk*, quoted by Albright, is doubtful (G. Posener, *Princes et Pays d'Asie et Nubie* pp. 26–28, where he read the word as *sqryw*). There is no difficulty in thinking that חניך is a *qatil* type noun deriving from the root חנך "train, dedicate." Therefore, Yahuda's original proposal is still valuable. It seems more likely that the word was borrowed by Egyptian.

חנית ? "spear"
--- *ḥny.t* 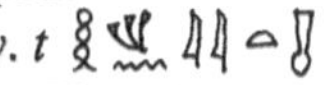 "spear"
Erman, *ZDMG* 46 p. 115; Calice no. 718; Ellenbogen p. 73; cf. Hoch no. 318
[Heb] 1Sam 17:7, 13:22 (47 x)
[Eg] *Wb* III.110.11 NK

The Eg word *ḥny.t* only occurs in NK, in which the Eg fem. ending *t* was lost. Therefore, it is impossible for Heb חנית to be an Eg loanword, unless we assume that the word was borrowed in a very early stage. The Eg *ḥny.t* occurs twice in the list of tribute from *Rṯnw* in Syria (*Urk* IV.719.727) and once in a magical text (A. Massart, *Leiden* I 343, recto V.2) as a weapon of Ba'al, suggesting that *ḥny.t* is Semitic loanword in Eg. Cf. Hoch no. 318.

חרי * "white cake?"
--- *ḥr(.t)*  "a kind of cake"
[Heb] Gen 40:16
[Eg] *Wb* III.148.16 end of MK–NK

That the word appears once in an Eg context is in favour of an Eg loanword. BDB, however, classified it under a root חור "be white", from which the meaning "white cake" was inferred. Though Eg origin is probable, it cannot be certain.

חרטם * "magician"

--- *ḥr(y)-tp* "who is upon, chief"

Stricker, *AO* 15 p. 164; Gardiner, *AEO* I p. 129*; Lambdin p. 151; Quaegebeur, in *Pharaonic Eg* pp. 162–172 (in which the more detailed bibliography and previous discussions are found, pp. 162–167); *SAK* 12 p. 368–389.

[Heb] Gen 41:8, 24; Ex 7:11, 22, 8:3, 14, 15, 19:11a, 11b; Dan 1:20, 2:2 [Aram] Dan 2:10, 27, 4:4, 6, 5:11

[Eg] *Wb* III.140.6ff since Pyr; [Demot] *ḥr-tb* (Erichsen p. 321, 325); [NA] *ḫar-d/ṭi-bi* (*KM* p. 37); [Gk] φεριτοβ, φεριτοβ(αυτης), φριτωβ, φριτ<ο>β, φριτοβ (see Quaegebeur p. 167)

The equation of חרטם with *ḥr-tp* has been long suspended because of phonetic problems: the representation of Eg *t* by Heb ט, and Eg *p* > *b* by Heb ם. However, the latter is certainly conceivable, because /b/ can become /m/ after [u] vowel (cf. χνουμις // χνουβις: חנום // חנוב, /m/ > /b/ after [u]). As for the former, which is more difficult, Quaegebeur presents inscriptional evidence that *ḥr-tb* and *ḥr-idb* (//) are written in parallel designating the same person. He thinks that "this can only be a sportive writing of *ḥry-tp*, *i.e.*, a kind of progressive spelling adapted more to the actual pronounciation than to the etymology. " If this is true, then all phonetic problems are resolved, because Eg *ḏ* > *d* is always represented by Heb ט. Especially the second item of evidence he presents seems to suggests strongly that *ḥr-tb* is written as *ḥr-(i)db*. However, the which is considered as a progressive spelling of *ḥr-tp* and read as *ḥr-idb* is attested as a different title *ḥr-wḏb* (*Wb* III.1–5), as Quaegebeur admits. It is not strange in Egypt that one person bears more than one title. Therefore, the question is how we can confirm that is a phonetic writing of *ḥr-tp* of a different title which was possessed by the same person. Further, it seems odd to write a title with another title for phonetic purposes. The phonetic change could be explained differently; /t/ > /ṭ/ before ם and after ח, though /r/ a resonant intervened between ח and ט (see the previous discussion p. 259). Therefore the identification is almost certain.

חשמל ? "some shining substance"

--- *ḥsmn*  "bronze"

Brugsch, *Wb* VI p. 853; Erman, *ZDMG* 46 p. 115; Calice no. 432

[Heb] Ezek 1:4, 27, 8:2

[Eg] see חשמן; [NA/NB] cf. *ešmarû* (hardly to be connected with Heb *ḥašmal*, *CAD* E p. 366f); [OB] cf. *elmešu* (*CAD* E p. 107f. "a precious stone of characteristic sparkle and brilliancy. In this peculiar quality, *elmešu* may well be connected with Heb *ḥašmal*"). Dr. Healey orally suggested a possible connection between *elmešu* and Heb *ḥallāmîš* "flint"(?). For the meaning of *elmešu*, see Landsberger, *VTS* 16 pp. 190–198

Cf. חשמן

The representation of Eg *n* by Heb ל at the end is conceivable in particular after or before a labial: *e.g.*, Eg *sbn* > *ⲤⲂⲖ (imperative ⲤⲂⲖⲦⲈ Černý p. 147), *tnm* > ˢⲦⲰⲖⲘ (Černý p. 186), *mnnn* > ᵇⲘⲒⲞⲖⲰⲚ (Černý p.81), *knm* > **knmnm* > ϬⲖⲞⲘⲖⲘ (Černý p. 328). However the word is more likely to be a cognate, because of Akk words above.

חשמן (in חשמנים) "meaning unknown"

--- *ḥsmn*  "bronze"

Spiegelberg, *ÄRAT*

[Heb] Ps 68:32 יאתיו חשמנים מני מצרים "Bronze/Envoys (?) will come out of Egypt"

[Eg] *Wb* III.163.14–24 since OK; [Ug] *ḫus/ḫasmannu* (*Syria* 28 p. 55f.) meaning unknown; [Akk] cf. *ḫašmānu* "a blue-green (wool)" (*CAD* Ḫ p. 142a), *ḫusmānu* "a blue shade (of wool)" (*CAD* Ḫ 257b)

Because of a single occurrence, the meaning of the word is unknown, though the contex favours the Eg loan word. If it is of Eg origin, it is most likely to be derived from Eg *ḥsmn* "bronze", though the correspondence between Heb שׁ and Eg *s* is a little troublesome.

חתם ** "seal"

--- *ḫtm* 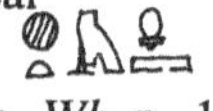 "seal"

Brugsch, *Wb* p. 1145; Erman, *ZDMG* 46 p. 117; Lambdin p. 151; Ellenbogen p. 74

[Heb] חתם (verb) Lev 15:3; Is 8:16 (16 x). חותם / חתם (masc.

noun) Gen 38:18; Ex28:11 (14 x). חותמת (fem. noun) Gen 38:25(1 x); [Ph/Pu] חתם; [Aram] חתם (*DISO* p. 98, Dan 5:18); [Arab] *ḫātm*; [Syr] *ḥātəmā*; [Eth] *māḫtam*
[Eg] *Wb* III.350.3ff. since OK [Copt] ϣⲱⲧⲙ, ϣⲧⲁⲙ, ϣⲑⲁⲙ; [Demot] *ḫtm* (Erichsen p. 372.2)

The long vowel /o/ of *ḥôtem* is a result of the Canaanite shift, because most Semitic nominal forms indicate a prototypte **ḫātam* (Lambdin p. 151). The fact that *ḫtm* does not occur in Akk (cf. Akk *kanaku* "seal") leads us to incline to think *ḫtm* is not a cognate but a borrowed word. The widespread occurrence of this word indicates that it was borrowed very early (Lambdin).

טבעת ** "signet-ring"
--- *ḏbʿ.t* 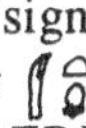 "seal"
Erman, *ZDMG* 46 p. 123; Lambdin p. 151; Ellenbogen p. 75
[Heb] Gen 41:42; 42 times in Ex; Num 31:50; Est 3:10, 8:2, 8a, 8b, 10; Is 3:21
[Eg] *Wb* V.566.5ff. since OK; [Copt] ^{s}ⲧⲃⲃⲉ (Černý p. 181), ⲧⲱⲱⲃⲉ "to seal"; [Demot] *tbʿ* (Erichsen p. 623)

The word *ḏbʿ.t* was borrowed in the early stage, perhaps in the third millennium, when Eg /ḏ/ had alrready become /d/, and Eg fem. ending was retained. The absence of a proper Heb etymology (cf. טבע "to sink") makes the Eg origin of this word most likely. It is almost certain that Semites borrowed טבעת "signet-ring" as well as חתם "seal."

טנא ** "basket"
--- *dni(.t)* 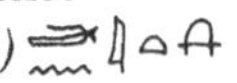 "basket"
Erman, *ZDMG* 46 p. 122; Yahuda, *Language* p. 97; Lambdin p. 151; Ellenbogen p. 77
[Heb] Deut 26:2, 4, 28:5, 17
[Eg] *Wb* V.467.2–8 since MK

Due to its isolated occurrences and the lack of Sem etymology, it is most likely that the word is an Eg loanword.

יאור ** "the Nile, river"
--- *i(t)r(w)*  , 
Erman, *ZDMG* 46 p. 108; Lambdin p. 151

[Heb] Gen 4:1, 2, 3; Ex 2:3, 5, 4:9 etc (total 65 x), cf. Amos 8:8 כאר *kā-ʾôr* "like the Nile"
[Eg] *Wb* I.146.10ff since NK; [Copt] ^{s}ⲉⲓⲟⲟⲣ, ^{b}ⲓⲟⲣ, ^{s}ⲓⲁⲁⲣ (Černý p. 48); [Demot] *yr* (Erichsen p. 50); [NA] ^{maru}*ya-ru-ʿu-ú* (*ìtrw-ʿ3* Ranke, *KM* p. 29; cf. Copt ⲉⲓⲉⲣ Černý p. 48).

From Dyn 18 onward the spelling without *t* occurs. The change *t* > *aleph* can be observed in the Coptic form but not in the NA form.

לוב (in לובים) ** "Libyans"
--- *rb(w)*  "Libyans"
[Heb] Dan 11:43; Nahu 3:9; 2Chr 12:3, 16:3
[Eg] *Wb* II.414.2–3

In the biblical contexts which refer to Egypt, the word is most likely an Eg loanword.

לשם ** "a precious stone"
--- *nšm(.t)*  "green felspar"
Erman, *ZDMG* 46 p. 113; Calice no. 227; Lambdin p. 152; Ellenbogen p. 97
[Heb] Ex 28:19, 39:12
[Eg] *Wb* II.339.19ff. since NK; Harris, *Lex. Stud.* p. 115, 231

The Heb לשם has no cognate in Semitic, making an Eg loan most likely. As far as the representation of Eg *n* by Heb ל is concerned, threre is no difficulty, because Eg /n/ often became /l/ at the initial position; see Eg *n(y)* > Copt ⲗⲁ; *nwẖ* > ⲗⲱⲃϣ; *nn* > ⲗⲉⲗⲟⲩ; *nsb* > ⲗⲁⲡⲥⲓ; *ns* > ⲗⲁⲥ; *nss* > ⲗⲱⲱⲥ; *nfnf* > ⲗⲟϥⲗϥ; *nhw* > ⲗⲉϩ; *nhm* > ⲗϩⲏⲙ (Černý pp. 69–76).

As for the identification, Harris comments "there is nothing to suggest that *nšmt* was other than green in colour, and its use for the green felspar. That it covered bluish varieties of the same stone seems likely, and it is also possible that other green stones were on occasion confused with it"(p. 115), and "*ňsmt* is the material not for a scarab, but (with *mfk3t* = נפך) for two uraei (p. 231)."

מזח ? "girdle"
--- *mdḥ* 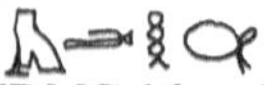 "fillet"
Erman, *ZDMG* 46 p. 112; Calice no. 643; Lambdin p. 152
[Heb] Ps 109:19

[Eg] *Wb* II.190.1 since MK; [Copt] sⲙⲟϫϩ, aⲙⲁϫϩ, bⲙⲟϫϩ (Černý, p. 101, says the word is probably a loanword from Sem מזח); [NB/SB] *mēzeḫu* "a scarf or belt" (*CAD* M 2 46); [SB/LB] *mēzeḫu* (relates to Heb *mēzaḥ*, Eg *mḏḥ AHw* 650a)

B. Gunn, "A Note on Brit. Mus. 828 (stela of Simontu)" *JEA* 25 p. 218f., opposed the identification on the following two grounds; (1) Eg *mḏḥ* is often wrongly translated "girddle" (*Wb* II.189), yet *mḏḥ* means "fillet" (Gardiner, *GE*^{3} p. 505 s. 10; *CDME* p. 123). Hence the neaning is not comparable. (2) Eg *ḏ* became *d*, which cannot be represented by Heb ז. Therefore, Heb מזח is not a loanword from Eg. Gunn assumed with G. R. Driver that there was perhaps a general Semitic root מזח / חזם "girdle" because of Arab *ḫazama*, Minaean *ḥzm* "strapped" and other Semitic forms. Copt ⲙⲟϫϩ, then, is a Semitic loanword in Copt as Černý notes (p. 101).

מטה ? "staff"

--- *mdw* 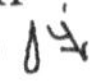 , late 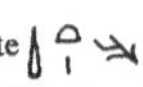 "staff"

Janssen, *ATO* p. 40 (in *KM*^{3})

[Heb] Gen 38:18, 25 onwards (250 x)

[Eg] *Wb* II.178 since OK; [Ug] *mṭ* "staff" (*UT* 164); [Gk] ('Εση)μητις = *(ns-p3-)mdw*

If this is a borrowed word, it must have entered Canaanite in the second millennium, because the *d* of *mdw* changed to *t*, at the latest, in the Late period (see above) and the *t* does not correspond to Heb ט,. However, Heb fem ending *-eh* has no correspondence in Eg *mdw*, unless we consider that it is a vowel letter, and that the *w* of *mdw* dropped. As C. Gordon pointed out, it is much more likely that Ug *mṭ* was drived from **nṭy* = Heb נטה "to extend", which is very productive. In Ezek 9:11, 12, 14 the word designates a branch of a vine. Therefore, it is no difficulty in thinking that the meaning "staff" comes from the root נטה.

מרח "rub"

--- *mrḥ(.t)* 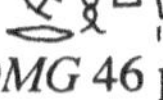 "rub"

Erman, *ZDMG* 46 p.112 (with Arab *mrḫ*); Calice No. 566; Lambdin p. 151

[Heb] Is 38:21

[Eg] *Wb* II.111.1-10 since OK (< *wrḥ* "to anoint" *Wb* I.334.8ff since OK); [Aram] *mrḫ;* [OB/SB] *marāḫu (?);* [Aram] מרחיא (*DISO* p. 168 meaning unknown)

It is difficult to discriminate between cognate and a loanword in this case. Von Soden (*AHw* 608b) compares Akk *marāḫu* with Heb מרח and Arab *mrḫ*. If this is so, since Akk *marrāḫu* is attested in OB texts, *mrḥ/ḫ* is a Semito-Eg loanword. If this is not the case, Heb מרח is likely to be an Eg loanword. Notice *CAD* does not have *marāḫu* as "to rub" but "to spoil."

משי "a coastly material for garments"

--- *mś.y* 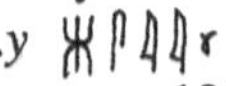 "a kind of garment"

Ellenbogen p. 109

[Heb] Ezek 16:10, 13 (used with שש (= Eg *šś*) "linen")

[Eg] *Wb* II.143.4–5 NK–Gk; [Arab] cf. *wašy*; [Hittite] *maššì(ya)*

Though that that the etymology of משי is unknown favours an Eg loanword, the identification is hindered by two difficulties; (1) different meaning: Heb משי indicates a material, while Eg *msy* "a kind of garment." (2) unusual correspondence between Eg *s* and Heb שׁ (see below [4] Notes on the Correspondences e) Sibilants). C. Rabin, "Hittite Words in Hebrew" *Or* NS 32 pp. 113–139, put forward the Hittite loanword; *maššì(ya)* "shawl." Therefore, the identification is open to the choice : (1) Eg loanword, (2) Hittite loanword, and (3) cognate.

נחת "descent"

--- *nḫt*  "strength, power"

Ellenbogen p. 112

[Heb] Is 30:30 נחת זרועו "strenghth of his arm"

[Eg] *Wb* II.316.7ff since Pyr; [Copt] ⲚⲀϢⲦⲈ (Černý p. 115); [Demot] *nḫtt*

As Ellenbogen points out, the expression *nḫt ḫpš* "strength of arm" is common and the meaning seems to fit the context (Is 30:30) well. However, the traditional interpretation is still possible, and the Heb root נחת is well attested. Futher נחת is used with זרע and יד in similar expressions; *e.g.*, ותנחת עלי ידך "your hand will descend upon me" (Ps 38:3); ונחתה קשת־נחושה זרעתי "my arms can bend a bow of bronze" (Ps 18:35, 2Chr 22:35). Therefore, an Eg explanation is unnecessary.

נפך ** "a precious stone"

--- *mfk(3.t)* 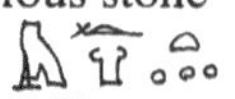 "(green/blue) turquoise"

Lambdin p. 152

[Heb] Ex 28:18, 39:11; Ezek 28:13, 27:16

[Eg] *Wb* II.56 sincePyr; Harris, *Lex. Stud.* p. 106–110, 231 (note Eg *fk3.t* in *Wb* I.580 is a misspelling of *mfk3.t*)

The representation of Eg *m* by Heb ן at initial position is not a problem because NA [alu]*Pi-ḫa-at-ti-ḫu-ru-un-pi-ki (pr-ḥtḥr-(nb.t)-mfk3.t)* shows that the initial Eg *m* became /n/ (Ranke, *KM* p. 32, his identification is *pr-ḥtḥr-nb.t-pr-k3.t,* yet see P. Montet, *Géographie* I p. 63). Supplementary evidence comes from the fact that some Eg *m*s became /n/ at the initial position; Eg preposition *m* > Copt Ⲛ; *mny.t* > ⲚⲎⲚⲒ; *mny.t* > ⲚⲞⲨⲚⲈ; *m-ḏr* > ⲚⲦⲈⲢⲈ; *m dwn* > ⲚⲦⲞⲞⲨⲚ; *m ki* > ⲚϬⲒ (Černý pp. 102, 109, 112, 113, 119). Therefore there is little doubt that נפך originated from Eg *mfk3.t*.

נתר ** "natorn"

--- *nṯr(i)*  "natron"

Erman, *ZDMG* 46 p. 113; Lambdin p. 152f; Ellenbogen p. 117

[Heb] Jer 2:22; Prov 25:20

[Eg] *Wb* II.366.8 since Pyr.; [Gk] νιτρον, λιτρον; [Akk] *nit(i)* (*AHw* 798a); [Nab] cf. נתר (?) (*DISO* p. 189); [Arab] *naṭūr, naṭrūn*; [Hittite] *nitri*; [Copt and Demot] not attested.

The Eg word *nṯri* was borrowed in Heb after Eg *ṯ* > *t* (NK onwards). The Heb, Gk, Akk forms indicate the original vocalization was *[nitr-], from which the Heb form took the usual shift of *qitl-* type; [nitr-] > [neter-]. The Arab form may be a later borrowing after Eg vowel shift [i] > [a] in closed accented syllables (1100–925 BC) (cf. Lambdin p. 145).

סוף ? "reed"

--- *ṯwf(y)*  "papyrus"

Brugsch, *Wb* p. 1580; Erman, *ZDMG* 46 p. 122; Calice no. 455; Albright, *VESO* p. 65 (he said "not syllabic"); Lambdin p.153.

[Heb] Ex 2:3, 5; Is 19:6; Jonah 2:6 "sea weed"; mostly in the combination ים־סוף Ex 10:19 etc. (many)

[Eg] *Wb* V.359.6–10 NK–Gk; [Copt] ϪⲞⲞⲨϤ (Černý p. 322); [Demot] *ḏwf*; [Arab] *ṣūf*

It seems likely that the word designating Eg papyrus is Eg. However there are other Eg words for Eg papyrus, such as *ḏ.t* (*Wb* V.511 OK–MK), *mnḥ* (*Wb* II.83 since MK) etc. Considering that the *ṯwfy* is a new word in the NK period, and is written in syllabic spelling (against Albright), the possibility that *ṯwfy* is a loanword in Eg is undeniable. Besides, there is a phonetic problem, that is, the correspondence between Eg *ṯ* and Heb ס. The phonetic value of Eg *ṯ* seems to remain unchanged in this word until Copt ϫⲟⲟⲩϥ, from which Arab probably borrowed the word *ṣuf.* W. Ward, for the same reason, opposes a borrowing in either direction, he supposes a protp–Canaanite word **sp* "reach", from which Eg *ṯwf,* Heb סוף developed ("The Semitic biconsonantal root *SP* and the common origin of Egyptian *ČWF* and Hebrew *SÛP*: "Marsh(-plant)" *VT* 24 p. 339–349).

סלעם "locust"
--- *snḥm* "locust"
Brugsch, *Wb* p. 1253; Erman, *ZDMG* 46 p. 117; Calice no. 782 (admits as Lw); Vycichl, *ZÄS* 84 p. 147
[Heb] Lev 11:22
[Eg] *Wb* III.461.6–7 since Pyr; [Cpot] ^{S}ⲥⲁⲛⲛⲉϩ

סלעם occurs once in Leviticus, and Eg *snḥm* is attested since the Pyr period, making an Eg loanword likely. However, the correspondence between Eg *ḥ* and Heb ע is questionable at the present. A Sem explanation is not impossible, as BDB suggests, *i.e.*, a root סלע "split" to which an afformative ם is added.

ערה (in ערות) ** "rush"
--- *ꜥr* "rush"
Thacker, *JTS* 34 p. 163f
[Heb] Is 19:7 ערות על־יאור "plants along the Nile"
[Eg] *Wb* I.208.4–7 since OK; *ꜥr.t* *Wb* I.208.8–9 Gk; cf. *ꜥr.t* "papyrus book roll"

That the word has no cognate in Sem and that it occurs only once in an Eg context (above) strongly suggest Eg etymology. BDB, considering the word ערה to be derived from ערה "be naked", translates it as "bare place." However, it is evident from the context that ערה designates a kind of plant, growing on the bank of the Nile.

Therefore, this עַרָה is a separate word from the root ערה "be naked."

As for Eg equivalents, the masc. form *ʿr* is attested since OK, while the fem. form, which would better fit Heb עַרָה, only occurs in the Gk period. So, we could assume either that Eg fem. form is accidentally not attested in the earlier period in Eg documents, or that Eg *ʿr* became a fem. noun when entering Hebrew.

פח ** "thin plate of metal"

--- *pḫ(3)*  "stone plate"

Erman, *ZDMG* 46 p. 110; Calice no. 605; Lambdin p. 153; Ellenbogen p. 130

[Heb] Ex 39:3; Num 17:3 (16:38)

[Eg] *Wb* I.543.12 Dyn 18

The word has no Sem cognate, so it is likely this is an Eg loanword.

פח ** "bird-trap"

--- *pḫ(3)*  "bird-trap"

Erman, *ZDMG* 46 p.110; Calice no. 605; Lambdin p. 153

[Heb] Josh 23:3; Ps 119:10; Job 18:9, 22:10; Is 24:17 etc. (total 25 x)

[Eg] *Wb* I.543.15; [Copt] ˢⲡⲁϣ, ᵇⲫⲁϣ; [Arab] *paḫḫ*

That פח has no cognate in Sem suggests the word is borrowed from the Eg common word *pḫ3* which is attested since NK. Heb verb from *פחח which once occurs in Is 42:22 is a denominative from פח.

פרעה ** "Pharaoh"

--- *pr-ʿ(3)* 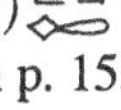 "great house"

Lambdin p. 153; Ellenbogen p. 139

[Heb] Gen 41:14 (274 x)

[Eg] see Aram פרעה.

צי ** "ship"

--- *ḏ(3)y* 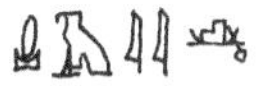 "river ship"

Brugsch, *Wb* p.1691; Erman, *ZDMG* 46 p. 123; Lambdin p. 153; Ellenbogen p. 145

[Heb] Num 24:24; Is 33:21; Ezek 30:9; Dan 11:30
[Eg] *Wb* V.515.6 since NK; [Copt] ϫⲟⲓ (Černý p. 310); [Demot] *ḏy* (Erichsen p. 674)

Notice the word has no cognate in Semitic.

קב ** "kab (a measure of capacity)"
--- *ḳb(.y)* 
Brugsch, *Wb* p. 1241; Erman, *ZDMG* p. 120; Ellenbogen p. 147
[Heb] 2k 6:25
[Eg] see Aram Lw קב.

קוף ** "ape"
--- *g(i)f*  , OK  , MK  "ape"
Brugsch, *Wb* p.1511; Erman, *ZDMG* 46 P. 121; Calice no. 451; Albright, *VESO* p. 61; Lambdin p. 154
[Heb] 1 K 10:22, 2Chr 9:21
[Eg] *Wb* V.158.12–16 since OK; cf. *gwf* (*Wb* V.16.9); [Demot] *kf*, *ḳf* (Erichsen p. 562, 536), [SB/LB] *uqūpu* (*AHw* 1427b); [Gk] κηβος, κηπος; [Aram] cf. קפא (*Ahikar* 117).

קוף has no cognate in Heb while Eg *gif* is attested since OK, making it very likely that קוף is an Eg loanword. The phonetic correspondence between Heb ק and Eg *g* is no problem, and Eg *gif* became *k*/*ḳf* in Demotic (cf. Heb קסת : *gesti*).

קלחת ** "pot, cauldron"
--- *ḳrḥ.t* 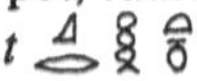 "vessel"
Brugsch, *Wb* p. 1469; Erman, *ZDMG* 46 p. 121; Bruchard, no. 258; Lambdin p. 154; Ellenbogen p. 149; Černý p. 329
[Heb] 1Sam 2:14; Mic 3:3
[Eg] *Wb* V.62.12ff since OK; [Copt] cf. ϭⲁⲗⲁϩⲧ (Crum p. 81 [Ug] *qlḥt* (*KTU* 5.22.16; ; Dietrich, Loretz and Sanmartin identified it with Heb קלחת, *UF* p. 166)

That קלחת has no cognate strengthens the possibility of a loanword. Since Heb קלחת preserves the Eg fem. ending *-t*, which had been lost by NK, the word was probably borrowed by Canaanite in the early second millennium. This early borrowing is also indicated by Ug *qlḫt*. After Eg *ḳrḥ.t* was borrowed, the final *t* was lost in Eg, on the other hand the *t* was kept in Canaanite until the first millennium. Therefore, Copt ϭⲁⲗⲁϩⲧ cannot be a direct descendant of Eg *ḳrḫ.t*. Lacau, "sur la chute du ⲁ (-*t*) final, marque de feminin" *Rd'E* 9 p. 83, considers that ϭⲁⲗⲁϩⲧ is a foreign word because of the final *t*. Therefore, we can safely assume that the קלחת re-entered Eg (Černý p. 329).

קסת ** "scribe's palette"

--- *gst(i)* 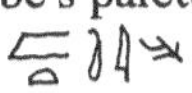 "scribe's palette"

Müller, *OLZ* 8 pp. 49–51; Eisler, *OLZ* 33 p. 585f; Lambdin p. 154; Ellenbogen p. 150; Ellenbogen p. 150

[Heb] Ezek 9:2, 3, 11

[Eg] *Wb* V.207.11ff. since OK; [Demot] *gst*; [Copt] ϭⲁⲥⲧ, ϭⲟⲥⲧ, ⲕⲁⲥⲧ (Černý p. 337; Crum p. 832); [Gk] κασтυ (Eisler, see above)

Lambdin notes that the only consonantal difficulty is the representation of Eg *ś* by Heb ס. However, this equation is normal (cf. פינחס: *p3-nḥśy*, רעמסס: *rᶜ-mś-sw*). Also the problem of the correspondence between Eg *g* and Heb ק can be resolved by the Eg phonetic change *g* > /k/, which is inscriptionally demonstrated  *ksd* (Gk),  *kst*, and Copt dialect ⲕⲁⲥⲧ (see Aram ק: Eg *g* in the previous chapter p. 211). The vocalization of *qeset* perfectly fits Copt and Gk forms [kast].

שׂכיות * "ship"

--- *śk.t(w)*  "ships"

Driver, "Difficult words" p. 52; Albright "Baal-Zephon" p. 4 n. 3; Alt, *AfO* 15 p. 70; Lambdin p. 155; Barr, *Comparative Philology* p. 280; Ellenbogen p. 154

[Heb] Is 2:16 // אניות "ship"

[Eg] *Wb* IV.315.9f. *skty* (NK), *sk.tw* (pl. Dyn 18); [Ug] *ṯkt* (*UT* 2680)

The Eg pl. form *sk.ty* phonetically and semantically fits the context well. Therefore the emendation: שׂכיות > שׂכתי (Driver, and *BHS*), being based upon the singular form *skty* is unnecessary. As for the correspondence between Eg *ś* and Heb שׂ, it is normal, if the word entered Hebrew directly. (Canaanite cf. Ug *ṯkt*: Ug *ṯ* = Heb שׂ). The Heb vocalization might be influenced by the parallel word אניות. The word cannot be confirmed because this is the single correspondence between Eg *ś* and Heb שׂ, though it is quite conceivable.

שׁוֹשַׁן ** "lily"

--- *sš(š)n* 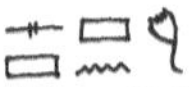

Brugsch, *Wb* p. 1314; Erman, *ZDMG* 46 p. 117; Lambdin p. 154; Ellengogen p. 159

[Heb] שׁוֹשַׁן: 1K 7:22, 26; Song of Solomon (6x); Ps 45:1, 69:1, 80:1 (total 11x); שׁוֹשַׁנָּה: 2Chr 4:5 etc. (4 x)

[Eg] *sššn Wb* III.487.9 OK–MK; *ssšn Wb* III.485 MK; *ššn* (K. Kitchen, *VA* 3 p. 29ff. for the disscussion, see Heb PN שׁוּשַׁן); [Copt] ϣⲱϣⲉⲛ; [Aram] שושן (*DISO* p. 322); [Gk] σουσαν; [Arab] *šwšan*.

שִׁטָּה ** "acacia"

--- *šnḏ(.t)*  "acacia"

Erman, *ZDMG* 46 p. 120; Calice no. 859; Lambdin p. 154; Ellenbogen p. 160

[Heb] Ex 25:5, 10 etc. (26 x); Deut 10:3; Is 41:19

[Eg] *Wb* IV.521.1ff. MK; cf. masc form *šnḏ* (*Wb* IV.520.9–13 Pyr and OK); [Copt] ^{s}ϣⲟⲛⲧⲉ, ^{b}ϣⲟⲛⲧ (Černý p. 247); [Demot] *šnt* (Erichsen p. 516); [Arab] *sanṭ*; [Akk] cf. *samṭu*[3]

Notice n-assimilation only in Hebrew. Inscriptional spellings clearly show the following phonetic change; *šnḏ.t* > *šnd.t*  (MK) > *šnt.t*  (NK). Because of the representation of Heb ט which corresponds only to Eg *d*, it is evident that Eg *šnḏ.t* entered Canaanite in the Middle Kingdom period after Eg fem. ending dropped yet before the *d* became *t*.

שַׁיִשׁ ** "alabaster"

--- *šś* 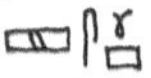 "alabaster"

Stricker, *AO* p. 12; Lambdin p. 155

[Heb] 1Chr 29:2

[Eg] *Wb* IV.540.10ff. since Pyr; [Aram] שש (*DISO* p. 321)

In the course of the phonetic change of Eg *šś*, there is no

[3] Akk *samṭu* is a foreign name of the acacia, see *šamṭu* (*CAD* S 125a). *ú sa-am-ṭu* is a name of *Ú.GIŠ.Ú.GÍR* in Meluḫḫa according to lexical series Uruanna I.182; *Ú.GIŠ.Ú.GÍR* is *ašāgu* a kind of acacia. Since Meluḫḫa stood for Nubia in NA texts, this could well be the Eg word (*CAD* A2 409a).

inscriptional evidence for *šś* > *šš*. Therefore, it may be reasonable to assume that Heb שׁ correspondence to Eg *ś* is due to the phonetic dissimilation of Heb ס > שׁ under the influence of the first שׁ. A parallel change is observed in שֵׁשׁ "linen."

(שׁן) הבים ?

--- (שׁן)-*3b(w)*  "Ivory of Elephants"

[Heb] 1K 10:22; 2Chr 9:21

[Eg] *Wb* I.7.16 since MK

Phonetically Eg *3* can hardly be represented by Heb ה. If Heb הב means "elephant," Heb and Eg *3b* could be cognate, both borrowed from a third language.

שׁסה "to spoil"

--- *š(3)ś(w)*  "Bedouin"

Albright, *BASOR* 89 p. 32 n. 7; Lambdin p. 155

[Heb] Judges 2:14, 16; 1Sam 14:48, 23:1, 2K17:20; Ps 44:11 etc. (12 x)

[Eg] *Wb* IV.412.10–11 Dyn 18; [Copt] ^{s}ϣⲱⲥ, ^{a}ϣⲁⲥ

Albright's identification seems to be groundless. If שׁסה is an Eg loanword, we must assume very early borrowing, because שׁסה is so hebraized that the secondary root שׁסס "to plunder" is produced. More likely, however, both words are independent.

שַׁעַטְנֵז "mixed stuff" (?)

--- **šʿd-nḏ* "cutting of thread"(?)

Lambdin p. 155 (following Albright's oral suggestion)

[Heb] Lev 19:19, Deut 22:11

[Eg] **šʿd-nḏ* (*Wb* IV.422 since NK, ^{s,f}ϣⲱⲱⲧ, ^{b}ϣⲱⲧ) "to cut" and *nḏ* (*Wb* II.376 ⲛⲁⲧ) "thread"

BDB's explanation using Copt ⲚⲞⲨϪ "false" is impossible because Eg of ⲚⲞⲨϪ is *nʿwḏ*, and the *'ayn* cannot be explained. Albright's theoretical reconstruction **šʿd-nḏ* is not impossible, though we cannot cite any evidence and the meaning does not really fit the context.

שֵׁשׁ ** "byssum"

--- *šś* 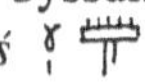 "linen"

Stricker, *AO* 15 p. 6; Lambdin p. 155; Ellenbogen p. 164
[Heb] Gen 41:42; Ex 25:4, 26:1 etc. (32x); Ezek 16:10, 13, 27:7; Prov 31:22 (total 38 x)
[Eg] *Wb* IV.539.12ff since MK; [Aram] שש (*DISO* p. 321); [Copt] cf. ˢϢΝϹ, ᵇϢЄΝϹ for *š(s)-ns(w)*

That שׁשׁ has no cognate in Heb, while *šś* is attested since MK in Eg make it very likely that the word is an Eg loanword. As for the phonetic problem of Heb שׁ and Eg *ś*, see the discussion in שׁישׁ. For the biblical evidence, see בוץ.

תבה ** "ark, box"
--- *ḏb(3.t)* , NK , MK , etc.
"shrine, coffin, chest, box"
Brugsch, *Wb* p. 1628; Erman, *ZDMG* 46 p. 126; Černý p. 180
[Heb] Gen 6:14–9:18 (26 x) "ark"; Ex 2:3, 5 "basket" made of papyrus גמא (see גמא).
[Eg] *Wb* V.561.8–12, 434.10, 261.11; [Gk] θιβις (LXX); [Copt] ΤΗΗΒЄ, ΤΑΙΒЄ

The Eg words *ḏb3.t* "shrine"(since OK), *ḏb3.t* "box" share a common origin. The progressive spelling *tbi* indicates that the initial *ḏ* already became /t/ in MK. Therefore, phoneticaly תבה corresponds well. The word has no cognate in Semitic, strengthening the Eg etymology. It is interesting that an Eg loanword is found in the flood story in Gesesis.

תחרא ? "collar" (?)
--- *dḥr* "the hide of an animal"
Lambdin p. 155 (with doubt)
[Heb] Ex 28:32, 39:23
[Eg] *Wb* V.481.13ff since MK

As Lambdin comments, there is a phonetic problem in this identification: Heb ת = Eg *d*, because it seems that the initial *d* of *dḥr* did not change into /t/ (*Wb* V.481). Also the meaning is not suitable in the context. More likely is the connection of תחרא with Eg *tḫr* "leather part of carriage" (*Wb* V.328.2; see Caminos p. 201), yet as shown by the syllabic writing, the word is a foreign word, which might have been borrowed from Semitic.

C. ANALYSIS OF PHONOLOGICAL CORRESPONDENCES

[1] Heb : Eg Phonetic Correspondences

Heb א : Eg *3*
Lw = אחו
Heb א : Eg *i*
PN = מיאמן; DN = אמון; GN = און, אן, נא; Lw = אטון, איפה, טנא
Heb א : Eg lost *r* in final position
PN = צחא, ציחא, פחא
Heb א : Eg probably lost *n* in initial position
PN = אסנת
Heb א : Eg lost *t* in middle position
Lw = יאור
Heb א : Eg ø or *y*
Lw = גמא
Heb א : Eg ø (prothetic *aleph*)
Lw = אחלמה
Heb ב : Eg *b*
GN = פיבסת; Lw = הובן, טבעת, לוב, קב, תבה
Heb ג : Eg *g*
Lw = גמא
Heb ד : Eg not attested
Heb ה : Eg *h*
PN = תרהקה; Lw = הובן, הין
Heb ה : Eg ø
(1) lost fem. ending *-t* [āh]
GN = סונה; Lw = אחלמה, איפה, ערה, שטה, תבה
(2) *mater lectionis*
PN = נכה, תרהקה; Lw = פרעה
Heb ו : Eg *w*
PN = נכו (?)[4] ; GN = סונה
Heb ו : Eg ø
(1) *mater lectionis*
PN = חור, חורי, כוש, כושי, פוטיאל, פוטיפרע, פשחור, שושק; DN = אמון; GN = און; Lw = אטון, הובן, יאור, לוב, קוף, שושה
(2) unknown (case ending?)

4 Or *mater lectionis* which is interchangable with ה; cf. נכה.

Lw = אחו

Heb ז : Eg not attested

Heb ח : Eg *ḥ*

PN = חור, חורי, חפרע, חרנפר, פחא, פינחס, פשחור, צחא, ציחא;
GN = חנס, שיחור, תחפנחס; Lw = קלחת

Heb ח : Eg *ẖ*

Lw = אחו, אחלמה, חתם, פח, פח

Heb ט : Eg *d*

PN = פוטיאל, פוטיפרע, פטיה, פט; Lw = אטון, טנא

Heb ט : Eg *ḏ* (> *d*)

Lw = טבעת, שטה

Heb י : Eg *i*

Lw = יאור

Heb י : Eg *y*

PN = חורי, מיאמן (or י could be a *mater lectionis*); Lw = צי

Heb י : Eg lost *r*

GN = פיבסת (the י is a vowel letter)

Heb י : Eg *w*

GN = סינין (probably confusion between סין and סון)

Heb י : Eg ø

(1) *mater lectionis* (see י : lost *r*)
PN = פוטיאל, פוטיפרע, פינחס, פפי, ציחא, שישק; GN = סין, שיחור; Lw = איפה, היה, שיש
(2) gentilic
PN = כושי

Heb כ : Eg *k*

PN = כוש, כושי, נכו, נכה; Lw = נפך

Heb ל : Eg *r*

Lw = לוב, קלחת

Heb ל : Eg *n* (> /l/)

Lw = אחלמה, לשם

Heb מ : Eg *m*

PN = מיאמן; DN = אמון; GN = מף, פתם, רעמסס; Lw = אחלמה, גמא, חתם, לשם

Heb נ : Eg *n*

PN = אסנת, חרנפר, מיאמן, נכה, נהו, פינחס, ששן; DN = אמון; GN = און, אן, חנס, נא, סונה, סין, סינים, צען, תחפנחס; Lw = הובן, הין, טנא, נתר, שושן

Heb נ : Eg *m*
GN = נף (change of the initial *m* > /n/ in Hebrew?); Lw = אטון (the final /m/ > /n/ after [u] vowel), נפך (the initial *m* > /n/ before a labial)

Heb ס : Eg *s*
PN = אסנת, פינחס; GN = חנס, סונה, סין, סינים, פיבסת, פתרוס, פתרסים, פעמסס, תחפנחס; Lw = קסת

Heb ע : Eg ᶜ
PN = חפרע, פוטיפרע; GN = צען, רעמסס, Lw = טבעת, ערה, פרעה

Heb פ : Eg *p*
PN = פוטיאל, פוטיפרע, פינחס, פשחור, פשחר, פפי, פחא, פטיה, פט; GN = פיבסת, פתם, פתרוס, פתרסים, תחפנחס; Lw = איפה, פח, פח, פרעה, קוף

Heb פ : Eg *f*
PN = חרנפר; GN = מף, נף; Lw = נפך

Heb פ : Eg *b*
PN = חפרע

Heb צ : Eg *ḏ*
PN = צחא, ציחא; GN = צען, צי

Heb ק : Eg *k*
PN = שושק, שישק, תרהקה; Lw = קב, קלחת

Heb ק : Eg *g* (> /k/ or /ḳ/)
Lw = קוף, קסת

Heb ר : Eg *r*
PN = חור, חורי, חפרע, חרנפר, פוטיפרע, פשחור, פשחר, תרהקה; GN = פתרוס, פתרסים, פעמסס, שיחור; Lw = יאור, נתר, ערה, פרעה

Heb שׁ : Eg *š*
PN = כוש, כושי, פשחור, פשחר, שושק, שישק, ששן; Lw = לשם, שושן, שיש, שטה, שש

Heb שׁ : Eg *s* (> /š/)
Lw = שושן, שיש, שש

Heb ת : Eg *t*
PN = אסנת, תרהקה; GN = פיבסת, פתם, פתרוס, פתרסים, תחפנחס; Lw = חתם, טבעת, קלחת, קסת

Heb ת : Eg *ṯ* (> /t/)
Lw = נתר

Heb ת : Eg *ḏ* (> /d/ > /t/)

Lw = תבה

[2] Eg : Heb Phonetic Correspondences

Eg *3* : Heb א
Eg *3* : Heb ø (excluding Eg article)
PN = חפרע, נכו, נכה; GN = פיבסת; Lw = נפך, פח, פח, פרעה, צי, תבה,
Eg *ỉ* : Heb א
Eg *ỉ* : Heb י
Eg *ỉ* : Heb ø
PN = חפרע, פוטיאל, פוטיפרע, פט, פטיהו; GN = פתם; Lw = אטון, נתר, קוף, קסת
Eg *y* : Heb י
Eg *y* : Heb ø
PN = פינחס; GN = פתרוס, פתרסים, תחפנחס; Lw = אחו (?), גמא (or Eg *y* : Heb א?), הובן, קב
Eg *ʿ* : Heb ע
Eg *w* : Heb ו
Eg *w* : Heb י
Eg *w* : Heb ø (Eg *w* dropped)
PN = חור, חפרע, נכה; GN = און, אן, סין; Lw = הין, יאור
Eg *b* : Heb ב
Eg *b* : Heb פ
Eg *p* : Heb פ
Eg *f* : Heb פ
Eg *m* : Heb מ
Eg *m* (> /n/) : Heb נ
Eg *n* : Heb נ
Eg *n* (> /l/) : Heb ל
Eg *n* (> /ʾ/) : Heb א
Eg *n* : Heb ø (n-assimilation)
PN = שׁושׁק, שׁישׁק; GN = מף, נף; Lw = שׁטה
Eg *r* : Heb ר
Eg *r* : Heb ל
Eg *r* (> ø) : Heb א (see *matres lectionis*)
Eg *r* (> ø) : Heb ø

PN = מיאמן; GN = מף, נף, פיבסת, פתם
Eg *h* : Heb ה
Eg *ḥ* : Heb ח
Eg *ẖ* : Heb ח
Eg *s* : Heb ס
Eg *s* (> /š/) : Heb שׁ
Eg *s* : Heb ø (Eg *s* assimilated into the following *s*)
Eg *š* : Heb שׁ
Eg *ḳ*: Heb ק
Eg *k* : Heb כ
Eg *g* : Heb ג
Eg *g* : Heb ק
Eg *t* : Heb ת
Eg *t* : Heb ø
(1) Eg fem. ending -*t* lost (see the discussion p. 300)
PN = נא; GN = סונה, פיבסת, צען, תחפנחס; Lw = אחמנה, איפה, טנא, לשם, נפך, ערה, שטה, תבה
(2) Eg *t* (> /ʾ/)
Lw = יאור
Eg *ṯ* : Heb ת
Eg *d* : Heb ט
Eg *d* : Heb ø (Eg *d* dropped: *ḏd* > *ḏ*)
Eg *ḏ* : Heb צ
Eg *ḏ* : Heb ט
Eg *ḏ* : Heb ת (Eg *ḏ* > /d/ > /t/)

[3] Table of Correspondences

	Heb	primary	secondary	Eg	primary	secondary
glottal stops	א	*3 i*	*r*[1] *n*[2] *t*[3] ø[4]	*3*	א	ø
				i	א י	ø
	ע	ᶜ		ᶜ	ע	
semivowels	י	*i y*	*r*[5] *w*[6] ø	*y*	י	ø
	ו	*w*	ø[7]	*w*	ו	י[6] ø
labials	ב	*b*		*b*	ב	פ
	פ	*p f*	*b*[8]	*p*	פ	
				f	פ	
nasals	מ	*m*		*m*	מ	נ
	נ	*n*	*m*	*n*	נ	ל[9] א[2] ø[10]
lateral	ל	*r*	*n*[9]			
trill	ר	*r*		*r*	ר ל	א[1] ø
pharyngals & laryngals	ה	*h*	ø	*h*	ה	
	ח	*ḥ ḫ*		*ḥ*	ח	
				ḫ	ח	
				ẖ	-	
sibilants	ס	*s*		*s*	ס	שׂ[11] ø[12]
	שׂ	*š*	*s*[11]	*š*	שׂ	
	צ	*ḏ*				
velars	ק	*ḳ*	*g*[14]	*ḳ*	ק	
	כ	*k*		*k*	כ	
	ג	*g*		*g*	ג	ק[14]
alveolars	ת	*t*	*ṯ*[15] *ḏ*[16]	*t*	ת	ø[18]
	ד	-		*ṯ*		ת[15]
				d	ט	ø
	ט	*d*	*ḏ*[17]	*ḏ*	צ	ט[17] ת[18]

*The above arrangement is based on the Eg alphabetical order, not phonology.

Notes 1. in the case of *ḥr* "face"
2. in the case of *ns* "He/She belongs to"
3. in the case of *itrw* "the Nile"
4. prothetic a *aleph* and the case of גמא
5. lost *r*
6. misspelling
7. *mater lectionis*
8. the secondary change *p* > *b*
9. the change *l* > /n/
10. n-assimilation
11. the secondary change *s* > /š/
12. s-assimilation to /š/
13. fem. ending or *mater lectionis*
14. the change *g* > /k/ or /ḳ/
15. the change *ṯ* > *t*
16. the change *ḏ* > *d* > *t*
17. the change *ḏ* > *d*
18. fem ending *-t*

[4] Notes on the Correspondences

a) Glottal Stops

Eg *3* once corresponds to Heb א at the initial position (אחו). The remaining examples of Eg *3* have no correspondences. Eg *i* is always realized by either א or י in the initial position (אמון, און, אן, אטון, איפה, יאור). In the final position, Eg *i* remains as א protected by the following elements (נא: *ni.t*, טנא; *dni.t*), yet it is elided when there is no protective element after it (אטון : *idmi*,; נתר : *ntri*; קסת : *gsti*). In the medial position, Eg *i* is elided except in אמן (מיאמן).

Heb א represents a lost *r* in the final, lost *n* in the initial and lost *t* in the middle position. It also occurs as a prothetic *aleph* (אחלמה). The א of גמא seems to be a *mater lectionis*.

b) Semi-vowels

Eg *y* probably corresponds to Heb י (חורי, מיאמן, צי), yet it is impossible to make a distinction between a consonant י and a vowel letter י except in the case of מיאמן. Eg *w* certainly corresponds to Heb ו as a consonant in סונה and most likely in נכו. However the majority of Eg *y* and *w* dropped.

Heb י and ו are frequently used as *matres lectionis*. The ו of אחו is difficult. It could be an old Eg case ending reflected in Heb.

c) Labials

There is nothing peculiar in correspondences between Eg and Heb labials. As in Aram and Ph, the פ of חפרע is the only case where Eg *b* is realized by Heb פ, probably because the following ר influenced the articulation of פ.

d) Nasals

Eg *m* and *n* are primarily represented by Heb מ and נ respectively. Eg initial *m* which becomes /n/ corresponds to Heb נ (נפך), and Eg *n* which becmes /l/in the initial position and between a labial and *ḫ* is realized as Heb ל.

Eg *mn-nfr* "Memphis" is realized as either מף or נף in Heb. The change מ > נ is not usual, yet the /m/ > /n/ before a labial is conceivable[5].

N-assimilation more frequently took place in Heb;

e.g. GN מף / נף (*mn-nfr*) --- cf. Aram מנף, Ph מנף

Lw שטה (*šnd.t*) --- cf. ϢΟΝΤЄ

PN שושק (*ššnk*) --- cf. Gk Σεσωγχις

e) Sibilants

It seems that there is no confusion in correspondences between

[5] Cf. in the case of Akk, von Soden, *GAG* § 31b; Millard, *MAARAV* 4 p. 90; cf. *m* > *n* (*GAG* § 84), *mt*, *mṭ* > *nt*, *nṭ* (*GVG* § 58).

sibilants, *i.e.*, ס : *s*, שׁ : *š* and צ : *ḏ*. Eg *ṯ*, which corresponds to Ph צ, and Aram שׁ is not attested in Heb. The representation of Eg *ś* by Heb שׁ has been long discussed. Only in the following cases does Heb שׁ represent Eg *ś*;

e.g. PN שׁשׁן --- *sšn* > /ššn/ (cf. Copt ϢЄϢЄN)
Lw שׁושׁן --- *sšn* > /ššn/ (cf. Aram שׁשׁן)
Lw שׁישׁ --- *šś*
Lw שׁשׁ --- *šś* > /ss/ (cf. Aram שׁשׁ)

Therefore, these indicate that Heb שׁ does not really correspond to Eg *ś*. It was Albright who advocated that PN ענמשׁ finally settles the problem of whether a Heb שׁ may represent an Eg *ś*, because he interpreted it as *'Anat-mâsey* "Born of Anat." However, Lemaire identified it with Eg *ʿn-m-š* , which is much more likely (see entry אנמשׁ). The loanword משׁי (Eg *mśy*) also suggested this possibility. Yet not only phonetically, but also semantically the identification cannot be confirmed (see also the discussion of Ph sibilants for אשׁרשׁלה, עבדשׁר). After examining all possibilities of correspondence between Heb שׁ and Eg *ś*, no certain evidence appears for it.

The equation of Heb שׂ and Eg *s* is suggested by two unconfirmed examples: אשׂראל (*3s-ir-*אל) and שׂכיות (*sk.tw*). The latter is probable though we cannot confirm it.

f) Pharyngals and Laryngals

Eg *ḥ* and *ḫ* (*ẖ* is not attested) are represented by Heb ח. As in Aram transliterations, Heb does not indicate any of spirantization of כ > /ḵ/, since Eg postvocalic *ḫ* consistently corresponds to Heb ח. This indicates that all Eg elements entered Heb before spirantization became operative.

g) Velars and Alveolars

The correspondences between Eg and Heb velars show consistency without any double realization.

Alveolars also show consistent correspondences with each other; *i.e.*, Eg *t* : Heb ת, Eg *d* : Heb ט, and Eg *ḏ* : Heb צ (Eg *ṯ* is not attested).

[5] Notes on the Hebrew Vocalizations

a) Eg article *p3*

In Heb transliteration of Eg names and words, Eg *p3* is realized as follows;

(1) Eg *p3* : פי [pî]
e.g., פינחס
(2) Eg *p3* :פו[pô]
e.g., פוטיאל (LXX φουτιηλ), פוטיפר (LXX πετεφρι פוטיפרע (LXX πετεφρης)[6].
(3) Eg *p3* : פ [pa]
e.g. פתרוס (LXX βαβυλωνια), פשחור (LXX πασχωρ etc.
(4) Eg *t3* : ת [ta]
e.g. תחפנחס

Corresponding to the divergences of vowel reflected in Heb forms of Eg *p3*, the cuneiform materials also show the variety of vocalization as follows (all examples are from Raneke, *KM* pp. 7–42);

(1) Eg *p3* : *pi-*
e.g., MB *pi-wi/e/a-ri (p3-wr)* (EA)
NA *pi-ša-an-ḫu-ru (p3-šri-n-ḥr)* (Assurb.)
NB *pi-sa-mi-is-ki (psmṯk)*
(2) Eg *p3* : *pu-*
e.g., MB *pu-ḫu-urr (p3-ḫr)* (EA)
NA *pu-ṭu-beš-ti (p3-di-b3st.t)* (Assurb.)
NB not attested
(3) Eg *p3* : *pa-*
e.g., MB *pa-ḫa-am-na-ta (p3-ḥm-nṯr)* (EA)
NA *pa-aḳ-ru-ru (p3-ḳrr)*
NB *pa-aṭ-e-si-i'*

Judging from the cuneiform materials, we conclude that therre is no consistent vocalization of the Eg article *p3*. The vowel value of Eg *p3* could be any short vowel [a/i/u]. It is most likely that Eg *p3* had a murmuring vowel, like Heb *shewa*. The phonetic context, dialectical

[6] These Gk forms indicate that when the translators of the LXX transcribed פוטיאל into Gk alphabets, they used the Gk form for the common Eg name *p3-di-p3-rˁ*.

variations, and chronological changes of sound value all affected the determination of the vowel value.

However, two Heb forms, פו and פי, seem to demand an explanation, because they indicate long vowel [û] and [î].

(1) Heb פי: probably due to a dialectal form; In Bohairic, a dialect of the Eastern delta where the Semites settled in the 2nd millennium B.C. the definite article has two forms, weak and strong;

	weak	strong
masc.	ⲡ-, ⲫ-	ⲡⲓ
fem.	ⲧ-, ⲑ-	ϯ

This strong article ⲡⲓ is used to indicate an individual, *e.g.*, ⲫ-ⲚⲞⲨϯ"god", ⲡⲓ-ⲚⲞⲨϯ "the god."[7] This usage of the strong article would explain the vocalization of [pî] of פינחס "The Nubian," because in this case פינחס represents an individual, not Nubians in general. We do not know whether [i] of ⲡⲓ is long or short. Yet the [i] vowel is explicitly articulated, no longer being a murmuring sound.

(2) Heb פו: probably due to an older form: In the midst of the considerable divergences of the cuneiform realization of Eg *p3*, it seems that the following chronological development of vowel sound is observable among the Eg names of *p3-di*-typte (Sem -פט); (all examples from Ranke, *KM* 33–42).

(a) *p3-di-* : *Put-* in NA (8–7th cent. BC)

pu-ṭi-ḫu-u-ru-u (p3-di-ḥr)	Johns 763
pu-ṭu-beš-ti (p3-di-b3st.t)	Assurb.
pu-ṭu-um-ḫe-e-šu (p3-di-m3-ḥs3)	Johns 307
pu-ṭu-pa-i-ti (p3-di-p3-?)	Johns 307
pu-du-pi-ya-ti (?)	Johns 99
pu-ṭi-ma-a-ni[(p3-di-?)	Johns 763
pu-ṭi-še-ri[(p3-di-?)	Johns 851

(b) *p3-di-* : *Pat-* in NB (6–5th cent. BC)

pa-ṭa-ᵈe-si-iʾ (p3-di-3s.t)	Clay X 39
pa-ṭa-ni-e-si-iʾ (p3-di-n.i-3s.t)	Clay X 15
pa-aṭ-e-si-iʾ (p3-di-3s.t)	Clay X
pa-aṭ-mi-us-tu-u (p3-di-imn-nswt-t3wy)	Dairus 301
pa-aṭ-ni-ip-te-e-mu (p3-di-nfr-tm)	Darius 301
pa-aṭ-u-as-tù (p3-di-b3st.t)	Cambyses 85

[7] A. Mallon, *Grammaire Copte*, p. 26f.

pa-ṭi(?)-e-su (p3-di-3s.t)

Since the phonetic context is fixed as *p3-di-* and the vowel change [u] > [a] is consistent, we may assume that the vocalization of *p3-di-* changed from [puṭ-] to [paṭ-] between the 7th and 6th centuries BC. The Heb form of this type -פוטי may be a reflection of the older pronounciation. Even though the Akk forms do not show a long [u] vowel as Heb forms do, if the [u] vowel is explicitly articulated, it would be no longer strange to use a *mater lectionis* ו for Eg *p3*. Likewise an alternative explanation may be possible, *i.e.*, the difference between [puṭ-] and [paṭ-] is a result of a different scribal convention between Assyrian and Babylonian.

b) Eg feminine ending *-t*

Eg fem. ending *-t* is realized in the following three ways;
(1) Eg fem. ending has no reflection:
e.g., GN = נא, פיבסת, צען, תחפנחס; Lw = טנא, לשם, נפך
(2) Eg fem. ending is realized as Heb ה:
e.g., GN = סונה; Lw = אחלמה, איפה, ערה, שטה, תבה
(3) Eg fem. ending is represented by Heb ת:
e.g., Lw = טבעת, קלחת

When the Eg fem. ending is indicated in Aram texts, the י is almost always used (see Chapter II, Eg : Aram Phonetic correspondences p. 209), indicating the normal fem. sound value [i] or [e] in the late period. However, it is characteristic that the Heb reflection of the fem. ending is ה, with vocalization [-āh] except for GN סונה [-ēh]. Though the ה is a Heb fem. ending, it is unlikely that Heb scribes, recognizing these as fem nouns, changed the vowel value of fem ending [i/e] > [ā], and added the ה. Neither is it likely that the words were first borrowed as *אחלמי like Aram forms, then underwent the secondary change אחלמה, attached with the sound change [ē] > [ā]. Apart from all these speculations, there are some indications that Eg fem. ending changed from [*at] > [a] > [e/i];

(1) The Eg fem. ending is realized as [a] in the following cuneiform writings in the second millennium:

(a) *mA-ma-an-ap-pa (imn-m-ip.t)* (EA *KM* p. 7)

(b) *na-am-ša (nms.t)* (EA *KM* p. 15)
(c) *ra-aḫ-ta (rhd.t)* (EA *KM* p. 24)
(d) *mMi-in!-mu-a-ri-a (mn-m3ᶜ.t-rᶜ)* (Bogasköi *KM* p. 12)

yet notice, if the ending is placed in medial position, the value [a] is often reduced to [i].

(a) *āluḪi-ku-up-ta-aḫ (ḥ.t-k3-ptḥ)* (EA *KM* p.10)
(b) *fNa-ap-te-ra (nfr.t-iry)* (Bogasköi *KM* p. 14)

(2) However, Eg fem ending is realized as [i] in NA and NB (6th-7th cent. BC) even at the end position;

(a) *ālubi-in-ṭi-ti (pr-b3-nb-ḏd.t)* (Assurb *KM* p. 27)
(b) *mma-an-ti-me-an(!)-ḫi-e (mnṯ.w-m-ḥ3.t)*(Assurb *KM* p. 30)
(c) *mpu-ṭu-beš-ti (p3-di-3s.t)* (Assurb *KM* p. 34)
(d) *mpa-ṭa-e-si-iʾ (p3-di-3s.t)* (Clay X *KM* p. 39)

Therefore, we could conclude that Heb forms of Eg loanwords reflect the older form of the Eg fem. ending. If the older form is [a], it is not difficult to infer that the original form was *[at], which is preserved in two Eg loanwords in Heb, *i.e.*, טבעת *(ṭabbaᶜaṯ)* and קלחת *(qallaḥaṯ)*. Since these two preserved the fem. ending, they will have entered Canaanite in the Middle Kingdom before the /t/ was lost in Eg.

c) Other Vowel Changes

(1) פיבסת *(pîḇesṯ)* : Eg *pr-b3st.t*

Through comparison with Gk βουβαστις, βουβατος and Copt ПОΥВⲀСТЄ, it seems that the vowel change /pī/ > /pū/ took place. It is well known that Eg *pr* became [pi] in NK, and *b3st.t* has a [u]-bowel at the initial as follows;

pr = /pi/ NA *alupi-šap-tu (pr-spdw)* Assurb
NA *alupi-in-ṭi-ṭi (pr-b3-nb-ḏd.t)* Assurb

b3st.t = /ubaste/ Ph אבסת
Aram -ובסת
NA *ubešti*

Hence, the vocalization of *pr-b3st.t* was *[piubasti], which became [p/bubasti] (Copt ПОΥВⲀСТЄ), then the [pi] for *pr* is usually reduced to [p] when it was followed by a [u]-vowel and even a nasal consonant;

e.g., *[pi-ušīru] > *alupu-ši-ru (pr-3s-ir)*

*[pi-nubu] > *[alu]pu-nu-bu (pr-nb)*

Yet if the [pi] is followed by a consonant, *pr* remains as [pi] as above. Therefore, we may infer from the Heb form פיבסת that the initial vowel [u] of *b3st.t*, which is never inscriptionally confirmed, was a secondary development in the first millennium. The Heb form might preserve the original form [pi-basti]. Yet apart from the Biblical form, we have no evidence.

The Heb form may be explained by an alternative vowel change [piubasti] > [pibasti] ([u] dropped rather than becoming [i]). The remainder of the Heb form took the analogy of *qatl*-form [basti] > [bast] > [beset].

(2) The vowel change [u/o] > [i/e]

(a) פתרוס *(paṯrôs)* : Eg *p3-t3-rsy*

The NA from *pa-tu-ri-si*, Copt -ⲣⲎⲤ "north" indicates the vowel change [ō] > [ē/ī], which took place between Ramesses II and Assy. period (see entry פתרוס).

(b) Lw שׁוּשַׁן *(šûšan)* and PN שֵׁשַׁן *(šēšan)*

Though one is a common noun and the other a proper noun, both originated from the same Eg root *sš(š)n > ššn* "lily," and show the vowel change [û] > [ē]. Down to copt ϢⲰϢⲈⲚ (even today in Susan), the [ū] vowel between the two שׁ never changed. The change is more lilely to be internal in Heb, as being sugested by LXX σωσαν foı *šēšān*.

(c) PN שׁוּשַׁק (LXX Σουσακιμ) and שִׁישַׁק (LXX Σουσακιμ) (cf. שָׁשָׁק *šāšāq*)

The phonetic change [u] > [ê/î] is suggested in the Gk forms Σεσωγχις, and Σεσωγχωσις (Manetho). If this the case, we can apply the same Eg phonetic change [u] > [e] to this PN. However K. A, Kitchen suggested that Manetho's form are due to metathesis. LXX Σουσακιμ for שׁוּשַׁק as well as שִׁישַׁק may indicate that there were no phonetic changes, and שִׁישַׁק is an internal change [u] > [i] in Heb, whether phonetic or merely script (ו / י).

(d) שַׁוְשָׁא *(šawšāʾ*, LXX Σουσα) and שִׁישָׁא *(šîšaʾ*, LXX Σηβα)

Since both names indicate the same person, it is impossible to assume phonetic change. Confusion in spelling is more probable, or even confusion of ו and י in the square script. It is noteworthy that the vowel variation between ו and י takes place between two שׁ three times.

This phonetic circumstance may cause the vacillation of vowels in the names and word שׁושׁא : שׁישׁא, שׁושׁק : שׁישׁק, שׁושׁן: שׁשׁן.

(e) סונה *(səsēnēh)* and סינים *(sînîm)*

From the context it is most likely that סינ(ים) is identical with סונה, rather than סין. This may be the result of misspelling.

IV

EGYPTIAN PROPER NAMES AND LOANWORDS IN UGARITIC

Eg PNs were studied by Gröndahl, *Die Personnamen der Texte aus Ugarit* (Roma 1967), in which he listed two Eg PNs, *amanmaššu* and *pmn* (p. 300). Though he did not explain them as Eg, there occur two more Eg names written in Akk, whose Eg identification is confirmed by the context, *pa'aḫi* and *ḫeḫea*. The other Eg names discussed below were taken from the list of PNs which were left unexplained by Gröndahl (pp. 304–314). We included Eg names written in Ug Akk, for it is most likely, that though letters are Akk, the scribes were Ugaritic.

We owe the comparative studies in Eg and Ug to W. Ward ("Comparative Studies in Egyptian and Ugaritic" *JNES* 20, 1961, pp. 31–40) and C. Gordon (chapter 19 of *UT* 1965). However their main concern seems to be with cognate words. Because of the lack of the context in which the names and words occur (mainly in name or material lists), the identifications of Eg names and loanwords are difficult. Thirty-nine possibilities are discussed below, of which only fifteen are used to establish phonetic correspondences.

A. INVENTORY OF EGYPTIAN PROPER NAMES AND LOANWORDS

[1] Personal Names

abdḥr (hybrid) **
--- *abd-ḥr* "The servant of Horus"
Gröndahl p. 136
[Ug] *KTU* 4.33.36; 4.40.11 *abdḥ[r]* (*UT* 19.16; Aist 14)
[Eg] see Ph בדחר

It seems that Ug *a* stands for ᶜ in the following PNs: *abdḥr* for *ᶜbdḥr,* for *abdᶜn* : *ᶜbdᶜn* (Gröndahl p. 136, 110); cf. also Ph אבדאבסת. However, Gordon does not consider that *abd-* is a variant of *ᶜbd-* (UT 19.16 and 1801), though he does not give any explanation of *abd.*

amanmaš(š)u **
--- *ỉmn-ms*  "Amun is born"
Gröndahl p. 300
[Eg] *PRU* IV 17.28.0 *ˡa-ma-an-ma-ši*; PRU IV 17.28.16, 27 *ˡa-ma-an-ma-aš-šu*
[Eg] Ranke I.29.8 m. NK–Late; [EA] *ˡa-ma-an-ma-ša*

Notice that *ỉmn-m-š* 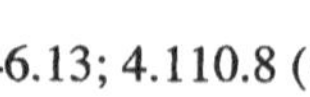 "Amun is on the lake" (Ranke I.29.3 m. NK) is not impossible. However *ỉmn-ms* is much more common in NK, making *ỉmn-m-š* less likely.

ḥr *
--- *ḥr(w)*  "Horus"
Gröndahl p. 136
[Ug] *KTU* 1.82.13; 4.46.13; 4.110.8 (*UT* 19.892; Aist 961f)
[Eg] see Ph חר
Gröndahl suggested the Eg god Horus, while Gordon proposed a Sem explanation: *ḥrr* I (< *ḥry*). Heb חור "be white" is also possible. The identification is open to choice.

ḫeḫea **
--- *ḥḥ*  "(God) *ḥḥ*"
[Ug] *PRU* III 16.136 *ˡḫé-ḫé-a amîl ^mat^mi-iṣ-ri*
[Eg] Ranke I.254.8 m. NK

The Eg name *ḥḥ* is probably a hypocoristicon of *ḥḥ-nḫw* "(God) *ḥḥ* is a protector" (Ranke I.254.10; probably *ḥḥ-n-* (Ranke I.254.11) is the same name, see also *KRI* I 409.8). The DN-*nḫw* type of name is common in NK, *e.g.*, *rʿ-nḫw* (Ranke I.219.11 Dyn 20), *ẖnm.w-m-nḫw* (Ranke I.275.13 Dyn 18). The final *aleph* /ʾa/ is a hypocoristic ending.

mn *

--- *mn* "The established" (?)

[Ug] *KTU* 4.350.13 *bn. mn* (*UT* 19.1496)

[Eg] Ranke I.149.29 m. MK–Late / f. Late; [EA] *^{l}ma-ne-e*

Gröndahl compared it with the root *mny* "to count" (Heb מני "fate"). However the Eg explanation is more probable because of its frequent occurrence; besides the *mn* above, *mn.ỉ* , *mn.y* (Ranke I.151.2f m. OK–NK / f. MK), *mn.w* (Ranke I.151.14 m. MK–Late). Notice that the text contains many foreign names; see Ug PN *pni*.

nmry

--- *n(b)-m(3ʿ.t)-r(ʿ)* "Reʿ is the lord of truth" (Amenophis III)

[Ug] *KTU* 2.42.9 epistle to the King (*UT* 19.1652) *nmry. mlk. ʿlm* "*nmry* the king of the Universe"

[Eg] Gauthier, *LR* II p. 306ff; [EA] *nibmuare(y)a, nimm(ʾ)wareya, mimmure(y)a, mimmureya, immure(y)a*; [Gk] Αμενωφις

The Ug form of Amenophis III's name is evidently based on the Akk transcription *nimmureya*, which does not mark the ʿ of the Eg, whereas the Ug script could mark them easily. This suggests the letter *KTU* 2.42 was translated from Akk into Ug.

snb **

--- *snb* "Being well"

[Ug] *KTU* 4.311.3 (*UT* 19.1772; Aist 1924)

[Eg] Ranke I.312.15 m.OK–Late /f. MK

This is one of the most common Eg names, which Gröndahl left unexplained (p. 313).

snt *

--- *s(3.t)-n.t* "Daughter of Neith"

[Ug] *KTU* 3.4.10 *snt bt ugrt* (*UT* 19.1777; Aist 1930)

[Eg] Ranke I.289.22 f. MK; cf. male name *s3-n.t* "Son of Neith" (Ranke I.282.15 m. MK–Late)

Gröndahl left the name unexplained (p. 313). Ug *snt* is.a female, to which Eg *s3.t-n.t* corresponds well. Note that the male name *s3-n.t* was used until the Late Period. However, the bearer of this name is explained as "a daughter (citizen) of Ugarit," making Eg identification uncertain.

ᶜbd-ḥr (hybrid) **

--- *ᶜbd-ḥr* "The servant of Horus"

[Ug] *KTU* 4.611.7 (*UT* 19.1801)

[Eg] see *abdḥr*

pa'aḫi **

--- *p(3)-(n?-)i(ᶜḥ)* 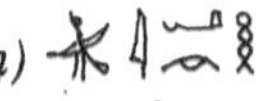 "He who belongs to the Moon"

[Ug] *PRU* III.16.136.9 [I]*pa-a-hi amîl* [mat]*mi-is-ri*

[Eg] Ranke II.279.23 m. NK (?); For the loss of *'ayn*, see Aram אחמס.

pa-pa-na

--- see *ppn*.

pwn

--- *p(3)-(n-)wn*  "He who belongs to the existing one" (?)

[Ug] *KTU* 4.70.8 (UT 19.2028)

[Eg] Ranke I.106.26 m. Gk; [Gk] cf. Παγωνις, Παγανις

Gordon suggested that *pwn* derived from **pw* (cf. *pwt* "red, purple dye"), yet the final *n* cannot be resolved. The Eg explanation is just possible in the absence of other identification.

pni **

--- *p(3)-(n-)ni(.t)*  "He who belongs to the town"

[Ug] *KTU* 4.350.8 (*UT* 19.2060) *bn pni* 4 // *[a]bmn bn qṣy* 4

[Eg] see Aram פנא

Gröndahl left the name unexplained. The name occurs in the text in which many foreign names appear such as *mn* (perhaps Eg), *drṣy, pry, qṣy, agmz, ibm, trn, gmz* etc. The Eg name *p3-n-ni.t* best fits the Ug *pni*. The questionable reading of the Eg word (*n.t / nw.t / niw.t / ni.t* is virtually confirmed by the Ug *pni*: the reading of is *ni.t* (see the discussion of Aram GN נא).

pnmn

--- *p(3)-n-mn*

[Ug] *KTU* 4.131 (*UT* 19.2066; Aist 2236)

[Eg] see *pmn*

Gröndahl left it unexplained. If the Eg preposition *n* is not assimilated, the Eg identification is likely.

pmn **

--- *p(3)-(n-)mn(.w)*  "He who belongs to Min"

Gröndahl p. 300

[Ug] *KTU* 4.63; 4.232 (*UT* 19.2058; Aist 2229)

[Eg] see Aram פמן.

ppn

--- *p(3)-(n-)pn(w)* "He who belongs to the Mouse"

[Ug] *KTU* 4.39.6 (*UT* 19.2084; Aist 2252)

[Eg] see Ph פפן

Cf. ^{m}*pa-pa-na* (Virolleaud, *Syria* 28 p. 50 line 34).

prḫ

--- *p(3)-(n-)rḫ(.t)*  "He who belongs to the knowledge" or "Knowledgeable one"

[Ug] *KTU* 4.134 a list of merchants (*UT* 19.2102; Aist 2267)

[Eg] Ranke I.109.20 m. Dyn 19

Gröndahl give no explanation for the name. There is a Semito-Hamitic cognate **prḫ*: Heb פרח, Arab *parḫa* "bud, sprout", Akk *pirḫu* "sprout" (*AHw* 856a), cf. Eg *prḫ* "bloom" (*Wb* I.532.7–11), Ug *prḫ* which is used as a PN in Akk. Therefore, a Sem explanation is equally possible.

ptm *

--- *p(3)-(n-ỉ)tm* "He who belongs to Atum"

[Ug] *KTU* 4.153.6 (*UT* 19.2131; Aist 2291)

[Eg] cf. *p3-n*-DN type: *p3-n-3s.t* etc. (Ranke I.105.21ff. mainly NK and Late). **p3-n-ỉtm* is accidentally not attested.

Gröndahl left it unexplained. The elision of *aleph* of *ỉtm* can be compared with Heb GN פתם (*pr-ỉtm*). Eg possibility is likely in the absence of a Sem explanation.

rwy *

--- *rw.y*  , *rw.i*  etc. "He of the lion" (?)

[Ug] *KTU* 4.103.9; 4.69.III.4 (*UT* 19.2310; Aist 2493)

[Eg] Ranke I.220.14–22.5 m./f. NK; cf. many similar names such as *rw.3, rw.i, rwy, rw.i, rw.y, rwiw* (except *rwy*  which may be group writing)

Gröndahl left it unexplained. As this type of name is common in NK, the Eg identification is very likely, though there is a Heb root רוי "be saturated" which is not attested in Ug as a word and not used as a PN.

rt **

--- *r(w)ḏ* MK  "Strong one"

[Ug] *KTU* 4.69.III.19 (*UT* 19.2357; Aist 2551)

[Eg] Ranke I.221.12 m. OK–NK / f. MK–Gk; [Copt] sⲣⲟⲟⲩⲧ, bⲣⲱⲟⲩⲧ for *rwḏ* (*Wb* II.410)

Gröndahl could not explain the name. Since Eg *rwḏ has* already become *rwd* in MK, it is most probable that *rwḏ* became /rwt/ in NK. Then it fits well with Ug *rt*.

[2] Divine Names

amn **

--- *imn*  "Amun"

[Ug] *KTU* 2.23.21 (*UT* 19.227; Aist 281) *l. pn. amn // w. l. pn.il. mṣrm*

[Eg] see Ph אמן.

[3] Loanwords

abyn ?

--- *bin* 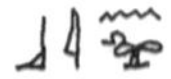 "evil"

Ward, *JNES* 20 p. 31f (denied)

[Ug] *KTU* 1.17:I:16 (*UT* 19.24; Aist 18)

[Eg] Heb אביון.

aḫ ** "meadow" "papyrus thicket"

--- *3ḫ(.y)*  "plant"

Rainey, *UF* 3 p.169
[Ug] *KTU* 1.10:II.9 (*UT* 19.129; Aist 134)
[Eg] see Heb אחו.

ap ** "chamber, court"
--- *ip(.t)* 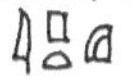 "harem, secret chamber"
Ward, *JNES* 20 p. 32
[Ug] *KTU* 1.3:V:[11], 27
[Eg] *Wb* I.67.13–15 since OK

No cognate of *ap* is found in Semitic. The meaning and phonetic form properly correspond to Eg *ip.t* "chamber."

ary * "kinsman"
--- *iry*  "companion"
Albright, *JPOS* 12 p. 197 n. 47; Ward, *JNES* 20 p. 32
[Ug] *KTU* 1.4:V:29; VI 44; 1.5:1:23, 25; 1.7:1.19, 20 (always parallel with "brother")
[Eg] *Wb* I.105.5–6; [Copt] ЄΡΗΥ.

irp
--- *irp*  "wine"
[Ug] *KTU* 4.123.20 (*UT* 19.371; Aist 417)
[Eg] *Wb* I.115.5–8 since OK; [Copt] ^{s,b}ΗΡΠ̄, ^{s}ΗΛΠ̄

Gordon suggested an Eg origin for Ug *irp*; however, Aistleitner rendered it "vessel", as the context requires a kind of vessel. Therefore, the equation is doubtful.

dd "pot, measure"
--- *dd(.t)* 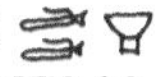 "bowl, pot, measure"
Ward, *JNES* 20 p. 4O
[Ug] *KTU* 4.55.1–4, 6, 7, 31, 33, 34; 6.21.1; 1.41.44; 4.14.7; 4.128.1
[Eg] *Wb* V.501.14–18 since OK; [Heb] דוד; [Aram] דודא; [Akk] *dudu* (since OB, *CAD* D 170)

The word is so common in Semitic that it is impossible to deal with it as a loanword. Most likely it is a cognate.

hbn **
--- *hbn(y)*  "ebony"
[Ug] *KTU* 4.402.6 (*UT* 19.743; Dahood, *UHP* p. 56)
[Eg] see Heb הובן

The text is a list of various items including lumber, tree (*tišr*). Therefore the equation of Ug *hbn* with Eg *hbn* is likely.

hdm ?

--- see Heb Lw *hdm*.

hn

--- *hn(w)* 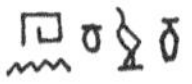 "a vessel"

[Ug] *KTU* 1.23.75

[Eg] see Heb *hyn*

Due to the uncertain context, the identification remains doubtful.

ḥtp **

--- *ḥtp(.t)* 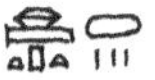 "offering"

Spalinger, *SSEA* 8 p. 55

[Ug] *RS* 24:266.V° 15 (*Ugaritica* VII p. 35) *[b]kr b[ʿ]l. nš[q]dš / ḥtp bʿ[l. n]mlʾu* "The first born for Baal we will consecrate / *ḥtp* for Baal we will fulfill" (by J. de Moor, Supp. of *IDB* p. 930)

[Eg] *Wb* III.183

Cf. Aram Lw חתפי

It seems that the word *ḥtp* is best explained by the Eg *ḥtp*. The meaning is fully supported by the context, while no Sem explanation can be offered.

mk * "lo!"

--- *mk*  "lo!"

[Ug] *KTU* 1.14.III.3; V.5; VI.31; VII.12 (parallel with *hn*) (*UT* 19.1472; Aist 1472)

[Eg] *Wb* II.5

Gordon commented that the word may have been borrowed into Ug during the period of Eg influence before the victories of Suppiluliuma. In the absence of a proper Sem etymology, an Eg explanation is conceivable. Aistleitner gave the rendering "then, there," comparing it with Akk *ammaka, maka* "there." However, since *mk* is used parallel with *hn*, *mk* is more likely to be a climactic word "lo!."

qlẖt **

--- *ḳrḥ.t* 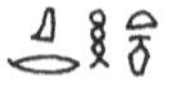 "vessel"

Dietrich-Loretz-Sanmartin, *UF* 7 p. 166

[Ug] *KTU* 5.22.16

[Eg] see Heb קלחת

The text is a list of items, in which *ḥ* is often replaced by *ḫ* such as *mptḫ* for *mptḥ*, *qmḫ* for *qmḥ* etc. (see *UF* 7 p. 166), Therefore, the representation of Eg *ḥ* by Ug *ḫ* is not a problem.

ṯkt “a kind of ship”

--- *sk.t(y)*  “sacred boat”

Alt, *AfO* 15 p. 70; Tsumura, *The earth and the waters in Genesis 1 and 2*, pp. 131–132

[Ug] *KTU* 1.4:V:7; 4.81:4, 5, 8, 9

[Eg] see Heb שׂכיות

Since the second sign can be read either as *k* or as *r*, *ṯrt* “moisture” is another possible reading Therefore the identification cannot be confirmed.

B. ANALYSIS OF PHONOLOGICAL CORRESPONDENCES

[1] Ug: Eg Phonetic Correspondences

Ug *a* : Eg *3*	Lw= *aḫ*
: Eg *ỉ*	DN= *amn*; Lw= *ap*
Ug *i* : Eg *ỉ*	PN= *pni*
Ug *b* : Eg *b*	PN= *snb*; Lw= *hbn*
Ug *h* : Eg *h*	Lw= *hbn*
Ug *ḥ* : Eg *ḥ*	PN= *abdḥr*, *ʿbdḥr*; Lw= *ḥtp*
Ug *ḫ* : Eg *ḫ*	Lw= *aḫ*
: Eg *ḥ*	Lw= *qlḫt* (in the text *ḥ* is replaced by *ḫ*)
Ug *l* : Eg *r*	Lw= *qlḫt*
Ug *m* : Eg *m*	PN= *pmn*; DN= *amn*
Ug *n* : Eg *n*	PN= *snb*, *pni*, *pmn*; DN= *amn*; Lw=*hbn*
Ug *s* : Eg *s*	PN= *snb*
Ug *p* : Eg *p*	PN= *pmn*; Lw= *ap*, *ḥtp*
Ug *q* : Eg *ḳ*	Lw= *qlḫt*
Ug *r* : Eg *r*	PH= *abdḥr*, *ʿbdḥr*, *rt*
Ug *t* : Eg *ḏ* (> /d/ > /t/)	PN= *rt*
Eg *t*	Lw= *ḥtp*, *qlḫt*

[2] Ug Akk : Eg Phonetic Correspondences

Ug Akk *a* : Eg *ỉ*	PN= *amanmaššu, paʾahi*
: Eg ø	PN= *ḫeḫea* (the *a* is a hypocoristic ending)
Ug Akk *ḫ* : Eg *ḥ*	PN= *ḫeḫea, paʾaḫi*
Ug Akk *m* : Eg *m*	PN= *amanmaššu*
Ug Akk *n* : Eg *n*	PN= *amanmaššu*
Ug Akk *p* : Eg *p*	PN= *paʾaḫi*
Ug Akk *š* : Eg *s*	PN= *amanmaššu*

[3] Eg : Ug Phonetic Correspondences

Eg *3* : Ug *a*	
: Ug ø	DN= *pni, pmn*
Eg *ỉ* : Ug *a*	

: Ug *i*	
Eg *y* : Ug ø	
Eg *w* : Ug ø	PN= *pmn* (final *w*), *rt* (middle *w*)
Eg *b* : Ug *b*	
Eg *p* : Ug *p*	
Eg *m* : Ug *m*	
Eg *n* : Ug *n*	
: Ug ø	PN= *pni*, *pmn* (Eg genitive *n* dropped)
Eg *r* : Ug *r*	
: Ug *l*	
Eg *h* : Ug *h*	
Eg *ḥ* : Ug *ḥ*	
: Ug *ḫ*	
Eg *ḫ* : Ug *ḫ*	
Eg *s* : Ug *s*	PN= *snr*
Eg *ḳ* : Ug *q*	
Eg *t* : Ug *t*	
: Ug ø	PN= *pni*; Lw= *ap*, *ḥtp* (Eg fem. ending *t* > ø)
Eg *ḏ* : Ug *t*	

[4] Eg : Ug Akk Phonetic Correspondneces

Eg *3* : Ug Akk ø	PN= *paʾaḫi*
Eg *ỉ* : Ug Akk *a*	PN= *amanmaššu, paʾaḫi*
Eg ʿ: Ug Akk ø	*paʾaḫi*
Eg *p* : Ug Akk *p*	
Eg *m* : Ug Akk *m*	
Eg *n* : Ug Akk *n*	
Ug Akk ø	PN= *paʾaḫi* (genitive *n*)
Eg *ḥ* : Ug Akk *ḫ*	
Eg *s* : Ug Akk *š*	

[5] Table of Correspondences

	Ug	primary	secondary	Eg	primary	secondary
glotta stops	*a*	*3 i̓*		*3*	*a*	ø
	i	*ı*		*i̓*	*a i*	
	u	-				
	ʿ	-		*ʿ*	-	
semi-vowels	*y*	-		*y*	-	ø
	w	-		*w*	-	ø
labials	*b*	*b*		*b*	*b*	
	p	*p*		*p*	*p*	
				f	*p*	
nasals	*m*	*m*		*m*	*m*	
	n	*n*		*n*	*n*	ø
lateral	*l*	*r*				
trill	*r*	*r*		*r*	*r l*	
pharyngals & laryngals	*h*	*h*		*h*	*h*	
	ḥ	*h*		*ḥ*	*ḥ*	*ḫ*
	ḫ	*h*		*ḫ*	*ḫ*	
				ẖ	-	
sibilants	*s*	*s*		*s*	*s*	
	š	-		*š*	-	
	ṣ	-				
	ś	-				
velars	*q*	*ḳ*		*k*	*q*	
	k	-		*k*	-	
	g	-		*g*	-	
alveolars	*t*	*t*		*t*	*t*	ø
	d	-		*ṯ*	-	
				d	-	
	ṭ	-		*ḏ*	-	

Ug Akk	primary	secondary
a	*i*	ø
h	*h*	
m	*m*	
n	*n*	
p	*p*	
s	*s*	

[6] Notes on the Correspondences

Since the number of Eg names and words in Ug is limited, there is not much to demand comment. However, two things should be noticed: (1) Eg *i* is represented by either Ug *a* or Ug *i*, so we may infer that, after Eg *3* was lost, Eg *i* stood for both /ʾa/ and /ʾi/. (2) It is most likely that the distinction between *ḥ* and *ḫ* was kept in Ug, as well as in Eg, as the correspondences are kept distinct.

V

EGYPTIAN PROPER NAMES AND LOANWORDS IN THE EL-AMARNA TABLETS

In 1910 H. Ranke thoroughly studied the Egyptian elements in EA tablets and published a monograph, *Keilschriftliches Material zur Altägyptischen Vokalisation* (Berlin). Then about forty years later two works followed: first, W. F. Albright studied Eg personal names in cuneiform texts "Cuneiform Material for Egyptian Prosopography 1500–1200 BC," *JNES* 5,1946, pp. 7–25 (this work is cited here with a number, *e.g.*, Albright no. 5). Secondly, T. Lambdin studied Eg words in EA 14 and 368[1] in his PhD dissertation in 1952 (see Introduction p. 16f.). Since 1952 there have been no systematic attempts made to analyze the Eg elements in the tablets. Those studies still remain the standard works, though each Eg element has been re-examined and some newly identified in small articles.

In this chapter, our aim is not to meet this need for a systematic study of Eg elements in the tablets, partly because of constraints on time and partly because the language used in these tablets is not NW Semitic on which our studies concentrate, although it is generally acknowledged that the language is heavily influenced by NW Semitic.

1 Prior to him, Egyptian in EA 368 was studied by T. E. Peet, "Additional Note," *JEA* 11 (1925) pp. 239–240; W. F. Albright, "The New Cuneiform Vocabulary of Egyptian Words" *JEA* 12 (1926) pp. 189–190; Then most recently by J. Vergöte, "La Chancellerie Royale d'Akhetaton" pp. 580–584. "Egyptological Studies" *Scripta Hierosolymitana* 27 (1982) pp. 105–116. M. Görg, "Anmerkungen zu EA 368" *UF* 7 (1975) p. 356f. E. Edel, "Zur Deutung des Keilschriftvokabulars EA 368 mit ägyptischen Wörtern" *GM* 15 (1975) pp. 11–16.

Our aim is restricted to looking into some phonetic features in the second millennium B.C., which are revealed in the light of Egyptian. In the following inventory, therefore, are listed without much discussion only Eg names and words whose identifications are unquestionable (hence, without the mark **) with an analysis of their phonetic correspondences.

A. INVENTORY OF EGYPTIAN PROPER NAMES AND LOANWORDS

[1] Personal Names

Amanap(p)a

--- *ỉmn-(m-)ỉp(.t)*  "Amun is in Luxor"

KM p. 7; Albright no.1

[EA] 73.1, 74.51, 77.1(?), 79.9, 82.1, 109.62, 117.23 *ˈa-ma-an-ap-pa*; 87.1 *a-ma-an-ap-pi*

[Eg] Ranke I.27.18 m. NK–Late / f. NK; *DemNB* I.64 (*ỉmn-m-ỉpy*), I.84 (*ỉmn-ỉpy*); [Gk] 'Αμενῶφις (*NB* p. 24).

Amanḫatpe

--- *ỉmn-ḥtp(.w)* 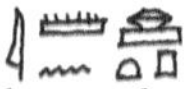 "Amun is gracious"

KM p. 8; Albright no. 2a

[EA] 185–186 (passim) *ˈa-ma-an-ha-at-bi*

[Eg] Ranke I.30.12 m. NK–Gk / f. MK–NK; *DemNB* I.67; [Gk] 'Αμενωθις, 'Αμενούθης, 'Αμενωθευς, 'Αμμενωθης (*NB* p. 24); 'Αμενωθου (*DemNB* I.67).

Amanmaša

--- *ỉmn-ms*  "Amn is born"

KM p. 8; Albright no.3

[EA] 113.36, 43, 114.51 *ˈa-ma-an-ma-sa*

[Eg] Ranke I.29.8 m. NK–Late / f. NK; *DemNB* I.65.

Cf. *ỉmn-m-š* "Amun is on the lake" (Ranke I.29.2 m. NK; much less common).

Api

--- *ipy* 

KM p. 21; Edel, *JNES* 7 p. 23

[EA] 138.8 *'a-p[i]*, 107 *'[a]-b[i]*, 107 *'[a]-b[i]*, 145.12 (?)

[Eg] Ranke I.22.22 m. MK–Late / f. MK–NK; *DemNB* I.62 (*ipe*/*ipy*). Cf. Ranke I.21.26–23.4.

Ap(p)iḫa

--- **ip(.t)-(m-)ḥ(3.t)*."(Goddess) *ʾIp.t* is in front"

Moran p. 567

[EA] 69.25, 29 *'ap-pi-ḫa*

[Eg] For the name type of: DN + *m-ḥ3.t*, see Ranke I.4.4; 28.8; 151.19 etc. m. MK–Late, *3s.t-m-h3.t*, *imn-m-ḥ3.t*, *mn.w-ḥ3.t*; for *ip.t* see *Wb* I.68.7.

Moran's interpretation "Api brille" by which he perhaps intends *ip.t-ḫʿi.ti* is impossible, because the final *ti* is retained.

Ataḫmaya

--- see *Taḫmaya*

Ḫaapi or *Ḫaip*

--- *ḥʿp(y)* 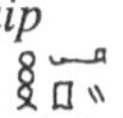 "The Nile"

KM p. 21; Albright no.4

[EA] 107.16, 132.40, 42, 133.9 *'ḫa-ip*; 149.37 *'ḫa-a-pi*

[Eg] Ranke I.234.7 m. NK (probably hypocoristicon).

Ḫaramas(s)a/-š(š)i

--- *ḥr-ms.w* 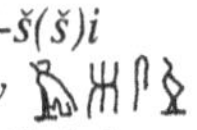 "Horus is born"

KM p.10; Albright no.11

[EA] 20.33 *'ḫa-a-ra-ma-aš-š[i]*, 36 *['ḫa-a-ra-]ma-aš-ši*, 49.25 *[a]-ra-ma(!)-sa*

[Eg] Ranke I.249.1 m. MK–Gk / f.MK–NK.

Ḫatip

--- *ḥtp* 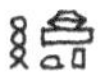 "The gracious one"

KM p. 10; Albright no.12

[EA] 161.38, 43, 164.4, 18, 26, 42, 165.15, 26, 166.12, 32, 167.14(?) *'ḫa-ti-ib*

[Eg] Ranke I.257.22 m. OK–Gk / f.MK–NK; [Gk] cf. ʽΑτπευς, ʽΑτπῆς, ʽΑτπηεις (*NB* p. 64, 65).

Leya

--- *r(3.3)i*  , *r(3.)i(3)*  etc.
KM p. 23; Albright no.20
[EA] 162.70 *'le-e-ia*
[Eg] Ranke I.216.22, 23; 28 (*ri3.y*), 29 (*ry*), 217.1 (*ry3*).

Manaḫpi(r)ya

--- *mn-ḫp(r)-rʿ* 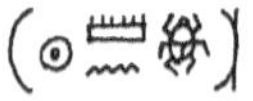 "May the form of Reʿ be enduring" (Thutmosis III)
KM p. 12; Albright no.22
[EA] 51.4 *'ma-na-aḫ-bi-ia*; 59.8 *'ma-na-aḫ-bi-ir-ia*
[Eg] Gauthier, *LR* II 253–270.

Manē

--- *mn(.i)*  , *mn(.y)* 
KM p. 12; Albright no.23
[EA] 19.17, 21, 20.8, 14, 18, 19, 23, 43, 64, 66, 69, 21.24, 24,1.53, 59, 71, 114, 11.7, 13, 16, 19, 57, 86, 91, 95, 100, 102, 107, 111, 116, IV.20, 21, 26, 27, 35, 52, 54, 55, 57, 26.15, 27.7, 70, 83, 96, 97, 28.17, 37, 29.70, 78, 89, 90, 151, 167, 174, 176 *'ma-ni-e*
[Eg] Ranke I.151.2 m. OK–NK / f. MK; I.151.4 m. MK–NK / f.MK.

Maya

--- *my* 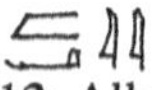
KM p. 12; Albright no.26
[EA] 62.26, 292.33, 337.26, 29 *'ma-a-ia*; 216,13, 217.16 (?), 218.14, 300.26, 328.24 *'ma-ia*
[Eg] Ranke I.146.10 m. NK / f. NK.

Mayati, Mayatu

--- *m(r)y(.t)-it(n)* 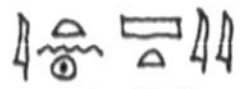 "Beloved of Aton" (Meritaton, daughter of Amenophis IV)
Albright no. 27
[EA] 10.44 *'ma-i-ia-a-tim*; 11.vs.26 *'ma-ia-tu-ma*; 155.8, 26, 29, 62 *ma-ia-a-ti*; 155.15, 22, 42, 50 *ma-ia-a-ti*

[Eg] Ranke I.161.18 f. Dyn 18.

Maireya

--- *m(r)y-rʿ* 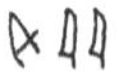 "Beloved of Reʿ"

Albright no. 21

[EA] 367.7 ^{I}*ma-i-ri-ia*

[Eg] Ranke I.160.23 m. MK–NK

Cf. *Miyare* (*mry-rʿ* ?) 289.31.

Naḫramaš(š)i

--- **nʿr-ms(.w)* "*Nʿr*-tree is born"

KM p. 13; Albright no.33

[EA] 21.33 ^{I}*na-aḫ-ra-ma-as-[s]i*

[Eg] cf. *t3-n.t-nʿr*  (Ranke II.369.7 f. Late); cf. *Wb* II.208.14–16 for *nʿr*.

The name has been identified with *in-ḥr.t-ms(.w)* "Onurig is born" (Ranke I.35.14; II,342 m. NK; cf. Copt ⲁⲛϩⲟⲩⲣⲉ, Gk Ονούρις for Onuris). However, as shown in Copt and Gk forms, the initial vowel (perhaps preceded by *aleph*: Eg *i*) is preserved and there is a vowel between *ḥ* and *r*, neither of which is reflected in this Akk form. Therefore, the identification is not likely. Although the sacred tree *nʿr* (*Wb* II.208.14–16) occurs so far only in late PNs, this identification is much more likely.

Napḫuru/areya or *Napḫuʾ/rreya*

--- *nf(r)-ḫ(p)r(.w)-rʿ* 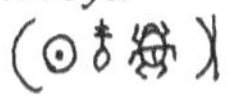 "Good is the Being of Reʿ"

(Amenophis IV)

KM p.14; Albright no.34

[EA] 7.1, 11.1 *na-ap-ḫu-ʾ-ru-ri[-ia]*; 8.1 *na-ap-ḫu-ʾ-ru-ri-[-ia]*; 10.1 *[na-ap-ḫu]-ra-r[i-i]a*; 14.1 *[*^{I}*na-ap-ḫu-ru-]ri-a*; 26.27, 32, 40, 46, 50, 54, 59, 27.1, 39 ^{I}*na-ap-ḫur-ri-[i]a*; 29.61, 63, 65, 67, 76 ^{I}*nap-ḫur-u-ri-ia*; 53.1, 55.1 ^{I}*n[am]-h[ur-i]a*

[Eg] Gauthier, *LR* II p. 343ff.

Nibhur(r)ereya

--- *nb-ḫpr(.w)-rʿ*  "Reʿ is the lord of Being"

(Tutankhamun)

KM p.14; Edel, *JNES* 7 p. 14

[EA] 9.1 *ni-ib-ḫu-ur-ri-ri-ia*
[Eg] Gauthier, *LR* II pp. 365ff.

Eg *nb* is always transcribed as *nib*, never being written as *nap*. Therefore the name is a designation of Tutanankhamun.

Nibmuare(y)a, Nimmu(ʾ)wareya, Mimmure(y)a, Mimmureya, Immure(y)a

--- *nb-m(3)ʿ(.t)-rʿ* 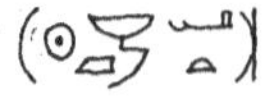 "Reʿ is the lord of truth" (Amenophis III)
KM p. 14; Albright no.36
[EA] 1.2 ^{I}*ni-ib-mu-a-ri-a*; 2.1 ^{I}*ni-mu-wa-ri-ia*; 3.1 *[*^{I}*ni-ib-m]u-ʾ-wa-ri-ia*; 5.1, 17.1 ^{I}*ni-ib-mu-a-ri-ia*; 19.1, 21.1, 22.IV.45, 47, 23.1 ^{I}*ni-im-mu-ri-ia*; 20.1 *[*^{I}*ni-im-]mu-ú-a-ri-ia*; 24.I.1, 29.6 passim ^{I}*ni-im-mu-u-ri-ia*; 24.I.84, III.106 ^{I}*ni-im-mu-u/ú-ri-i-aš*; 24.III.104 ^{I}*im-mu-u-ri-ia*; 24.III.106 ^{I}*im-mu-u-ri-aš*; 24.IV.128 ^{I}*im-mu-u-ri-i-an*; 26.8–35 passim, 27.9 ^{I}*mi-im-mu-ri-ia*; 27.14, 20 ^{I}*mi-im-mu-ú-ri-ia*; 27.38 ^{I}*mi-mu-ri-ia*
[Eg] Gauthier, *LR* II, p. 306ff.; [Ug] *nmery*.

Nimmaḫe

--- *nb-mḥ(y.t)* 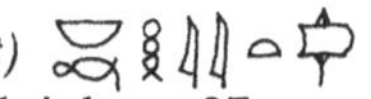 "The Lord of the north wind"
KM p.24; Albright no.37
[EA] 162.77 ^{I}*ni-im-ma-ḫe-e*
[Eg] Ranke I.185.7 m. NK.

Paapu

--- *p(3)-(n-)ip(.t)* 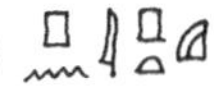 "He who belongs to Luxor"
Albright no. 39
[EA] 333. [2], 22 $^{(I)}$*pa-a-bu*
[Eg] Ranke I.106.7 m. Dyn 18; *DemNB* I.349; [Gk] Παωπις (*NB* p. 297); for *apu* for Luxor, see *a-ma-an-ap-pa* (*imn-ip.t*).

Paḫa(m)natale

--- *p(3)-ḥm-nṯ(r)* 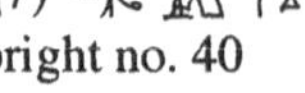 "Servant of god"
KM p. 15; Albright no. 40
[EA] 60.8, 20, 30, 62.1 ^{I}*pa-ḫa-na-te*; 68.22, 131.35 ^{I}*pa-ḫa-am-na-ta*
[Eg] Ranke I.115.16 m. NK–Late; II.354; *DemNB* I.204.

Puḫuru/i, Paḫura, Piḫura

--- *p(3)-ḫr(.y)* 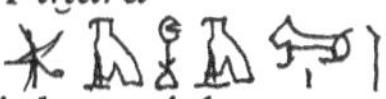 "The Syrian"

KM p. 15; Albright no.4 1

[EA] 57.6, 10, 189.18, 208.11 *ᴵpu-ḫu-ru*, 117.61, 123.13, 34, 132.47 *ᴵpi-ḫu-ra;* 122.31 *ᴵpa-ḫu-ra*; 189.17, 190.2 *ᴵpu-ḫu-ri*; 207.17 *ᴵpu-ḫu-ur*

[Eg] Ranke I.116.17 m. NK–Dyn 22ff.; *DemNB* I.210 (*p-ḫr*); [Gk] Πχόιρης, Πχοῖρις (*NB* p. 352); [Aram] פחורה.

Pamaḫu

--- *p(3)-(n-)mḥ(y.t)*  "He who belongs to (goddess) *Mḥy.t*"

KM p. 15; Albright no. 42

[EA] 7.76 *ᴵPa-ma-ḫu[-]*

[Eg] Ranke I.108.15 m. NK–Gk; *DemNB* I.375 (*pa-mḥy*); [Ph] פמחו

Cf. *Nimmaḫe* (*nb-mḥy.t*).

Pawara, Pa/uuru, Piwa/uri

--- *p(3)-wr* 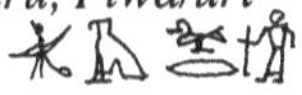 "The great"

KM p.16, 17, 24; Albright no. 45

[EA] 117.47, 124.44, 132.38, 171.15 (?), 263.21 *[ᴵpa]-wa-ra*; 131.22 *ᴵpi-wa-ri*; 287.45 *ᴵpa-ú-ru*; 289.38 *ᴵpu-ú-ru*; 362.69 *ᴵpi-wu-[ri]*

[Eg] Ranke I.104.4 m. NK; *DemNB* I.176; [Gk] Ποῦρις, Πουερ,

Πουερις, Ποῆρις (*NB* p. 335, 341, 342).

Peya, Pieya

--- *pi(3)y* 

Albright no. 46

[EA] 292.42, 51 *ᴵpi-e-ia*; 294.16, 24, 30 *ᴵpi-i-ia*

[Eg] Ranke I.129.25 m. NK.

Pišyari

--- *p(3)-sr* 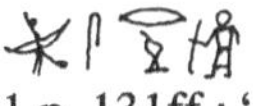 "The prince"

Edel, *SAK* 1 p. 131ff.; "Brief" p. 120f.

[EA] 162.71 *ᴵpi-iš-ia-ri*

[Eg] Ranke I.117.12 m. NK; [Copt] CIOYP "eunuch" (Crum p. 371a);
[Gk] Ψιοῦρις; for the extra *y*, see also the late spellings  *sỉr*,  *syr* (*Wb* IV.188). EA has the oldest attestation.

Reanap(a)
--- *rᶜ-nf(r)*  "Re' is good"
KM p. 18; Albright no. 49
[EA] 292.36 *'ri-a-na-ap*; 315.13, 326.17 *'[r]i-a-na-pa*
[Eg] Ranke I.219.10 m. OK.

Reyamanū
--- *rᶜ-ỉmn* "Re' is Amun"
KM p. 24; Edel, "Neue Deutungen" p. 15
[EA] 347.3 *'ri-ia-ma-nu-[---]*
[Eg] cf.*rᶜ-ptḥ* "Re' is Ptah" (Ranke I.217.14 m. NK) and perhaps *rᶜ-sbk* "Re' is Sobek" (Ranke I.220.4 m. MK); also f. *Amanmasa* in which *ỉmn* is realized as *aman*.

šuta
--- *st(ỉ)* 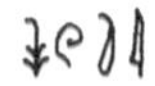 ,  "Seth" or "Sute(kh)"
KM p. 25; Albright no. 56; Edel, *JNES* 7 p. 19
[EA] 234.14, 23 *'šu-ta*; 5.19 *'šu-ut-ti*; 288.19, 22 *'šu-ú-ta*
[Eg] Ranke I.321.17 m. NK.

Taḫmaya, Ataḫmaya
--- *(p)tḥ-my* 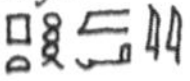 (a short form of *ptḥ-ms*)
KM p. 18; Albright no. 59
[EA] 265.9 *'ta-aḫ-ma-ia(!)*; 316.15 *['ta]ḫ-m[a-i]a*; 364.13 *'a-taḫ-ma-ia*
[Eg] Ranke I.140.6 m. NK; see *taḫmašši*.

Taḫmaš(š)i
--- *(p)tḥ-ms(w)*  "Ptah is born"
KM p. 18; Albright no. 60
[EA] 303.20 *'táḫ-[m]a-aš-ši*
[Eg] Ranke I.140.9 m. NK.

Teye
--- *ty* 𓂉𓇋𓇋 , 𓂋𓏤𓇋𓇋 etc.
KM p. 18; Albright no. 61
[EA] 26.1, 27.4, 112, 28.43, 45, passim in 29 ^{aêlu}te-i-e
[Eg] Ranke I.377.22 m./f. MK-NK.

Tuya
--- *t(w)y* 𓏏𓅱𓇋𓇋
KM p. 25; Albright no. 63; Edel *JNES* 7 p. 20; SAK 1 p. 16ff.
[EA] 162.69 ^{I}tu-u-u-ia
[Eg] Ranke I.379.8 m./f. NK.

[2] <u>Divine Names</u>

Aman(u)
--- *imn* 𓇋𓏠𓈖 "Amun"
KM p.7
[EA] 1.46, 19.15, 24, 76 ^{ilu}a-$m[a$-$n]u$-um; 20.26, 27.87 ^{ilu}a-ma-a-nu; 20.74, 369.29 ^{ilu}a-ma-nu; 24.I.76, 101, 24.II.65, 77, 24.IV.118 ^{ilu}a-ma-a-nu-$ú$; 71.4, 86.3, 87.5, 95.3, 164.40(?) ^{ilu}a-ma-na
[Eg] see Ph אמן.

[3] <u>Geographical Names</u>

Ḥikuptaḫ, Ḥikutaḫ
--- *ḥ(.t)-k(3)-ptḥ* 𓉗𓂓𓏏𓊪𓏏𓎛 "The House of the ka of Ptah"
(another name for Memphis)
KM p.10
[EA] 84.37 $^{alu}ḫi$-ku-up-ta-$aḫ$ (!); 139.8 $ḫi(!)$-ku-ta-$aḫ(!)$
[Eg] *Wb* III.5.20; Gauthier, *DG* IV p. 137f.; Montet, Géograpie I. p.32.

[4] Loan Words

anaḫū
--- *ʿnḫ* (name of a vessel in *ʿnḫ* form)
Lambdin, *Or* NS 22 p. 363
[EA] 14.1.36 *a-na-ḫu-u* / *na-ḫu-u* (Moran read as *anaḫu*)
[Eg] *Wb* I.204.15.

daši
--- *ds* "jar"
KM p.26; Lambdin, *Or* NS 22 p. 364
[EA] 14.I.48 *da-ši*
[Eg] *Wb* V.485.3ff. since Pyr.

ḫapši
--- *ḫpš* "arm"
Knudtzon p. 1549
[EA] 147.12 *ḫa-ab-ši*
[Eg] *Wb* III.268 early MK (cf. *ḫpš* "thigh, leg" since Pyr); [Copt] [s]ϣⲱⲡϣ̄ (Černý p. 250).

ḫaman
--- *ḫmn* "eight"
For bibli., see p. 384
[EA] 368.13 *ḫa-ma-an*
[Eg] *Wb* III.282.10–11; [Copt] [s]ϣⲙⲟⲩⲛ, [b]ϣⲙⲏⲛ.

ḫamtu
--- *ḫmt* "three"
For bibli., see p. 384
[EA] 386.8 *ḫa-am-tu*[4]
[Eg] *Wb* III.283; [Copt] [s]ϣⲟⲙⲛⲧ̄ , [b]ϣⲟⲙⲧ, [a2]ϩⲁⲙⲧ

ḫanūnu šaḫū
--- *hnn sʿḥʿ* "an upright box or chest"
Lambdin, *Or* NS 22 p. 365; Edel, "Weitere " p. 112f
[EA] 14.11.52 *ḫa-nu-u-nu sa-ḫu-u*
[Eg] *hn* "box, chest" (*Wb* II.491.9ff since OK; *sʿḥʿ* "rise up" (*Wb* IV.53 – 4 since Pyr) Copt [s]ⲥⲟⲟϩⲉ, [b]ⲥⲟϩⲓ

ḫatupu

--- *ḥtp* "table"

For bibli., see p. 384

[EA] 368.rev.11 *ḫa-tu?-pu*

[Eg] *Wb* III.183.6 since Pyr.

Notice that all Eg words (except numbers) in EA 368 end with *u*, which may be the Eg case ending.

ḫina

--- *hn(w)* "a liquid measure"

Lambdin, *Or* NS 22 p. 365; Edel, "weilter Beiträge" p. 105

[EA] 14.111.62 *ḫi-na*

[Eg] see Heb הין.

ḫubunu

--- *hbn(.t)* "a large jar for votive offering"

Morgan, *JA* 203 p. 152f.; Lambdin, *Or* NS 22 p. 365

[EA] 14.1.58, 60, II.51 *ḫu-bu-un-nu*

[Eg] *Wb* II.487.13–19 since OK.

kuiḫku

--- *k(3)-ḥ(r)-k(3)* (name of temple vessel)

Erman, *ZÄS* 34 p.165f; *KM* p. 11; Lambdin, *Or* NS p. 366

[EA] 14.III.43, 55 *ku-i-iḫ-ku*

[Eg] *Wb* V.93.4–5 since Dyn 20 (name of temple vessel).

Cf. Aram month name כיחך

The first attestation of this Eg word is found in EA, belonging to Dyn 18.

miši

--- *mšʿ* "soldiers, army"

Lambdin, *JCS* 7 pp.75–77

[EA] 101.4, 33, 105.27, 110.48 (?), 52, 111.21 (?), 126.63 Knudtzon read *mi-lim*, yet Ebeling's suggestion is *miši* (p. 1550)

[Eg] *Wb* II.155.2–19 since OK; [Copt] ^{s}ⲘⲎⲎϢⲈ, ^{b}ⲘⲎϢ.

muṭu

--- *mḏ* "ten"

For Bibli. see p. 384
[EA] 368.15 *mu-ṭu*
[Eg] *Wb* II,184.1–2 since OK; [Copt] ΜΗΤ.

nabnasu
--- *n(3)-bnš* "the door posts"
For bibli. p. 384
[EA] 368. rev.8 *na-ab-na-su*
[Eg] *bnš*  "door post" *Wb* I,464.3 since NK.

namša
--- *nms(.t)* 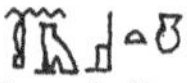 "a kind of jar"
KM p. 13; Lambdin *Or* NS 22 p. 367
[EA] 14.I.32, 67, II.50, III.37, 67 *na-am-ša*
[Eg] *Wb* II.269.7–8 since Pyr.

naš(š)a
--- *nš(w)*  "a kind of pot or a measure"
KM p. 14; Lambdin, *Or* NS 22 p. 367
[EA] 14.III.48, II.80 *na-aš-ša*
[Eg] *Wb* II.338.14–15 since MK.

paḫatu
--- *p(3)-ḥˁt*  "the bed"
For bibli., see p. 384
[EA] 368.rev.10 *pa-ḫa-tu4*
[Eg] *Wb* III.43.15 NK.

pawira/i
--- *p(3)-wr* "the great"
KM p. 16 and 24
[EA] 117.47(?), 149.30 *pa-wi-ra*; 151.59 *pa-wi-ri*
[Eg] *Wb* I.328.14ff since OK.

pazite
--- *p(3)-ṯ(3)t(y)*  "vizier"
Albright, 13a; Moran, p. 246 n. 1
[EA] 71.1 *pa-zi-t[e?]*
[Eg] *Wb* V.343.8ff since OK.

piparu

--- *p(3)-pr(y.t)* , "the houses"

For bibli., see p. 384

[EA] 368. rev. 5 *pi-pa-ru*

[Eg] for *pry.t*, see *Wb* I.518.12–13 MK–NK (for the final *r* pronounced, see Edel, *GM* 15 p. 15).

pisiṭ

--- *psḏ* "nine"

For bibli., see p. 384

[EA] 368.14 *pi-si-it*

[Eg] *Wb* I.558.10; [Copt] [s]ⲯⲓⲧ(ⲯⲓⲥ), [b]ⲯⲓⲧ.

piṭāti/u/a/e(u)

--- *pḏ.t(y)* "bowmen, foreigner"

KM p. 16

[EA] 287.17 *pi-ta-ti-ú*; 286.53 etc. *pi-ṭa-ti*; 285.16 *pi-ṭa-tu*; 287.21 etc. *pi-ta-tù*; 269.12 etc. *pi-ta-ta*; 174.21, 176.16 *pi-ta-a-te*; 166.4 etc. *pi-ta-te*

[Eg] *Wb* I.570.4 MK (for *ḏ* > *d*, see *pd.t*)

pusbiú

--- *p(3)-sb3* "the door"

For bibli., see p. 384

[EA] 368. rev.6 *pu-us-bi-ú*

[Eg] *Wb* IV.83.9–17 since Pyr; [Copt] [s]ⲥⲃⲉ, [b]ⲉⲃⲏ.

qapqapu

--- *ḳfḳf* (a cult utensil)

Edel, "weitere Berträge" p. 101ff.

[EA] 14.1.67 *qáp-qá-pu*

[Eg] *Wb* V.33.5 Dyn 18.

raḫta

--- *rhd(.t)* "vessel"

KM p. 24; Lambdin, *Or* NS 22 p. 367

[EA] 14.I.46 *ra-ah-ta*

[Eg] *Wb* II.441.5–7 NK; [Copt] ⲣⲁϩⲧⲉ, ⲣⲟϩⲧⲉ.

ruḫi

--- *rḫ(-nsw.t)*  "(king's) acquaintance"

KM p. 25

[EA] 288.11 *amêluru-ḫi (šarri[ri])*

[Eg] *Wb* II.446.9–447.3 since Pyr.

šaḫšiḫa

--- *sš.šʿ(.t)* 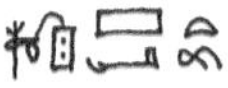 "letter scribe"

Albright, no. 53; Helck, Beziehunngen[2] p. 435 n. 6; Schulman, *JARCE* 3 p. 60 n.73; Moran p. 540 n.4

[EA] 316.16 *ʾša-aḫ-ši-ḫa-ši-ḫa* (the final *-ši-ḫa* is a dittography)

[Eg] *Wb* III.480.9 since end of Dyn 18; cf. *sš* "scribe" attested since OK. (Note Eg *sš* > /šs/ > /šḫ/ cf. Copt [s]ⲥⲁϩ, [b]ⲥⲁϧ, [a]ⲥⲁⳉ).

šapḫa

--- *sfḫ*  "seven"

For bibli. see p. 384

[EA] 368.12 *šap-ḫa*

[Eg] *Wb* IV.115.15; [Copt] [s]ⲥⲁϣϥ, [b]ϣⲁϣϥ

šau

--- *si(s)*  "six"

For bibli. see p. 384

[EA] 368.11 *ša-ú*

[Eg] *Wb* IV.40.7; [Copt] ⲥⲟⲟⲩ.

šina

--- *šn(w)ty* 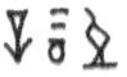 "two"

For bibli., see p. 384

[EA] 368.7 *ši-na*

[Eg] *Wb* IV.148.6; [Copt] [s,b]ⲥⲛⲁⲩ, [a]ⲥⲛⲉⲩ, ⲥⲛⲟ.

šunuti

--- *šn(w)ty* 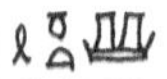 (dual)"granary"

Helck, *MDOG* 92 p. 11; Moran p. 524 n. 2

[EA] 294.22 *šu-nu-ti*

[Eg] *Wb* IV.510.1 since Pyr; [Copt] sg. forms [s]ϣⲉⲩⲛⲉ, [b]ϣⲉⲩⲛⲓ.

tasbu, taasbu

--- *t(3)-isb(.t)* 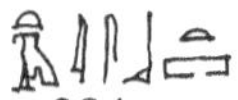 "the stool"

For bibli., see p. 384

[EA] 368. rev. 9 *ta-as-bu* "the stool"

[Eg] *Wb* I.132.2–8 NK.

ṭiban

--- *dbn*  "Eg measure of weight"

For bibli. see p. 384

[EA] 368.12 *ṭi-ba-an*

[Eg] *Wb* V.438.2 – 10 since OK.

ṭiu

--- *di͗(w)*  "five"

For bibli., see p. 384

[EA] 368.10 *ti-u*

[Eg] *Wb* V.420.9 – 12; [Copt] ϯⲟⲩ.

uruš(š)a

--- *wrs* 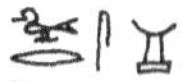 "head support"

KM p. 19

[EA] 5.22 ^{iṣu}*ú-ru-[u]š-ša ša* ^{iṣu}*ušî*

[Eg] *Wb* I.335.9 OK – NK.

weḫu, ueḫ, wea/u, ue, ui/eu

--- *wʿ(w)* 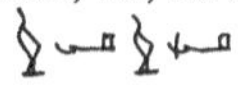 "a low officer"

KM p. 19

[EA] 129.12 *wi-ḫi*; 230.11 *w[i]-ḫu*; 287.69 *ú-e-eḫ*; 109.39 *wi-a*; 150.9 *wi-ú*; 287.47 *ú-e-e*; 288.10 *ú-e-ú*; 285.6 *ú-i-ú*

[Eg] *Wb* I.280.3 – 8 Dyn 18 – end of NK.

zabnakū

--- *ṯ(3)b-n-k(3)* 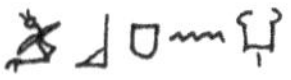 "ka-vessel"

KM p. 20; Lambdin, *Or* NS 22 p. 369

[EA] 14.111.54 *za-ab-na-ku-u*

[Eg] *Wb* V.354.8–9 since Dyn 19.

B. ANALYSIS OF PHONOLOGICAL CORRESPONDENCES

[1] Akk : Eg Phonetic Correspondences

Akk *b* : Eg *b*
Akk *d* : Eg *d*
Akk *g* : Eg -
Akk *ḫ* : Eg *h*
: Eg *ḥ*
: Eg *ḫ*
: Eg *š* (*s* > /š/ > /ḫ/)
Akk *y* : Eg *y*
: Eg *ỉ*
: Eg *ʿ*
Akk *k* : Eg *k*
Akk *l* : Eg *r*
Akk *m* : Eg *m*
: Eg *b*
Akk *n* : Eg *n*
Akk *p* : Eg *p*
: Eg *f*

Akk *q* : Eg *ḳ*
Akk *r* : Eg *r*
Akk *s* : Eg *s*
: Eg *š*
Akk *ṣ* : Eg -
Akk *š* : Eg *s*
: Eg *š*
Akk *t* : Eg *t*
: Eg *ṯ* (> /t/)
: Eg *d* (> /t/)
: Eg *ḏ* (> /d/ > /t/)
Akk *ṭ* : Eg *d*
: Eg *ḏ* (> /d/)
Akk *z* : Eg *ṯ*

[2] Eg : Akk Phonetic Corresnondences

Eg *3* : Akk ø (mostly)
Eg *3* : Akk /ʾ/ between two vowels
Lw = *pusbiu (pu-us-bi-û) /pusbiʾu/*
Eg *ỉ* : Akk vowel in the beginning
PN = *amanap(p)a (a-ma-an-ap-pa) / ʾamanʾapa /, Amanḫatpe, Amanmassa, api, ap(p)iḫa, mayati (ma-ia-tu-ma)*
Eg *ỉ* : Akk /ʾ/ between a consonant and a vowel in the middle
PN = *amanap(p)a, Mayati* /mayʾati/
Eg *ỉ* : Akk /ʾ/ between two vowels in the middle
PN = *paapu (pa-a-pu)* /paʾapu/; Lw= *šau, taasbu, ṭin*
Eg *ỉ* : Akk *y*
PN = *Leya, peya*
Eg *ỉ* : Akk ø at the end

Lw = *šūta (šu-ta)*

Eg ᶜ: Akk vowel at the beginning

Lw = *anaḫu (a-na-ḫu-u)*

Eg ᶜ: Akk /ᶜ/ between a vowel and a consonant in the middle

Lw = *paḫatu (pa-ḫa-tu)* /paḫaᶜtu/

Eg ᶜ: Akk /ᶜ/ between two vowels at the middle

PN = *Ḫaapi (ḫa-a-pi)* /haᶜapi/, *Nibmuare(y)a, Reanap*; Lw= *ḫanūnušaḫū, wea/u*

Eg ᶜ: Akk ø at the end

Lw = *miši (mi-ši)*, /mišiᶜ/, *šaḫū (ša-ḫu-ū)* /saḫuᶜ/ or /šaḫuᶜu/?

Eg ᶜ: Akk *y* (*ia*-sign; restricted to the spelling of Re')

PN = *Manaḫpi(r)ya, Maireya, Naphu/areya, Nibḫur(r)eya, Nibmuare(y)a, Reyamanū*

Eg ᶜ: Akk *ḫ*

PN = *Naḫramas(s)i*; Lw= *šaḫšiḫa, wueḫ/ueḫ*

Eg *y* : Akk *y*

PN = *Maya, Mayati, Peya, Taḫmaya, Teye, Tuya*

Eg *y* : Akk *i*

PN = *Maireya*

Eg *y* : Akk ø at the end

PN = *Api, Ḫaap, Puḫura, Pamaḫu*; Lw= *piparu, piṭātu, šunuti*

Eg *w* : Akk *w*

PN = Pawara

Eg *w* : Akk *u* (restricted *u*-sign)

PN = *Pa/uuru*; Lw= *uruš(š)a, ueḫ*

Eg *w* : Akk ø

(1) Eg final *w* dropped: PN= *Amanḫatpe, Naḫramašši, Nibḫur(r)ereya, Taḫmašši*; Lw= *ḫina, našša, šina, šunuti, ṭiu,weʾḫu*

(2) Eg middle *w* dropped: Lw= *šunuti* (Eg *šnwty*)

Eg *b* : Akk *b*

PN = *Nibḫur(r)ereya, Nibmuare(y)a*; Lw= *ḫubunu, nabnasu, pusbiu, taasbu, ṭiban, ẓabnakū*

Eg *b* : Akk *m* (/b/ > /m/ before *m*)

PN = *Nimmu(ʾ)wareya, Mimmur(y)a*

Eg *b* : Akk ø

PN = *Immure(y)a*

Eg *p* : Akk *p*
PN = *Amanap(p)a, Amanḫatpe, Api* etc GN= *Ḫikuptaḫ*; Lw= *ḫatupu, ḫapši, paḫatu*, etc
Eg *p* : Akk ᵓ (Eg *p* > /ᵓ/)
PN = *Napḫuᵓrureya*
Eg *p* : Akk ø (Eg *p* is not supported by a vowel)
(1) Eg *ḫpr* > *ḫr* : PN= *Napḫuru/areya, Nibḫur(r)ereya*
(2) Eg *ptḥ* > *tḥ* : PN= *Taḫmaya, Taḫmaš(š)i*; Lw= *Ḫikkutaḫ*
Eg *f* : Akk *p*
PN = *Napḫuru/areya, Reanap(a)*; Lw= *qapqapu, šapḫa*
Eg *m* : Akk *m*
PN = *Amanap(p)a* etc.; DN= *Aman* etc.; Lw= *ḫaman* etc.
Eg *m* : Akk ø
(1) Eg prep. *m* > /ø/: PN= *Appiḫ*
(2) *m* > /ø/ before *n*: PN= *Paḫa(m)natate*
Eg *n* : Akk *n*
Eg *n* : Akk ø
(1) Eg prep. *n* dropped: PN = *Paapu, Pamaḫu*
(2) the final *n* dropped: PN = *Mayati*
(3) the initial *n* dropped: PN = *Immure(y)a*
Eg *r* : Akk *r*
PN = *Manaḫpi(r)ya, Naḫramašši* etc.; Lw= *pawira/i* etc.
Eg *r* : Akk *l* (Eg *r* > /l/ at the initial)
PN = *Leya*
Eg *r* : Akk ø
PN = *Manaḫpi(r)ya (mn-ḫpr-rᶜ), Mayati, Maireya*; Lw= *kuiḫku*
Eg *h* : Akk *ḫ*
Lw = *ḫanūnu šaḫū, ḫina, ḫubunu, raḫta*
Eg *ḥ* : Akk *ḫ*
PN = *Amanḫatpe, Appiḫa,* etc.; GN= *Ḫikuptaḫ* etc.; Lw= *ḫatupu* etc.
Eg *ḫ* : Akk *ḫ*
PN = *Manaḫpi(r)ya, Paḫura,* etc.; Lw= *anaḫu, ḫapši,* etc.
Eg *s* : Akk *š*
PN = *Amanmaš(š)a*, etc.; Lw= *daši*, etc.
Eg *s* : Akk *s*
PN = *Ḫaramas(s)a (cf. Ḫaramašši)*; Lw= *pusbiu, taasbu*
Eg *s* : Akk ø (Eg final *s* dropped)
Lw = *šau* (Eg *sis* > *si*)

Eg *š* : Akk *š*
Lw = *ḫapši, miši, nšw, šaḫšiḫa, šunuti*
Eg *š* : Akk *s*
Lw = *nabnasu*
Eg *š* : Akk *ḫ* (Eg *š* > /ḫ/)
Lw = *šaḫšiḫa*
Eg *ḳ* : Akk *q*
Lw = *qapqap*
Eg *k* : Akk *k*
GN = *Ḫikuptaḫ*; Lw= *kuiḫku, zabnakū*
Eg *t* : Akk *t*
PN = *Amanḫatpe*, etc; GN= *Ḫikuptaḫ*; Lw= *ḫamtu* etc
Eg *t* : Akk ø (Eg fem.ending *t* dropped)
PN = *Amanappa*,etc; GN= *Ḫikuptaḫ*; Lw= *ḫamtu, ḫatupu*, etc,
Eg *ṯ* : Akk *z*
Lw = *zabnakū, pazite* (?)
Eg *t* : Akk *t* (Eg *ṯ* > /t/)
PN = *Paḫa(m)nate*
Eg *d* : Akk *d/ṭ*
Lw = *daši, ṭiban, ṭiu*
Eg *d* : Akk *t* (Eg *d* > /t/)
Lw = *raḫta*
Eg *ḏ* > /d/: Akk *ṭ / d*
Lw = *muṭu, piṭatu*
Eg *ḏ* : Akk *d / ṭ / t*
Lw = *pišiṭ*

[3] Table of Phonetic Correspondences

	Akk	primary	secondary	Eg	primary	secondary
glottal stops	*ʾ*		*p*	*3*	ø (vowel)	
				ỉ	vowel *y* ø	
				ʿ	vowel *y h* ø	
semi vowel	*y*	*ỉ ʿ y*		*y*	*y i*	ø
	w			*w*	*w u*	ø
labials	*b*	*b*		*b*	*b*	*m*
	p	*p f*		*p*	*p*	*ʾ* ø
				f	*p*	
nasals	*m*	*m*		*m*	*m*	ø
	n	*n*		*n*	*n*	ø
lateral trill	*l*	*r*				
	r	*r*		*r*	*r l*	ø
pharyngal & laryngal	*ḫ*	*h ḥ ḫ*	*š*	*h*	*ḫ*	
				ḥ	*ḫ*	
				ḫ	*ḫ*	
				ẖ	-	
sibilants	*s*	*s š*		*s*	*š s*	ø
	š	*s š*		*š*	*š s*	*ḫ*
	ṣ	-				
	z	*ṯ*				
velars	*q*	*ḳ*		*ḳ*	*q*	
	k	*k*		*k*	*k*	
	g	-		*g*	-	
alveolars	*t*	*t*	*ṯ d*	*t*	*t*	ø
	d	*d*	*ḏ*	*ṯ*	*z*	*t*
	ṭ	*d*	*ḏ*	*d*	*d ṭ*	*t*
				ḏ	-	*d ṭ*

[4] Note on the Corresoondences

a) Glottal Stops

All Eg *3* are elided except one: *pusbiu* (*p3-sb3*), in which the final *3* of *sb3* is realized as /ʾ/ between two vowels, *i* and *u*. This indicates that Eg *3* is still preserved at the final position (there is no example of an initial *3*) Eg *ỉ* is preserved well. It is realized (1) by a vowel at the initial, (2) between two vowels in the middle, (3) between a consonant and a vowel. The suggestion that Eg *ỉ* corresponds to Akk *y* in the two names, *i.e., Leya, Peya (q.v.)*, in which the spelling of Eg *y* and *ỉ* is interchangable, is weak.

The Akk treatment of Eg ᶜ is very similar to that of Eg ʾ. The above three reflections are also used for Eg ʿ. However, the representation of Eg ᶜ by Akk *y* (in the case of Re', with *ia*-sign) and *ḫ*. is unique.

b) Semi-Vowels

Eg *y*, which was lost at the end, is represented by Akk *y* and *i*. Eg *w*, which was lost at the end, is represented by Akk *w* and *u* (always *ú*-sign), both of which seem to be interchangable.

c) Labials & Nasals

Eg *b* normally corresponds to Akk *b* and to Akk *m* before *m*. Eg *p* is elided, becoming ʾ or ø before a consonant.

Eg *m* and *n* correspond to Akk *m* and *n* respectively. Yet Eg prep. *m* was elided once, and Eg *m* assimilated to the following *n* (notice that *pa-ḫa-na-te* could be normalized as *Paḫannate*, cf. *Paḫamnate*). Eg prep. *n* in the name of type *p3-n-* "He who belongs to" is already elided and *p3-n-* becomes [pa] (*e.g., Paapu, Pamaḫu* etc.). In two cases (*Immure(y)a, Mayati*) the initial and final Eg *n* are not realized by Akk.

d) Pharyngal and Laryngals (Eg *h*-consonants)

Akk *ḫ* stands for all Eg *h* sounds. If we could apply the correspondence between Eg *ḫ* and NW Sem spirantized /k̲/, the result suggests that there was no spirantization in EA Akk, because the postvocalic Eg *ḫ* is represented by Akk *ḫ*, not *k*.

e.g.,(1) *Manaḫpi(r)ya* (Eg *mn-ḫpr-rʿ*):
(2) *Paḫura* (Eg *p3-ḫr.y*)
(3) *anaḫu* (Eg *ʿnḫ*)
(4) *ruḫi* (Eg *rḫ*)

e) Sibilants

It seems that there are no fixed correspondences between Eg and Akk sibilants. Eg *s* is normally represented by Akk *š*; however there are three cases in which Eg *s* is realized as Akk *s*. The fact that *Ḫaramassa* is replaced by *Ḫaramašši* indicates that they are interchangable. Eg *š* is usually equated with Akk *š*. However, once Eg *š* is represented by Akk *s*.

Due to the secondary change in Eg, Eg *š* is represented by Akk *ḫ* or lost. As for Akk *z*, see below.

f) Velars and Alveolars

There is no confusion among velars; Eg *ḳ* : Akk *q*, Eg *k* : Akk *k*.

Due to the Akk writing system, which is incapable of showing the exact phonetic value among voiced, voiceless and emphatic consonants, the determination of the correspondence is more difficult. However, Eg *d* corresponds not only to Akk *ṭ*, but also to Akk *d*. The correspondence between Eg *d* and NW Sem *d* is exceptional. Yet in EA the correspondence seems to be usual.

Unique to EA is the correspondence between Eg *ṯ* and Akk *z*.

[5] Phonetic Changes between EA and the Late Period

Within the considerable time span between EA and the Late Period there are some phonetic changes observable.

a) Consonants

As shown above, Eg *ṯ* corresponds to Akk *z*. However, Eg *ṯ* is represented by Ph *ṣ* (mid 5th cent. BC) and Aram *š* (6th cent BC) (not attested in Heb). This correspondence suggests that the consonantal value of Eg *ṯ* has changed. However as this is the case of a sibilant, the conclusion cannot be conclusive.

b) Vowels

The following Eg vowel changes has been generally accepted by Egyptologists since Albright and Sethe (see Heb פתרוס);

accented CvC : a > o i > a u > e

accented Cv : a > o i = i u > e

The vowel changes that appear in our studies are these:

(1) /a/ > /o/ in open and closed syllable

(a) Eg *imn*: EA [ʾaman] > Aram, Heb [(ʾ)amo/un]

EA: *Aman*, (unaccented: *Amanap(p)a, Amanḫatpe, Amanmaš(š)a*). Yet Aram: פטמון, פמון, אמון; Heb: אמון

(b) Eg *ip.t:* EA [ʾapu/a/i] > Aram [ʾope]

EA: *Paapu, Amanap(p)a* (unaccented: *Ap(p)iḫa*). Yet Aram: אופתשתו.

(c) Eg *ḥtp*: EA [ḫat(i/u)pe/u] > Aram [ḥotpi]

EA: *Amanḫapte, Ḫatip, ḫatupu*. Yet Aram: ימחות (cf. Ug: חתף, Ph: ימחת, Aram: אחתף)

(d) Eg *nf(r)*: EA [nap] > Aram [nope]

EA: *Napḫuru/areya, Reanap*. Yet Aram: חרנופי, כנופי, פתחנופי

(cf. Heb חרנפר (*ḥarnep̄er*) perhaps derived form *harnapr*, indicating [nap]).

(e) Eg *nṯ(r)*: EA [nata/e] > Aram [note]

EA: *Paḫa(m)nata/e*. Yet Aram: פקנותי, פסחמצנותי

(2) /i/ = /i/ in closed syllable
(a) Eg *hn(w)*: EA [hina] = Heb [hin]
EA: *hina*. Heb הין.

(3) /o/ > /e/ (see Heb GN פתרוס)

(4) /e/ > /a/ or /a/ > /e/ (?)
(a) Eg *ʿnḫ*: EA [anaḫ] cf. Heb [ʿneaḫ]
EA: *anaḫu* Heb צפנתפענח *(-paʿneaḥ)*

Most of them are in accordance with the above rules of vowel changes. However, as far as Eg *hn(w)* is concerned we would expect [han] because *hn(w)* consists of a single syllable (Copt ϩΙΝ). Yet the example tells that vowel [i] can remain as [i] even in the closed syllable.

VI

CONCLUSIONS

[1] Consonantal Correspondences

The historical correspondences between Eg and North-West Semitic are as follows (the table below contains only the primary correspondences);

	Eg	Ph/Pu	Aram	Heb	Ug	Akk
glottal stops	*3* *ꞽ* ʿ	ʾ ʾ *y* ʿ	ʾ ʾ *y* ʿ	ʾ ʾ *y* ʿ	*a* *a i* -	by vowel ø by vowel ø *y* by vowel ø *y ḫ*
semi vowels	*y* *w*	*y* *w*	*y* *w*	*y* *w*	- -	*y i* *w u*
labials	*b* *p* *f*	*b* *p* *p*	*b* *p* *p*	*b* *p* *p*	*b* *p* -	*b* *p* *p*
nasals	*m* *n*	*m* *n*	*m* *n*	*m* *n*	*m* *n*	*m* *n*
trill lateral	*r* *l*[1]	*r*	*r l* *l*	*r l*	*r l*	*r l*
pharyngal & laryngal	*h* *ḥ* *ḫ* *ẖ*	*h* *ḥ* *ḥ k* *k*	*h* *ḥ* *ḥ* *ḥ*	*h* *ḥ* *ḥ* -	*h* *ḥ* *ḫ* -	*ḫ* *ḫ* *ḫ* -

sibilants	*s*	*s*	*s*	*s*	*s*	*s* *š*
	š	*š*	*š*	*š*	-	*s* *š*
velars	*ḳ*		*q*	*q*	*q*	*q*
	k	*k*	*k* *q*	*k*	-	*k*
	g	-	-	*g*	-	-
alveolars	*t*	*t*	*t*	*t*	*t*	*t*
	ṯ	*š*[4]	*š*	-	-	*z*
	d	*ṭ*	*ṭ* *d*[2]	*ṭ*	-	*ṭ* *d*[3]
	ḏ	*ṣ*	*ṣ*	*ṣ*	-	-

Notes
1 Demotic
2 Once attested in GN אבוד (*3bḏw*), could be dialectal.
3 Due to the inadequacy of Akk writing system.
4 Perhaps dialectal

[2] Notes on the Correspondences

As the above table shows, the consonantal correspondences between Eg and NW Semitic are remarkably stable in the course of history of two languages. we can conclude that the phonetic values of each consonant did not change much. Semitic scribes seem to have had no difficulty in transcribing the Eg language. They carefully transcribed Eg and their results show great consistency. Semi-vowels, labials, nasals, trills, laterals, and sibilants have no double realization.

a) Glottal Stops etc.

Two of three Eg glottal stops have no double realizations. The fact that Eg *ỉ* is realized by NW Semitic both א and י simply indicates that Eg *ỉ* has an *aleph* + /i/ sound value. When the *aleph* value was elided Eg *ỉ* is represented by Sem י.

However, Akk scribes obviously had a great problem transcribing Eg glottal stops, resulting in various realizations of Eg glottal stops. While they often disregarded the existence of the two Eg *alephs*, there is a clear tendency for Akk scribes to try to represent the value of *'ayn* as a consonant: Akk *y* or *ḫ* . Since this was caused by the lack of glottal stops in Akk, we should not extend this correspondence to the relations between NW Sem and Eg, such as פער = Eg *p3-ḫr.y* (Benz p. 394).

The *aleph*-value of Eg *3* was evidently preserved at the initial position until the Late Period. The fact is demonstrated in Heb Lw אחו, Ph DNs אסר "Osiris" and אס "Isis", Aram GN אבוט "Abydos." Akk *pusbi'u* (*p3-sb3*) also demonstrates that the *aleph* was pronounced at the end in the New Kingdom. However, in the majority of cases Eg *3* was completely elided, esp. in the middle position.

b) Sibilants

Against the general assumption of the confusion of sibilants, the NW Semitic transcriptions do not provide any evidence of confusion. The difference in the phonetic value /s/ and /š/ was undoubtedly recognized by NW Semitic scribes who represented Eg *s* by Sem ס, Eg *š* by Sem שׁ, while in Akk confusion of /s/ and /š/ is evident. There seems to be no fixed rule on how to represent the difference between Eg *s* and *š*. However, again, this confusion should not be extended to the correspondences between Eg and NW Sem (*e.g*. Ph פסר = Eg *p3-šrỉ* Benz p.193).

It was unfortunate that we could not confirm the equation of Heb שׂ. There is one unconfirmed Eg loanword in Heb, *i.e.*, שׂכיות (*sk.tw*) which suggests that Heb שׂ represents Eg *s*. Eg scribes represented NW Sem שׂ by both Eg *s* and *š*. Yet from the NW Sem side the equation is open to further investigation.

c) Pharyngals and Laryngals (Eg *h* consonants)

The realizations of Eg strong *h* consonants are most interesting. Due to the different number of pharyngals and laryngals between NW Sem and Eg, NW Sem scribes were compelled to transcribe them differently. These different realizations of the three strong Eg *hs* in

NW Semitic sheds new light upon the existence of spirantization, which has been long discussed. Although there is general agreement, except in German scholarship, concerning the existence of spirantization in NW Semitic, the double realization has never been confirmed. What was observed here in the light of Egyptian transcribed into NW Semitic is revolutionary:

(1) In Ph, spirantization was completed by the fifth century B.C., because all postvocalic Eg *ḫ* and *ẖ* consistently correspond to Ph כ.

(2) In Imperial Aram, spirantization was not operative, because the expected evidence in Aram transcriptions is not found. All postvocalic Eg *ḫ* and *ẖ* are spelled by Aram ח.

(3) In Heb, our evidence is not determinative, because postvocalic Eg *ḫ* is attested in only two loanwords (אחלמה, פח) and we do not know when these loanwords entered into Hebrew. It is most likely that the loanwords containing Eg *ḫ* were transcribed into Heb before spirantization began to be operative.

Therefore, the general view that Heb spirantization was a result of the influence of the Aram spirantization needs to be changed. It is more likely that spirantization started in either Ph or Heb and that Aram spirantization was caused by Ph or Heb spirantization.

As for Ug, since Ug has two strong *h*s, our method is inapplicable. In EA Akk, we may say that there is no evidence of spirantization, because EA Akk *k* does not correspond to postvocalic Eg *ḫ*. However, it should be kept in mind that the phonetic value of EA Akk *ḫ* seems to be very broad, because all Eg *h*-consonants (including soft Eg *h*) are represented by EA Akk *ḫ*.

We can reconstruct Eg laryngals and pharyngals in terms of NW Sem as follows:

Eg	NW Sem
h	*h*
ḥ	*ḥ*
ḫ	*ḥ*
postvocalic *ḫ*	spirantized *k* (/ḵ/) in Ph and Heb
ẖ	*ḥ*
postvocalic *ẖ*	spirantized *k* (/ḵ/) in Ph and Heb

d) Alveolars

Among alveolars, Eg *t, d, ḏ* consistently correspond to Sem ת, ט, צ. However, the representation of Eg *ṯ* shows a great variety. It seems that Eg *ṯ* is the only consonant with which NW Semitic scribes had trouble. Eg *ṯ* is represented by Ph צ, Aram שׁ and EA Akk *z* (it is not attested in Heb). In terms of the realizations in NW Semitic, we can conclude that Eg *ṯ* is not an alveolar, but rather a sibilant or the like. It is not impossible to say that the variant realizations of Eg *ṯ* are a simple result of the inability of the NW Semitic consonantal system to transcribe Eg *ṯ*. However since the correspondence is consistent within each NW Semitic language, *e.g.*, in Aram, Eg *ṯ* is always represented by שׁ, it is more likely that there was some phonetic difference between Ph and Aram צ / שׁ. Likewise, the problem of representing Eg *ṯ* by Ph צ and by Aram שׁ was partly caused by dialectical differences. It is known that some Eg *ṯ* became /ḏ/ (Copt ϫ) in Sahidic (see Chapter I, p. 73). Ph realization צ may be a case of this, because the names containing Eg *ḏ* came from Elephantine. Since NW Sem צ always represents Eg *ḏ* (Copt ϫ) and Aram שׁ represents Eg *ṯ* we can conclude that NW Sem צ represents Eg *ṯ* which became /ḏ/. He can reconstruct, therefore, the Eg alveolars in terms of NW Sem as follows;

Eg	NW Sem
t	*t* /t/
ṯ > /ḏ/ (Copt ϫ)	*ṣ* /ṣ/ (could be *š* in Aram)
ṯ > /ṯ/ (Copt ϭ)	*š* /š/
d	*ṭ* /ṭ/
ḏ > (Copt ϫ)	*ṣ* /ṣ/

The historical change of the phonetic value of Eg *ṯ* is suggested by the correspondence between EA Akk *z* and Eg *ṯ*. This is the only indication which allows us to infer the historical change of an Eg consonantal value. However, the limited attestation of the correspondence (twice in Akk) prevents us from confirming this historical change. Moreover, as this is the case of sibilants, the value of the evidence is reduced.

The correspondence between Eg *ṯ* and NW Sem seems not to be as big a problem to Eg scribes as to NW Sem scribes, because Eg scribes mostly used the *ṯ* for NW Sem ס, rarely for ז (Burchardt I § 143). However, this difference between the correspondence from the Eg side and that from the NW Sem side indicates that Eg *ṯ* did not have an exact phonetlc counterpart in NW Semitic.

NW Semitic ג, ד hardly appear to represent Eg consonants. Aram ד once represents Eg *d* (Aram GN אבוד as a variant of אבוט), Heb ג once represents Eg *g* (Heb Lw גמא). This is because Eg lost these two phonetic values (/g/ and /d/) by the New Kingdom (perhaps much earlier). This is reflected in the fact that Coptic does not normally use Δ and Γ, which is a positional variant of Copt K in a very small set of forms (Lambdin, *Introduction to Sahidic* p. x). Eg *g*, being prepalatalized, became /k/ or /k̯/ (cf. Vergote, *Phonétique* p. 40), Eg *d* became /t/ or /t̯/. However some rare examples of NW Sem transcriptions prove that Eg *g* and *d* originally corresponded to NW Sem ג and ד as shown above. In the Late Period, therefore, Eg *g* is represented by NW Sem ק (Aram PN פקרקפתח = *p3-n-grg-ptḥ*, Heb Lw קוף = *gif*, קסת = *gsti*).

NW Sem ז is the only consonant which represents no Eg consonant. NW Sem ז could not find any phonetic counterpart in Eg in the Late Period, as Eg *ṯ* could not in NW Semitic. This is reflected in the fact that Copt does not use Z, which may occur for Copt C in a few words. Eg scribes evidently had trouble in representing NW Sem ז, which was represented by Eg *ṯ* and *ḏ* (Burchardt I § 138 and 153).

[3] Phonetic Changes

It is almost impossible to list all Eg internal phonetic changes, such as *mry.t* > *m(y)t*. These Eg cases were discussed in each entry. Here listed are only phonetic changes which are somehow or another related to NW Sem phonology and which are noteworthy. There are some cases, however, where we cannot discern whether the change took place in Eg or in NW Sem.

a) Changes of Consonants[1]

(1) ʿ > ʾ --- It seems that in Ug hybrid names ʿ is replaced by ʾ at the initial, as Ph and Pu hybrid: *e.g.* *abdḥr* (= *ʿbdḥr*); cf. Ph אבדאס (= עבדאס). Yet *abd* and *ʿbd* could be different words.

(2) *b* > *p* --- *b* became *p* before *r*. The example is restricted to Eg *w3ḥ-ib-rʿ*: *e.g.* Ph וחפרע, Aram וחפרע, וחפרעמחי, Heb חפרע. Cf. Akk *Uḫ-pa-ra*.

(3) *b* > *w* --- *b* became *w* at the final due to assimilation to the previous [u] vowel: *e.g.* Aram הריו (*hr-ib*).

(4) *b* > *m* --- *b* was partially or entirely assimilated to the following *m*: *e.g.* Akk *Nimm(ʾ)wareya* (*nb-m3ʿ.t-rʿ*); cf. Aram Lw נמעתי (probably *nb-m3ʿ.ty*).

(5) *p* > *b* --- *p* became *b* at the final position: *e.g.* Aram פחטב (*p3-ḥtp*).

(6) *k* > *ḳ* --- *k* became emphatic *ḳ* at the initial and final position: *e.g.* Aram פטסבק, קלבי.

(7) *m* > *b* --- *m* was dissimilated to *m* at the end due to the previous [ū] vowel: *e.g.* Aram חנוב (*ḫnm.w*). cf. חנום.

(8) *m* > *w* --- *m* became *w* as an allophone in the case of Eg goddess Mut: *e.g.* פסתות, תות (*-mw. t*).

(9) *m* > *n* --- in Heb *m* became *n* before a labial: *e.g.* Heb GN נף (cf. Ph and Aram forms מנף, מנפי: *mn-nfr*); The change is *mn-nfr* > מנף > מף > נף. Another example is נפך (*mfk3.t*), whose change maybe occurred in Eg. Akk *paḫamnata/e* and *paḫanata/e* also shows the assimilation of *m* to *n*.

(10) *n* > *m* --- *n* became m before a labial (cf.above): *e.g.* Akk *Mimmure(y)a, Mimmureya* (*nb-m3ʿ.t-rʿ*).

(11) *n* > *l* --- in Eg it is commonly observed that the initial *n* became *l*: e.g. Heb Lw לשם. However, the same change also occurs between ח and a labial: *e.g.* Heb Lw אחלמה (*ḫnm.t*), for other Copt examples, see the entry for אחלמה.

(12) *s* > *š* --- *s* is assimilated into *š* under the influence of another *š* placed near: *e.g.* Aram שש (*šs*), Heb שושן (*sšn*), שיש (*šs*), שש (*šs*). Cf. Ph PN אשרשלה, עבדשר discussed on p. 72.

(13) *t* > *ṭ* --- *t* became *ṭ* between a labial and *ḥ*: e.g. Aram פחטמוני (*p3-ḫ.t-mni.t*), פטחרטים (*ptḥ-ir-di-sw*), אחטף (*ii-ḥtp*),

[1] Vowel changes were discussed on p. 298–303. and 339.

פחטב (*p3-ḥtp*). The same change occurs between a labial and *'ayn*: *e.g.* Aram: פפטעונית (*p3.f-ṯ3w-ʿ.wy-n-nyt*). The change, voiceless *t* > emphatic *ṭ*, took place under the influence of pharyngals or laryngal maybe in Aram (cf. the change *n* > *l* between *ḥ* and a labial).

(14) *nn* > *m* --- in Eg *nn* became *m* (probably *nn* > *n* > *m*): *e.g.* Aram month name פרמותי (*p3-n-rnnwt.t*). The *n* became *m* due to phonetic assimilation to the following long vowel [ū].

b) Dropping of Consonants

In many cases Eg consonants disappeared in words. Here common cases, such as Eg preposition *n*, *mry.t* > *my*, are excluded.

(1) *b* > ø at the medial position: *e.g.* Ph פטבנטט (*-nb-* > *-n-*).

(2) *p* > ø at the end: *e.g.* אמחות, ימחות (*ḥtp* > *ḥt* with long vowel [ū]). However there are some cases that the *ḥt* was realized without *mater lectionis*, *e.g.* Aram חרחת from Saqqara where *matres lectionis* were less developed, Ph ימחת.

(3) *p* > ø at the initial in Akk: *e.g.* *Taḫmaya (ptḥ-my)*, *Taḫmaš(š)i* (*ptḥ-ms*), note that the *p* is followed by a consonant. Yet in NW Sem the initial *p* was always retained.

(4) *n* > ø before *ḥ* in Aram: *e.g.* מחנית, מחפרע, ענחחרי (cf. עחחפי). Perhaps n is assimilated into the following strong h.

(5) *n* > ø before *r* in Aram: *e.g.* אמורטים (*imn-ir-di-sw*).

(6) *n* > ø at the end in Akk: *e.g.* *Mayati*, *Mayatu* (*mry-itn*).

(7) *n* > ø at the initial in Akk: *e.g.* *Immure(y)a* (*nb-m3ʿ.t-rʿ*).

(8) *w* > ø at the initial in Heb: *e.g.* חפרע (*w3ḥ-ib-rʿ*), cf. Aram וחפרע.

c) N-assimilation

N-assimilation is hardly observable in the documents from Elephantine. However in other places n-assimilation is observable: *e.g.* Eg *ʿnḫ* > ענח in Eleph, yet *ʿnḫ* > עח in Saqqara and AD, Eg *mn-nfr* > מנפי in Eleph, Saqq and Padua, yet *mn-nfr* > מפי in Hermopolis. Although generally n-assimilation is not common in Eg Aram, its occurrence is geographically differentiated. In Hebrew n-assimilation most frequently occurs: *e.g.* before a labial *mn-nfr* > מנף or נף; before emphatic *šnḏ.t* > שטה (cf. Aram שנטא), *links ššnk* > שושק.

d) Prosthetic *Aleph*

In the transcription of Eg words, NW Sem recorded the initial vowel of Eg words, which is not reflected in the Eg writings;

(1) Heb Lw אחלמה (*ḫnm.t*): [a] vowel was protected by א.

(2) Ph DN אבסת (*b3st.t*): [u] vowel was protected by א.

[4] Matres Lectionis

The frequent use of *matres lectionis* is prominent in NW Sem transcriptions of Eg PN, as well as Lws. Although the Ph language is famous for its rigid consonantal system, the *matres lectionis* are observable at the final position in Ph, *i.e.*, כנפי, פטאסי, possibly צחא. We can confirm that Ph scribes were conscious that consonant י can stand for a vowel [i], and probably א for a vowel [o].

In Aram the use of *matres lectionis* is fully developed and the evidence strongly suggests that they were used on the accented syllables, *i.e.*, normally the final syllable. The accented syllable usually has the *matres lectionis*, and it seems that the non-accented syllable is not capable of bearing the *matres lectionis*. This fact supports the hypothesis that Eg usually had an accent at the final syllable. The sound values of *matres lectionis* are mostly in accordance with BA, except for the final ה, indicating [o].

Naturally the *matres lectionis* developed most in Heb, and the use of *matres lectionis* extended to unaccented syllables. It is peculiar that even Eg article *p3* is vocalized by the *matres lectionis*.

The *matres lectionis* are used not only in proper nouns, but also commonly used in loanwords. The *matres lectionis* occur in more than half of Eg loanwords in both Aram and Heb.

[5] Quantitative Analysis of the Eg Loanwords

When Eg loanwords are categorized by semantic groups, that reveals which areas of the NW sem-speaking worlds were most influenced by the Eg culture.

		Heb	Aram
Natural products	Mineral terminology Botanic terminology	8(26%)[1] 6(19%)[3]	1(4%)[2] 4(15%)[4]
Domestic materials	Tools and Utensils Measure Textiles and Cloths	6(19%)[5] 3(10%)[7] 2(6%)[9]	2(7%)[6] 3(11%)[8] 2(7%)[10]
Officials of titles		0	5(19%)[11]
Buildings	Architecture Nautical terminology	2(6%)[12] 1(3%)[14]	2(7%)[13] 2(7%)[15]
Scribal terminology		1(3%)[16]	0
Others		3[17]	5[18]
Total		31	26

1 שׁישׁ, פח, נתר, נפכ, לשׁמ, פח, נתר, אחלמה
2 שׁשׁ
3 שׁטה, שׁושׁן, ערה, הובן, גמא, אחו
4 שׁישׁ, שׁשׁן, שׁנטא, אחו
5 תבה, פח, קלחת, חתמ, טבעת, טהא
6 חתמ, קלול
7 קב, הין, איפה
8 סףּ, קב, הן
9 שׁשׁ, אטון
10 שׁנטא, שׁשׁ
11 פסחמצנותי, תמנחא, מנחה, חסיתמח, חסי
12 תבה, פרעה
13 תחית, פרעה
14 צי

15 תמיס, פחטמוני
16 קסת
17 לוב, יאור, קוף
18 חתפי, תרי, רסי, תמא, קלבי

The above table shows that the largest percentage (45 % in Heb; 19 % in Aram) of Eg loanwords are from terms for natural products in Eg, such as הבון "ebony", which were purely foreign to the Heb and Aram worlds. The second largest category (35 % in Heb; 25 % in Aram) is the daily domestic material culture. Contrarily Eg loans of administrative and political terminology are completely lacking in Heb and quite rare in Aram. When we compare it with Akk loanwords in Aram, an entirely opposite result is seen. According to S. A. Kaufman (*The Akkadian Influences on Aramaic*, p. 166ff), the largest percentage of Akk loanwords comes from the realm of politics and law. Another sphere in which the NW Sem world lacks Eg loanwords is religion. Eg religious terms are not found in Heb, and only one (חתפי "offering") in Aram. When we look at Akk loanwords in Aram we find that, although some religious terms were attested, the percentage is relatively low (3–4%) in contrast to words from politics and law. In this connection, we should take it into account that terms for natural products and buildings are by and large belong to the realm of material culture. We may say that only in the realm of material culture Eg had a heavy impact on the Heb and Aram worlds. Only Aram has a significant percentage (15 %) of Eg loanwords relating to a kind of title, and they are not found in Heb at all. Though in most cases they are qualifications of certain persons, not the official title, one Eg official title is attested (פסחמצנותי). Here some administrative influence may be observable. However, since Arameans lived in the land, it may not be right to ascribe it to Eg influence. For the same reason, it is not legitimate to discuss the different percentage between Heb and Aram in the table. The twelve Eg month names found in Aram documents are not included in the table, because they are most likely to be a case of foreign words written by Aram in the land of Egypt.

[6] Light on the Age and Character of Egyptian Terms in the Old Testament

Within the long time span of the Old Testament, we might expect divergent consonantal correspondences between Eg and Heb to be attributable to different periods, which might help in dating sources or sections of the Hebrew texts. However, there is no unique correspondence attested so far. The consonantal correspondences are the same as those found in Ph and Aram documents. The only correspondence newly attested in Heb is the representation of Eg *g* by Heb ג, which is expected. However, since Eg *g* became /k/ or /ḳ/ (see above), it indicates the borrowing was early, yet it can not be dated exactly. Heb Lw שׁנטה (*šnḏ.t*) is another indication that the borrowing was in MK, because *šnḏ.t* became *šnt.t* [šnti] in NK.

Though the consonantal correspondences are stable, some vocalizations and words reveal evidence that they were borrowed early. Notable are the two Lws טבעת (*ḏbʿ.t*) and קלחת (*ḳrḥ.t*) which preserve the Eg fem. ending *-t*. Since the Eg ending was lost in NK, these words must have been borrowed into Canaanite in the early second millennium.

The vocalization of פתרוס and פתרסים (*paṯrusîm*) indicates that the Eg word *p3-t3-rs(y)* "Upper Egypt" probably entered Heb in the second millennium, because, if the word had been borrowed in the first millennium, it would have been vocalized as פתריס (cf. NA *pa-tu-ri-si*, see Heb GN פתרוס). The vocalization of Heb PN חרנפר (*ḥarnep̄er* , Eg *ḥr-nfr.w*) also indicates that the name was borrowed in the second millennium, because the vocalization of Eg *nfr(.w)* was [nap(r)] in EA (cf. *Renap* etc.), which changed to [nūf(r)] in the Late Period (cf. Copt ΝΟΥϤΡ). We can safely assume that Heb *ḥarnep̄er* derived from the earlier vocalization [ḥarnapr].

Heb vocalization of פוטיפרע and other names of the same type suggest that they reached their Heb forms no later than the seventh century B.C.. And the same criteria can be applied to Eg Lws which have [ā] (Heb ה) vowel for the Eg fem. ending. The vocalization of פינחס could be traced back to the second millennium.

Since we are not informed when these vowel changes took place in Eg (roughly between Ramesses II and the NA period) and internal vowel changes are always conceivable, these can not give strong evidence for the purpose of dating. These observations, however, do indicate that there were close relationships between Egypt and Canaan even in the early second millennium.

[7] Hybrid Names (Eg religious Influences)

The spread of hybrid names is also noticeable. The following table eloquently tells us the distribution of the influence of Eg religion over the NW Sem world:

		Ph	Aram	Heb	Ug
Eg gods in hybrid	Number of Eg gods	12	4	1	1
	Number of hybrid names	28	5	1	2
	Number of attestations	52	5	1	2
Eg gods as DN		5	8	1	1
Eg religious terms		0	1	0	1

This is striking evidence of the influence of Eg religion in the Ph world. When we consider that the quantity of Ph documents is relatively small in comparison with that of Aram, the percentage of the occurrence of Eg gods is much higher. The most popular Eg god is "The lion" (*p3-m3i*), which has long been unidentified. They are also fond of "Bastet" (lioness godess) and "Isis." Contrarily, Eg theophoric elements are hardly found in Aram PNs, though Arameans actually lived in the land of Egypt. This result is in accordance with the quantitative analysis of Eg loanwords in Aram (above). Eg gods were most welcomed by Ph, but were not acceptable to Aram people. In the Heb world only one hybrid name is confirmed (חרנפר). However, several other possibilities can be mentioned here; אחירע, אשראל, אחימות, בנחור. Although these cannot be confirmed as hybrid names, Eg theophoric elements are suggested. Whatever the identifications of these names are, as with the Arameans, Eg religion was not acceptable to the Heb world.

BIBLIOGRAPHY

Abel, F. M. *Géographie dela Palestine*. 2 vols. Paris: 1933/38.

Aharoni, Yohanan. *The Land of the Bible: a Historical Geography*, translated by A. F. Rainey. London: 1968.

——— "Three Hebrew Ostraca from Arad." *BASOR* 197 (1970) 16–42.

——— *Arad Inscriptions*. Jerusalem: 1981.

Aimé-Giron, M. Noël, "Fragments de papyrus araméens provenant de Memphis." *Journal Asiat* 18 (1921) 56–64.

——— "Note sur une tome découverte près de Cheikh-Fadl par Monsieur Flinders Petrie et contenant des inscriptions Araméennes." *AE* 23 (1923) 38–43.

——— "Glanures de Mythologie Syro-Egyptienne." *BIFAO* 23 (1924) 3–25.

——— "Trois Ostraca Araméens d'Elephantine." *ASAE* 26 (1926) 23–31.

——— *Textes Araméens d'Egypte*. Caire: 1931.

——— "Adversaria Semitica." *ASAE* 39 (1939) 339–363.

——— "Adversaria Semitica." *BIFAO* 38 (1939) 1–63.

Aistleitner, J. *Wörterbuch der ugaritischen Sprache*[3] Berlin: 1967.

Albrecht, Alt. "Ägyptisch-Ugaritisches." *AfO* 15 (1945–51) 69–74.

Albright, W. F. "Notes on Egypto-Semitic Etymology. " *AJSL* 34 (1918) 81–98.

——— "Note on Egypto-Semitic Etymology II." *AJSL* 34 (1918) 215–255.

——— "New Light on Magan and Meluẖa." *JAOS* 42 (1922) 317–322.

——— "The Principles of Egyptian Phonology." *Rec. de. Trav* 40 (1923) 64–72.

——— "The Evolution of the West-Semitic Divinity 'AN-'ANAT-'ATTÂ." *AJSL* 41 (1924–25) 73–101.
——— "The New Cuneiform Vocabulary of Egyptian Words." *JEA* 12 (1926) 189–190.
——— "Notes on Egypto-Semitic Etymology III." *JAOS* 47 (1927) 198–237.
——— "Mitannian maryannu «chariot-warrior» and the Canaanite and Egyptian Equivalents." *AfO* 6 (1930/31) 215–221.
——— "The North-Canaanite Epic of 'Al 'êyân Ba'al and Môt." *JPOS* 12 (1932) 185–208.
——— *The Vocalization of the Egyptian Syllabic Orthography.* New Haven: 1934.
——— "The Egyptian Correspondence of Abimilki Prince of Tyre." *JEA* 23 (1937) 190–203.
——— "An Archaic Hebrew Proverb in an Amarna letter from central Palestine." *BASOR* 89 (1943) 29–32.
——— "The Furniture of El in Canaanite Mythology. " *BASOR* 91 (1943) 39–44.
——— "A Prince of Taanach in the Fifteenth Century B.C." *BASOR* 94 (1944) 12–27.
——— Review of *Phonétique historique de l'Egyptien*, by J. Vergote. *JAOS* 66 (1946) 316–320.
——— "Cuneiform Material for Egyptian Prosopography 1500–1200 BC." *JNES* 5 (1946) 7–25.
——— "Exploring in Sinai with the University of California African Expedition." *BASOR* 109 (1948) 5–20.
——— "Baal-zephon." in *Festschrift Alfred Bertholet*, p. 1–14. Tübingen: 1950.
——— "The smaller Beth-Shan Stele of Sethos I (1309–1290 BC)." *BASOR* 125 (1952) 24–32.
——— "Notes on Amonite History." in *Miscellanea Biblica B. Ubach.* (Montserrat: 1954) 131–136.
——— "New Light on Early Recensions of the Hebrew Bible." *BASOR* 140 (1955) 27–33.
Altenmüller, Hartwig. "Letopolis und der Bericht des Herodot über Papremis." *JEOL* (1959–1966) 271–279.
Amadasi, M. G. G. *Le Iscrizion Fenicie e Puniche delle Colonie in Occidente.* Roma: 1967.

Anonymous. “En-gedi.” *IEJ* 12 (1972) 145–146.
Avigad, N. “Three Ornamented Hebrew Seals.” *IEJ* 4 (1954) 236–238.
——— *Hebrew Bullae from the Time of Jermiah: Remnants of a Burnt Archive*. Jerusalem: 1986.
——— “Another group of West-Semitic seals from the Hecht collection.” *Michmanim* 4 (1989) 7–21.
Babelon, E. *Traité des monnaies grecques et romaines*. 2 vols. Paris 1907.
Barnett, R. D. “A Review of Acquisitions (1955–1962) of Western Asiatic Antiquites.” *BMQ* 27 (1963–64) 79–88.
Barr, James. “St. Jerome and the sound of Hebrew.” *JSS* 12 (1967) 1–36
——— *Comparative Philology and the Text of the Old Testament*. Oxford: 1968.
Bauer, Hans and Leander, Pontus. *Historische Grammatik der Hebräischen Sprache des Alten Testaments*. Hildescheim: 1962.
——— and Meissner, B. “Ein aramäischer Pachtvertrag aus dem 7 Jahre Darius I.” *SBPA* (1939) 414–424.
Beer, G. and Meyer, R. *Hebräische Grammatik*. 4 vols. Berlin: 1952ff.
Beeston, A. F. L.; Ghul, M. A.; Müller, W. W. and Ryckmans, J. *Dictionaire sabéen*. Beyrouth: 1982.
Benz, Frank. *Personal Names in the Phoenician and Punic Inscriptions: A Catalog, Grammatical Study and Glossary of Elements*. Rome: 1972.
Bergsträßer, Gotthelf. *Hebräische Grammatik*. Hildesheim: 1962.
——— *Introduction to the Semitic Languages: Text Speciments and Grammatical Sketches*. Winona Lake, Indiana: 1977.
Berthier, André and Charlier, R. *Le Sanctuaire puniqué d'El-Hofra à Constantine*. Paris: 1952–55.
Biella, Joan Copeland. *Dictionary of Old South Arabic: Sabaean Dialect*. Chico, CA: 1982.
Bietak, Manfred. *Tell el -Dab'a*. Wien: 1975.
——— *Avaris and Piramesse: Archaeological Exploration in the eastern Nile Delta*. London: 1979.
——— “Comments on the “Exodus”” in *Egypt, Israel, Sinai*. pp. 163–171. Edited by Anson F. Rainey. Tel Aviv: 1987.
Bondi, J. H. “Die Bezeichnung der ägyptischen Spanne.” *ZÄS* 32 (1894) 132–133.

Bordreuil, Pierre. *Catalogue des Sceaux Ouest-Semitiques Inscrits.* Paris: 1986.

——— and Lemaire, André. "Nouveaux Sceaux Hébreux et Araméen." *Semitica* 32 (1982) 21–34.

Borger, R. "Das Ende des Ägyptischen Feldherrn Sib'e = סוא." *JNES* 19 (1960) 49–53.

Breasted, J. H. Review of *Ägyptologische Randglossen zum Alten Testament*, by W. Spiegelberg. *AJSL* 21 (1905) 247–250.

Bresciani, Edda. "Un pariro aramaico da El-Hibeh del Museo Archeologico di Firenze." *Aegyptus* 39 (1959) 3–8.

——— "Papiri aramaici egiziani di epoca persiana presso il Museo Civico di Padova." *RSO* 35 (1960) 11–24.

——— "Frammenti di un Testo Aramaico da Saqqara del V. Sec. A. CR." in *Studi in Onore di E. Volterra VI.* pp.529–532. Milano: 1971

——— "Ancora su Papremi: Proposte per una nuova etimologia e una nuova Localizzazione." *Studi Classici e Orientali* 21 (1972) 299–303.

——— and Kamil, M. *Le Lettero aramaiche di Hermopoli, Atti della Accademia Nazionale dei Lincei, Memorie, Classe di Scienze morali, Storiche e filologiche*, Series VIII, 12 / 5 (1966) 358–428 + 10 plates.

Bright, John. *Jermiah: Introduction, Translation, and Notes.* New York: 1965.

Brockelmann, Carl. *Grundriß der vergleichenden Grammatik der semitischen Sprachen.* 2 vols. Berlin: 1908.

Brønno, E. "Samaritan Hebrew and Origen's Secunda." *JSS* 13 (1968) 192–201.

Brugsch, Heinrich. *Hieroglyphisch-Demotisches Wörterbuch.* 7 vols. Leipzig: 1867ff.

——— "Geographica." *ZÄS* 13 (1875) 5–8.

Burchardt, M. *Die Altkanaanäischen Fremdworte und Eigennamen im Ägyptischen.* Leipzig: 1910.

Calice, Franz. *Grundlagen der Ägyptisch-Semitischen Wortvergleichung.* Wien: 1936.

Caminos, Rocardo. *Late-Egyptian Miscellanies.* London: 1954.

Gazelles, H. "Les localisations de l'Exode et Critique Littéraire." *RB* 62 (1955) 321–364.

Černý, Jaroslav. "The Name of the Town of Papremis." *Archiv Orientalni* 20(1952) 86–89.

——— *Coptic Etymological Dictionary*. Cambridge: 1976.

——— and Groll, S. I. *Late Egyptian Grammar*. Rome: 1978.

Chabot, J.-B. "Punice" *JA* series II vol 10 (1917) 1–79.

Chéhab, Maurice. "Nouvelles Steles d'Oum el-'Awamid." *BMB* 13 (1956) 43–52.

Clay, Albert. T. *Business Documents of Murashû sons of Nippur*. The Babylonian Expedition of the University of Pennsylvania Series A: Cuneiform Texts. Edited by H. V. Hilprecht vol.10. Philadelphia: 1904.

——— *Personal Names from Cuneiform Inscriptions of the Cassite Period*. Yale Oriental Series vol.1. New Haven: 1912.

Clermont-Genneau, Ch. "Sceaux et cachets." *JA* Series 8 vol.1 (1883) 123–59.

——— and Chebot, Jean B., ed. *Répertoire d'épigraphie Sémitique*. 5 vols. Paris: 1900–29.

Cody, Aelred. "Le Titre Ègyptien et le nom propre du scribe de David." *PB* 72 (1965) 387–393.

Cohen, Marcel. *Essai Comparatif sur le Vocabulaire et la phonetique du Chamito-Sémitique*. Paris: 1947.

Cooke, G. A. *A Text-Book of North-Semitic Inscriptions*. Oxford: 1903

Corpus Inscriptionum Semiticarum. pars prima, inscriptiones phoeniciae. Paris: 1881ff.

Corpus Inscriptionum Semiticarum. pers secunda, inscriptiones aramaicas continens. Paris: 1889ff.

Couroyer, B. Review of *The Brooklyn Museum Aramaic Papyri*, by E. G. Kraeling. *RB* 58 (1951) 252–253.

——— "Termes Égyptiens dans les Papyri Aramée de Brooklyn." *RB* 61 (1954) 554–559.

——— Review of *Joseph en Égypte*, by J. Vergote. *RB* 66 (1959) 582–600.

——— "Apropos dele Stèle de Carpentras." *Semitica* 20 (1970) 17–21. with "Post-Scriptum" by Pierre Grelot, pp.17–21.

Cowley, A. "Some Egyptian Aramaic Documents." *PSBA* 25 (1903) 202–208, 259–266, 311–316.

——— "Another Aramaic Papyrus of the Ptolemeic Period." *PSBA* 37 (1915) 217–223.

——— Aramaic Papyri of the Fifth Century B.C. Oxford: 1923.
——— "Two Aramaic Ostraka." *JRAS* (1929) 107–112.
Crim, Keith. ed., Supplementary Volume of *The Interpreter's Dictionary of the Bible*. Abingdon: 1976.
Croatto, J. Severino. "'Abrek 'Intendant' dens Gén. 41,43." *VT* 16 (1966) 113–115.
Cross, F. M. "An Ostracon from Nebī Yūnis." *IEJ* 14 (1964) 185–186
——— and McCarter, P. K. "Two Archaic Inscriptions on Clay Objects from Byblos." *Rivista di Studi Fenici* 1 (1973) 3–8.
Crum, W. E. *A Coptic Dictionary*. Oxford: 1979.
Dahood, Mitchell. *Ugaritic-Hebrew Philology*. Biblica et Orientalia vol.17. Rome: 1965.
Dalman, Gustef, *Grammatik des jüdisch-palästinischen Aramäisch nach den Idiomen des palästinischen Talmud des Ondelos argum und Prophetentargum und der Jerusalemischen Targume*. Darmstadt: 1960.
de Buck, *A. Grammaire Élémentaire du Moyen Égyptien.* Translated by B. van de Walle and J. Vergote. Leiden: 1967.
Degen, von Rainer. *Altaramäische Grammatik der Inschriften des 10. - 8. Jh. v. Chr.*. Wiesbaden: 1969.
——— "Der Name Harpokrates in Phönizischer und aramäischer Umschreibung." *Die Welt des Orients* 5 (1968–70) 218–221.
——— Müller, Walter W. and Röllig, Wolfgang. Neue Ephemeris für Semitische Epigraphik. 3 vols. Wiesbaden: 1972–78.
del Monte, Giuseppe F. and Tischler, Johann. *Die Orts- und Gewässernamen der hethitischen Texte*. Répertoire Géogrephigue des Texts Cunéiformes. vol 6. Wiesbaden: 1978.
de Meulenaere, H. "Notes d'onomastique tardive." *RdE* 11 (1951) 77–84
——— "Anthroponymes Égyptiens de Basse Époque." *Cd'E* 38 (1963) 213–219.
de Morgan, Jacques. "L'Égypte et l'Asie aux temps antéhistoriques." *JA* 203 (1923) 117–159.
de Vaux, R. "Titres et Fonctionnaires Égyptiens a la Cour de David et de Salomon." *RB* 48 (1939) 394–405.
Dietrich, M. ed. *lišan mitḫurti*. *AOAT* vol.1. 1969.
——— Loretz, O. and Sanmartin, J. "Zur Ugaritischen Lexikographie XIII." *UF* 7 (1975) 157–169.

——— *Die Keilalphabetischen Texte aus Ugarit. AOAT* vol. 24. 1976

Donner, H. and Röllig, W. *Kanaanäische und aramäische Inschriften.* 3 vols. Wiesbaden. 1962 64.

Douglas, J. D., et al. ed., *The New Bible Dictionary.* London. 1962.

Driver, G. R. "Difficult Words in the Hebrew Prophets." in *Studies in Old Testament Prophecy presented to Prof. Theodore H. Robinson*, pp. 52–72. Edited by H. H. Rowley. New York: 1950.

——— *Aramaic Documents of the Fifth Century B.C.* Oxford. 1954.

Dunand, Maurice. *Fouilles de Byblos.* 5 vols. Paris: 1939.

——— "Nouvelles Inscriptions Phéniciennes du Temple d'Echmoun a Bostan Ech-Cheikh, prè Sidon." *BMB* 18 (1965) 105–109.

Dupont-Sommer, André M. "Un Ostracon araméen inédit d'Elephantine." *RESem* (1941–45) 65–75.

——— "Un papyrus araméen d'époque Saite découvert a Saqqarah." *Semitica* 1 (1946) 43–68.

——— "Ostraca Araméens d'Éléphantine." *ASAE* 48 (1948) 109–130.

——— "Deux Nouvelles Inscriptions Sémitiques Trouvées en Cilicle." *JKF* 1 (1950) 43–47.

——— "Un Ostrecon Araméen inédit d'Éléphantine." *RSO* (1957) 403–409.

——— *Les Inscriptions Araméennes de Sefiré.* Paris: 1958.

Dussaud, René. "Inscription Phénicienne de Byblos d'Époque Romaine." *Syria* 6 (1925) 269–273.

——— *Mélanges Syriens Offerts a Monsieur.* 2 vols. Paris: 1939.

Edel, Elmer. "Neue keilschriftliche Umschreibungen ägyptischer Namen aus den Bogezköytexten." *JNES* 7 (1948) 11–24.

——— "Zwei Originalbriefe der Königsmutter Tuja in Keilschrift." *SAK* 1 (1974) 105–146.

——— "Zur Deutung des Keilschriftvokabulars EA 368 mit ägyptischen Wörtern." *GM* (1975) 11–16.

——— "Der Brief des ägyptischen Wesirs Pašijara an den Hethiterkönig Ḫattušili und verwandte Keilschriftbriefe." *Nachrichten der Akademie der Wissenschaften in Göttingen, 1 Philologisch-Historische Klasse* 4 (1978) 17–158.

——— "Neue Deutungen keilschriftlicher Umschreibungen Ägyptischer Wörter und Personennamen." *Österreichische Akademie der Wissenschaften.* Wien: 1980.

——— "Weitere Beiträge zum Verständnis der Geschenklisten des

Amarnabrifes Nr.14." in *Documentum Asiae Minoris Antiquae, Festschrift für Heinrich Otten.* Wiesbaden: 1988.

Eilers, W. *Iranische Beamtennamen in der keilschriftlichen Uberlieferung I.* Abhandlungen für die Kunde des Morgenlandes Bd. 25 Nr. 5. Leipzig: 1940.

Eister, Robert. "  *gśti* = κα στυ του γραμματεως = סֶת הַסֵּפֶר im Danielkommentar des Hippolytos von Rom." *OLZ* 33 (1930) 585–587.

Ellenbogen, Maximilian. *Foreign Words in the Old Testament: Their Origin and Etymology.* London. 1962.

Ember, A. "Kindred Semito-Egyptian Words. *ZÄS* 51 (1912) 110–121; 53 (1917) 83–90.

——— *Egypto-Semitic Studies.* Leipzig: 1930.

Erichsen, W. *Demotisches Glossar.* Kopenhagen, 1954.

Ermen, Adolf. "Zum Namen des Osiris." *ZÄS* 46 (1909) 92–95.

——— "Das Verhältnis des Ägyptischen zu den semitischen Sprachen." *ZDMG* 46 (1982). 93–129.

——— "Das Gefäss *kuihku.*" *ZÄS* 34 (1896) 165–166.

——— and Grapow, Hermann. *Wörterbuch der Ägyptischen Sprache.* Berlin. 1971.

Estañol, Maria and José Fuentes. *Vocabulario Fenicio.* Biblioteca Fenicia vol.1. Barcelona: 1980.

Faulkner, R. O. *A Concise Dictionary of Middle Egyptian.* Oxford 1986

Ferron, J. "La inscripcion cartaginesa en el Arpocrates madrileño." *Trabajos de Prehistoria,* N.S. 28 (1971).

Fevrier, J. "Inscriptions Puniques et Néopuniques." in *Inscriptions Antiques du Maroc.* Paris. 1988.

Fitzmyer, Joseph A. *The Aramaic Inscriptions of Sefire.* Rome: 1967.

Foraboshi, D. *Onomasticon alterum papyrologicum, Supplemento al Namenbuch di F. Preisigke.* Milano: 1967.

Fraser, P. M. "Bibliography: Graeco-Roman Egypt Greek Inscriptions (1952–3)" *JEA* 40 (1954) 124–141.

Friedrich, Johannes. "Kleinigkeiten zum Phönizischen, Punischen und Numidischen." *ZDMG* 114 (1964) 225–231.

——— and Röllig, Wolfgang. *Phönizisch-Punische Grammatik*[2]. Analecte Orientelis vol. 44. Rome: 1970.

Gerbini, G. *Il Semitica di nord-ovest.* Napoli: 1960.

Gardiner, Alan H. "The Delta residence of the Ramessides." *JEA* 5 (1920) 127–138, 179–200, 242–271.

——— "The Geography of the Exodus." in *Recuil d'Études Egyptologiques, dédiées à la Memoire de Jean-François Champollion*, pp. 203–215. Paris: 1922.

——— "The Egyptian Origin of some English Personal names." *JAOS* 56 (1936) 189–197.

——— *Ancient Egyptian Onomastica.* 2 vols. Oxford: 1947.

——— *Egyptian Grammar3* London: 1973.

Gauthier, M. Henri. *Le Livre des Rois d'Égypte.* 5 vols. Caire: 1907–1917.

——— *Dictionaire des Nomes Géographiques contenus dans les Textes Hiéroglyphiques.* Caire: 1925.

Gelb, I. J., Purves. P. M. and McRae, A. A. *Nuzi Personal Names.* Chicago: 1943.

Ginsberg, H. L. "The Brooklyn Museum Aramaic Pepyri." *JAOS* 74 (1954) 153–162.

Glanville, S. R. K. "Records of a Royal Dockyard of the Time of Tuthmosis III: Papyrus British Museum 10056." *ZÄS* 68 (1932) 7–41.

Glédat, J. "Notes sur l'isthme de Suez." *BIFAO* 23 (1924) 27–84.

Goetze, A. "Accent and Vocalism in Hebrew." *JAOS* 59 (1939) 431–459.

Gordon, Cyrus H. *Ugarit Textbook.* 3 vols. Rome: 1965.

Görg, M. "Anmerkungen zu EA 368." *UF* 7 (1975) 356–357.

Grelot, Pierre. "Sur 1a Stèle de Cerpentras." *Semitica* 17 (1967) 73–75.

Grdseloff, Bernhard. "Édôm d'après les Sources Égyptiennes." *Revue de l'Histoire Juive en Égypte* 1 (1947) 69–99.

Greenberg, J. "The Patterning of root morphemes in Semitic." *Word* 6 (1950) 162–181.

Grelot, P. *Docunents araméens d'Égypte.* Paris: 1972.

Griffith, F. Ll. "Herodotus II, 90. Apotheosis by drowning." *ZÄS* 46 (1909) 132–134.

——— "On the Early Use of Cotton in the Nile Valley." *JEA* 20 (1934) 5–12.

Griffiths, J. Gwyn. "Is Chalbes a Greek Names?." *ASAE* 51 (1951) 219–220.

Griffiths, J. W. "The Egyptian Derivation of the Name Moses." *JNES*

12 (1953) 225–231.
Gröndahl, F. *Die Personennamen der Texte aus Ugarit.* Rome: 1967.
Gunn, Bettiscombe. "A Note on Brit. Mus. 828 (Stela of Smontu)." *JEA* 25 (1939) 218–219.
Halff, Giselle. "L'Onomastique Punique de Carthage." *Karthago* 12 (1963–64) 63–145.
Hammond, Philip C. "An Ammonite Stamp Seal from 'Amman." *BASOR* 160 (1960) 38–41.
Harding, Lankester. *An Index and Concordance of the Pre-Islamic Arabian Names and Inscriptions.* Toronto: 1971.
Harris, Zellig S. *A Grammar of the Phoenician Language.* New Haven: 1936.
——— *Development of the Canaanite Dialects: An Investigation in Hinguistic History.* New Haven: 1939.
Harris, J. R. *Lexicographical Studies in Ancient Egyptian Minerals.* Deutsche Akademie der Wissenschaften zu Berlin Institut für Orientforschung, no. 54. Berlin: 1961.
Healey, J. P. "The Kition Tariffs and the Phoenician Cursive Series." *BASOR* 216 (1974) 53–60.
Helck, Wolfgang, "Die ägyptische Verwaltung in den syrischen Besitzungen." *MDOG* 92 (1960) 1–3.
——— *Beziehungen Ägyptens zu Vorderasien im 3. und 2. Jahrtausend vor Christus.* Wiesbaden, 1962.
——— "*Ṯkw* und die Ramses-stadt." *VT* (1965) 35–48.
Herdner, A. "Nouveaux Textes Alphabetiques de Ras Shamra-XXIVe Campagne, 1961." *Ugaritica II*, Mission de Ras Shamra vol.18. Paris: 1978.
Herr, Larry G. *The Scripts of Ancient Northwest Semitic Seals.* Missoula, Montana: 1978.
Heuser, Gustav. *Die Personennamen der Kopten.* Leipzig: 1929.
Hill, George Francis. *Catalogue of the Greek Coins of Cyprus*, A Catalogue of the Greek Coins in the British Museum, ed. by Arnaldo Forni. Bologna: 1964.
Honeymenn, A. M. "Inscriptions from Cyprus." *JRAS* (1960) 111–114.
Huffmon, Herbert Bardwell. *Amorite Personal Names in the Mari Texts: A Structural and Lexical Study.* Baltimore: 1965.
Hurvitz, Avi. "The Usage of שׁשׁ and בוץ in the Bible and its Implication for the Date of P." *HTR* 60 (1967) 117–121.

Israelit-Groll, Sarah. *Pharaonic Egypt: The Bible and Christianity.* Jerusalem: 1985.

Jackson, Kent P. *The Ammonite Language of the Iron Age*, Harvard Semitic monographs 27. Chicago: 1983.

——— "Ammonite Personal Names in the Context of the West Semitic Onomasticon." in *The Word of the Lord Shall Go Forth: Essays in Honor of David Noel Freedman in Celebration of his Sixtieth Birthday*, pp. 507–521. Edited by C. Meyers, M. P. O'Connor, N. C. Durham. Winona Lake: 1983.

James, T. G. H. *The Ḥeḳanakhte Papers and other early Middle Kingdom Documents.* New York: 1962.

Jean, Cherles-F. and Hoftijzer, Jacob. *Dictionnaire des Inscriptions Sémitiques de l'ouest.* Leiden: 1960–65.

Johns, C. H. W. *Assyrian Deeds and Documents.* 3 vols. Cambridge: 1898–1901.

Jones, Dilwyn. *A Glossary of Ancient Egyptian Nautical Titles and Terms.* London: 1988.

Jouön, P. Paul. "Notes grammeticales, lexicographiques et philologiques sur les papyrus araméens d'Egypte" in *Melanges de l'Université Saint-Joseph*, Beyrouth, XVIII.

Kahle, Paul E. *The Cairo Geniza.* London: 1949.

Kaufman, Stephen A. *The Akkadian Influences on Aramaic*, Assyriological Studies, no. 19. Chicago: 1974.

Keimer, Ludwig. "Flechtwerk aus Halfagras im alten und neuen Ägypten." *OLZ* 30 (1927) 145–154.

Kitchen, Kenneth A. Review of *Joseph en Égypte*, by J. Vergote. *JEA* 47 (1961) 158–164.

——— *Ramesside Inscriptions: Historical and Biographical.* Oxford: 1975ff.

——— Review of *A Study of the Biblical Story of Joseph (Genesis 37–50)*, by D. B. Redford. *Oriens Antiquus* 12 (1973) 233–242.

——— *The Third Intermediate Period in Egypt (1100–650 BC)*[2]. Werminster: 1986.

——— "Lotuses and Lotuses, or --- Poor Susan's older than we thought." *VA* 3 (1987) 29–31.

——— "Egypt and Israel during the first Millennium BC." *VTS* 40 (1988) 107–123.

——— "Raamses, Succoth and Pitom." (forthcoming).

Knudsen, E. E. "Spirantization of Velars in Akkadian." in *Lišān mitḫurti*, pp. 147–155. Edited by M. Dietrich.

Knudtzon, J. A. *Die El-Amarna-Tafeln.* 2 vols. Leipzig: 1915.

Koehler, Ludwig and Baumgartner, Walter. *Hebräisches und Aramäisches Lexikon zum Alten Testament.* Leiden: 1967.

——— *Lexicon in Veteris Testamenti Libros.* Leiden: 1953.

Kornfeld, Walter. "Aramäische Sarkophage in Assuan." *WZKM* 61 (1967) 9–16.

——— "Jüdisch-aramäische Grabinschriften aus Edfu." *AÖAW* 110 (1973) 123–137.

——— "Neues über die phönikischen aramäischen Graffiti in den Tempeln Abydos." *AÖAW* 115 (1978) 193–204.

——— *Onomastica Aramaica Aus Ägypten.* Wien: 1978.

Kreeling, E. G. *The Brooklyn Museum Aramaic Papyri: New Documents of the Fifth Century B.C. from the Jewish Colony at Elephantine.* New Haven: 1953.

Kuhlmann, Klaus P. *Der Thron im Alten Ägypten.* Glückstadt: 1977.

Kutscher, E. Y. "New Aramaic Texts." *JAOS* 74 (1954): 233–248.

——— "Contemporary Studies in North-Western Semitic." *JSS* 10 (1965) 21–51.

——— "Yemenite Hebrew and Ancient Pronunciation." *JSS* 11 (1966) 217–225.

——— "Aramaic." *Current Trends in Linguistics* 6 (1970) 347–412.

Laceu, Pierre. "Sur la Chute du final, Marque de feminin." *RdE* 9 (1952) 82–90.

Lambdin, Thomas O. "Egyptian Loanwords and Transcriptions in the Ancient Semitic Languages." Ph.D. dissertation, Johns Hopkins University, Baltimore: 1952.

——— "Egyptian Loanwords in the Old Testament." *JAOS* 73 (1952) 145–155.

——— "The *Miši*-people of the Byblian Amarna Letters." *JCS* 7 (1953) 75–77.

——— "Egyptian Words in Tell-El Amarna Letter No. 14." *Or* NS 22 (1953) 362–369.

Landes, G. M. "The Material Civilization of the Ammonites." *BA* 24 (1961) 66–86.

Lendsberger, B. "Akkadisch-hebräische Wortgleichungen." *VTS* 16 (1967) 176–204.

Leroche, Emmanuel. *Les Noms des Hittites*. Paris: 1966.

Leahy, A. "«ḤARWA» and «ḤARBES»." *Cd'E* 55 (1980) 43–63.

Leander, P. *Laut- und Formenlehre des Ägyptisch-aramäischen*. Göteborg: 1928.

Ledrein, E. "Quelques Inscriptions Inédites Entrées au Musée du Louvre." *Revue d'Assy* 2 (1888–92) 93.

Lemaire, A. *Inscriptions Hebräiques*. Tome I: *Les Ostraca*. Paris: 1977.

——— "Notes d'Épigraphie Nord-Ouest Sémitique." *Semitica* 30(1980) 2–32.

Levy, M. A. *Siegel und Gemmen mit aramäischen, phönizischen, althebräischen, himjarischen, nabathäischen und altsyrischen Inschriften*. Breslau: 1869.

Lidzbarski, Mark. *Ephemeris für Semitische Epigraphik*. 3 vols. Giessen, 1900–1915.

——— *Phönizische und aramäische Krugaufschriften aus Elephantine*. Anhang zu den Abhandlungen der Königlich preussischen Akademie der Wissenschaften, philosophisch-historische Klasse. Berlin: 1912.

——— "Zu den phönizischen Inschriften von Byblos." *OLZ* 30 (1927) 453–458.

——— *Handbuch der nordsemitischen Epigraphik, nebst ausgewählten Inschriften*. Hildesheim: 1962.

Lipinski, Édouard. Review of *Documents araméens d'Éypte*, by P. Grelot. *Bibl. Or*. 31 (1974) 119–124.

——— Review of *Personal Names in the Phoenician and Punic Inscriptions*, by F. L. Benz. *Bibl. Or* 32 (1975) 77–81.

——— "*p3-(n)-ḤR*, Fils de Raučāka" *OLP* 6/7 (1975.76) 381–388.

——— "Emprunts suméro-akkadiens enhébreu biblique." *ZAH* 1 (1988) 61–73.

Loret, Victor. "Le Champ des Souchets." *Rec. de Trev*. 13 (1890) 197–201.

Lüddeckens, Erich. *Demotisches Namenbuch*. Wiesbaden: 1980ff.

Magnanini, Pietro. *Le Iscrizioni Fenicie dell'Oriente Testi, Traduzioni, Glossari*. Rome: 1973.

Melion, Alexis. *Grammaire copte*[4]. Beyrouth: 1956.

Maraqten, Mohammed. "Neue aramäische Ostraka aus Elephantine." *MDIK* 43 (1987) 170–172.

Massart, Adhémar, *The Leiden Magical Papyrus I 343 + I 345*. Leiden: 1954.

Masson, Olivier, "Recherches sur les Phéniciens dens le Monde Hellénistique." *BCH* 93 (1969) 679–700

Mayrhofer, Manfred. *Onomastica Persepolitana: Das altiranische Namengut der Persepolis-Täfelchen*. Wien: 1973.

Mettinger, Tryggve N.D. *Solomonic State Officials: A Study of the Civil Government Officials of the Israelite Monarchy*. Lund: 1971.

Milik, J. T. "Deux Documents inédits du Désert de Jude." *Biblica* 38 (1957) 245–268.

Millard, Alan R. "Assyrien Royal Names in Biblical Hebrew." *JSS* 21 (1976) 1–15.

——— "The Etymology of NB̲RAŠTAʾ" *MAARAV* 4 (1987) 87–92.

——— "Ebla Personal Names and Personal Names of the first Millennium B.C. in Syria and Palestine." *ARES* 1 (1988) 159–1644.

Montet, Pierre. *Géographie de l'Éypte Ancienne*. 2 vols. Paris: 1961.

Moran, William L. *Les Lettres d'El -Amarna*. Paris. 1989.

Muchiki, Yoshiyuki. "The unidentified god *PMY* in Phoenician texts." *JSS* 36 (1991) 7–10.

——— "On the transliterarion of the name Osiris." *JEA* 76 (1990) 191–194.

——— "Spirantization in fifth-century B. C. North-West Semitic." *JNES* 53 (1994) 125–130.

Müller, Max W. "Zwei ägyptische Wörter im Hebräischen." *OLZ* 3 (1900) 49–51.

Naveh, Joseph. *The Development of the Aramaic Script*. Jerusalem: 1970

——— "The Palaeography of the Hermopolis Papyri." in *Israel Oriental Studies*, pp. 120–122. Edited by Tel Aviv University, Department of Arabic. Tel Aviv: 1971.

——— Review of *Aramaic Texts from North Saqqara*, by J. B. Segal. *IEJ* 35 (1985) 210–212.

——— and Shaked, Shaul. "A Recently Published Aramaic Papyrus." *JAOS* 91 (1971) 379–382.

Naville, E. *The Store City of Pithom and the Route of the Exodus*, EES

Noth, Martin. *Die israelitischen Personennamen im Rahmen der gemeinsemitischen Namengebung*. Hildesheim: 1966.

Nougayrol, *Jean. Le Palais royal d'Ugarit, III:* Textes accadiens et hourrites des Archives Est, Ouest et Centrales. 2 vols. Mission de Ras Shamre, vol. VI. Paris: 1955.

——— *Le Palais royal d'Ugarit, IV: Textes accadiens des Archives Sud*. 2 vols. Mission de Ras Shemra, vol. IX.

Oppenheim, A. L., et. at., eds. *The Assyrian Dictionary of the Oriental Institute of the University of Chicago*. Chicago: 1964ff.

Osing, Jürgen. "Leutsystem." *LÄ* III pp. 944–949.

Parpola, Simo. *Neo-Assyrian Toponyms*, *AOAT* 6. Kevelaer: 1970.

Peckam, J. Brian. *The Development of the Late Phoenician Scripts*, Harvard Semitic Series, vol.20. Cambridge: 1968.

Peet, T. Eric. *Egypt and the Old Testament*. Liverpool: 1922.

——— "Additional Note." *JEA* 11 (1925) 239–240.

Petrie, W. M. Flinders. *Hyksos and Israelite Cities*. London: 1906.

Porten, Bezalel and Greenfield, Jonas C. *Jews of Elephantine and Arameans of Syene (Fifth Century B.C.E.): Fifty Aramaic Texts with Hebrew and English Translations*. Jerusalem: 1974.

——— "Une lettre Areméenne Conservée à l'Académie des inscriptions et Belles-lettres (AI 5-7): Un nouvelle reconstruction." *Semitica* 33 (1983) 89–100.

——— "Aramaic Papyrus Fragments in the Egyptian Museum of West Berlin." *Or* NS 57 (1988) 14–54.

——— and Yardeni, Ada. *Textbook of Aramaic Documents from Ancient Egypt: Newly Copied, Edited and Translated into Hebrew and English*: vol. 1: Letters. Jerusalem: 1986.

——— and Yardeni, Ada. *Textbook of Aramaic Documents from Ancient Egypt: Newly Copied, Edited and Translated into Hebrew and English*: vol. 2: Contracts. Jerusalem: 1989.

——— and Yardeni, Ada. *Textbook of Aramaic Documents from Ancient Egypt: Newly Copied, Edited and Translated into Hebrew and English*: vol.3: Literature·Accounts·Lists. Jerusalem: 1993.

Posener, G. *Princes et Pays d'Asie et de Nubie*. Bruxelles: 1940.

Postgate, J. N. *Fifty Neo-Assyrian Legal Cocuments*. Warminster: 1976.

Preisigke, F. *Namenbuch enthaltend alle griechischen* --

Menschennamen--. Heidelberg: 1922.
Quaegebeur, Jan. "On the Egyptian Equivalent of Biblical *ḤRṬUMMÎM*." in *Pharaonic Egypt*, pp. 162–172. Edited by Sarah Israelit-Groll. Jerusalem: 1985.
——— "La Designation *(p3-) ḤRY-TP: PHRITOB*." *SAK* 12 (1987) 368–394.
Rabin, C. "Hittite Words in Hebrew." *Or* NS 32 (1963) 113–139.
Rebinowitz, Isaac. "Aramaic Inscriptions of the Fifth Century B.C.E. from a North-Arab Shrine in Egypt." *JNES* 15 (1956) 1–9.
——— "Another Aramaic Record of the North-Arabian Gooddess Han-'Ilat." *JNES* 18 (1959) 154–155.
Rainey, Anson F. *El Amarna Tablets 359–379: Supplement to J. A. Knudtzon, Die El-Amarna Tafeln, AOAT* vol. 8. Kevelaer: 1970/8.
——— ed., Egypt, *Israel, Sinai: Archaeological and Historical Relationships in the Biblical Period.* Jerusalem: 1987.
Ranke, Hermann. *Keilschriftlisches Material zur altägyptischen Vokalisation.* Berlin: 1910.
——— *Die ägyptischen Personennamen.* 3 vols. Glückstadt: 1935–76.
Redford, Donald B. "Exodus I 11." *VT* 13 (1963) 401–418.
——— *A Study of the Biblical Story of Joseph: Gen 37–50, VTS* vol. 20. Leiden: 1970.
Reisner, George Andrew, Fisher, C. Stanley and Gordon, Lyon D. . *Harvard Excavations at Samaria 1908–1910*, Harvard Semitic Series vol.1. Cambridge: 1924.
Röllig, Wolfgang. "Beiträge zur nordsemitischen Epigraphik (1–4)." *Die Welt des Orients* 5 (1969–70) 108–126.
——— "Paläographische Beobachtungen zum ersten Auftreten der Phönizier in Sardinien." in *Antidoron Jürgen Thimme*, pp. 125–130. Karlsruhe: 1982.
Sachau, Eduard. *Aramäische Papyrus und Ostraka aus einer Jüdischen Militär-Kolonie zu Elephantine.* Leipzig: 1911.
Sayce, H. A. "Gleanings from the land of Egypt § 4." *Rec. de Trav.* 17(1895) 164.
——— "Aramaic Inscriptions from Egypt." *PSBA* 26 (1904) 207–208.
——— "Karian, Aramaic and Greek Graffiti von Heshân." *PSBA* 30

(1908) 28.
——— "An Aramaic Ostracon from Elephantine." *PSBA* 33 (1911) 183–184.
Scheder, Hans Heinrich. *Iranische Beiträge I*. Halle: 1930.
Schiller, A. *Ten Coptic Legal Texts*. New York: 1932.
Schulman, Alan A. "Some Remarks on the Military Background of the Amarna Period." *JARCE* 3 (1964) 51–69.
——— "On the Egyptian Name of Joseph: A New Approach." *SAK* 2 (1975) 235–243.
Segal, J. B. *Aramaic Texts from North Saqqâra with some Fragments in Phoenician*. London: 1983.
Segert, Stanislav. *Altaramäische Grammatik mit Bibliographie, Chrestomathie und Glossar*. Leipzig: 1975.
Sethe, K. "Der Name des Gottes Suchos." ZÄS 50 (1912) 80–83.
——— "Die Vokalisation des Ägyptischen." *ZDMG* 77 (1923) 145–207.
——— "Zur ägyptischen Herkunft des hebräischen Maßes Epha." *ZÄS* 62 (1927) 61.
Spalinger, A. J. "A Canaanite Ritual Found in Egyptian Reliefs." *SSEA* 8 (1978) 47–60.
Speiser, E. A. "Progress in the Study of the Hurrian Language." *BASOR* 74 (1939) 4–7.
Spiegelberg, W. "Die Gruppe  *'3ẖ(Y)*" *Rec. de Trav.* 24 (1902)180–182.
——— "אברך" *OLZ* 15 (1903)317–321.
——— "Die Tefnachthosstele des Museums von Athen." *Rec. de Trav* 25 (1903) 190–198.
——— *Aegyptologische Randglossen zum Alten Testament.* Straßburg: 1904.
——— "Aegyptisches Sprachgut in den aus Aegypten stammenden aramaeischen Urkunden Perserzeit." in *Orientalische Studien Theodore Noeldeke zum 70. Geburtstag*, pp. 1093–1115. Edited by C. Bezold. Giessen: 1906.
——— " נפתחים (Gen x. 13)." *OLZ* 9 (1906) 276–279.
——— "Ägyptische Lehnwörter in der ältesten griechischen Sprache." *ZVS* 41 (1907) 127–132.
——— "Der ägyptische Name von Pelusium." *ZÄS* 49 (1911) 81–84.
——— "Die ägyptischen Personennamen in den kürzlich

veröffentlichten Urkunden von Elephantine." *OLZ* 15 (1912) 1–10.
——— "Zu den aegyptischen Personennamen der Urkunden von Elephantine." *OLZ* 16 (1913) 346–347.
——— *Koptisches Handwörterbuch*. Heidelberg: 1921.
Stamm, J. J. *Akkadische Namengebung*. Leipzig: 1939.
Stark, J. Kurk. *Personal Names in Palmyrene Inscriptions*. Oxford: 1971.
Stricker, B. H. "Trois études de phonetique et de morphologie coptique." *AO* 15 (1937) 1–20.
Sznycer, Maurice. *Les Passages Puniques en Transcription Latine dans le «Poenulus» de Plaute*. Paris: 1967.
——— "Trois Fragments de Papyri Araméens d'Egypte d'Époque Perse." in *Hommages a André Dupont-Sommer*, pp.161–176. Paris: 1971.
Tallqvist, Kunt L. *Assyrian Personal Names,* Acta societatis scientiarum fennicae, vol. 48 part 1. Helsingfors: 1918.
Teixidor, Javier. "Un Nouveau Papyrus Araméen du Règne de Darius II." *Syria* 41 (1964) 285–290.
——— Bulletin d'Épigraphie Sémitique (1964–1980). Paris: 1986.
Thacker, T. W. "A note on עָרוֹת (Is. xix:7)." *JTS* 34 (1933) 163–165.
Tigay, Jeffrey H. *You Shall have no other gods: Israelite Religion in the Light of Hebrew Inscription*. Altanta, Georgia: 1986.
Tomback, Richard S. *A Comparative Semitic Lexicon of the Phoenician and Punic Languages*, SBL Dissertation Series 32. Missoula, Montana: 1978.
Torrey, Charles C. *Aramaic Graffiti on Coins of the Demanhur Hoard*, Numismatic Notes and Monographs no. 77. New York: 1937.
Tsevat, Matitiahu. "The Canaanite God ŠÄLAḤ." *VT* 4 (1954) 42–49.
Uberti, M. L. "Scarabeo punic del Museo Archeologic Nazionale di Cagliari." *Atti del I° Convegno italiano sul Vicino Oriente Antico*, Or, Coll. XIII, pp. 157–162. Rome: 1978.
Ungnad, Arthur. "Joseph, der Tartan des Pharao." *ZAW* 41 (1923) 204–207.
Ussishkin, David. "Excavations at Tel Lachish 1973–1977." *Tel Aviv* 5 (1978) 1–97.
Vattioni, F. "I sigilli ebraici." *Biblica* 50 (1969) 357–388.
——— "I sigilli ebraici II." *Augustinianum* 11 (1971) 447–454.

——— "I sigilli ebraici III." *AION* 38 (1978) 227–253.

——— "I sigilli fenici." *AION* 41 (1981) 177–193.

Vergote, J. *Phonétique Historique de l'Égyptien: les Consonnes*, Bibliotheque du Muséon vol. 19. Louvain: 1945.

——— *Joseph en Égypte: Génèse Chap. 37-50 à la Lumière des Études Egyptologiques Récentes*. Louvain: 1959.

——— "La chancellerie Royale d'Akhetaton et la tablette Ashm. Mus., Tell el Amarna 1921, 1154" in *Zetesis Festschrift E. de Strijocer*, pp. 580–584. Antwerp-Utrecht. 1973.

——— " Egyptological Studies." *Scripta Hierosolymitana* 27 (1982) 105–116.

Vittmann, G. "Zu den ägyptischen Entsprechungen aramäisch überlieferter Personennamen." *Or* NS 58 (1989) 213 229.

——— "Zu den in den phönikischen Inschriften enthaltenen ägyptischen Personennamen." *GM* 113 (1989) 91–96.

——— "Zu einigen keilschriftlichen Umschreibungen ägyptischer Personennamen." *GM* 70 (1984) 65–66.

Vonel, Sidon A. "Six ostraca phéniciens trouvés au temple d'Echmoun près de Saide." *BMB* 20 (1965) 45–95.

von Soden, W. *Akkadisches Handwörterbuch*. Wiesbaden: 1965ff.

——— *Grundriss der Akkadischen Grammatik*, Analecta Orientalia 33/47. Roma: 1969.

Vycichl, Werner. "Ägyptische Ortsnamen in der Bibel." *ZÄS* 76 (1940) 79–93.

——— "Ägyptisch-semitische Anklänge." *ZÄS* 84 (1959) 145–147.

——— *Dictionnaire étymologique de la langue Copte*. Leuven: 1983.

Ward, William A. "Notes on Egyptian Group Writing." *JNES* 16 (1957) 198–203.

——— "Comparative Studies in Egyptian and Ugaritc." *JNES* 20 (1961) 31–40.

——— "Notes on Some Semitic Loan-Words and Personal Names in Late Egyptian." *Or* NS 32 (1963) 412–436.

——— "The Semitic biconsonantal root *SP* and the common origin of Egyptian *čwf* and Hebrew *sûp*: "marsh(-plant)." *VT* 24 (1974) 339–349.

Weidner, Ernst F. "Jojachim, König von Juda, in Babylonischen Keilschrifttexten." in *Melanges Syriens offerts à R. Dussaud*.

Raymond, Weill. "Un Document Araméen de la Moyenne-Egypte."

REJ 65 (1913) 16–23.

Weippert, Manfred. *The Settlement of the Israelite Tribes in Palestine: A Critical Survey of Recent Scholarly Debate.* Translated by James D. Martin. London: 1971.

Wiseman, D. J. "Some Egyptians in Babylonia." *Iraq* 28 (1958) 154–158.

Wolf, Walther. "Neue Beiträge zum 'Tagebuch eines Grenzbeamten.'" *ZÄS* 69 (1933) 39–45.

Worrel, William H. *Coptic Sounds.* AnnArbor: 1934.

Yahuda, A. S. *The Language of the Pentateuch in its Relation to Egyptian.* London: 1933.

Yaron, Reuven. "The Schema of the Aramaic Legal Documents" *JSS* 2 (1957) 33–61.

Yadin, Yigael. *Hazor: with a Chapter on Israelite Megido.* London: 1972.

Yoyotte, Jean. "Des Lions et des Chats contribution à la Prosopographie de l'Epoque Libyenne." *RdE* 39 (1988) 155–178.

Zadok, Ran. "On Some Egyptians in First-Millennium Mesopotamia." *GM* 26 (1977) 63–68.

——— *The Jews in Babylonia during the Chaldean and Achaemenian Periods according to the Babylonian Sources.* Haifa: 1979.

——— "On Some Egyptians in Babylonian Documents." *GM* 64 (1983) 73–75.

——— *Geographical Names According to New- and Late-Babylonian Texts,* Répertoire Géographique des Textes Cuneiformes VIII. Wiesbaden: 1985.

Zauzich, Karl Th. "Ägyptologische Bemerkungen zu den neuen aramäischen Papyri aus Saqqara." *Enchoria* 13 (1985) 115–118.

INDEXES

[A] Egyptians PNs

3ḫ-pp.y 64
3s-ỉr.w 208
3s.t-ỉỉr-dỉ-s.t 67
3s.t-ʿ3.t 15
3s.t-wr.t 67, 68
3s.t-m-p 68
3s.t-ršw.ty 71
3s.t-t3-ʿ3.t 16, 68
ỉỉ-m-ḥtp 25, 66, 88
ỉʿḥ 64
ỉʿḥ-ỉỉr-dỉ-sw 65
ỉʿḥ-mn 14, 64
ỉʿḥ-ms 14, 64
ỉw.f-ʿ3 89
**ỉw.f-r.ỉ* 72
ỉw.f-rr 72
ỉwỉ 207
ỉbỉ 14
ỉpỉ 72
ỉpy 291
ỉpw 72
ỉpn 16
**ỉp.t-m-ḥ3.t* 291
ỉp.t-t3-šd.t 63
ỉpt.y 25
ỉmy.t-ḥpy 15
ỉmn 66
ỉmn-ỉr-dỉ-sw 66
ỉmn-m-ỉp.t 290
ỉmn-nḫw 15
ỉmn-ms 276, 290
ỉmn-ḥtp.w 290
ỉr.t-n.t-ḥr-ỉr.w 89
**ỉrt-ḥʿỉ* 212
**ỉḥ.t-w3ḏ.t* 87
ỉḥ3 63
ỉḥ3-pp.y 64
ỉky 66
ỉkn.ỉ 63
ỉkš 26, 66, 91
ỉtm 17
ỉtf 17
ỉdỉ 65
ʿ3-ptḥ 33
ʿ3-ḥr 16, 31
ʿn-m-š 220
ʿn-mw.t 219
ʿnḫ-p3-ms 32f.
**ʿnḫ-p3-n-m3ʿ.t* 102
**ʿnḫ-p3-rmṯ-n-ny.t* 103
ʿnḫ-mr-wr 101
ʿnḫ-ḥp 102
ʿnḫ.f-n-m3ʿ.t 102
ʿḥ3 63

ꜥš 103
**ꜥš3-ḥrw* 103
**w3ḥ-ib* 75
w3ḥ-ib-rꜥ 20, 76, 211
w3ḥ-ib-rꜥ-m-3ḫ.t 76
**w3ḥ-ib-rꜥ-nḫt* 76
**w3ḥ-t3-n-rw* 76
w3s3rkni 218
wi3 20
wnn-nfr.w 76
wrš-nfr 77
wḏ3-ḥr 77
b3b3 17
b3k-n-rn.f 73
b3k.i 18
bi.ty.t 210
**bik.n* 73
bb.i 17
bb.iw 17
bl 18
br 18, 73
**bḫ* 73
bs.y 74, 210
bš3w 19, 74
p3-iwn.y 104
p3-ꜥ3 221
p3-ꜥ3-ṯb 129
**p3-ꜥn-n.i* 129
p3-ꜥr 38
p3-wi3-mni.w 106
p3-wnw 106
p3-wnš 106
p3-wr 295
p3-by 104
p3-m3i 33, 36
p3-miw 123
p3-ms 124
p3-msḥ 124
**p3-md.w* 123, 125
p3-n-3s.t 127
p3-n-3s-ir 38, 129
p3-n-iꜥḥ 104, 278
p3-n-iwn.y 104
p3-n-iwny 104
p3-n-iwnw 104
p3-n-ip.t 294
p3-n-imn 123
p3-n-inpw 37
**p3-n-ir.t-rši.ti* 121
p3-n-itm 134, 279
p3-n-wi3 20
p3-n-wn 278
p3-n-wnw 106
p3-n-wsr 107
p3-n-wsḫ.t 33
p3-n-b3.w 104
p3-n-bnr 105
p3-n-py 104
p3-n-pnw 39, 130, 279
**p3-n-mw.t* 37, 125
p3-n-mn 123, 279
p3-n-mn.w 124, 279
p3-n-mḥy.t 295
p3-n-msḥ 124
p3-n-niw.t 125, 278
p3-n-rꜥ 223
p3-n-rw 131
p3-n-rwḏ 131
p3-n-rḫ.t 279
p3-n-niw.t 121, 125, 278
**p3-n-nfr-tm* 126
p3-n-niw.t 121, 278
p3-n-ḥ3.t 108
p3-n-ḥw.t 108
p3-n-ḥp 111
p3-n-ḥr 107, 221

p3-n-ḥr 108
p3-n-ẖnm.w 110
p3-n-s3w 126
**p3-n-k3* 121
**p3-n-k3-nṯr* 131
p3-n-k3-ʿs.t 122
**p3-n-k3-n-mw.t* 222
p3-n-km.t 122
p3-n-t3 40, 133, 134
**p3-n-t3-ipw* 138
**p3-n-t3-ʿnḫ.i* 138
**p3-n-t3-šd.t* 139
p3-n-t3.wy 134
p3-n-t3w 137
p3-n-t3.wy-p3-n-ʿ3-str.t 134
p3-n-t3-wsḫ.t 33
p3-n-t3-m3ʿ.t 137
**p3-n-t3-mrw.t* 137
p3-n-t3-n.t-iḥw.t 41
**p3-n-ṯni-wḏ3.w* 137
p3-nfr 37
p3-nfr-ii 37
p3-nḥsy 87, 222
p3-nsy 125
**p3-rwḏ* 122
p3-ḥm-nṯr 294
**p3-ḥr-ḳ3y-ḏ3ḏ3* 110
p3-ḥry 111
p3-ḫy 108
**p3-ḫy-r-ḳ3y-ḏ3ḏ3* 110
p3-ẖm 109
p3-ẖr 109, 295
p3-sn 120
**p3-sr* 126
p3-sr 295
**p3-sṯ3w-ḳns* 129
p3-šri 40
p3-šri-n-p3-wr 132
p3-šri-n-p3-m3i 133
p3-šri-n-ptḥ 133
p3-šri-n-mḥy.t 39
**p3-šri-n-t3-sp.t* 133
**p3-šd-w3ḏy.t* 133
p3-ḳd-nṯr 130
p3-k3p.w 121
p3-k3my 122
p3-kmy 121
**p3-gry-m-p.t* 105
**p3-t3.wy-p3-ʿ3-sty* 134
p3-twt 139
p3-tri 138
**p3-ṯ3w* 137
**p3-ṯ3w-rwḏ.w* 137
**p3-ṯni-k3* 138
p3-di 114, 222
p3-di-3s-ir 113
p3-di-3s.t 34, 112
p3-di-iʿḥ 112
p3-di-imn 116
**p3-di-ihy* 115
p3-di-itm 119
**p3-di-b3-nb-ḏdw.t* *35*
p3-di-b3st.t 113
**p3-di-p3-iry* 221
p3-di-p3-rʿ 221
p3-di-ptḥ 119
p3-di-m3i-ḥs3 115
p3-di-mw.t 116
p3-di-mn 116
p3-di-mḥ.t 115
p3-di-n.i 117
p3-di-ni-3s.t 117
p3-di-nfr-ḥtp 117
p3-di-nṯr 117
p3-di-nṯr.w 118
p3-di-ḥr 115

p3-di-ḥr-p3-ẖrd 114
p3-di-ẖnm.w 113
p3-di-ḫns.w 35
p3-di-sbk 118
p3-di-t3-wr.t 120
**p3-di-t3-wsr.t* 119
p3.f-ṯ3w-m-ʿ.wy-n-ny.t 130
p3y.w-m3i 33
**p3y.w-ḥry-ib* 105
pi3 120
pi3y 295
pp 223
pp.i 130
ppy 38, 130
psmṯk 127, 128, 222
psmṯk-m-3ḫ.t 129
psmṯk-mry 128
psmṯk-ḥsy 128
psmṯk-s3-n.t 127
**psmṯk-s3-n-s-ny.t* 37
psš-imn 132
**psš-b3st.t* 132
**psš-ḥr* 223
ptḥ 40, 40
ptḥ-ir-di-sw 114
ptḥ-wr 136
ptḥ-m-wi3 135
ptḥ-my 296
ptḥ-nfr 136
ptḥ-msw 296
ptḥ-ḫns.w 135
ptḥ-ḳ3i 136
ptḥ.y 40
m3i 27
my 292
mm 92
mn 277
mn-ḫpr-rʿ 92, 292
mn.i 292
**mnḫ-ny.t* 92
**mnṯ.w-ḥr* 27
**mr-iḥy* 27
mr-ptḥ 93
mr.t-mw.t 215
mry-imn 213
mry-bʿr 215
mry-rʿ 293
mry-ḥmn 94
mry.t 215
mry.t-itn 292
mrr.i 216
mrr.y 216
ms 216
msw.ti 93
**msḥ-nh.t* 93
**mšʿ* 217
n.t 97
**n3-snw* 96
n3.f-ʿ3-rd 97
ny.t-iir-di.t-s.t 95
**nʿr-ms.w* 293
nb-ḫpr.w-rʿ 293
nb-m3ʿ.t-rʿ 277, 294
nb-mḥy.t 294
nb.i-sbk 27
nb.y 217
nbs 94
nfr-3s.t 96
**nfr-n-n.t* 96
**nfr-rpw* 97
nfr-ḫpr.w-rʿ 293
nfr.w 28, 94, 97
nfr.t-ii.ti 97
**nḥm-sw-iʿḥ* 94
nḫt-ḥr.w 95
**ns-p3-ʿ3-mrw.t* 70, 100

ns-p3-mdw 17, 70
ns-p3-šn 71
**ns-p3-di-n.i-sn.t* 70
ns-ptḥ 72
ns-mn.w 69
**ns-mdw-špsy* 69
**ns-ny.t* 208
**ns-nw.t* 208
ns-ḥr.w 67
ns-ẖnm.w 68
ns-ḳ3y-šw.y 69
ns-ḳ3y-šw.ty 69
**ns-tḫ* 72
nk3.w 95, 218
nky 95
r3.3i 292
r3.i3 292
rᶜ-imn 296
rᶜ-m-wi3 142
rᶜ-nfr 296
rᶜ.i3 142
rᶜ.iy 143
rw.y 280
rwḏ 280
rnp.w 141
rnp.t-nfr.t 142
ll 91
hr-ib 19, 75
hr-w3ḏ.t 75
hr.t 19
ḥ.t-ḥr.w 78
ḥ3py 79
ḥᶜpy 291
ḥb.y 21
ḥp 23
ḥp-iw 23
ḥp-iw 81
ḥp-ᶜnḫ w 82
ḥp-mn 81
ḥp.y 81
ḥp.w 81
ḥpt 24
ḥfnr 211
**ḥm-nḫt* 23
ḥm.t 22
**ḥnw.t-ny.t* 80
ḥnt3sw 23
ḥr 21, 24, 82, 276
ḥr-iny 84
ḥr-wn 83
ḥr-wḏ3 24, 82, 83
**hr-w3ḏ.t* 75
ḥr-bik 82
ḥr-p3-bik 86
ḥr-p3-nḥsy 86
**ḥr-p3-šd* 87
ḥr-m-3ḫ-bi.t 83
ḥr-m-3ḫ.t 85
ḥr-m-nb-t3.w 86
**ḥr-m3ᶜ-ḫrw* 85
ḥr-mn.w 85
ḥr-ms.w 25, 291
ḥr-n-t3-bwi3 87
ḥr-nfr 85
**ḥr-nfr.w* 212
**ḥr-ḥs.w* 212
ḥr-ḥtp 84
ḥr-s3-3s.t 86
ḥr-k3p 24
ḥr.y 78, 84, 211
ḥr.w 77, 211
ḥry-ḥr 212
ḥrbs 22
ḥḥ 276
**ḥk3-ir-di-sw* 79
ḥkn.t 79

ḥtp 291
ḫ3y-ḥr 78
ḫ3y-šb 87
ḫns.w 80
**ḫnm.w-ỉw* 80
**ḳn-m3ỉ* 26
k3 89
k3.ỉ-nfr 26, 91
k3.ỉ-nfr-wp 26
k3.ỉ3 90
k3mn 90
kf3 91
km.w.n.ỉ
kš 213
kkỉ 90
glhb 74
gm.w-ḥp 141
grhb 74
**s-n-mṯk* 99
s3-ptḥ 29
s3-nr.t 28
s3-sr 28
s3.t-ʿnḫ 99
s3.t-ptḥ 29
s3.t-n.t 277
sp-n-mw.t 100
sm3-t3.wy 99
sn.w 96
snb 277
**snb-ny.t* 99
sr-3s-ỉr 29
**sḫm-r3.ỉ* 98
sšn 100, 227
skr 28
sgry 98
stỉ 296
**š3ʿ-nfr* 227
**šp-n-ỉtm* 144
**šp-n-ny.t* 144
**šrỉ-n-w3ḏ.t* 144
**šrỉ.t-n-n3-hb.w* 144
šš 226
šš.ỉ 226
ššnḳ 227, 228
t3-w3.t 146
t3-wr.t 147
t3-bỉ 146
t3-ms 151
t3-n.t-3s-ỉr 153
t3-n.t-3s.t 145, 153
**t3-n.t-wỉ3* 146
t3-n.t-wb3 146
**t3-n.t-b3.w* 145
**t3-n.t-p3-n-mw.t* 154
**t3-n.t-p3-n-ḫnm.w* 153
**t3-n.t-p3-ḫy* 153
**t3-n.t-p3-dỉ* 42
t3-n.t-mỉw 150
t3-n.t-mw.t 151
t3-n.t-mn.w 151
**t3-n.t-ny.t* 152
**t3-n.t-nfr* 151
t3-n.t-rw 154
t3-n.t-rwḏ 155
**t3-n.t-ḥ.t-p3-nsw* 228
**t3-n.t-ḥ3.t* 148
t3-n.t-ḥw.t 147, 148
t3-n.t-ḥp 149
t3-n.t-ḫy 148
**t3-n.t-ḫpry* 149
t3-n.t-ḫnm.w 149
t3-n.t-š3 155
**t3-n.t-t3-p.t* 156
**t3-nr.t* 152
t3-r.t 155
t3-rwḏ 155

t3-rḫ.t 154
t3-ḥnw.t 149
t3-ḥr 147
t3-ḫ3w.t 42
t3-ḫ3bs 148
**t3-ẖrd.t* 149
t3-s3w 152
**t3-šri͗.t-n.t-p3-wi͗3* 155
t3-šri͗.t-n.t-p3-nbs 94
t3-di͗.t-3s-i͗r 149
**t3-di͗.t-ḥr-wr.t* 150
t3-di͗.t-ḥr-p3-ẖrd 150
t3-di͗.t-ḥr-n-p 150
ty 297
**twi͗3* 147
twy 297
twt 156
trw 154
thrḳ 146, 229
ṯ3y-i͗m.w 42, 143
ṯ3y-ḥp-i͗m.w 41, 143
ṯ3y-ḫns.w-i͗m.w 41
ṯn 140
ṯn3 140
ṯni͗ 140
di͗.t-sṯi͗t 88
**ḏf3.i͗-nṯr, p3-ʿnḫ* 224
ḏḥwty-m3ʿ.w 148
**ḏd-mḥy.t* 140
ḏd-ḥr 41, 139, 224
**dḏ-ḥr-ẖnmw* 140

[B] Hybrid PNs

[1] with Egyptian gods

<Amon>
אל-*i͗mn* 15
עבד-*i͗mn* 29

<Apis>
בן-*ḥp* 18
יתן-*ḥpy* 25
עבד-*ḥp* 101

<Bastet>
אחת-*b3st.t* 65
עבד-*b3st.t* 29, 30
פעל-*b3st.t* 38

<Chons>
עבד-*ḫns.w* 101

<a crocodile god>
בעל-*ḫnty* 18

<a frog god>
עבד-*ḳrr* 30

<Isis>
3s.t-ברכ 15
3s.t-יתונ 68
3s.t-רחמ 71
3s.t-תכני 16
אבד-*3s.t* 14
בד-*3s.t* 18
בנ-*3s.t* *18*
עבד-*3s.t* 29, 31, 100
פד-*3s.t* 33

<Horus>
ḥr-זבד 83
abd-ḥr 276
ʿbd-ḥr 278
בנ-*ḥr* 210
עבד-*ḥr* 30
עמי-*ḥr* 217
פלס-*ḥr* 36
שמ-*ḥr* 144

<Khnum>
ẖnm.w-נתנ 80

<the Lion god>
p3-m3i-חויא 36
p3-m3i-יתנ 37,
p3-m3i-סרכא 36
p3-m3i-שמע 36
p3-m3i-שמר 37
עבד-*p3-m3i* 31

<Min>
אח-*mn.w* 14

<Mut>
אחי-*mw.t* 207
ירי-*mw.t* 213
עבד-*mw.t* 30

<Osiris>
3s-ir-אדר 16
3s-ir-אל 209
3s-ir-גנ 16
3s-ir-שמר 16
3s-ir-תני 16
אמת-*3s-ir* 15
עבד-*3s-ir* 30

<Ptah>
עבד-*ptḥ* 31

<Ra>
אחי-*rʿ* 207
עבד-*rʿ* 31

<Sokar>
עמ-*skr* 32

[2] with Semitic gods

<Baal>
ʿn-בעל 32
ʿn-בתבעל 32
mr-ib-בעל 216
mry-bʿr 215
hr-בעל 19
ḥm-בעל 22

<El>
hr-אל 210
mry-אל 214
p3-di-אל 220

<Yahweh>
hr-יהו 210
ʿn-יהו 219
p3-di-יהו 222

[C] Eg Divine Names

3s-ir 43, 156, 157, 158
3s-ir-ḥp 157
3s.t 43, 157
imn 43, 229, 280, 297
b3s.t.t 43

ptḥ 157, 158
ḥp 229
ḥr 158
ḥr-p3-ẖrd 44
ẖnm.w *158*, 15
sti.t 159
ḏḥwty 159

[D] Eg Place Names

3bw 160, 257
3bḏw 159
iwnw 45, 229, 230
ip.t 159
itm 230
p3-iw-rḳ 162
**p3-n-p3-rmṯ* 163
**p3-grg-ptḥ* 163
**p3-t3-rsy* 234
p3-dmi.t-n-ḥr 164
pr-itm 234
pr-b3st.t 233
pr-rʿmss 235
**pr-ḥpy-m3ʿ.t* 162
pr-sẖm.t 163
m3ʿ 161
mn-nfr 45, 161, 231
mr-wr 161
mry-n-ptḥ 230
**n3-p3-idḥw* 213
n3-ẖnm.t-mr.n-ptḥ
nb.y.t 162
niw.t 161, 231
**ḥw.t-nni-nsw* 230
ḥ.t-k3-ptḥ 297
**ḥ.t-t3-hr.t-ib* 160
ẖ3sw-t3-mḥw 160
sin 232
swn.t 162, 232
š-ḥr 235
**t3-ḥ.t-p3-nḥsy* 45, 236
t3-ḥw.t-wḏ-nʾ.t 164
**t3-šdy.t-rs.t* 164
ṯkw 232
**dmi-n-3s-ir* 164
ḏʿn.t 164, 235
ḏb3 160

[E] Eg Loan Words

3ẖ.y 165, 238, 280
iw 45, 239
ib-r.k 236
ibhty 240
iry 281
irw.t 165
irp 281
ip.t 239, 281
ipip 178
ips 165
itrw 247
id-šri 165
idmi 239
ʿnẖ 298
ʿr 252
ʿẖ 238
w3ḏ.t 240
wʿw 303
wrs 303
bin 236, 280
bnd 237
bẖn.w 241
bẖn.t 241
p3-imy-r-šn 170

p3-ʿrʿr 171
p3-wr 300
p3-wg 170
p3-pry.t 301
p3-n-ỉp.t 176
p3-n-ỉmn-ḥtp 177
p3-n-ỉn.t 178
p3-n-rnnwt.t 177
p3-n-ḫns.w 178
p3-ḥʿt 300
**p3-ḫt-mnỉ* 169
p3-sb3 301
p3-sḫ-mḏ3.t-nṯr 170
p3-sḫ-nsw 170
p3-ṯ3ty 300
pr-ʿ3 171, 253
pḫ3 253
pḫ3 253
psḏ 301
pg3 171
pḏ.ty 301
mfk3.t 251
mnḫ.t 168
mrḥ.t 249
mḫyr 177
msw.t-rʿ 178
msd.t 168
mś.y 250
mšʿ 299
mk 282
mdw 249
mḏ 299
mḏḥ 248
n3-bnš 300
nb-m3ʿty 168
nfr.t 168
nms.t 300
nḫt 250
nšw 300
nšm.t 248
nṯrỉ 251
ry.t 242
rbw 248
rhd.t 301
rḫ-nsw.t 302
rsy 172
hbn.t 299
hbny 243, 281
hnw 166, 243, 282, 299
hnn sʿḥʿ 298
hdm.w 242, 282
ḥ.t-ḥr 176
ḥny.t 244
ḥnk 243
ḥr.t 244
ḥry.t 167
ḥry-tp 245
ḥsy 167
ḥsmn 246
ḥsmn 246
ḥtp 299
ḥtp.t 167, 282
ḫpš 298
ḫmn 298
ḫmt 298
ḫnm.t 238
ḫtm 45, 167, 246
ẖyr 166
ẖr 166
s3w 169
s3w 169
sis 302
**sʿ3-bl* 169
swn.t 169
sfḫ 302
snḥm 252

sšsn 173, 256
sš.šʿ.t 302
śk.tw 255, 283
š3św 257
**šʿd-nḏ* 257
šmy.t 173
šnwty 302
šnwty 302
šnḏ.t 256
šnḏy.t 173
šsp 173
šś 173, 256
šś 173, 257
ḳb.y 171, 254
ḳfḳf 301
ḳlby 172
ḳnḥ.t-nṯr 172
ḳrḥ.t 254, 282
k3-ḥr-k3 176
k3-ḥr-k3 299
krr 172
gỉf 172, 254
gmy 241
gstỉ 255
t3-ỉsb.t 303
t3-ʿ3b.t 177
t3-mỉ.t-nṯr 174
t3-mnḫ.t 175
t3-rỉ.t 175
t3-ḫ3ty 174
t3-shr.t 175
tmsw 175
ṯ3b-n-k3 303
ṯwfy 251
dỉw 303
dbn 303
dp.w 167
dmỉ 174
dnỉ.t 247
dḥr 258
ds 298
dd.t 281
ḏ3y 253
ḏb3.t 258
ḏbʿ.t 247
ḏr.t 166, 243
ḏry.t 166
ḏḥwty 176

www.ingramcontent.com/pod-product-compliance
Lightning Source LLC
Chambersburg PA
CBHW021352290426
44108CB00010B/202
* 9 7 8 1 5 8 9 8 3 1 3 3 9 *